A WORLD BANK COUNTRY STUDY

Russia

Forest Policy during Transition

The World Bank
Washington, D.C.

Manufactured in the United States of America
First printing March 1997

World Bank Country Studies are among the many reports originally prepared for internal use as part of the continuing analysis by the Bank of the economic and related conditions of its developing member countries and of its dialogues with the governments. Some of the reports are published in this series with the least possible delay for the use of governments and the academic, business and financial, and development communities. The typescript of this paper therefore has not been prepared in accordance with the procedures appropriate to formal printed texts, and the World Bank accepts no responsibility for errors. Some sources cited in this paper may be informal documents that are not readily available.

The World Bank does not guarantee the accuracy of the data included in this publication and accepts no responsibility whatsoever for any consequence of their use. The boundaries, colors, denominations, and other information shown on any map in this volume do not imply on the part of the World Bank Group any judgment on the legal status of any territory or the endorsement or acceptance of such boundaries.

Cover photograph by Louis H. Carbonnier.

ISSN: 0253-2123

Library of Congress Cataloging-in-Publication Data

Russia : forest policy during transition.
p. cm. — (A World Bank country study)
Includes bibliographical references. (p.).
ISBN 0-8213-3896-X
1. Forest policy—Russia (Federation)—20th century. 2. Forest management—Russia (Federation)—20th century. 3. Forest products industry—Russia (Federation)—20th century. I. World Bank. II. Series.
SD629.R87 1997
333.75'0947—dc21 97-1111
CIP

CONTENTS

LIST OF TABLES, BOXES, AND FIGURES

FOREWORD

Russia's forest sector is of global importance in terms of its size (22 percent of the world's forest resources), carbon storage capacity (15 percent of the estimated global terrestrial capacity and 75 percent of total boreal forest capacity), production (21 percent of the world's estimated standing timber volume and until recently more than 10 percent of its timber production), and biodiversity (contains the most important habitats for Eurasia's biodiversity). It is equally important nationally for its contribution to gross domestic product (over 2 percent), export earnings (over 5 percent), and employment (2 million people) and for its vital role in the lives of the indigenous peoples.

A long history of forest management has made Russia a recognized leader in forest conservation, research, and development. However, central planning policies led to unsustainable forest management practices, which were exposed during transition to a market economy. Despite vast resources and strong global demand for forest products, the Russian forest sector has been experiencing severe management problems that threaten the socioeconomic stability and environmental integrity of the forests. These issues are a severe impediment to the sustainable development of the forest sector and need to be addressed with a sense of urgency.

In this context, the Government of the Russian Federation invited the World Bank to assemble a team of international experts to undertake a comprehensive review of the forest sector and of the forest policies underpinning its development. World Bank staff worked very closely with Russian experts, who made an invaluable contribution to the preparation of this report. The report outlines the significance of the Russia's forest resources, reviews the sector's performance, identifies the key challenges and opportunities for the sector during transition, proposes an agenda for forest sector reform, and assesses the need for public investment and assistance (both technical and financial) from the international community.

Promoting sustainable sector development during transition to a market economy will require action on many fronts. Government needs to establish and enforce an enabling forest policy environment and regulatory framework that ensures sustainable management and helps maximize the benefits from utilizing and conserving forest resources. Several steps in this direction are envisaged in the proposed new Forest Code of the Russian Federation. However, completing this work will require a firm commitment to accelerate fundamental reforms in the management and conservation of forest resources at all levels of government and to ensure their enforcement. This will also require close cooperation between public and private sectors.

The report is intended for policymakers and their advisors in the Russian Federation as well as for a broad range of stakeholders in the sector, including indigenous communities, nongovernmental and academic organizations, domestic and international private sector concerns, bilateral agencies, and international financial institutions. All those who are interested in promoting sustainable development of Russia's forest sector and its critical role in facilitating a successful transition to a market economy should find the report useful.

Yukon Huang
Director
Country Department III
Europe and Central Asia Region

PREFACE

This World Bank report, *Russia: Forest Policy during Transition,* represents a unique effort at a comprehensive analysis of the challenges that the world's largest national forest sector is facing under the dynamic changes occurring on the eve of the new millennium.

It should be noted that the main conclusions and recommendations of the report reflect the views of the World Bank staff and not necessarily the views of the Federal Forest Service of Russia. However, I hold the preparation and timely publication of this report in high regard. Of special importance, in our view, is the assessment of the global role of the Russian forest sector, as well as the Report's integrative, intersectoral approach to the analysis of the environmental, economic, financial, social, legal, and administrative aspects of the forest sector and its sustainable development.

Preparation of this report would not have been possible without the active contributions of Russian specialists -- foresters, economists, ecologists, sociologists, and lawyers -- in preparing of extensive background working papers and in reviewing the draft report. I would like to express confidence that the publication and broad dissemination of this report will promote a deeper dialogue between the Russian forest agencies and the international financial institutions, bilateral agencies, nongovernmental organizations, and private sector. I hope that such a dialogue will result in joint projects and programs designed to promote sustainable development of Russia's forest sector.

Valery Shubin
Chief
Federal Forest Service of Russia

ABSTRACT

Russia's forest sector is of major national and global significance because it accounts for the world's largest forest resources and for globally important values in terms of biodiversity and effects on global climate change. The stabilization and structural reform measures introduced in Russia during the past five years have considerably improved the prospects for sectoral efficiency. However, much more remains to be done to promote sustainable development of the forest sector. This report examines forest policy in Russia during the transition to a market economy and beyond.

The report deals with forest resources and sector performance, key challenges facing the forest sector during transition, suggested solutions to some of the major problems, and the role of private sector, NGOs, bilateral agencies, and international financial institutions. The report makes recommendations for promoting sustainable sector development during transition, emphasizing that any future forest programs must be designed to support environmentally, socially, and economically viable forest projects based on efficiency and sustainability. The recommendations include integrating the forest sector into the overall process of economic reform, making forest management sustainable, rationalizing public investment and expenditures, and, in consultation with all the stakeholders, strengthening the role of the international community.

Implementation of these recommendations will establish a national policy framework for resource sustainability that protects the environment, strengthens traditional economies, and ensures the long-term productive potential of the forest sector, at both regional and national levels. The report contains eleven annexes that provide detailed technical information and analysis on selected aspects of Russia's forest sector, such as forest resources, forest management, forest institutions, and forest legislation; forest industry, trade, prices, and tax revenues; protected area system and wildlife management; and international best practices in sustainable forest development.

ACKNOWLEDGMENTS

This project was managed by Mohinder S. Mudahar and Horst Wagner (joint Task Managers) and coordinated by Hilmar Foellmi. They prepared the initial version of this report. Mohinder S. Mudahar led the discussions with the Russian Government and prepared the final version of this report, with contributions from the following Bank staff: Roger J. Batstone, Louis H. Carbonnier, David S. Cassells, Andrey V. Kushlin, William B. Magrath, Justin R. Mundy, Evgeny V. Polyakov; and international consultants: Kathy Abusow, Nicolaas Bech, Suzanne Gnaegy, Karl Kehr, Goetz Schuerholz, and William Turner.

Significant input was provided by the Russian working group co-chaired by Alexander S. Isaev and Nikolai A. Burdin. The members of the working group were Georgy N. Korovin, Nikolai A. Moiseev, Dmitry V. Mozhaev, Anatoly P. Petrov, Anatoly I. Ryzhenkov, Elena N. Samolyotova, Vladimir M. Shlykov, Pavel A. Sokolov, Valentin V. Strakhov, Vasily I. Sukhikh, Victor K. Teplyakov, Galina A. Verzhevikina, and Anatoly N. Yamskov.

We want to thank the Russian Government for its support without which this project would not have been possible. This includes the participation and review by the Federal Forest Service, former Ministry of Environmental Protection and Natural Resources, Russian Academy of Sciences, Ministry of Finance, Ministry of Economy, and the former Russian State Forest Industry Company. We gratefully acknowledge the contributions made by Anatoly I. Pisarenko (forestry) and Amirkhan M. Amirkhanov (environment) who played leading roles, on behalf of the Russian Government. The support provided by the Khabarovsk and Krasnoyarsk Regional Administrations and Regional Institutes is also acknowledged with thanks.

The report was reviewed by Bank staff members: Mary Canning (social services and employment), Shelton H. Davis (sociological and aboriginal issues), Philippe H. Le Houerou (macro-economic and fiscal issues), Dennis B. Whittle (macro-economic issues), and Lev Freinkman (fiscal issues). Luis F. Constantino, Kathleen S. Mackinnon, and Andrew H. Bond served as the peer reviewers. The report greatly benefitted from comments by Michael A. Gould, Pradeep K. Mitra, Costas Michalopoulos, Marcelo Selowsky, and Laura Tuck. The report was edited by Meta de Coquereaumont and processed by Rathna Chiniah.

Valuable comments were provided by Sten Nilsson, International Institute for Applied Systems Analysis (Russian forest resources); Gail Osherenko, Institute of Arctic Studies, Darmouth College (indigenous people and traditional economies); Doug Norlen, Pacific Environment and Resources Center (protection of forests in Siberia and the Far East); Pat Rasmussen, Taiga Forest Project of EarthKind, USA and EarthKind, Russia; Josh Newell, Siberian Hotspot Project of Friends of the Earth - Japan; David Ostergren, Division of Forestry of West Virginia University; and D. Carl Freeman, Department of Biological Sciences of Wayne State University. Steven Johnson, International Tropical Timber Organization and Thomas Waggener, College of Forest Resources of University of Washington facilitated the search for forest product prices.

The report benefitted a great deal from the contributions made by Russian and international NGOs. Alexei Grigoriev, Socio-Ecological Union (Moscow), was NGO liaison throughout the preparation of this report. Cindy Buhl, The Bank Information Center (Washington, D.C.) provided valuable comments and also facilitated comments from the international community. Sergei Ponomarenko, World Wildlife Fund (WWF) - Russia; Sergei Tsyplenkov, Greenpeace Russia; and Evgeny Simonov, Biodiversity Conservation Center - Russia participated in the final review of the report in Moscow. John Clark of the Bank's NGO Liaison Office facilitated discussions with NGOs.

The staff of the World Bank Resident Mission in Moscow facilitated work on this project. The valuable contributions made by many other individuals in the Bank and in Russia as well as by international forestry experts are also gratefully acknowledged. Besides Bank funding, significant cofinancing for this project was provided by the Canadian and the Dutch Trust Funds.

The project was carried out under the general direction of Michael Gould, Costas Michalopoulos and Yukon Huang.

ABBREVIATIONS

AAC: Annual Allowable Cut
BOD: Biological Oxygen Demand
CAS: Country Assistance Strategy
CEM: Country Economic Memorandum
CIS: Commonwealth of Independent States
COD: Chemical Oxygen Demand
CPI: Consumer Price Index
EBRD: European Bank for Reconstruction and Development
ECE: Economic Commission for Europe (United Nations
EIA: Environmental Impact Assessment
EMP: Environment Management Project
FAO: Food and Agriculture Organization of the United Nations
FFS: Federal Forest Service (Russia)
FMP: Forest Management Plan
FPR: Forest Policy Review
FSA: Forest State Account
FSU: Former Soviet Union
FTO: Foreign Trade Organization
GDP: Gross Domestic Product
GEF: Global Environment Facility
GIS: Geographic Information System
GKI: State Committee for the Management of State Property (Russia)
GNP: Gross National Product
IFC: International Finance Corporation
IIASA: International Institute for Applied Systems Analysis
ILO: International Labor Organization of the United Nations
IMF: International Monetary Fund
ITTO: International Tropical Timber Organization
IUCN: International Union for Conservation of Nature - World Conservation Union
MEPNR: Ministry of Environmental Protection and Natural Resources (Russia)
MEWB: Massive Edge-glued Wood Boards
NASA: National Aeronautic and Space Administration (USA)
NGOs: Non-Governmental Organizations
NIPF: Non-Industrial Private Forest
OECD: Organization for Economic Cooperation and Development
PERC: Pacific Environment and Resources Center (USA)
RAAS: Russian Academy of Agricultural Sciences
RAS: Russian Academy of Sciences
RFE: Russian Far East
RSFSR: Russian Soviet Federative Socialist Republic
SEU: Socio-Ecological Union (Russia)
SOEs: State Owned Enterprises
TACIS: Technical Assistance to the Commonwealth of Independent States
UNCED: United Nations Conference on Environment and Development
UNEP: United Nations Environment Program
USAID: U.S. Agency for International Development
USSR: Union of Soviet Socialist Republics
VAT: Value Added Tax
WTO: World Trade Organization
WWF: World Wildlife Fund

WEIGHTS AND MEASURES

Metric System

FISCAL YEAR

January 1 - December 31

GLOSSARY OF RUSSIAN TERMS

Dallesprom:	Far Eastern regional forest industry holding company in Khabarovsk Krays; subsidiary of the former Roslesprom
Goskomlesprom:	State Committee for Timber, Pulp and Paper, and Woodworking Industry; a federal agency established in June 1996 by reorganizing Roslesprom
Kray:	Administrative region; a constituent part of the Russian Federation
Les:	Forest or timber
Leskhoz:	A forest management district; the primary operational unit (forestry administrative and managerial body) of the Federal Forest Service
Lesnichestvo:	A forest range; subunit of a Leskhoz
Lespromkhoz:	A forest industry (logging) enterprise
Lesprojekt:	Former association of forest inventory enterprise
Oblast:	Administrative region; a constituent part of the Russian Federation
Okrug:	Formerly an administrative subdivision within an oblast or a kray; set up especially for indigenous people; currently a constituent part of the Russian Federation
Prom:	Russian abbreviation for Industry or industrial
Rayon:	Administrative district; a constituent part of a kray, oblast, or republic
Republic:	Administrative region; a constituent part of the Russian Federation, but with relatively more autonomy than others
Roskomzem:	Russian State Committee for Land Resources and Land Administration
Rosleskhoz:	Federal Forest Service of Russia
Roslesprom:	Russian State Forest Industry Company; a state holding established on the basis of the former Ministry of Forest Industry (Minlesprom) and recently reorganized into Goskomlesprom
State Forest Fund:	Government-owned forest and non-forest lands that are managed by the authorized forest management agencies, primarily by the Federal Forest Service of Russia.
Zakaznik:	A nature reserve and wildlife refuge set aside for the preservation of small ecosystems and particular animal or plant species
Zapovednik:	A nature reserve that is strictly protected

Currency Equivalents

Unit of Currency = Ruble (RB)

Exchange Rate: Rubles per US Dollar
Moscow Inter-Bank Foreign Currency Exchange/Foreign Exchange Auction Market (VEB) Rates

Period	*Period Average*	*End of Period*
1989	9	9
1990	19	23
1991	62	169
1992		
I Quarter	177	160
II Quarter	134	144
III Quarter	178	254
IV Quarter	396	415
1993		
I Quarter	580	684
II Quarter	968	1,060
III Quarter	1,028	1,169
IV Quarter	1,206	1,247
1994		
I Quarter	1,591	1,753
II Quarter	1,877	1,989
III Quarter	2,166	2,633
IV Quarter	3,191	3,550
1995		
I Quarter	4,311	4,899
II Quarter	4,931	4,539
III Quarter	4,467	4,499
IV Quarter	4,554	4,640
1996		
I Quarter	4,764	4,856
II Quarter	4,980	5,105
III Quarter	5,271	5,407
IV Quarter[1]	5,463	5,525

1 As of December 10, 1996

Executive Summary

Russia is endowed with abundant forest resources. With a total forested area of some 764 million hectares, Russia accounts for over 22 percent of the world's forested area and 21 percent of its estimated standing timber volume, and its forests provide the largest land-based carbon storage in the world. Of Russia's total forested area, 78 percent is in Siberia and the Far East and 22 percent is in European Russia. Although many people view these forests as a vast reservoir of timber that can be mobilized for the world timber economy, much of Russia's forest resource is located in remote areas with low growth potential and fragile environments that are sensitive to disturbance. It is also an area of great cultural diversity, the home of numerous indigenous peoples many of whom still practice traditional economies based on hunting, fishing, reindeer herding, and the use of a multitude of non-timber forest resources.

A long history of forest management experience has made Russia a recognized leader in forest conservation, research, and development. However, central planning policies led to unsustainable forest management practices which were exposed with the introduction of a market economy. Many wood-based enterprises are now isolated from any economically accessible forest resource, a fact that became clear once wood processors were no longer paying artificially low prices for energy, transport, and other production inputs. Roundwood harvesting levels have fallen dramatically over the past few years, from 375 million cubic meters a year in 1989-91 to 115 million cubic meters in 1995. Roundwood harvesting in 1996 is projected to be 110 million cubic meters. Russia, which once ranked second after the United States, now ranks third (behind the United States and Canada) in industrial forest output and even lower in total wood output. The decline in wood output and lack of appropriate value-added processing capacity in remote locations have virtually isolated these forest communities from domestic and international markets. This has brought economic and social hardships and has increased pressures for the utilization of more accessible protected forests.

Russian forests, with their surviving areas of extensive wilderness, have immense global importance because of their broad expanse, their biodiversity, their role in the global carbon cycle, and their potential influence on international trade in forest products. Although European Russia still possesses many significant areas of old growth forests and unique ecosystems that need attention, many environmental concerns are focused on the vast areas of forests in Siberia and the Far East, including large areas still untouched by industrial utilization. About 85 percent of the roughly 600 million hectares of forest lands east of the Ural mountains are covered with closed-stand forests, much of it still unaffected by industrial harvesting.

Protection is afforded to some of the more ecologically important areas by the Russia's protected area system. However, the national system of nature reserves established during the Soviet era is now threatened by the economic difficulties of the transition to a market economy. Large areas of more economically accessible greenbelt and protection forests established near major population centers are coming under increasing pressure for more intensive utilization. Where this has occurred, the incidence of fires, pests, and diseases has risen dramatically. The Federal Forest Service of Russia estimates that some 2 million hectares of forest are damaged annually because of inadequate management of fires, pests, and disease. While such disturbances are a natural element of boreal forest ecosystems, inadequate forest management is increasing their impact to the point of irreversible destruction of these ecosystems in the accessible areas.

The recent collapse in production in the forest sector is also the result of the unsustainable resource exploitation that occurred under central planning and decades of neglect of some forest management and environmental considerations. This crisis is aggravated by the serious financial problems facing forest-related public agencies and private enterprises. However, despite these problems but with appropriate management and policy reform, the forest sector still has considerable potential to contribute to national environmental, social, and economic development goals, including as much as US$5.5 billion as tax revenue. But, significant changes are needed in the management of forest resources if Russia is to meet its stated goals of protecting the environmental values of its forests and promoting the sustainable development of the forest sector during its transition to a market economy.

Achieving these goals will require fundamental change in forest management, particularly in harvesting and regeneration methods. Development of any new forest areas must be restricted to areas that are environmentally, socially, and economically suitable for wood production and must use appropriate forest management practices. Industrial capacity and output need to be consistent with environmental constraints and the sustainable supply of the forest resource. Under this approach, levels of production in many areas will be lower than they used to be. Preliminary resource data and market information suggest that the overall sustainable production level in Russia for the next few decades are likely to continue to be below pre-1991 levels; because of past exploitation patterns, much of the easily accessible commercial forest land may not be ready for new harvesting and the distance between mature stands and the domestic or international markets is increasing.

Because of immediate concerns for the environmental sustainability of the remaining accessible primary forests of the Asian part of Russia, which have become particularly vulnerable during the transition period, the discussion in this report focuses more on Siberia and the Far-East - all land East of Ural Mountains. Nevertheless, the proposals for national forest policy reform and many of the recommendations apply to the forest sector as a whole. In addition, more detailed sectoral and sub-sectoral studies will also be required for both the Asian and the European parts of Russia.

The report is based on several sources of information, including: (a) a 1995 Bank mission to Krasnoyarsk (in Siberia) and Khabarovsk (in the Far East) regions; (b) many meetings in Moscow with experts, policymakers and government officials dealing with the national forest sector; (c) secondary data provided by the Russian Federal Forest Service related to different aspects of the national forest sector; (d) papers on specific topics prepared by a working group of fifteen Russian forest experts and policymakers; and (e) comments by government officials, forestry experts, and NGOs (both national and international) who reviewed the draft version of the report. This report does not, however, attempt to offer solutions to all the problems of the forest sector. Rather, it focuses on a few key issues that inhibit environmentally, socially, and economically sustainable development in the forest sector and on recommendations to promote sustainable sector development during transition. Additional work needs to be done on the potential for enhancing the sustainability of the traditional economies of Siberia and the Far East.

Framework for Sector Analysis

Rebuilding the forest sector and setting it on a sustainable path will require action on many fronts. The most important area for government is to establish and enforce an enabling policy and regulatory framework that ensures sustainable management of forest resources and helps maximize the benefits from utilizing and conserving forest resources. Several steps in this direction are envisaged in the proposed Forest Code (July 1996). However, completing this work will require a firm commitment to accelerate fundamental reforms in forest resource administration, management, and conservation at all levels of government and ensure their enforcement and close cooperation between the public and private sectors.

Establishing the Jurisdictional Prerequisites of Forest Resources

Reform is needed to resolve the conflicting claims to forest tenure and resource access rights by various levels of government (federal, regional and local) and indigenous people. In consultation with the sector stakeholders, particularly the indigenous people and other inhabitants of the various forest regions, the federal agencies should oversee the development of appropriate forest policies to meet Russia's national objectives and its international commitments and responsibilities. There is a need for transparency in decisionmaking and a clear definition of responsibilities for different levels of government, particularly for mechanisms of enforcement. A first step is to sort out the jurisdictional concerns, establishing who is in charge of what. A coherent, enforceable national policy framework is needed that clearly assigns jurisdictional and management responsibilities with respect to ownership, regulatory and enforcement powers, and administrative and budgetary authority to appropriate levels of government.

This consistent national policy framework should strengthen the ability of regional and local administrations to handle the day-to-day implementation, monitoring, and enforcement of policies and the direct administration of forest resources. There is also a need to resolve any contradictions between forest legislation and regulations dealing with natural resources and indigenous peoples. The framework should incorporate effective controls and incentives for private sector involvement, reflecting the economic changes that have occurred in Russia as it moves to a market economy. Broadly, the private sector should be responsible for promoting sustainable development and for the processing and marketing of forest resources in areas designated for sustainable wood production.

In addition to developing the overall policy framework, the federal Government should establish and maintain a national data and information base for broad strategic planning and monitoring of the forest sector. The federal Government should have jurisdiction over forestry issues of national importance, including national protected areas, and over the regions' implementation of international forestry and environmental commitments. The federal Government must also ensure that the timber industry does not dominate decisionmaking at the expense of environmental and social concerns. Targeted forest research programs, including the model forest network, should be under the jurisdiction of the federal Government, which is better positioned to coordinate research activities and disseminate findings nationwide.

Regional administrations should take over more of the day-to-day administration, management, and funding of forest sector activities within broad national guidelines. The regions should have the authority to develop regulations and standards consistent with national legislation and principles of sustainable resource management and to make decisions of a regional nature about the administration, protection, utilization, and renewal of forest resources. Regional administrations should also monitor and evaluate the performance of the private sector, enforce regulations and environmental management standards, and collect and distribute resource rental charges. At the local level, the preferences, practices, and interests of traditional users of land, forest, and other resource should be integrated into government policies and programs.

In conjunction with a new framework for forest resource administration and management, a new fiscal formula should be designed to unify and simplify the resource revenue system (based on market pricing) and to share revenues among different levels of government responsible for forest management activities. Funding for regional and local authorities should be transparent, with each level accountable for forest-related revenues and expenditures, and consistent with the sustainable management of the resource. Care should be taken to avoid establishing incentives for the forest administrations to log a greater volume of timber than is environmentally or economically sound, through actions such as the linking of public sector funding solely to timber volume extracted. Where appropriate, part of revenue from commercial forest production should be used to strengthen the economies of indigenous peoples and local communities.

Within the federal Government's overall forest policy and regulatory framework, the activities of the private sector will be determined largely by market conditions. Resource sustainability should be the core objective, and tenure agreements should reflect the rights and obligations of both the concession holder and the land owner. Performance-based tenure agreements should be developed from detailed information on resources, which would permit long-term business and operational planning within the overall regulatory framework. The private sector, guided by the market, should be encouraged to make significant investments for restructuring the industry to ensure profitability and sustainability, developing and maintaining production and processing capacity, and extending and maintaining the transport infrastructure for harvesting. Targeted public investment is needed, to facilitate participation by the private sector and to ensure that commercial interests do not compromise environmental integrity and forest sustainability or undermine traditional economies and communities.

Promoting Resource Sustainability, Environmental Integrity, and Economic Viability

Appropriate land and resource allocation as well as sound management policies should be the core of the new forest policy framework. Wood demand is expected to increase nationally and internationally, and supplies from traditional supply areas are likely to continue to decline in the short to medium-term. Sustainable forest resource management must be the overriding objective in the conservation, protection, and utilization of forest resources for environmental and commercial ends. If properly managed, this valuable resource will yield abundant economic, social, environmental, and recreational benefits in perpetuity. Users must adjust to the fact that environmental and economic costs matter, an approach that will greatly limit the areas currently available for commercial harvesting. Still, the economic potential of the forest sector remains strong, even though vast areas of forests are economically inaccessible and another significant portion will be off limits for harvesting for reasons of forest conservation and protection. There is also a need to promote wood recycling and alternatives to forest products for building materials and paper products.

A fundamental requirement to meet these objectives is to clarify the nature, location, and distribution of forest resources in environmental, economic, and social terms. Gap analyses are needed to identify and determine how much the protected area needs to be expanded to preserve environmentally significant forests. Such work is being addressed in the current Russian Biodiversity Conservation Project supported by the Global Environment Facility (GEF). More rigorous definition of the criteria for sustainable management must be developed to identify the forest resource base that is suitable for responsible industrial utilization, as well as the areas that should remain under subsistence production. This information is required to ensure adequate representation of biodiversity in the nature conservation system and the protection of fragile environments. Urgent clarification of the resource base for sustainable production is also required to aid investment and planning for industrial adjustment.

Forest enterprises must be restructured to make them sensitive to real costs and benefits and to create incentives to use wood resources more efficiently and to facilitate the transition from exploitative to sustainable resource use management. For the forest industry, optimizing returns from resources will mean adapting to market requirements and systematically applying resource renewal practices within the framework of environmentally driven sustainable resource management. New technology in value-added processing is an important step toward more efficient resource utilization and improvements in regional economies and the industrial competitiveness of marginal wood production areas.

Extracting a fair share of resource value for the government (as resource owner) will play an important role in securing sustainable management. The forest taxation system needs to be rationalized, so that issues of economic rent for the resource are separated from issues of enterprise taxation. Current taxation and stumpage charges undervalue the forest resource (including non-timber forest products and other benefits), cause over-exploitation, and create disincentives to investment. Much potential tax revenue is also lost due to illegal logging and poor record keeping. Resource rentals should be structured to ensure full internalization of costs, the sustainability of the resource, and an equitable return to forest owners that is shared appropriately among federal, oblast, and local governments. Enterprise taxation rates should be the same as for all other industries in Russia.

Russia's boreal forests are important in stabilizing atmospheric gases and global climatic conditions. Much more research is needed to better understand the relationship between the global climate and the boreal forests, but it is already clear that forest utilization, fire control, and regeneration practices can greatly influence the amount of carbon released to the atmosphere. Improving the way these forests are managed and protected is critical since logging, fires, and other injurious agents damage 2 to 3 million hectares annually. These losses mobilize the carbon currently stored in the biomass and the soil in these areas. Healthy stands will maximize carbon sequestration and storage in the long run.

Safeguarding the Social Welfare of Forest Communities

Another important concern is addressing the issues of economically vulnerable forest communities while the economic transformation occurs. The remote logging communities in the Asian part of Russia are home to more than 1.8 million people. With the transition to a market economy and the need to account for higher production costs, local enterprises have been forced to drastically curtail wood production, resulting in the loss of employment, income, and social services and an increase in poverty. The problem is most severe in single-enterprise forest communities, where people rely almost exclusively on forest activities for their livelihoods. Social services and poverty alleviation measures require a national perspective. Creation of gainful, sustainable employment through diversification into value added manufacturing and processing of non-wood products in the forest sector should be a long-term objective. But, immediate action is also needed to provide social services for the most seriously affected communities, including the aboriginal people. Aboriginal land and resource rights need legal clarification and protection, and other measures are needed to strengthen traditional economies and establish appropriate consultation mechanisms. These should include the development of the market potential for the sustainable utilization of non-timber forest products.

Agenda for Reforming the Forest Sector

The agenda for forest sector reform focuses on four critical issues: integrating the forest sector into overall economic reform, making forest management sustainable, rationalizing public investment and expenditures, and clarifying the role of the international community.

Deepening the integration of the forest sector into overall economic reform is particularly challenging because of the legacy of the Soviet central planning system. Under this regime, economic costs and benefits did not influence decisions to allocate forest resources since these allocations were made to state-owned processing enterprises on the basis of noncompetitive production targets. The transition to a market economy has led to considerable disruption in past resource utilization patterns as forest industries have had to incorporate something approaching the real costs of production into their operations. However, the long-term sustainability of the resource will depend on removing the remaining distortions in markets and prices and enhancing competitiveness by putting effective antimonopoly policies in place in the forest processing sector. Competitive markets should enable the Government to generate potentially large tax revenues from resource exploitation and fund essential management activities to ensure resource sustainability by promoting freedom of entry for new firms and competitive bidding for forest resource utilization.

The role of the public sector is to protect the public good aspects associated with the environmental and social values of the forests and to create an enabling environment for responsible private sector investment in sustainable production. This role is important since, as international experience shows, the private sector rarely promotes sustainable sector development when it is left to its own devices. However, the Government also needs to rationalize and prioritize public investment and expenditures and to ensure that all levels of government work within a framework of sustainable forest management. That will involve revising land allocation criteria and procedures, adjusting forest management practices and expanding public investment in forest protection. It will also involve clarifying the role of the international community in providing technical and financial assistance. In establishing and implementing a policy and regulatory framework for the forest sector, the Government should carefully assess the impact of policy reforms.

Integrating the Forest Sector into Overall Economic Reform

Forest sector policies must be consistent with the Government's broader environmental, economic, and social objectives, and forest sector reforms should be integrated with the country's overall economic reform program. Trade barriers between regions and any remaining price subsidies (for energy and transport) and other indirect forms of economic protection, which distort resource allocation and investment decisions, should be phased out. The government should not be involved in commercial activities in the sector, and private activities in the sector should be carried out within a clearly defined regulatory framework to ensure transparency, environmental integrity, and resource sustainability. Special measures are needed to ease social adjustment problems in remote areas, to clarify aboriginal land rights, to strengthen traditional economies, and to create job reorientation and training programs to assist workers in changing jobs as the sector restructures.

Since 1992, ***price liberalization*** has increased rail tariffs dramatically as energy prices moved toward world levels, thereby raising the price of wood and reducing demand. Though some interest groups in now-privatized enterprises are calling for the resumption of energy and transport subsidies, the government should resist the temptation to do so and should instead work to ensure that enterprises are held to the rigors of market prices. Domestic timber prices are still much lower than international prices and this is partly due to low stumpage charges.

Rent-capture mechanisms should ultimately channel a much larger share of the economic value of commercially exploited forest resources to the public sector, as resource owner and manager. However, prospects for significantly increasing rent capture are limited in the short run because of inefficiencies, high nominal enterprise taxes but very low recovery, and declining production of timber and non-timber forest resources. Nonetheless, as recovery takes place, government should experiment more aggressively with a range of rent-capture instruments, particularly higher stumpage charges. These charges should not only reflect the replacement value of timber but also the opportunity costs of forgone benefits, including non-timber forest products.

Implementing and enforcing ***antimonopoly regulations*** should also support reform in the forest sector. Notwithstanding general progress with privatization in the forest industrial sector, quasi-monopolistic holding companies in the regions still tend to enjoy unfair competitive advantage, using their influence to obtain preferential treatment in forest land allocations, timber sales, processing, and exports. Many of them still dominate the industry in their regions and are often able to influence stumpage charges and output prices and secure preferential, below-market transport rates. While, on a case by case basis, the economies of scale argument could be a legitimate reason for the government to defer the breakup of the monopolies that have developed in remote forest communities, the government must ensure that any preferential treatment of regional holding companies be removed and that strict antimonopoly regulations are enforced in the forest sector. This would improve efficiency by encouraging competition through the entry of new firms and competitive bidding for forest resource utilization rights. Merely replacing public monopolies with private monopolies does not promote competition or sustainable sector development.

The severe budgetary stringency facing all levels of government is affecting the ability to handle forest management responsibilities. Additional resources are needed to promote sustainable development of the forest sector. However, the ***budget allocation process*** should consider the sector's financial needs on their merits. Expenditures should be organized by management objectives and prioritized across and within sectors. Within the forest sector, priority should be given to determining the status of forest resources, resource protection, and resource renewal and to ensuring greater compliance with environmental and sivilcultural standards specified in timber sale agreements. As management responsibility is transferred to regional and local administrations and new fiscal formulas are developed for sharing resource revenues and defining resource management responsibilities, more efficient resource allocation decisions should be possible at the local level. Budget allocations themselves should not be solely linked to logging volumes since that creates distorted incentives to increase logging unsustainably. Significant changes in the forest management budget allocation process are being considered in the new Forest Code (July 1996 draft).

Many remote forest-dependent areas are in urgent need of alternative employment opportunities and government sponsored ***social services*** during the transition. Social services have deteriorated severely in these areas, lowering living standards to below the poverty line for many people. Local governments may need to have more direct responsibility for these programs to ensure adherence to national standards and to meet the special needs of people in these areas. There needs to be a clear recognition of the importance of protecting and strengthening traditional economies, as a means of economic and natural survival for the region's indigenous peoples and other subsistence resource users. Aboriginal land claims have to be resolved so that native people are less susceptible to economic fluctuations and are able to enjoy the use of the land that belongs to them. Job creation should receive top priority to help alleviate poverty. A range of new jobs and economic activities are needed to implement national and regional forest sector strategies and policies, including increased value-added processing of timber and non-timber forest products. This will create new employment opportunities and will reduce reliance on the social services system. It will also reduce mass emigration from the northern areas into already overburdened urban and more-developed areas in the south.

Making Forest Management Sustainable

Sustainable forest management is the basis for the economic prosperity and social stability in forest resources-based communities. Achieving it requires improving the efficiency of forest land management through land use planning, ecosystem management to ensure protection of all forest values, and the integrated development of other economic activities that affect the forest sector. Establishing consultation procedures among numerous stakeholders is fundamental to achieving sustainable forest management. The forests in Siberia and the Far East offer one of the last chances to demonstrate whether forestry enterprises can engage in sustainable production without destroying biodiversity.

The first step is to ***clarify the status of the resource base*** and guide government resource management and private sector investment decisions by identifying areas that are environmentally, economically, and socially suitable for sustainable timber production. Much of Russia's forest area is in economically inaccessible areas or on environmentally sensitive sites that are unsuitable for timber production. The use of modern remote sensing and geographic information system (GIS) technology is critical for effective management and analysis of forest resource data, as well as for identifying areas that have aboriginal claimants or are being used for subsistence purposes.

Land use planning is the key to a comprehensive and multipurpose forest management approach for optimizing the environmental, social, and economic benefits of sustainable forest resource use for the Russian population and for protecting the environmental heritage of Siberia and the Far East. Comprehensive land use planning is needed to identify and protect areas with significant biodiversity values, social values, or protective functions and areas sensitive to disturbance from commercial logging activities. International experience indicates that successful land use planning is usually based on systematic stakeholder identification, consultation, and participation.

Even on lands that are to be managed primarily for industrial wood production, there are strong economic and environmental justifications for adopting an ***ecosystem management approach*** that clearly defines both the environmental and the economic objectives of forest management. This will better protect biodiversity, minimize net carbon emissions, provide protection of wildlife populations, aid soil and water conservation, and meet local demands for wildlife and other non-timber forest products. The forest legislation needs to be fully harmonized with the new stringent laws on environmental protection, a requirement that the proposed Forest Code has failed to achieve. Local stakeholders should be systematically involved in the planning and implementation of forest management operations. The Russian State Committee for Land Resources and Land Administration (Roskomzem), the Federal Forest Service, the State Committee for Environmental Protection (which, along with the new Ministry of Natural Resources, replaces the former Ministry of Environmental Protection and Natural Resources), regional authorities, aboriginal communities, scientific research establishments, NGOs, and other stakeholders should all be involved in land use planning activities.

Standards for harvesting, postharvest land treatment, and regeneration need to be examined, and systems for ensuring better compliance with established standards need to be put into practice. Russia has scores of documents dealing with forest standards, but enforcement seems to be ineffective. Government agencies should establish refundable performance bonds to encourage compliance with established standards. In view of national sensitivities about private investment in the forest sector, the Government should consider independent certification of such compliance in operations involving joint ventures and foreign funding. Independent certification could be organized under the auspices of internationally recognized organizations such as the Forest Stewardship Council to ensure maximum transparency and incentives for adopting best practices.

Regulations on harvesting practices, postharvest land treatment, and regeneration should encourage the retention of desired stand characteristics and the use of desired regeneration methods, according to the land use management plan. The forest management authorities need to set priorities for the areas to be regenerated and to designate the methods to be used to achieve economic and environmental objectives.

Cooperation between Russia and other countries with boreal forests on improving the effectiveness of ***resource protection systems*** could help reduce the staggering annual forest losses due to fire, insects, and disease. Early detection and rapid mobilization of resources for protection efforts within a rigorous forest health management system should be a top priority, although international cooperation should include a broader array of issues as well. Such an exchange of technology and know-how would benefit all partners.

Considerable threats to forest ecosystems arise from ***economic activities in other sectors***, in particular in oil and gas, mining, and infrastructure. While environmental legislation and policy are adequate, their application and enforcement falls short of adequately protecting forest resources. An important first step is to clarify management jurisdiction over land and forest resources so that the responsible agencies can proceed with the development and enforcement of environmental standards.

The expansion of the ***protected areas system*** (including those areas that may be most appropriately managed by indigenous peoples) should be an integral part of the planning process for sustainable forest management. The southern boundary of the northern protected zone should be shifted south to coincide with the line proposed by Russian scientists. The new protected zone would ban commercial harvesting in the most fragile permafrost areas covering some 15 to 20 percent of the forested land of Siberia and the Far East. The network of protected areas would be gradually adjusted as the resource information needed for assessing the environmental and biodiversity values of a given area becomes available.

Rationalizing Public Investment and Expenditures

As the major land and forest resource owners, the various levels of government need to commit substantial resources to administer, manage, and protect commercially viable forest areas; to define the timber supply areas as part of their land use management planning; to renew already degraded or nonproductive forest land; to expand and protect essential noncommercial and protected areas; to strengthen the scientific and management capabilities of the public sector; to create an enabling environment for private sector participation; and to provide other services needed to get the restructuring process going.

An assessment of immediate needs and implementation capabilities indicates that additional public funds, beyond current budget allocations, could beneficially be invested in the sector over the next few years. This ***public investment*** should be targeted to priority areas that are currently underfunded and that would encourage private sector involvement and have an immediate impact on resource sustainability. These priority areas include developing policy, strengthening institutions, clarifying the resource base for sustainable wood production, expanding the protected areas network, improving management of fire and other injurious agents (such as pests, diseases, and pollution), expanding forest regeneration programs, strengthening targeted scientific research capabilities, developing and enforcing environmental standards in other sectors, and strengthening indigenous communities and traditional economies. Although the public sector may have to assume responsibility for these investments, there is still broad scope for contracting with communities and private sector firms to provide many of these management services. Where feasible, such investments should build on Russian and international programs already underway.

A successful public investment program will require significant changes in the way public spending on forests is targeted and managed in Russia. Budgetary procedures need to be developed that properly distinguish between current expenditure and capital investment and that allow periodic evaluation of spending performance. As a first step, the federal Government should initiate a ***review of public expenditure*** in the forest sector and examine opportunities for improved management, identification, and reordering of priorities.

Public investment in ***forest health management and protection*** could yield immediate benefits by saving old-growth forests from destruction by fire, insects, and disease and by protecting habitats that harbor unique biodiversity. Research is needed on an integrated approach to fire management based on a comprehensive understanding of fire ecology and fire behavior. Plans should be developed for all aspects of fire management, including fire suppression, nonintervention and the prescribed use of fire for hazard reduction and habitat manipulation. A stronger focus is also warranted on research and extension of integrated forest pest management techniques, including the use of environmentally safe biological control agents, efficient application equipment, and comprehensive pest monitoring systems. It should be noted that in response to a request by the Russian Government and NGOs, the World Bank in the summer of 1996 financed the purchase of a biological control agent to control pest infestation in Krasnoyarsk Kray and support for a pest monitoring system and associated environmental impact assessment studies.

At the field level, ***fire management*** regulations should prohibit the accumulation of excessive logging waste, which increases the fuel load and intensifies the destructive force once a fire takes hold. Training programs and educational campaigns should be considered to increase public awareness of the dangers and effects of fire. Satellite surveillance and computer technology should be used to detect and monitor fires. International initiatives such as the joint Russia-U.S. National Aeronautics and Space Administration (NASA) project that is exploring the use of satellite imagery for detecting and monitoring large fires and efforts to coordinate the development and exchange of fire management technologies should be continued and expanded. The State Program of Forest Fire Control for 1993-97 could form an initial basis of an investment and action program.

Forest research institutes, squeezed by shrinking government funding, are losing staff at an alarming rate, severely impairing their ability to contribute to forest and land use planning. Adequate funding should therefore be provided for essential targeted research in support of resource management objectives, particularly for the collection and recording of baseline information needed for forest inventories, resource mapping, and environmental assessments. ***Information management technologies*** that give decisionmakers and interested stakeholders better access to information are an immediate priority for improving management efficiency. The model forest network initiated by the Federal Forest Service could serve as a nucleus for developing a community-based planning process and as a source of additional environmental and economic forest management information.

To ensure sustainability, the ***regeneration costs*** associated with future harvesting should be recovered or internalized in forest pricing policies and ultimately borne by consumers of wood products. For areas already logged that remain nonproductive because of inappropriate natural regeneration or planting, public funding will be needed to ensure rehabilitation. The costs for regeneration are high, however, and new planting may not be cost efficient. The government should therefore use environmental and comprehensive cost-benefit analyses to determine which areas should be harvested and what harvesting and regeneration systems to apply. The type of harvesting system used determines what regeneration method (natural or artificial) is most appropriate. Accelerating wood production in easily accessible areas and protecting environmental benefits should be important considerations. Other measures include improving stand productivity and management of forest fires, replacing low-grade hardwood stands with conifers, and reducing inefficient harvesting.

Integrated planning for resource sustainability requires government investment to facilitate forest sector restructuring. Developing the skills and capacity to conduct planning activities at the regional and local government levels is a critical first step. The technical and managerial skill requirements for this planning process should be matched to site-specific information about wood and other resources, environmental values, and the economies and cultures of local communities. The absence of such expertise could be an important limiting factor and deserves attention. Finally, broad-based input by local stakeholders should be sought at every stage of the planning process.

Role of the International Community

The forest policy framework outlined above is an ambitious undertaking. Russia has a well-developed network of forest research institutes, scientists and technical experts. However, this network is facing serious budget constraints, and scientists and other research institute staff are not trained to cope with conditions created by transition to a market economy. Russia does not have all the necessary resources to carry out the whole restructuring process in the next few years. The international community, recognizing that it has a tremendous stake in the future health and sustainability of Russia's forest environment and forest enterprises, is involved in several efforts in the sector. This involvement focuses on providing assistance for reforms that will promote sustainable and conservation-oriented forest management.

Russia has mobilized external and domestic support to work on forest resource assessment, sustainable forest management, reforestation, resource protection, protection of biodiversity, maintenance of the carbon balance, and development of ecotourism and the recreation potential of Russian forests. Although these projects are broadly consistent with the overall policy framework proposed in this report, they are functionally and geographically dispersed and lack the focus to act as catalyst to accelerate restructuring of the forest sector.

A more concerted effort is needed by the global community to assist the Russian Government, as the custodian of the largest land-based carbon-store, to fulfill its ***international environmental commitments*** and in planning, financing, and implementing the restructuring of the forest sector. One purpose of this forest policy review is to provide a framework for a comprehensive forest policy dialogue between the Russian Government and the international community, which should lead to the development of an appropriate program of technical and financial assistance.

A joint national and international approach is needed that focuses, within a strong and consistent national policy framework, on formulating and implementing key policies; decentralizing responsibility for forest resource management to the regions; strengthening institutional, administrative, and managerial capabilities at each level of government; collecting and analyzing appropriate resource data and information; implementing an overall land use planning system; introducing sustainable forest management concepts; defining an appropriate role for the private sector; encouraging stakeholder participation (particularly indigenous people); protecting and strengthening indigenous communities and traditional economies; and creating an enabling policy environment for private sector investments. This joint approach should lead to the development of options that the Russian Government can consider in determining its own environmental, economic, and social objectives related to the forest sector and in meeting its international obligations.

Technical and financial assistance are needed to accelerate the integration of the forest sector into the overall economic reform process, make forest management sustainable, rationalize public expenditures, and create an enabling environment for private sector investment in sustainable forest-based enterprises. Human resource development, particularly for indigenous people, is urgently needed to mitigate the negative social effects of the transition and to facilitate future development of the forest sector, especially at the regional level.

At the international level, a new country-driven approach to rationalize assistance for sustainable forest sector development is emerging from an initiative of the joint multilateral-bilateral donors Forest Advisors Group. In consultation with national stakeholders, international and bilateral institutions, and NGOs, Russia should use this report to assess its needs and coordinate international resources for technical and financial assistance. The consultative process should lead to a consensus on sectoral polices and development priorities. This partnership agreement concept is currently being discussed by a number of countries for consideration by the Intergovernmental Panel on Forests appointed by the U.N. Commission on Sustainable Development in April 1995.

The idea of partnership is also vital to the U.N. *Decade of the World's Indigenous People,* to which the Russian Federation has made a strong commitment. Many of the issues confronting the indigenous peoples of Siberia and the Far East can be fruitfully approached through cooperative agreements between the Russian Federation and indigenous associations and governments of the other countries of the North (e.g. Canada and the United States).

As a basis for future dialogue on support for reforming the forest sector, the following priority areas have been identified for promoting sustainable sector development during transition and for providing technical and financial assistance:

Short-Term Support (over the next two years)

(a) ***Ongoing policy reform***: Short-term support for policy reform would accelerate the economic transition and help to ensure the sustainability and integration of the forest sector into the overall economic reform framework. This would consist of carrying out the proposed follow-up studies to close information gaps and develop specific options for reform. These options could then be discussed in a series of regional and national forestry conferences in Russia to work out the details of sectoral reform for consideration by the Government. Priorities are to:

- Examine the rent generation capacity of the major forest producing regions and the mechanisms for ensuring sufficient rent capture to support sustainable forest management. This is a high priority activity since the preliminary analysis indicates large potential for generating tax revenues (from both the stumpage charges and taxes on enterprise profits). This activity needs to be integrated with proposed activities for clarifying the status of the resource base for existing enterprises and determining the market prospects for the Russian forest sector. It should also identify essential tasks for achieving sustainable management in each region in order to determine and prioritize forest management budgets.

- Examine the antimonopoly measures employed by other countries with large forest resources in order to develop appropriate measures for the forest sector in Russia (as well as for the other related sectors such as transport and energy).

- Examine the influence of transport and energy monopolies on the sustainable management of the forest sector.

- Develop environmental, economic, and social criteria and indicators that will allow analysis of available information to identify status and quality of forest resources and their division into logical supply zones.

(b) ***Clarifying the status of resource base and market prospects***: The first step would be a rapid appraisal of the status of the resource base serving all existing forest-based enterprises in order to identify enterprises with a viable resource base that is capable of supporting future investment and sustainable employment. Nonviable enterprises also need to be identified to determine the magnitude of social adjustment needed as the sector moves from a nonsustainable, command driven, resource-mining approach to environmentally, economically, and socially sustainable production. A rapid appraisal of domestic and international market prospects for products from the major forest regions in Russia should also be undertaken. Overall this consists of four steps:

- Strengthen the national strategic planning capacity with expertise in the environment, economics, social anthropology, community-based development, forest resource management, and forest planning.

- Develop regionally appropriate rapid resource assessment processes (remote sensing, mapping, enterprise questionnaires) to synthesize information and close information gaps on the status, distribution, and quality of forest resources in the logical supply zones for existing enterprises. There is also a need to clarify land and resource rights in the various forest zones, particularly in terms of aboriginal land claims and areas to be set aside for biodiversity conservation.

- Provide guidance for undertaking international market studies to identify areas of comparative advantage and disadvantage in relation to potential domestic and international markets. These studies should define the limits to economic resource utilization under a range of price scenarios for both inputs (e.g., forest resources, energy, transport, labor) and outputs. Particular attention should be paid to the implications of the emergence of sustainable timber buyers groups in Europe and elsewhere and the growing demand for timber whose sustainability has been certified by independent third parties. These studies should examine both the opportunities and obstacles such trends will create for enhanced market access in the future.

- Prepare status reports for each enterprise and region.

(c) ***Forest Health and Protection***: Proper management of fire, pests, and other injurious agents has been identified as a high priority in protecting the environmental and economic values of Russia's forest resources. Urgent steps are needed to address immediate problems and to set the stage for longer-term strategic responses to these problems, including financing. In the immediate future:

- Strengthen the ability of forest management authorities to determine the magnitude, temporal distribution and spatial distribution of fire, pest, and disease management problems.

- Identify the remote sensing, resource monitoring, and direct management requirements for effective forest protection planning and management, particularly for high risk and vulnerable areas to facilitate targeted intervention.

- Establish at least three regional pilot projects to develop forest protection regimes and to determine long-term investment needs for forest protection.

- Accelerate the implementation of appropriate regeneration mechanisms on disturbed forest lands.

Medium-Term Support (over the next two to five years)

- Establish institutional arrangements for a new national-regional forest management system that clearly defines rights and responsibilities for resource planning, resource allocation, revenue collection, and field management.

- Initiate detailed resource assessment and land use planning for the national forest system.

- Develop modern resource information management systems at all levels (national, regional, local) of forest management responsibility.

- Develop strategic planning capacity at the national, regional, and local levels, including among indigenous communities.

- Develop an improved operational management and planning capacity for local forest management units that is consistent with modern ecosystem-based concepts of sustainable forest management.

- Establish regional systems to provide information to private and community investors on markets and investment opportunities in sustainable forest production and processing.

- Establish and promote independent environmental certification (based on the criteria of sustainable management of forests) of timber and timber products to comply with international market requirements.

Long-Term Support (over the next decade)

- Develop a comprehensive system of rent capture mechanisms that increases tax revenue generation, improves efficiency, and promotes sustainable sector development.

- Develop comprehensive ecosystem-based forest management systems for all forest production areas including transparent planning systems, trained personnel, environmentally appropriate equipment, and environmentally and economically sound regeneration of large disturbed areas.

- Develop human resources at all levels, from appropriate short-term technical training programs to long-term university undergraduate and post-graduate programs. Ensure that indigenous and other traditional communities have access to such programs.

- Rationalize the forest research system to establish and maintain a world class capacity for targeted forest ecosystem research and provide information for policy formulation in all the ecological, social, and economic aspects of forest resource management.

- Establish a comprehensive system for achieving a sustainable socioeconomic development in forest-based communities.

Activities that would promote transition to sustainable forest management and sectoral development will require considerable technical and financial assistance. Financial requirements for these activities alone could reach US$700 million over the next decade (about US$70 million per year). Investment at this level is necessary to achieve sustainable resource management and to create an enabling environment for private investment in the sector. Within a decade, such investment should be able to transform the sector from a net drain on the national budget to a net contributor to the economy through self-financing forest protection and renewal programs, capture of resource rentals, taxation of forest enterprises, and generation of employment and income. In a worst case scenario of a further reduction in annual wood production to 75 million cubic meters, investment in these activities can be supported by resource rental capture of about US$1 per cubic meter over the next decade, a level that is well within the capability of the sector and consistent with the global experience.

The potential for a pilot forestry project, as an initial phase of Bank assistance, was discussed between the Government and the World Bank during the review of this report. During subsequent discussions related to the Country Assistance Strategy (CAS), the Government has requested the Bank to assist it in preparing a forestry project. Once formally included in the Bank's lending program, this pilot project would support a range of targeted activities at the federal level and in two or three regions. It would address strategic planning and selected reform issues by testing reform models in representative forest management situations. These would include the development and testing of new management and governance arrangements designed to link the capture of resource rentals with management responsibility. A comprehensive forest protection strategy and forest information system would be developed in each pilot region to facilitate management and investment planning in the sector. Preparatory activities, targeted on the pilot areas, will include analyses of the forest health and protection system, the forest information system and market prospects; development of national and regional guidelines for sustainable forestry; and identification of ways to strengthen the regulatory and enforcement systems, including options for establishing a certification process.

Conclusions and Recommendations

The forest sector in Russia is of major national and global significance. Approximately, 60 percent of Russia's total land base in under forest. About 2 million people are employed in the forest sector, accounting for 3 percent of total employment. Over 2 percent of GDP comes from the forest sector. In 1995, the exports of forest products (US$4.2 billion) accounted for 5.4 percent of total export earnings. Furthermore, the sector is a major source of potential tax revenues. At the global level, Russia's forest sector accounts for 22 percent of world's forested area (largest), 15 percent of the global terrestrial carbon pool, 75 percent of the carbon sink capacity of the total boreal forests and 21 percent of world's standing timber volume (largest).

The potential for tax revenue from the forest sector in Russia is substantial. There are at least three main sources of tax revenue: stumpage charges, taxes on harvesting companies and taxes on wood processing activities. At present, the average stumpage charges in Russia are less than US$1 per cubic meter whereas under auction the stumpage charges in Russia and some neighboring countries are over US$10 per cubic meter. In Scandinavia, the stumpage charges could be as high as US$30 per cubic meter.

The estimated potential tax revenues in 1996 U.S. dollars from the forest sector in Russia vary between US$0.9 billion and US$5.5 billion per year. Unless the government is able to reform the forest sector policy, increase stumpage charges and improve tax recovery, they will not be able to recover the potential tax revenues. The potential tax revenue is adequate not only to finance all the expenditures related to forest management, regeneration, protection and sustainability but also make a major fiscal contribution to the treasury. Furthermore, higher stumpage charges will discourage over-exploitation of the forest resources and waste of harvested wood, thereby, promoting efficiency and sustainable sector development.

With clarification of land and resource rights and appropriate management, Russia's forest resource can continue to make valuable contributions to the country's regional and national economies and to the global environment while protecting and strengthening the region's traditional communities and economies. In the longer term, increases in domestic and global demand should create opportunities for viable investment in environmentally sound value-added production in areas with high resource capability. The creation of appropriate value-added production capability is likely to expand economic accessibility and to bring new life to some of the areas that have become economically marginalized as a result of high transportation costs.

The real challenge will be to establish a national forest policy framework for resource sustainability that protects environmental values, strengthens traditional communities and economies, and ensures the productive potential of the forest resource, at both the regional and national levels. This forest policy review outlines the significance of Russia's forest resources, the key challenges and opportunities faced by the sector, an agenda for reforming the forest sector, and the need for public investment and assistance (both technical and financial) from the international community. Table 1 provides an overview of the key conclusions, recommendations, and issues for a dialogue with various stakeholders, experts, and policymakers related to the forest sector in Russia.

Table 1: Key Recommendations for Forest Sector Reform in Russia

A. Integrating the Forest Sector in Overall Economic Reform

Issue	*Status*	*Proposed policy objectives*	*Proposed strategy*
Liberalization of key prices (in particular, energy and transport)	Adjustment toward world prices has led to significant curtailment of output and employment	Incorporation of real fuel costs and benefits in decisionmaking; efficiency improvements in industrial utilization of forest resource	• Continue to further liberalize input prices and provide market discipline • Continue to further liberalize forest product prices • Remove inter-regional trade barriers
Rent capture of forest resources	Only a small share of the value of commercial forest resource harvests are captured for resource renewal and public purposes, leading to overharvesting and excessive and poorly located industrial capacity	Collection of a significant portion of the value of harvests from users to ensure resource renewal and a fair return to forest owners.	• Introduce market-based mechanisms (auctions, bidding) to increase rent capture • Incorporate enhanced rent- capture provisions in agreements with foreign-owned and joint ventures • Properly enforce rent capture mechanisms and tax laws to improve recovery of tax revenues
Antimonopoly measures and privatization	Reform has had limited impact on industrial structure in the processing sector; this sector is still dominated by inefficient, interrelated, and monopsonistic holding companies	Efficient and sustainable resource use by competitive enterprises	• Break-up monopolies and monopsonies, including the holding companies • Apply antimonopoly regulations and privatization measures more effectively to increase competitiveness of forest industry • Ease restrictions on joint ventures and forest investment • Increase efficiency in use of timber and other resources in processing sector • Competitive bidding for forest utilization rights
Budgetary stringency on forest management agencies	Reduced budgets have adversely affected forest management and protection; low rent capture from forest utilization	Meeting environmental and forest protection needs	• Scrutinize budgetary process to increase rent capture and maximize efficiency to achieve environmental and forest protection • Increase budget to ensure sustainability, private sector participation, and protection
Social welfare needs of remote forest communities	Significant populations are at risk due to unemployment and declining sectoral output	A minimum social safety net for populations at risk; long- term adjustment in labor markets; development of markets for nontimber forest products; strengthened indigenous communities and traditional economies.	• Target assistance to neediest populations, using local government structures to channel resources • Ease constraints on migration • Clarify land rights to enhance aboriginal welfare through benefits from the management of aboriginal land by aboriginal people • Restructure unemployment compensation, adjusting levels and duration of benefits • Design employment service systems to meet local needs • Organize skill transfer and training programs • Promote community-based credit and development schemes for traditional trades

Table continued on the next page

Table 1: Key Recommendations for Forest Sector Reform in Russia (Contd.)

B. Making Forest Management Sustainable

Issue	*Status*	*Proposed policy objectives*	*Proposed strategy*
Knowledge of resource base	Inadequate national and regional diagnosis of forest resources and their real potential for various uses, including wood production and conservation of biodiversity	Framework and guidelines for sustainable forest resource management in place, with the necessary allocations, for carrying out broad-scale appraisal; participatory resource appraisal system for sustainable forest resource management	• Promote the use of modern information management techniques for efficient resource assessment and planning • Obtain reliable information on forest resources suitable for planning purposes at different planning levels • Analyze data and stratify total forest land according to land allocation procedures • Undertake a rapid appraisal of the resource base of existing enterprises to clarify investment opportunities and restructuring needs
Land use planning	The three-group classification system used to designate forests for protection and commercial uses is not specific enough	A rational system of land allocation that protects environmental values and facilitates sustainable management for multiple objectives	• Ensure compatibility of land allocation criteria with the interests and capabilities of proposed management structure and governance • Incorporate logical wood supply zone concept into design of commercial forest management areas • Identify key areas needed to close gaps in existing protected area system • Include environmental protection criteria in designating forests for commercial utilization • Formalize aboriginal land allocations and ensure protection of these land rights • Incorporate local participation at all levels of planning process
Management of intersectoral environmental impacts	A significant source of fire risk and other damage to forest resources arises from poor environmental practices in the energy, mining, and infrastructure sectors	Planning process that includes appropriate environmental assessments and enforcement of measures to minimize deleterious effects of various activities	• Review and improve on environmental impact assessment procedures • Revise jurisdictional responsibilities for enforcement of regulations on forest land to reflect decentralized responsibilities and capabilities
Ecosystem management to promote multiple forest values	Timber extraction and impacts from other sectors are excessively destructive and impede satisfactory regeneration	Careful management of forest lands, especially commercial areas, to provide a high level of protection to environmental values; environmentally, economically, and socially sustainable forest utilization and management practices	• Revise and enforce implementation of management guidelines that incorporate ecosystem management and multiple-use concepts • Impose a regulatory and incentive framework to monitor, assess, and motivate concern for effective regeneration

Table continued on the next page

Table 1: Key Recommendations for Forest Sector Reform in Russia (Contd.)

Issue	*Status*	*Proposed policy objectives*	*Proposed strategy*
Forest regeneration	Large logged-over and fire-damaged areas remain without sufficient regeneration; harvesting practices are inconsistent with heavy reliance on natural regeneration	Productivity of degraded forest land restored to satisfy economic and environmental objectives; harvesting practices regulated so that they are consistent with desired regeneration methods	• Prioritize degraded areas in relation to environmental costs and future economic potential • Allocate public funding for regeneration of existing degraded land on a priority basis • Restrict and enforce the size of clear-cutting and monitor regeneration efforts to prevent continued degradation • Update guidelines on regeneration and sustainable management to incorporate ecosystem management concepts
Resource protection	About 1.6 million ha of forest is being damaged annually by fire, insects and diseases	Improved efficiency and effectiveness of forest resource protection through the use of appropriate technology, methodology, and funding	• Develop comprehensive forest health monitoring and management strategies • Expand cooperation with other countries in technology transfer • Increase protection area according to specified economic, social, and environmental criteria

C. Rationalizing Public Investment and Expenditures

Issue	*Status*	*Proposed policy objectives*	*Proposed strategy*
Planning for resource sustainability	Little sectoral capacity for long-term strategic planning in the context of a market economy; budget process does not correctly distinguish between investment and current expenditure, leading to chronic misallocation of resources to activities that do not promote sector sustainability	Sectoral capability to assess consequences of policy changes and to disseminate findings to stakeholders and policymakers; economically rational levels and patterns of sectoral reinvestment and resource flows	• Decentralize institutional planning capacity and involve stakeholders, including indigenous people, in an integrated resource planning process
Forest health and protection	Fire, insects, and disease annually cause substantial economic and environmental losses	An integrated management process for forest protection	• Invest in fire, insect, and disease monitoring, management, and control systems and technology to minimize losses of economic and environmental values
Research and technology	Budgetary restrictions have reduced the rate of investment in forest research and slowed implementation of results of new findings	Targeted scientific research support to properly manage forest resources	• Rationalize the allocation of resources to targeted forest research according to forest management objectives • Support research on ways to strengthen traditional economies, technologies, and resource use practices

Table continued on the next page

Table 1: Key Recommendations for Forest Sector Reform in Russia (Contd.)

D. Role of the International Community

Issue	*Status*	*Proposed policy objectives*	*Proposed strategy*
Global environmental sustainability	International interest in the application of sustainable management principles is not matched by adequate financial or technical support	Meeting financial and other obligations for management of nationally owned resources in ways consistent with international environmental commitments	• Adapt international frameworks on criteria and indicators for sustainable forest management to produce nationally and regionally relevant policies, procedures, and performance indicators • Identify specific policies, investments, and management practices with international environmental consequences that go beyond national economic priorities • Convene donor meetings to mobilize resources for priority activities
Technical assistance	International technical assistance covers wide range of topics and geographic areas but is uncoordinated and of limited impact	International technical assistance focused on key national priorities with the potential to produce systemic change in resource management policy and practice	• In consultation with sectoral stakeholders, donors and financiers, prepare assessment of technical assistance needs and prospective sources of assistance • Promote cooperative agreements between indigenous associations of Russian Federation and other countries of the North for strengthening traditional communities and economies • Develop multidonor partnership agreements to provide systematic targeted assistance
Financial assistance	Financial needs for restoring and maintaining resource sustainability extend beyond the current ability and willingness of the private sector to invest and of the domestic public sector to pay	Adequate financial resources to pursue long-term resource management objectives	• Finance economically, environmentally, and socially viable projects and activities in a coordinated manner to promote sustainability and efficiency in areas that are key to protecting resources, protecting the standards of living of the remote forest population, and attracting private investment

I. Forest Resources and Sectoral Performance

With over 22 percent of global forests (764 million hectares, 78 percent of them in Siberia and the Far East and 22 percent in European Russia), Russia holds more of the world's forest resources than any other country. Forests have played a central role in Russia's economic, social, and cultural development and are a key component of the national and global environment. In addition to wood products, Russian forest resources provide the largest land-based carbon storage in the world and a wide range of nonwood products, including fish and game, berries, mushrooms, and herbs, which are important to the livelihood of forest communities. A long history of forest management experience has made Russia one of the recognized leaders in forest conservation, research, and development.

However, the forest sector in Russia faces a constellation of problems stemming from the conflicting needs to conserve and use the country's varied ecosystems and the rapid political and economic changes sweeping the country in its transition to a market economy. Despite vast resources and strong global demand for forest products, the Russian forest sector has been experiencing severe sector management problems that threaten the socio-economic stability of the forest communities and the environmental integrity of the forests. These problems call for a fundamental change in Russia's approach to forest resource management. This report examines the Russian forest sector in the context of these larger challenges and presents a coherent framework within which to develop policies, regulations, and investment programs for promoting sustainable sector development during the transition.

Because of immediate concern for the environmental sustainability of the remaining accessible primary forests of the Asian part of Russia, which have become particularly vulnerable during the transition period, the discussion in this report focuses more on Siberia and the Far east - all land east of Ural Mountains. Nevertheless, the proposals for national forest policy reform and many of the recommendations apply to the forest sector as a whole. In addition, more detailed sectoral and sub-sectoral studies will also be required for both the Asian and the European parts of Russia.

The report is based on several sources of information, including: (a) a 1995 Bank mission to Krasnoyarsk (in Siberia) and Khabarovsk (in the Far East) regions; (b) many meetings in Moscow with experts, policymakers and government officials dealing with the national forest sector; (c) secondary data provided by the Russian Federal Forest Service related to different aspects of the national forest sector; (d) papers on specific topics prepared by a working group of fifteen Russian forest experts and policymakers; and (e) comments by government officials, forestry experts, and NGOs (both national and international) who reviewed the draft version of the report. This report does not, however, attempt to offer solutions to all the problems of the forest sector. Rather, it focuses on a few key issues that inhibit enviromentally, socially, and economically sustainable development in the forest sector and on recommendations to promote sustainable sector development during transition.

Before 1989, Russia was second only to the United States as an industrial wood producer. Annual wood production of more than 300 million cubic meters contributed over 2 percent of Russia's gross domestic product (GDP) and employed some 2 million people. The forest sector is also a major source of export earnings and potentially large tax revenues. Since the beginning of the transition to a market economy, however, forest output has fallen to about one-third of that level. Roundwood harvesting plummeted from estimated 375 million cubic meters in 1989-91 (annual average) to about 115 million cubic meters in 1995 and is projected to be about 110 million cubic meters in 1996 (Figure 1.1). The unsustainable forest production systems of central planning collapsed under the pressure of market realities, as producers began to face the real costs of transport and other factors of production. Many forest enterprises are located in areas with low growth potential and fragile environments that are sensitive to disturbance and are isolated from any economically accessible resource.

Russia's forest sector is of major global significance and accounts for 22 percent of world's forested area (largest), 21 percent of world's standing timber volume (largest), 15 percent of the global terrestrial carbon pool, and 75 percent of the carbon sink capacity of the total boreal forests. Russian forests also have enormous global importance because of their biological diversity and carbon sequestration capacity--especially the vast pristine forest ecosystems in Siberia and the Far East (Box 1.1). In European Russia, after some 300 years of intensive forest exploitation, more than 60 percent of the forests have been affected by industrial utilization and have lost significant biodiversity values.

East of the Ural Mountains, however, large areas of old growth forests remain intact. These vast ecosystems offer one of the greatest and last opportunities to conserve unique assemblages of species that surpass those found elsewhere in temperate forests in levels of diversity and endemism. The Siberian and Far Eastern forests also provide a major carbon store that is essential in balancing the world's greenhouse gases. If the problems afflicting the forest sector are ignored and appropriate public and private actions are not forthcoming, conditions in the forests east of the Ural Mountains may be irreversibly altered to the detriment of the region's environment and economy.

The time is opportune for joint national and international action to promote the sustainable and conservation-oriented management of Russia's forest resources. Russia's current forest policy framework does not adequately support the Government's international environmental commitments, makes private investors hesitant to enter this potentially lucrative sector, and presents obstacles to environmental, social, and economic development and to the achievement of its forest resource management objectives. This report develops options for the government to consider in reforming these policies and suggests an action program aimed at restoring sectoral performance and maintaining environmental integrity by promoting sustainable forest management.

Four issues are critical: refining the ***legal*** and regulatory framework governing ownership and management of forest land, promoting forest resource sustainability and maintaining ***environmental*** integrity, restructuring the sector to ensure ***economic*** sustainability and viability, and strengthening the ***social*** safety net for the most threatened communities, developing alternative employment opportunities, and ensuring the conditions for the continuity of traditional communities and economies. Accomplishing these objectives will require integrating forest policy into the broader process of economic and social reform, making resource management sustainable, prioritizing public investment in the sector, and creating an enabling policy and regulatory environment for private sector investment.

Figure 1.1: Wood Harvesting Volume in Russia, 1980-96

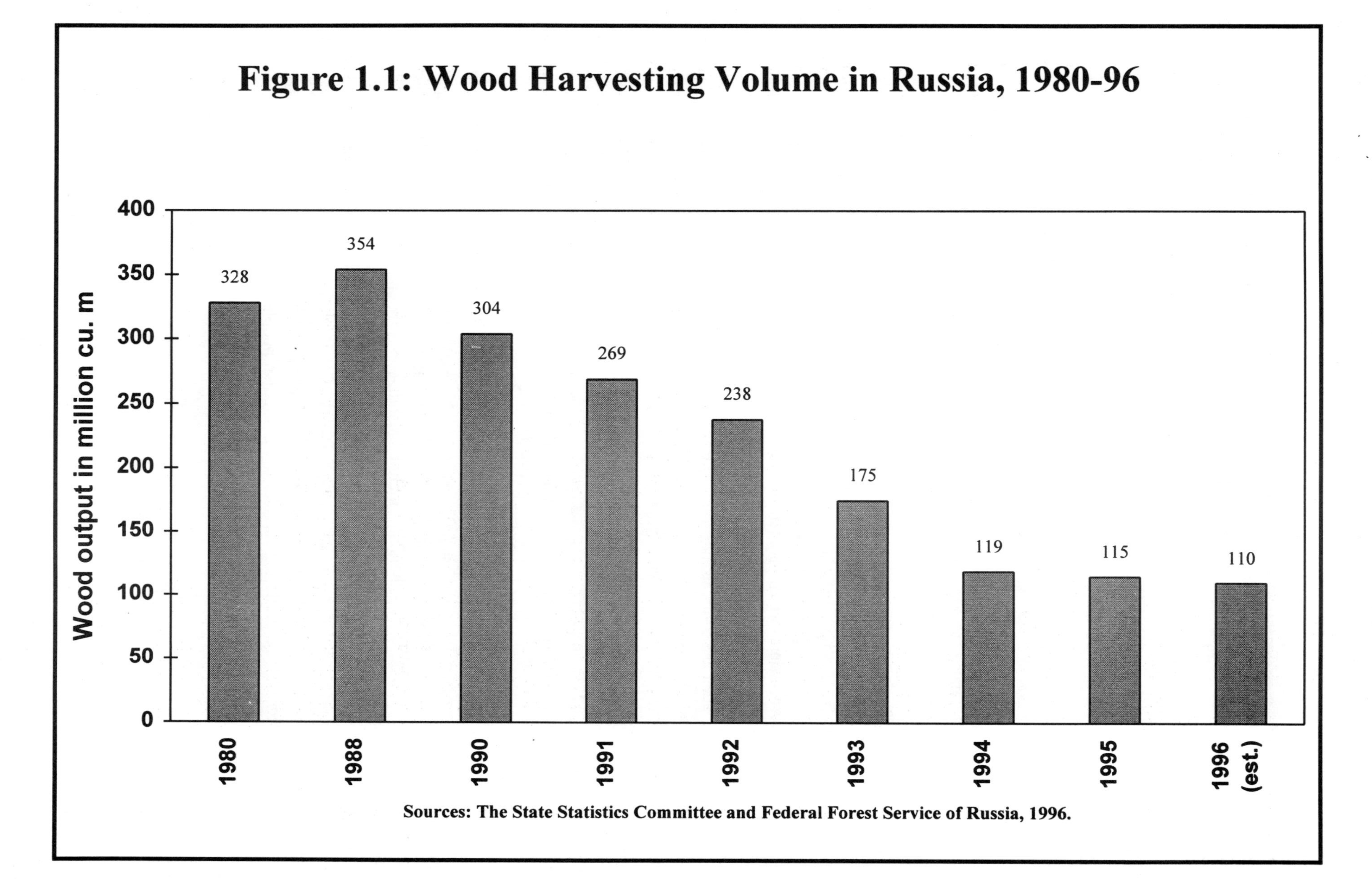

Sources: The State Statistics Committee and Federal Forest Service of Russia, 1996.

Box 1.1: The Global Significance of Russia's Forests

The vast, relatively intact ecosystems of Russia offer one of the last opportunities to conserve natural landscapes on a scale large enough to preserve genuine wilderness and allow ecological processes and wildlife populations to fluctuate naturally. The unique assemblages of species in the Greater Caucasus and the Russian Far East surpass the diversity and endemism found in temperate forests anywhere in the world. Russian forests also support a diversity of human cultures of the indigenous people living in Siberia and the Far East (see Annex G for details).

The Amur-Sakhalin Bioregion in the Far East has particular significance because much of the region escaped past periods of glaciation. As a consequence, these areas became a climatic refuge for many species and communities and have a high level of plant and invertebrate endemism (Krever and others 1994; Charkiewicz 1993). Similar forests once covered areas of China, Korea, and Japan, but they have been largely destroyed. The region's unique biogeographic history has resulted in unusual assemblages of plants and animals. Amur tigers, Amur leopards, musk deer, and Himalayan bears share the same habitat with brown bears, reindeer, and salmon.

Undisturbed boreal forest islands and other forests close to the tundra boundary are also valuable for monitoring the effects of global climate change because their reproductive status should provide an indication of any consistent increase in high latitude temperatures (Nichols 1993). Russia's vast expanses of forest also provide a major carbon store, which may represent as much as one-seventh of the Earth's terrestrial carbon pool (Kolchugina and Vinson 1993). With appropriate management of stand productivity, forest fires, and logging practices, these forests will continue to help minimize the release of greenhouse gases. Without appropriate conservation and management practices, however, increased intensity of utilization and fire could exacerbate global atmospheric carbon accumulation problems by releasing current carbon stores (Krankina and Harmon 1994; Krankina and Dixon 1994; FIRESCAN 1994).

Russia's forests are also important for the international timber economy. Though production has fallen from its highs in the 1980s, the vast extent of the Russian forest resource should, with proper management, allow the forest industries to continue to make a significant contribution to regional and national economies. The challenge will be to establish a framework for resource sustainability that will protect both the environmental values of the forests and their productive potential.

Because forest policy is a social process, policymakers need to build on the open and participatory processes that are now at work to ensure a broad base of support for reform. Inclusion of a wide range of interested stakeholders, including indigenous peoples, in policy evaluation and development is vital for the identification of socially and environmentally sustainable reforms. The analytical approach proposed in this report can assist Russian policymakers in the more detailed examination of specific policy interventions and changes. With environmentally and economically sound management, the forest sector's resources can be sustained for the benefit of future generations, continuing to provide valued goods and services to the Russian people and the world community.

A. Sector Problems

Legacy of Overuse

The Ural Mountains have been historically an important dividing line between European and Asian Russia. Less than two centuries ago, forest sector activities were almost entirely limited to the European part of Russia. The concept of national sovereignty over forest lands was introduced in Russia in the late seventeenth to early eighteenth century in response to growing national interest in forest utilization and ownership. The forest policies that were developed at that time were aimed primarily at securing sovereign control over forests for strategic purposes (navy, industry, and construction of St. Petersburg) and included a juridical code governing the rights and responsibilities of owners. Beginning in the 1780s, revenue generation became a key objective of forest policy, and private forest owners regained full control over their forests. Intensive commercial utilization increased significantly and by the second half of the nineteenth century had led to massive forest destruction, mostly in European Russia. The reform period of late 1860s and early 1870s brought about the eventual introduction of the Principles of Forest Conservation, which set the stage for the earliest attempts at forest management and conservation at the turn of the twentieth century.

The 1917 revolution radically changed the structure of the forest sector in Russia. Legislation in 1918 abolished all rights to private ownership of forest land. Forests were declared the property of the people, to be managed on the basis of planned regeneration for the common good of the nation. The state took control of foreign trade in wood and forest materials as well. In the early 1930s, forest enterprises were brought within the centralized planning system and assigned production targets. Rather than promoting the common good of the nation, this change led to a new era of "forest mining" since neither incentives for economic efficiency nor funds for sustainable forest management were provided. By 1940 processing capacity had expanded significantly.

During the 1930s and 1940s, forest policy began to distinguish between production forests and protection forests, first for water protection purposes and later for the protection of forest ecosystems. Although forest mining continued, the sector's goals were expanded to include improved forest harvesting technology, management, and regeneration. After World War II, opening up of new harvesting areas in the north and east of the country was given top priority. Forest management enterprises were given harvesting rights, so that they might achieve their production quotas, and were assigned responsibility for reforestation in the harvested areas. By 1960, annual harvesting had reached 369 million cubic meters. Seeding, planting, and other forest management activities such as natural regeneration, draining, and stand-tending increased, requiring tremendous investments in infrastructure and new technology. However, these efforts never kept pace with the rapid timber removal in many management areas, and the sector's production growth rate began to decline in the late 1970s.

By the end of the 1980s, the sector was unable to satisfy national and export markets despite adequate industrial processing capacity. Harvesting and transportation problems and the depletion of easily accessible harvesting areas, contributed to the decline in production. To ease the shortages, the USSR State Forestry Committee was given the authority to engage directly in industrial wood harvesting. Because harvesting generated substantial revenue, it received disproportionate attention while forest management languished. Still, some protection, conservation, and socioeconomic concerns began to emerge, culminating in a plan to modestly expand the area of protected forest reserves and nature parks.

Russia's new constitution and its move toward a market economy following the breakup of the former USSR in 1991 brought radical political, legal, and economic changes that shook all sectors of the economy, including the forest sector. The production concept that had developed under the central planning system proved unsustainable and ceased to function effectively, resulting in sharp production declines and widespread social hardship, particularly in the remote logging communities of Siberia and the Far East.

Inconsistencies in the Forest Legislation

The rapid and far-reaching economic and political changes in Russia had rendered the Soviet legal and regulatory framework in the forest sector obsolete and disfunctional. To provide interim ground rules for forest management and utilization, the "Principles of Forest Legislation of the Russian Federation" were enacted by the Parliament and signed into law in March 1993 to replace the old Forest Code. Work on drafting a new forest code began in 1994, initially to accommodate the provisions of the new Russian Constitution adopted in December 1993. However, subsequent major changes in other branches of law (changes in the Civil Code, new environmental laws) and lack of consensus on other fundamental legal issues (such as land ownership) have significantly delayed approval of the new forest legislation. As of December 10, 1996, the new Forest Code had not yet been signed into law.

The 1993 Principles of Forest Legislation, which constitute the current legal framework for forest management, together with the proposed new Forest Code (see Annex C) strengthen the focus on sustainable forest utilization and environmental protection. The July 1996 draft Forest Code identifies the principal objective of the forest legislation as "ensuring sound, nondepleting use of forests, as well as their conservation, protection, and reproduction based on the principles of sustainable forest management and preserving the biological diversity of forest ecosystems, increasing the ecological and resource potential of forests, and satisfying society's need for forest resources on the basis of scientifically substantiated, multi-purpose forest use." Moreover, according to the Federal Forest Service the main goal of national programs for the period 1994-99 is to "manage forests with the objective of protecting biodiversity of forest ecosystems, regulating the carbon budget and ensuring sustainable development of the forest sector of the economy" (Shubin 1994).

Though the interim Principles are in line with current international social, economic, and environmental thinking about sustainable forest development, they lack specificity in administrative and fiscal processes and vest many interested parties with control over forest resources without properly defining their responsibilities. The Constitution vests authority over natural resources jointly in the federal and regional governments. This provision of joint ownership has been variously interpreted with regard to the State Forest Fund.[1] Many so-called subjects of the Russian Federation (republics, krays, and oblasts) have declared themselves owners of territorial forests and have introduced their own legislations. These unilateral actions have caused tensions between the federal and regional governments.

---

1 *The State Forest Fund (Gosydarstvennyi Lesnoy Fond) is an official Russian term denoting government-owned forest and non-forest lands that are managed by the authorized forest management agencies, primarily by the Federal Forest Service of Russia. About 60 percent of Russia's total land base belongs to this fund (for further details, see Annex A).*

The new Forest Code passed by the Duma (the lower house of the Parliament) on July 5, 1996, contained a provision declaring all forests of the State Forest Fund to be federal property. However, ten days later, the Federation Council (the Parliament's upper house, composed of regional leaders) rejected the Duma's draft for its noncompliance with the Constitution and environmental legislation. Subsequent consultations between the two houses of the Parliament and the Government (in October-November 1996) have reportedly resulted in softening the corresponding language of the new Code allowing the possibility of regional ownership of forests. Nevertheless, the fundamental issues of land and forest resource ownership and consequent management responsibilities are unlikely to be adequately addressed until appropriate land legislation is in place. (A more detailed discussion on the recent evolution of forest legislation in Russia[2] is provided in Annex C).

Even though 95 percent of Russia's stocked forest land is under federal administration, the forest legislation transfers to the regions the rights and responsibilities of forest management, including responsibility for establishing leasing arrangements, the location and size of harvesting areas, and stumpage payments. A new leasing system is to replace the current method of allocating resources by establishing one-to-forty-nine year lease agreements between resource owners and resource users. The forest legislation also provides for national and international sales of timber through auctions by local administrations, with the participation of the Federal Forest Service. The Federal Forest Service, in coordination with the Russian Ministry of Economy, is supposed to establish a new payment system for the use of forest resources.

The forest legislation calls for certain areas to be set aside for exclusive use and management by indigenous people, to allow them to continue their traditional way of life. But, because no enforceable framework is yet in place, unsustainable commercial logging continues in areas where indigenous people have land and resource interests. The definition and protection of aboriginal land and resource rights are critical to the sustainable management of forest resources in Siberia and the Far East and need to be resolved before there is widespread investment and development. The International Labor Organization (ILO), which has been providing technical assistance to the Russian Federation on the development of legislation relating to indigenous people, has the international experience and expertise to help complete this task.

Difficulty in Meeting Environmental Commitments

Russia's international environmental commitments (Box 1.2) help to define the nation's broad forest policy framework and forest management objectives. However, because of the uncertainty of national forest management policy, Russia has difficulty fulfilling these commitments.

There are compelling reasons for the global community to be concerned about the future of Russia's forest resources, which are huge by any standard (Table 1.1 and Figure 1.2). Looming threats are the environmental degradation of 22 percent of the world's forest area, loss of unique ecosystems and other types of biodiversity, and the cultural disappearance of aboriginal ethnic groups. Russian boreal forests, which cover roughly the same area as the forests of Central and South America combined, make up about 60 percent of the world's boreal forests and 95 percent of all Russian closed forests. These

---

2 *An historical overview of forest legislation in Russia from 1918 to 1993, including problems with the 1993 Principles of Forest Legislation, is also provided by Sheingauz, Nilsson, and Shvidenko, 1995.*

forests play an important role in the global carbon balance, accounting for an estimated 75 percent of net boreal carbon storage capacity (Table 1.2 and Figure 1.2). Russia also harbors areas of unique biodiversity that constitute a valuable global heritage. These and other transboundary issues make forest policy and forest management in Russia a matter of global importance deserving of the support of the international community.

Box 1.2: Russia's Commitment to International Accords on Forest Resources

The Federal Forest Service represents the Russian Government in global discussions and international agreements on forestry. Since the 1992 United Nations Conference on Environment and Development (UNCED), Russia has participated in the Helsinki process, the 1993 Montreal workshops on the Sustainable Management of Temperate and Boreal Forests, the 1994 meetings of the Intergovernmental Working Group on Global Forests convened by Canada and Malaysia, and the 1994 Olympia Dialogue on Criteria and Indicators for the Conservation and Management of Temerate and Boreal Forests, and it was one of the sponsors of the Montreal Process Santiago Declaration in March 1995. At the meeting on the International Tropical Timber Agreement in January 1994, the Russian Federation was one of the twenty-four consumer countries that made a commitment to achieving sustainable management of their own forests by the year 2000. Russia has signed and ratified the Framework Convention on Climate Change and the Convention on Biological Diversity. Russia also plays a significant role in the International Panel on Forestry (under the UN Commission for Sustainable Development).

Table 1.1: Forest Area and Wood Volume in Selected Countries, 1990

Country	*Total forest area (millions of hectares)*	*Share of global forested area (percent)*	*Total wood volume[a] (million m^3)*	*Share of global wood volume (percent)*	*Wood production 1989-91 (million m^3)*	*Share of global production (percent)*
Russia	764[b]	22	82,110	21	375[b]	11
Brazil	566	16	65,088	17	262	8
Canada	247	7	28,671	7	179	5
United States	210	6	24,730	6	508	15
China	134	4	9,789	3	281	8
Indonesia	116	3	19,609	5	167	5
Zaire	113	3	23,108	6	39	1
Nordic countries	53	2	4,942	1	109	3
All other	1,239	36	125,979	33	1,542	46
World	**3,442**	**100**	**383,726**	**100**	**3,462**	**100**

[a] Excludes tropical plantations.

[b] Forest area and wood production estimates vary from one source of data to another.

Source: UN Food and Agriculture Organization (FAO); World Resources Institute 1994.

Figure 1.2: Selected Global and Russian Forest Sector Indicators in the 1990s

a. Distribution of Forest Land in the World, 1990s

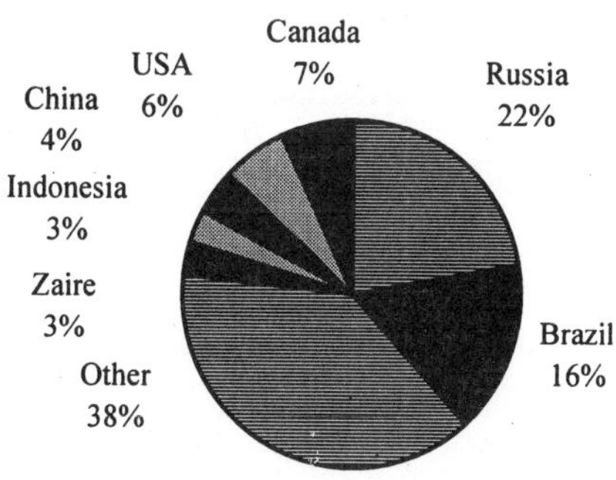

Sources: FAO and World Resources Institute, 1994.

b. Distribution of Annual Net Carbon Store in Boreal Forest Ecosystems, 1990s

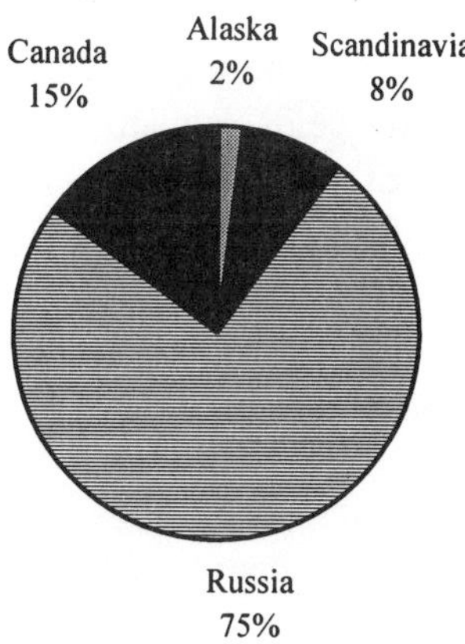

Source: Bemmann, 1995.

c. Distribution of Forested Land in Russia, 1990s

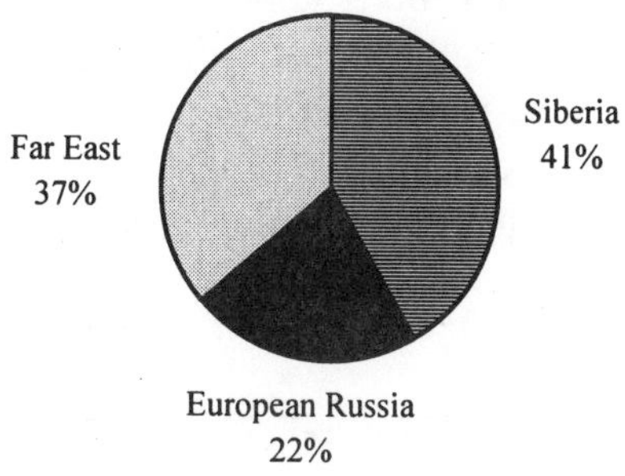

Source: The Federal Forest Service of Russia, 1996.

Table 1.2: Estimated Net Carbon Store in Boreal Forest Ecosystems (millions of tons of carbon per year)

Location	*Forest ecosystems*		*Swamps*		*Wood products*		*Total*	
	Amount	*Percent*	*Amount*	*Percent*	*Amount*	*Percent*	*Amount*	*Percent*
Alaska	6	1	3	6	<1	<1	9	2
Canada	63	10	26	57	19	33	108	15
Russia	493	82	11	24	26	46	530	75
Nordic countries	43	7	6	13	12	21	60	8
Total	**605**	**100**	**45**	**100**	**57**	**100**	**707**	**100**

Source: Bemmann 1995.

Reduced Accessibility and Weakened Health of Forest Resources

Some 78 percent of Russia's 764 million hectares of forested land is in Siberia (318 million hectares) and the Far East (279 million hectares), with the remaining 22 percent (167 million hectares) in European Russia[3] (see Figure 1.2). Most of the forests east of the Urals are classified as taiga (boreal forest consisting mainly of conifers), with yields at maturity ranging from 50 cubic meters of wood per hectare in northern taiga forests to 200-250 cubic meters per hectare in southern taiga forests. Pretundra forests, a subtype of taiga forests in a transition zone between the open tundra and the other taiga forests, have little potential for commercial harvest. There are also some temperate broadleaf forest types along the southern fringes of Siberia and the Far East. Detailed characteristics of these forest types are presented in Annex A; see also map IBRD 27086R.

Age and species composition are important considerations in assessing the economic potential of Russia's timber resources. In 1993, 85 percent of the total forested land in Siberia and the Far East (and up to 95 percent in European Russia) was covered by closed forest stands consisting of primary forests and second-growth stands of various age groups (Figure 1.3). Primary (mature and overmature) forests constitute 50 percent of closed forests in Siberia and the Far East and 39 percent in European Russia (Table 1.3). Other categories of forest lands comprise free growing stands, including young plantations and nurseries (2 percent of total forest lands in European Russia and 0.2 percent in Asian Russia), natural open woodlands (located only in Asian Russia, with over 10 percent of the regional total forest lands in the Far East), and nonstocked forest lands, including burned or dead stands, cutover areas, glades, and barrens (3 percent in European Russia and over 8 percent in Asian Russia). The land categories within the State Forest Fund in Russia are summarized in Figure 1.4.

---

3 *The estimates of stocked forest land vary between 735 and 770 million ha, with about 72 percent of it coniferous. Russia's total land area is 1707.5 million ha. In other words, about 45 percent of Russia'sland area is under stocked forest. On the average, the estimated growing stock is 106 cubic meters per hectare. Additional information on the development and utilization of Russian forest resources is available in Strakhov and Pisarenko (1996) and Isayev, ed. (1991); on the socio-economic assessment of boreal forests is available in Pisarenko and Strakhov (1996); and on production, consumption, and export prospects is available in Backman (1996).*

Figure 1.3: Forest Land Distribution by Region and Land Category in Russia, 1993

a. Total Forest Land Distribution by Category

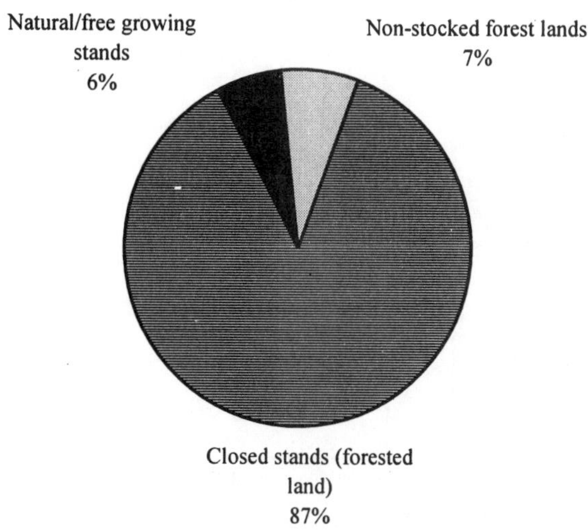

b. Forest Land Distribution by Region and Category

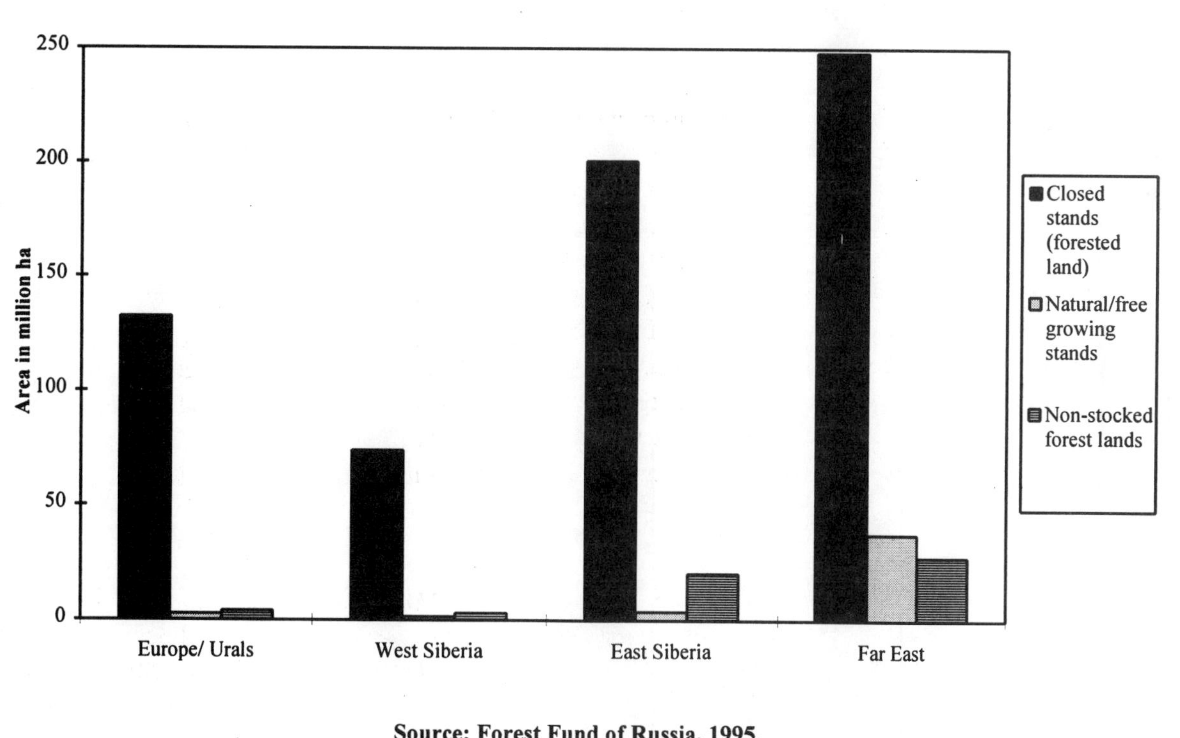

Source: Forest Fund of Russia, 1995.

Figure 1.4: Land Categories within the State Forest Fund in Russia

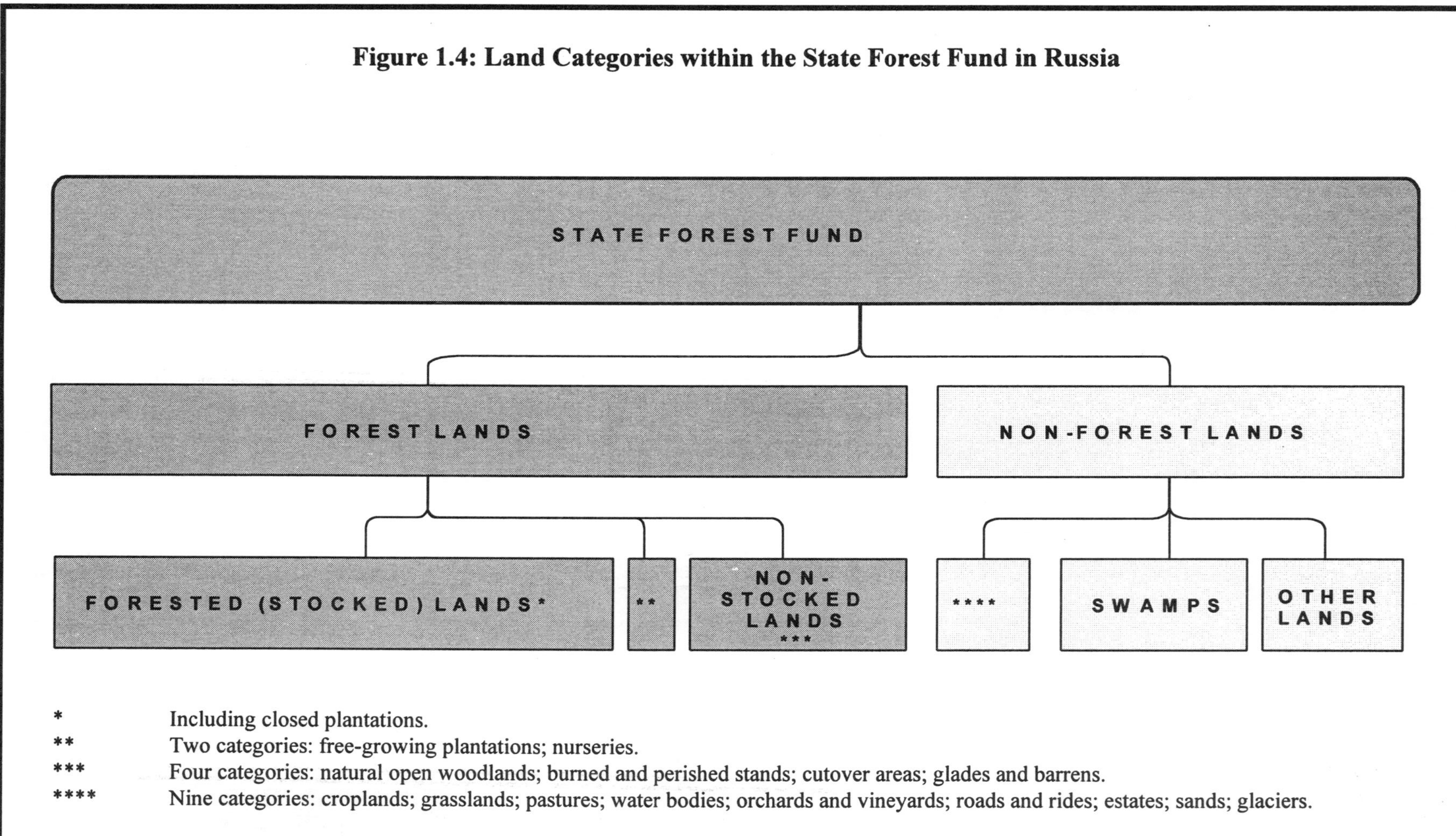

* Including closed plantations.

** Two categories: free-growing plantations; nurseries.

*** Four categories: natural open woodlands; burned and perished stands; cutover areas; glades and barrens.

**** Nine categories: croplands; grasslands; pastures; water bodies; orchards and vineyards; roads and rides; estates; sands; glaciers.

Source: The Federal Forest Service of Russia, 1996.

Table 1.3: Forest Land Distribution by Region and Land Category in Russia, 1993 (millions of hectares)

Region of Russia	*Total forest lands*	*Closed stands*	*Free-growing stands*	*Natural open wood-lands*	*Nonstocked forest lands*			
					Total in 1993	*Dead stands in 1988*	*Cutover areas in 1988*	*Glades/ barrens in 1988*
Europe/Urals	139.1	132.3	2.7	0.0	4.0	0.2	3.2	0.4
West Siberia	78.4	73.9	0.4	1.1	3.1	1.0	0.9	0.4
East Siberia	224.8	200.6	0.4	3.3	20.4	8.9	1.8	0.9
Far East	312.9	248.2	0.3	37.0	27.4	16.4	2.5	2.5
Total	**755.2**	**655.0**	**3.8**	**41.4**	**54.9**	**26.5**	**8.4**	**4.2**

Note: Refers only to the lands of the State Forest Fund managed by the Federal Forest Service and timber companies. In 1988, an additional 94.4 million hectares of forest lands (or about 10.9 percent of the total) were managed by other entities (such as federal agencies and agricultural enterprises).

Source: Forest Fund of Russia 1995.

The major coniferous species in these forests are pines, larch, spruce, and fir. Among the deciduous species, birch and aspen are most prevalent. These species are found in both Siberia and the Far East, though their distribution and composition vary (see Box 1.3). There is an urgent need to clarify the nature, distribution, quality, and condition of these forest resources in Russia, both to ensure adequate representation of biodiversity and protection of fragile environments in conservation plans and to guide investment and industry adjustment. Accurate estimates are needed to assess the real forest potential and to determine a sustainable annual allowable cut level that is relevant for industrial planning and control.

Box 1.3: Krasnoyarsk and Khabarovsk Krays: a Snapshot of Diversity

To explore some issues of regional diversity, the territories of Krasnoyarsk and Khabarovsk Krays were selected as representative samples for Siberia and the Far East, respectively. In Khabarovsk, climax species such as spruce and larch dominate, while in Krasnoyarsk the species composition is more varied containing pine, spruce, fir, birch, and aspen. The relatively high proportion of pioneer species (birch and aspen) inkrasnoyarsk is a direct result of insufficient regeneration following fifty years of heavy exploitation. Forests average 104 years of age in Krasnoyarsk and 82 years in Khabarovsk. A large portion of mature forests, however, is located in extremely remote areas that may never be economically accessible or that should not be harvested for environmental reasons. Young stands near industrial complexes and communities and alongside rivers, railways, and roads make up an increasing proportion of the easily accessible forests, but most are still decades away from harvesting age.

Forests are dynamic biological systems, and timber resources are affected by both natural and anthropogenic factors. In addition to the average annual clear-cut harvest of 860,000 hectares between 1987 and 1993, fire, insects, disease, and pollution take a tremendous toll, especially in Siberia and the Far East. Official estimates put the average area damaged by these factors during 1984-92 at 1.6 million hectares a year. Unofficial estimates are much higher, putting forest damage from various disturbance factors as high as 2 million hectares a year (IIASA 1995). Some estimates put the cumulative effect of such damage at 26.5 million hectares of dead forest in Russia today, 99 percent of it in Siberia and the Far East (Krankina and Dixon 1994). A more detailed description of the extent of this damage is provided in Annex A (also see Table 1.3 and Figure 1.7 later in this section).

The commercial losses due to fires and insect damage can be significant, destroying the economic base of a community or even the community itself. Equally serious is the environmental degradation, loss of wildlife habitat, and biodiversity implied by losses on this scale. For example, a catastrophic outbreak of Siberian silkworm (*Dendrolimus sibiricus*) infestation that developed in the forests of East Siberia in 1994-96 has damaged at least 700,000 hectares of valuable coniferous forest stands, with 300,000 hectares of trees - a standing volume of about 40-50 million cubic meters of timber - already drying. This volume is equal to 3.3 times the annual allowable cut for Krasnoyarsk Kray and 17 times its actual 1994 conifer timber harvest.

The World Bank responded to the Russian Government's request to provide emergency assistance to the Federal Forest Service and the regional administration in implementing the first phase of the Emergency Program of Integrated Forest Pest Control in the Forests of Krasnoyarsk Kray in 1996/97. Some US$5 million was reallocated from the Environment Management Project (EMP) in the summer of 1996 to finance the procurement of an environmentally safe biological control agent and efficient application equipment and to implement an integrated environmental impact assessment and pest monitoring system. An additional US$3 million may be on-lent to Krasnoyarsk Kray through the EMP's National Pollution Abatement Facility to help finance the salvaging of affected timber.

Overharvesting of Wildlife, Fish, and Other Nonwood Forest Products

Some 190,000 aboriginal people depend entirely on forests (timber and nontimber products) for their livelihoods and cultural and social traditions. Nonwood forest products provide important economic and social values for many Russians and are often essential for aboriginal and indigenous people to maintain their traditional relationship with the forests. Fish and game are a valuable source of meat and fur for home use, and commercial sales provide an essential income supplement for the population. About seventy animal species are identified for legal hunting under quotas, but the management, control, and enforcement of fishing and hunting regulations have seriously deteriorated, allowing overharvesting to occur. As wage incomes and employment have declined in the forest, mining, and oil and gas sectors, there has been a tendency for newcomer populations to overexploit wildlife resources and, in turn, to compete with indigenous peoples who are dependent on forest and nontimber forest resources for their livelihoods.

Other nonwood forest resources also contribute to the Russian economy. Some 5 to 7 million tons of nontimber forest products such as fruits and berries, nuts, mushrooms, honey, and a variety of medicinal herbs and ingredients are gathered and processed annually for consumption and local sales. These activities depend critically on the health of forests. (Additional information on the use of nonwood products is provided in Annex A and Annex G). Lack of funding is steadily weakening a once-sophisticated inventory and information collection system. (Wildlife management and sustainable forest development is further described in Annex I).

Wildlife resources and management, including the setting of quotas for commercially exploited game animals, fall under the jurisdiction of the newly created State Committee for Environmental Protection (until August 1996, the Ministry of Environmental Protection and Natural Resources[4]) and the Game Department of the Ministry of Agriculture and Food. Fish resources are regulated and controlled by the autonomous Russian Committee on Fisheries. Nongame species are not protected by law, and it is unclear whether all nongame species (including the 250 animal and 500 plant species listed as endangered) are under the jurisdiction of the newly established State Committee for Environmental Protection. Russia's hunting laws and regulations have not kept pace with the dramatic changes in Russia that have increased pressures on nongame species--changes in authority over resources and over conservation of biodiversity, privatization of state property, changes in the pricing structure of licenses and leases, and the breakdown of established support structures at the regional level.

Weakening of Forest Research Capabilities

Over the years, Russia had developed broad scientific capabilities at its numerous forest research and technology institutes, funded almost entirely through federal budget allocations (see Annex B and map IBRD 28354). Funding has been sharply curtailed in recent years, however, and the number of forest research institutes has fallen considerably because of the severe budgetary stringencies facing the federal Government. With budget allocations at the remaining institutes cut back to less than 25 percent of their pre-1991 levels, it is becoming very difficult to retain scientists and researchers (Box 1.4).

While the loss of so much research capacity is a serious concern at a time when the need for targeted information on forest resources is critical, the lack of goal orientation, priority setting, and coordination are fundamental issues in forestry research. Accurate and comprehensive information is needed on the nature and distribution of resources. Gap analyses are needed for extending the coverage of the nature reserve system and for securing the protection of environmentally fragile forests. A more rigorous definition of local criteria for sustainable management is also needed to help identify the forest resource base that is suitable for responsible and economically viable industrial use.

Box 1.4: When Forest Research Capability Breaks Down

Lack of funds and the disintegration of the support structure are jeopardizing fifteen years of good quality ecological and biological baseline data on all major game animals and rare and endagered animal species throughout Krasnoyarsk Kray. The data had been systemataically collected by twenty highly skilled and experienced professionals in the Sukachev Forest Institute. Because of inadequate funds, surveys concentrate on lands to be leased, neglecting other areas. The result will be a break in the continuity of data. The core of the Institute's research team is now working full time at the Krasnoyarsk Technological Academy, while trying to continue with the most essential wildlife inventory and research work for the local Game Department on an ad hoc, contract basis.

---

4 *Following the August 1996 restructuring of the Government, the former Ministry of Environmental Protection and Natural Resources (MEPNR) was reorganized into two new federal agencies - the State Committee for Environmental Protection and the Ministry of Natural Resources. As of October 1996, distribution of responsibilities between these two new entities was not yet finalized.*

B. Environmental Significance

The sheer size of the forests of Siberia and the Far East and the diversity of their plant and animal life and habitats make these forests an environmental factor of tremendous importance to Russia and the world. Loss of habitat from harvesting, fire, disease, and inappropriate management is the most serious threat to the unique biodiversity of climax forests. The survival of endangered species such as the Siberian tiger (*Panthera tigris altaica)* depends on the maintenance of large, undisturbed forest areas. The need to protect fragile permafrost areas is another special environmental concern, as is the importance of the forests' large contribution to carbon sequestration, which must not be jeopardized. Such environmental considerations are not adequately incorporated in the planning process or properly attended to in forest management and harvesting activities. As a general requirement in meeting these environmental concerns, large areas of forests have to be retained undisturbed, and forests that are not within protected areas need appropriate, complementary management.

National Protected Area System to Conserve Biodiversity

Forest conservation in Russia takes place through the unified National Protected Area System and the classification system applied to forests in the State Forest Fund. The National Protected Area System was established to conserve biodiversity and foster research on natural processes and phenomena (Box 1.5). There are concerns, however, that the National Protected Area System does not provide effective coverage for boreal forest areas. The State Committee for Environmental Protection, with the assistance of a US$20.1 million grant from the Global Environment Facility (GEF), has embarked on a strategy for systematically integrating biodiversity concerns into sectoral and cross-sectoral plans, programs, and policies.[5] This reflects the need for a country as large and ecologically as diverse as Russia, to have regional biodiversity strategies that are well-integrated in national strategy and that are based on cooperation among forest resource users in an integrated land-use planning process.

Permafrost forests constitute a special environmental protection issue. Half the forested areas in Siberia and the Far East are in permafrost areas, which are very sensitive to natural and anthropogenic disturbances (see map IBRD 27086R). Permafrost conditions create land surface instability from frost heave and subsidence and present challenging management issues, regeneration problems (mortality, leaning trees), and infrastructure concerns (roads breakup more easily under permafrost conditions).

---

5 *The details of the Russian Biodiversity Conservation Project are provided in the Project Document, World Bank (1996a). In this context, a very good overview of forests, biodiversity hotspots, and industrial developments in the Russian Far East is available in Newell and Wilson (1996).*

Box 1.5: Russia's National Protected Area System

The National Protected Area System in Russia has four components:

- Zapovedniks are strict nature reserves in which all economic activity that might threaten the natural ecosystems is forbidden. Currently there are eighty-three nature reserves covering some 28 million hectares (Krever and others 1994), a little over 1 percent of the territory of Russia (see map IBRD 27086R).[1] A recent presidential decree declared the Government's intention to expand the system to 150 reserves covering 3 percent of the territory.

- National Natural Parks are areas with a special ecological, historical, or aesthetic value and are intended for environmental, recreational, educational, scientific, and cultural activities. There are plans to expand the current system of twenty-four National Natural Parks (a total area of about 13 million hectares) to seventy-one (15 million hectares) by 2005.

- Protected Territories, or Zakazniks, are designated for the preservation of specific aspects of biodiversity, from natural ecosystems to individual species, through the preservation, reproduction, and restoration of natural resources. Protected Territories (which cover an additional 11.5 million ha) are a potentially more flexible instrument for conserving biodiversity because they are numerous and easy to establish and their conservation regime is adaptable to specific conservation regime is adaptable to specific conservation management objectives.

- National Monuments are small, natural objects or areas of value that are preserved and protected in their natural condition. These areas are often poorly documented, and few resources are devoted to their conservation and management.

Annex H provides more detailed information about the current status of the protected area system in Russia.

----

[1] *These figures, from Krever and others 1994, are at variance with the information obtained by the World Bank, which indicates that there are 80 Zapovedniks covering an area of 16 million hectares.*

Since 1959 a special protection zone has been established to shield the northern pre-tundra forests from commercial exploitation (see map IBRD 27086R). Protection has not been complete, however, and commercial development in the northern permafrost region has resulted in the destruction of some 1 million hectares. Until management of permafrost areas can ensure resource extraction without irreparable environmental damage, a very cautious approach should be taken to the granting of harvesting rights. Based on extensive research in permafrost areas and on a model of the northern region, the Sukachev Forest Institute has proposed moving the strict protection zone further south, which would greatly increase protection of some of the most fragile landscape in Siberia and the Far East. The proposed line is shown on map IBRD 27086R.

Russia's Forest and Global Carbon Balance

Russia's vast expanse of forest provides a major carbon store that may represent as much as one-seventh of the earth's terrestrial carbon pool (Kolchugina and Vinson 1993) and about 75 percent of estimated net carbon storage capacity of the total boreal forest ecosystems (see Table 1.2). The role of Russia's forests in regulating atmospheric carbon content is significant, and they merit careful management on these grounds alone. The impact of forest utilization, regeneration, and protection on the carbon balance is considerable, as is that of forest fire management. Krankina and Dixon (1994) estimate that replacement of old growth forests with forests intensively managed for wood production (harvest rotations of 60-100 years, site preparation, thinning and salvage) reduces the total woody biomass averaged over the rotation to between 10 and 25 percent of that in the natural old growth forest. Forest fires and other injurious agents also have a significant influence on carbon emissions from forests. Estimates for emissions from forest fires in Russia range from 150 million tons carbon per year (Shvidenko and others 1995) to 170-330 million tons carbon per year and (Krankina and Dixon 1993). Shvidenko and others (1995) also estimate that additional emissions of 130-165 million tons carbon per year result from biotic and abiotic agents other than fires.

Krankina and Dixon (1994) estimate that forest fires account for some 17 percent of carbon emission from forests in Siberia and the Far East. They also estimate that improvement in fire management systems and the extension of these systems to areas not currently covered would result in a 20 percent reduction of the annually burnt area, with a consequent reduction in carbon emission of some 49 million tons carbon per year. Shvidenko and others (1995) suggest that implementation of forest protection systems similar to those in use in Canada and the Nordic countries could reduce fire emissions by two-thirds and emissions from biotic sources by one-third. They estimate that this would reduce total annual emission by some 150-170 million tons carbon per year (also see ECE/FAO/ILO 1996). Either way, it is clear that forest fire management is potentially one of the more immediate and effective means for reducing carbon dioxide emissions.

Boreal forests play an important role in the global carbon balance and carbon cycle. This role can be enhanced through sustainable forest management designed to increase carbon sequestration. According to Shvidenko, Nilsson, Roshkov and Strakhov (1996), the present forest management regime can be significantly improved and should consist of the following: reforestation of unforested, clear-cut, and burnt areas; replacement of less productive and soft deciduous stands; reconstruction of climax stands; improvements in fire, pest, and disease control; implementation of thinning; and efficient utilization of forest resources.

Carbon sequestration in the boreal forest environment is an area that needs much more research, and all countries with boreal forests have joined in an effort to coordinate research and management activities. The Russian Federation has signed and ratified the Framework Convention on Climate Change and the Convention on Biological Diversity. These conventions commit the federal Government to manage forests to protect their biodiversity and ecosystems, to regulate atmospheric carbon, and to ensure the sustainable development of the forest sector. The stated national objectives of Russia are consistent with these international conventions, but a new forest policy framework is needed to make full compliance possible.

Other Sources of Environmental Impact

Policies and activities in other sectors of the economy also have a large impact on forest resources in Russia, particularly oil field development. Roads originally built for oil fields increase fire risks and enable timber harvesting activities to take place with less planning, management, and control than in officially designated harvesting areas. Native vegetation is destroyed during construction of roads and oil well pads for drilling operations. Reclamation of areas criss-crossed by vehicle tracks takes years, and in the meantime the ecological disruption may cause irreversible loss of biodiversity.

Oil field development often intercepts the migration routes of wildlife and is disruptive in other ways as well. The well pads, roads, pipelines, heavy vehicles, drilling rigs, and noise drive animals away, while the removal of native vegetation can also harm wildlife, since there is great competition for what little biomas is produced in the taiga and tundra. The fires used to "clean up" oil spills often spread well beyond the spill area. In some northern reaches of Russia, exploration activities have left the land unsuitable for hunting and fishing or as reindeer pasture, thus affecting the livelihoods and cultures of indigenous communities.

C. Economic Significance

Under the current forest classification system, approximately 70 percent of the forested area of Siberia and the Far East is considered to be potentially available for harvesting (Group III); the remaining 30 percent is either strictly protected (Group I) or subject to some type of harvesting restrictions (Group II) (see Box 1.6 and Annex A). About 90 percent of harvested wood comes from Group III forests, and the annual allowable cut is derived primarily from this group of forests.

Box 1.6: Management Status of Forest Groups in the Russian State Forest Fund

Forests in the State Forest Fund are divided into three broad groups, each further subdivided according to its biodiversity, ecological, and social functions.

Group I forests (21 percent of State Forest Fund area) are designated as "protective" forests. Group I forests are further subdivided into seven protective categories and include noncommercial forests that satisfy environmental needs such as watershed and riparian protection, erosion mitigation, landscape and other land protection and preservation functions, and sanitary and health-enhancing functions, as provided by the greenbelt forests around cities, townships, and industrial sites. Only sanitary harvesting (felling of trees that are fifty years older than their optimum cutting age) is allowed in these forests.

Group II forests (8 percent) are located in densely populated areas, limiting their potential for wood production. They are mainly protective forests with limited commercial value. Final harvest is allowed in parts of these forests, based on the principles of sustainable yield, though no clear felling may be allowed in certain areas of sensitive forests (for example, along river banks).

Group III forests (71 percent) are designated commercial forests. However, this designation refers more to legal status than actual commercial potential since the group includes both economically accessible and inaccessible forests. They are managed primarily for industrial wood production, with few restrictions on final cutting. Forest management in these areas is expected to adhere to principles of sustained yield and the safeguarding of environmental protection.

Wood Production Potential

From inventory data collected for each defined management area, the Federal Forest Service calculates the annual allowable cut -- a measure of the total biological potential for sustainable yield harvests -- for the entire country, region by region. In the current planning period the federal total annual allowable cut is set at about 530 million cubic meters (down from an estimated 800 million cubic meters or more in the mid-1980s); Siberia and the Far East account for about 63 percent of the total (332 million cubic meter; see Table 1.4). The annual allowable cut is based on periodic net volume changes in forests as a whole (normally over a ten-year period), including areas that are economically inaccessible or noncommercial.

The inclusion of inaccessible and uneconomic areas, that published figures on the annual allowable cut do not indicate, inevitably leads to overestimation of the level of harvesting that can be sustained from the effective productive area of the forest, and so this measure cannot serve as a reliable basis for planning sustainable forest management. Accurate determination of an annual allowable cut is crucial to achieving resource sustainability (see Chapter 2 and Annex A). However, it is impossible with the data at hand to verify the sustainability of current harvesting levels. More detailed information on resource productivity and costs for the effective productive areas is urgently needed to determine the environmentally and economically sustainable wood supply. In addition, areas that can be environmentally and economically managed on a sustainable basis need to be carefully identified if wood production potential is to be realistically assessed. Until such an assessment is made, the current estimate of the annual allowable cut level in Russia cannot be used to guide the sustainable development of the sector.

Table 1.4: Estimated Biological Forest Potential for Various Regions of Russia (thousands of cubic meters)

Region of Russia	*Total annual allowable cut*	*Conifers*	*Deciduous (hard)*	*Deciduous (soft)*
Siberia	233,286	187,720	--	55,566
Far East	98,546	81,853	4,187	12,506
Europe/Urals	197,575	49,554	5,043	132,978
Total	**529,407**	**319,127**	**9,230**	**201,050**

Source: Based on State Forest Account of 1993 and obtained from the Federal Forest Service of Russia, 1995.

An additional problem in the assessment of the wood production potential is the legacy of past patterns of overexploitation. As noted, a large proportion of the mature forests are in remote areas that may never be economically accessible or that should not be harvested for environmental reasons. And 1.47.most of the young forest stands growing in areas of past exploitation that are more accessibly located (near industrial complexes or along major transport corridors) are many decades away from harvesting age. Considerable loss of environmental and social amenity values will occur if increased intensity harvesting of accessible Group I and Group II forests (about 30 percent of Russian Forest Fund) continues or accelerates.

Thus before there can be any meaningful determination of the potential for wood production in Russia, the current status of the resource base for sustainable forestry has to be determined. Detailed information is urgently needed on the spatial distribution of age classes in economically accessible forests that are environmentally suitable for sustainable wood production. In the long run, sustainable wood production will require a commitment to comprehensive land use planning for the forest resource. In the short term, it will require rapid assessment of the status of the forests in the logical supply zones for existing enterprises to help frame investment opportunities and to determine the full extent of restructuring needed in the sector.

Wood-Dependent Domestic Industries

Forest industry accounts for about 5 percent of total industrial output and 7 percent of the total number of industrial employees. However, by 1993, domestic production of wood products (the output of logs, lumber, plywood, reconstituted wood boards, and pulp and paper products in roundwood equivalent) had plunged to 57 percent of its 1989 level. The decline continued in 1994 and 1995, aggravating the supply problem for wood processing industries. Except for furniture production, all major producers of wood products suffered a major contraction in output (see Table 1.5). The domestic production of major wood and paper products in the first five months of 1996 was lower than that in the corresponding period in 1995.

Housing and railways have been especially hard hit by the reduction in the supply of wood products. In 1993 the housing construction industry claimed a wood shortfall of at least 10 million cubic meters, while the national railways received only half the required railway wooden sleepers and a third of wooden traffic light poles. Although these shortfalls may be based on needs prevailing under central planning, which may since have changed, recent studies confirm significant shortages in building materials (World Bank 1995d) and inadequate replacement of railways sleepers (Holt 1993).

Table 1.5: Wood Products Consumption in Russia, 1989 and 1993
(millions of cubic meters)

	Roundwood equivalent consumption		
User group	*1989*	*1993*	*Percentage change*
Machine industry	15.0	6.0	-60.0
Consumer products	21.0	9.7	-53.8
Construction	49.0	26.2	-46.5
Railway sleepers	14.5	7.8	-46.2
Pulp and paper	44.5	24.0	-46.1
Maintenance	32.0	17.4	-45.6
Packaging	38.0	24.7	-35.0
Furniture	20.3	20.9	+0.6
Other users	23.0	10.3	-55.2
Total	**257.3**	**147.0**	**-42.9**

Source: The State Statistics Committee of Russia, 1995.

Export Market Potential

Exports of wood products have accounted for a significant portion of total output and have been a significant source of foreign exchange. Logs, the main forest export, are shipped to forty countries, while lumber, pulp and paper, and furniture products are shipped to some seventy countries. Japan has emerged as a major importer of Russian logs (unprocessed timber). Reported export earnings fell sharply between 1990 and 1992, from US$3.87 billion to US$1.49 billion, with the adjustments in the foreign exchange rate accounting for most of the decline in export earnings. Since then there has been a recovery and even some growth in export volumes of timber products (Table 1.6). In 1995, the total value of forestry product exports had risen to US$4.2 billion (Table 1.7 and Figure 1.5). Unprocessed timber (18.5 million cubic meters) was the largest export item, accounting for 25 percent of total exports, 97 percent of it to countries outside the Commonwealth of Independent States (CIS). Other important forestry product exports were sawn timber, pulp and paper, and newsprint. (Additional details on international forest trade are provided in Annex D).

The export market potential for wood should be good, particularly for the high-quality wood that Russia can provide. However, Russia can maintain or even increase its export earnings from forest products while reducing its raw wood requirements and strengthening local economies by increasing exports of value-added processed timber rather than raw logs. Undamaged slow-growing trees in Russia's northern regions yield fine-textured wood with narrow rings and small, well-dispersed knots. Larch is widely popular for special end-uses in foreign markets, spruce and fir are also in demand, while the even-textured Korean pine and Siberian red pine have ready markets in Japan and the United Kingdom. Demand projections for European and the Pacific Rim markets indicate a growing supply shortfall from traditional wood-exporting countries (tropical and temperate), promising likely expanded markets for Russian wood products. China is also an excellent prospect, since current per capita consumption of wood products (including paper products) is extremely low and is expected to rise with income growth. Following economic recovery, Kazakstan and other Central Asian countries are also likely to be important potential markets for wood products from Russia.[6]

Table 1.6: Exports of Roundwood and Sawn Timber from Russia, 1992-94
(millions of cubic meters)

Exports	*1992*	*1993*	*1994*	*1995*
Roundwood[a]	16.90	14.20	14.85	18.45
Sawn timber	3.80	4.60	5.40	6.15[b]
Total solid wood	**20.70**	**18.60**	**20.25**	**24.60**

[a] Unprocessed timber.
[b] Estimate.

Source: Ekonomica I Zhizn 1995; and the State Customs Committee of Russia.

---

6 *Additional analysis on the prospects for timber trade between Russia and the former Soviet Republics is available in Backman (1995 and 1996). An assessment of the supply and demand of industrial wood and other forest products is provided in Nilsson (1996).*

Trade barriers to exports of forest products have been substantially reduced or abolished (Box 1.7). However, despite the forest sector's importance to Russia's international trade, structural barriers to trade remain, from government control of forest production to legal system and policies on taxation, banking, and business licensing that interfere with open market mechanisms. The sector still lacks the infrastructure, institutions, information, and incentives necessary for establishing free market prices that will foster appropriate private investment and sustainable production. In this context, however, there is a need to address the growing problems of illegal logging and timber trade, unregulated exports of unprocessed logs, and lack of enforcement of environmental laws. Furthermore, particularly in the European market, independent certification of compliance with international standards on sustainable production norms will be increasingly important in terms of developing or maintaining market access.

Table 1.7: Export of Forest Products from Russia, 1995

	Total		*Non-CIS countries*		*CIS countries*	
Product	*Quantity (thousand tons)*	*Value (million dollars)*	*Quantity (thousand tons)*	*Value (million dollars)*	*Quantity (thousand tons)*	*Value (million dollars)*
Timber and timber products	--	2,107.9	--	1,940.3	--	167.6
Fuel wood	737.8	27.8	701.4	27.0	36.4	0.8
Timber, unprocessed (m^3)	18,446.0	1,064.5	17,948.8	1,040.8	497.1	23.6
Sleepers	168.6	25.3	4.9	0.7	163.7	24.6
Timber, sawed	--	709.4	--	640.1	--	69.2
Wood filing panels	--	21.5	--	3.6	--	18.0
Wood fiber panels	--	32.0	--	21.1	--	10.9
Plywood (m^3)	670.5	193.2	657.0	188.9	13.5	4.3
Wood containers	102.8	12.8	44.0	6.6	58.9	6.2
Wood construction products	8.8	5.6	3.4	2.0	5.4	3.6
Paper-pulp	--	951.3	--	919.0	--	32.3
Cellulose sulfate, soluble	79.5	85.8	76.7	82.5	2.8	3.3
Cellulose sulfate, insoluble	1,092.7	762.7	1,062.6	743.5	30.1	19.2
Cellulose sulfite, insoluble	159.6	96.4	151.5	90.7	8.1	5.8
Paper and products	--	1,175.9	--	950.1	--	225.8
Newsprint	1,005.1	598.3	916.4	542.3	88.7	56.0
Paper and cardboard, nonchalked	219.2	153.4	150.2	108.2	69.0	45.1
Craft-paper and cardboard, nonchalked	251.7	143.3	233.9	130.0	17.8	13.4
Other paper and cardboard, nonchalked	296.5	166.0	241.0	128.3	55.6	37.7
Paper and cardboard chalked	8.5	7.9	5.7	3.4	2.8	4.5
Paper and cardboard saturated	34.1	22.9	29.7	17.3	4.4	5.6
Wallpaper	4.9	7.2	1.1	1.0	3.8	6.2
Paper hygiene products	3.6	4.8	1.5	2.2	2.1	2.6
Paper or cardboard containers	34.8	33.5	9.4	8.0	25.4	25.5
Paper or cardboard labels	--	4.5	--	0.1	--	4.4
Other paper and cardboard products	4.2	6.9	1.1	0.8	3.1	6.1
Total	**--**	**4,235.1**	**--**	**3,809.4**	**--**	**425.7**

Source: Customs Statistics of Foreign Trade of the Russian Federation, 1995.

Figure 1.5: Export Composition and Trends for Forest Products from Russia

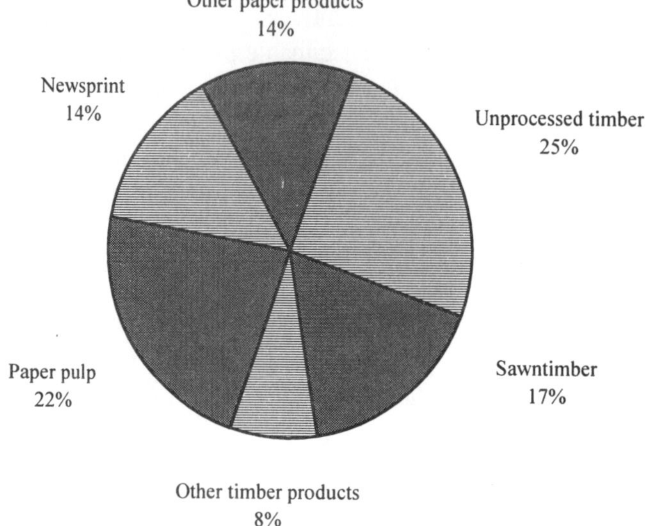

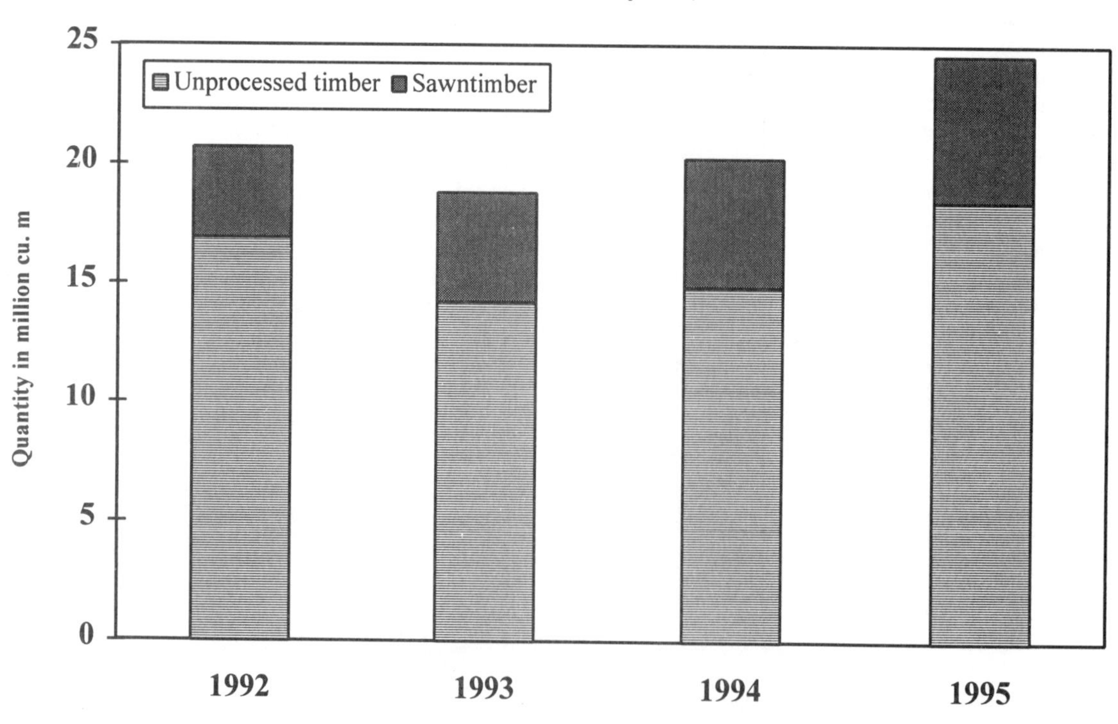

Source: The State Customs Committee of Russia, 1996.

Box 1.7: Reduction in Barriers to Exports of Forest Products

As part of Russia's overall trade liberalization, many barriers to exports of forest products have been eliminated. Before these reforms, exporters of forest products in Russia were required to register their contracts with the local branch of the Ministry of Foreign Economic Relations and with the Russian State Forest Industry Company, Roslesprom, and its regional counterparts. Exporters were also required to contract their sales through designated special exporters. Though these exporters were limited by law to charge fees of no more than 1.5 percent of the contract value for placing their seal on the contract, they often charged much more for additional "consulting" or other services. Some of these companies established subsidiaries to handle insurance, banking, and import operations, giving them near-monopoly power over export licensing. One such regional organization, Dalles in Khabarovsk, essentially dominates the log export market in the region. The export controls thus simply resulted in higher rents to privileged companies.

This system of special exporters, export licenses, quotas and mandatory contract registration was formally abolished on April 1, 1995. Registration of export contracts with the State Customs Committee has been continued on a voluntary basis. All exporters are required to file a report on foreign trade transactions with the Central Bank of Russia, to control the repatriation of foreign currency. Export taxes (which used to be 8 percent on sawn and unsawn timber and 10 percent on cellulose) were abolished in April 1996. Another promising sign of competition-promoting change occurred in early 1995, when the Russian Far Eastern Association of Small Private Nongovernmental Timber Users registered in Khabarovsk, announcing its intention to remain independent of government and large established enterprises such as Dalles.

Taxation and Stumpage Charges

Russia's forest enterprises complain that their tax burden is extremely high, claiming that more than 90 percent of revenues go to taxes (for a discussion of general Russian taxation law and fiscal management, see World Bank 1995c; Sunley 1995; and World Bank 1996b). Overall tax recovery, however, is very poor. During the first nine months of 1994, the sector's profits were 909.3 billion rubles. Of that amount, 327.6 billion rubles (36 percent) was paid in profit tax and 64.3 billion rubles (7 percent) in employee payroll taxes. According to unconfirmed reports, the enterprises retained only 517.4 billion rubles, one-fourth the amount needed to cover their liabilities to territorial and local government for social, cultural, housing, and infrastructure expenses and repayment of bank loans and interest and debt to the federal budget (*Izvestia,* February 16, 1995).

However, despite this apparently heavy tax burden on forest enterprises, actual tax revenues from the sector were low in 1994 because of the sector's poor performance, with total tax receipts being little more than US$1 per cubic meter harvested. *Izvestia's* figures indicate total federal tax payments of only about US$184 million (at 2,125 rubles to the dollar). An equal amount should have been collected at the territorial and local levels to cover social, housing, infrastructure, and related expenditures. Stumpage revenues to local governments are estimated at about $40 million (based on an average stumpage of 800 rubles per cubic meter on a total of 123 million cubic meters of chargeable wood production). A 5 percent federal forest conservation tax, intended to recover forest regeneration costs but amounting to only 6 percent of operating costs in 1994, was abolished in April 1995.

Until the new Forest Code becomes effective, three charges are still being levied on forest utilization: stumpage charges, land use taxes, and timber lease charges. Stumpage charges are assessed by the territorial authorities and, the revenues go to their general revenue funds.[7] Stumpage charges seem to be determined through one-on-one negotiations between territorial officials and enterprises. In Khabarovsk, stumpage charges vary by species (from approximately 2,000 rubles per cubic meter for spruce in 1994 to 500 rubles for birch). Quality and distance from the market are not generally considered in determining stumpage charges. The land use tax (5 percent of the stumpage charge) is assessed annually for the right to use timberlands. Charges for long-term leases for logging rights are based on the primary species found on the leased land and the length of the lease. Average timber lease charges in Khabarovsk are 40 percent of the annual stumpage charge.

The new Forest Code, if signed into law, is expected to bring about significant changes in system of forest utilization charges. Minimum stumpage charges would be determined by the federal authorities and the proceeds would be distributed to federal and regional budgets according to a pre-determined ratio. Forest lease charges, determined by auction, would be channeled directly to the local Forest Management Districts (leskhozes) after the mandatory minimum stumpage charge had been deducted (see Annex C for details on the proposed Forest Code).

However, the potential for tax revenue from the forest sector in Russia is substantial. There are at least three main sources of tax revenue: stumpage charges, taxes on harvesting companies and taxes on wood processing activities. Because of the high level of uncertainty about sustainable levels of wood production and future costs and prices, the potential tax revenue is estimated in 1996 U.S. dollars at two levels of wood production and three levels of costs and prices. The domestic prices at present are lower than the assumed international prices. However, with the continuing liberalization of prices and trade, the domestic prices are expected to converge to international prices. Since the underlying assumptions are conservative, the potential tax revenue estimates are on the conservative side. For example, at present, the average stumpage charges in Russia are less than US$1 per cubic meter whereas under auction the stumpage charges in Russia and some neighboring countries are over US$10 per cubic meter. In Scandinavia, the stumpage charges could be as high as US$30 per cubic meter. Furthermore, tax recovery in Russia is also very low.

The potential tax revenues from the forest sector in Russia, under the most conservative assumptions, are estimated to be at least US$0.9 billion per year. They could be as high as US$5.5 billion depending on assumptions about wood production and profitability of harvesting companies and wood processors (see Table 1.8 and Annex Table D.13). Unless the government is able to reform the forest sector policy, increase stumpage charges and improve tax recovery, they will not be able to recover the potential tax revenues. The potential tax revenue is adequate not only to finance all the expenditures related to forest management, regeneration, protection and sustainability (the forest management operations budget in 1996 is approximately US$425 million) but also make a major fiscal contribution to the treasury. Furthermore, higher stumpage charges will discourage over- exploitation of the forest resources and waste of harvested wood, thereby, promoting efficiency and sustainable sector development. The reforms suggested in this report are essential to realize the potential tax revenues through sustainable sector development which is consistent with maintaining the environmental integrity of country's forest resources.

---

7 *The term "stumpage" here refers to the royalty level or charge paid at stump for the harvest of timber. These charges are fixed administratively and are not strictly stumpage charges in the technical sense of western forest management. In the latter case, stumpage charges are determined by subtracting the cost of harvesting and transport from the price for logs in a designated market (see glossary of forest terms).*

Table 1.8: Potential Annual Tax Revenues from the Forest Sector in Russia
(million 1996 U.S. dollars)

Tax scenarios	*Under wood production of*	
	110 mill. cu. m (current level)	*300 mill. cu. m (possible maximum sustainable level)*
Stumpage charges		
Scenario 1: $3 per cu.m	330	900
Scenario 2: $6 per cu.m	660	1,800
Scenario 3: $10 per cu.m	1,100	3,000
Taxes on harvesting companies[a]		
Scenario 1	77	210
Scenario 2	154	420
Scenario 3	193	525
Taxes on wood processing activities[b]		
Scenario 1	514	1,400
Scenario 2	616	1,680
Scenario 3	719	1,960
Total tax revenue		
Scenario 1	**921**	**2,510**
Scenario 2	**1,430**	**3,900**
Scenario 3	**2,012**	**5,485**

[a] Based on three levels of the cost of harvesting.
[b] Based on three levels of prices for paper-pulp and sawn wood.

Notes:
1. Tax on harvesting companies and wood processing activities consists of profit tax.
2. Additional details on tax calculations are provided in Annex Table D.13.

Source: World Bank staff estimates, 1996.

Forest and Wood Product Enterprises

Most logging enterprises *(lespromkhoz)* were privatized in 1993 as joint-stock companies. Many of them are still partly owned (about 20-30 percent) by the federal Government and are managed by Goskomlesprom, which replaced Roslesprom in June 1996.[8] Recently, the shares managed by the

8 *Goskomlesprom is a State Committee for Timber, Pulp and Paper and Woodworking Industry. This new federal agency was established in June 1996 by reorganizing the former state holding company Roslesprom (see Annex B).*

Government were put up for sale, a move meant to reduce government involvement in the commercial aspects of the forest industry. As of July 1, 1995, 62 percent of the logging industry had been privatized, 95 percent of wood processing, 95 percent of pulp and paper, and 100 percent of the furniture industry. (Privatization and enterprise reform in the forest sector are described in more detail in Annex F).

In the Soviet era, most of the timber harvested in Siberia and the Far East was shipped east for export as raw material (logs) or west for processing. The current industrial structure still relies heavily on the transportation link between the raw material producers in the east and the industrial capacity that is still heavily concentrated in the west. Although European Russia has less than 40 percent of the country's timber resources (see Table 1.4), it accounts for more than 60 percent of Russia's total wood processing (see map IBRD 27087R). Only seven of the country's twenty-five major pulp and paper facilities, 14 percent of its plywood production capacity, and 20 percent of its particle board capacity are located in Siberia and the Far East. The tremendous costs of this inefficient arrangement were hidden under central planning, when prices were controlled and the cost of transporting wood to distant locations for processing was largely ignored. The elimination of subsidies and the emergence of a market economy have exposed the true costs of delivering wood to the west, and they have been shown to be prohibitively high (see Annex E).

There is a growing tendency to form integrated arrangements between forest harvesting enterprises and wood processing enterprises through stock acquisitions. Such integration which should help to stabilize timber supply and industrial production, is easier to accomplish in areas with a broad mix of processing capacity. Remote areas with no processing capabilities may not be able to use this option, at least in the near term. There has been a remarkable increase in the number of small-scale enterprises, especially in the sawmilling industry, although their share in production is still small.

Processing Technology and Investment

Under appropriate management and sustainable sector development programs, the forest sector in Siberia and the Far East (particularly the Far East) can contribute significantly to recovery of the Russian economy. However, the sector must overcome the serious comparative disadvantages it faces, including high transport costs, rapid deterioration in technology and a resulting inability to produce products that meet international standards, and a lack of capital, stemming in part from an under developed domestic credit network and in part from the relative unprofitability of production enterprises. Over the medium to long term, reform and investment measures will be needed to overcome these obstacles and encourage participation by the private sector on a sustainable basis.

Russia's industrial capacity in roundwood and pulp and paper production increased steadily until the late 1980s, making Russia the second largest wood processor in the world. Since then, Russia has fallen behind its global competitors in many important areas. Roundwood production went from over 300 million cubic meters at the end of the 1980s to about 115 million cubic meters in 1995 (see Figure 1.1). Pulp and paper production capacity, which had grown an average of 2.7 percent a year from 1976 to 1988, has since declined to pre-1970 levels (Simons 1992).

Most wood processing plants use obsolete technology and are poorly maintained. Outdated machinery in sawmills, plywood mills, and pulp and paper mills severely handicaps the production of wood products for export. In the absence of standard equipment such as edgers and kiln-drying facilities, for example, sawn-wood is shipped green or incompletely air dried and is often delivered unsorted. As a result, Russian wood products do not meet the standards of an increasingly quality-oriented international market. They are competitive only at the lower end of the price scale in world markets, in products such as standard-grade plywood. A few joint-venture enterprises with foreign partners have installed modern equipment and produce good quality output for foreign markets, but their capacity is still very limited.

Outdated technology also holds back the particle board and pulp and paper industries. Russia is unable to produce the medium-density fiberboard currently in high demand on global markets. Much of the pulp and paper sector operates with old, poorly maintained equipment, and several heavily polluting mills have been forced to shut down. A survey of seventeen pulp and paper facilities found that they accounted for 50 percent of the biological oxygen demand, 90 percent of chemical oxygen demand, and 49 percent of suspended solids in the combined effluent of all industries (Simons 1992).

These conditions are not surprising in an industry that has seen very little capital investment in the past twenty years. Only three new particle board mills have been established since 1989, one in Siberia (240,000-cubic-meter capacity) and two in the Moscow area (combined capacity of 220,000 cubic meters). No new sawmills or pulp and paper facilities have been built since 1989, but some equipment has been modernized or replaced in sawmill, plywood, particle board, and fiberboard plants, affecting about 0.5 percent of the total wood processing capacity. One-third of this maintenance work was in Siberia and the Far East, the rest in European Russia. Relatively little investment has gone into the pulp and paper industry, most of which is located in European Russia.

Roslesprom had estimated investment requirements for the Russian forest sector at about US$8 billion for the remainder of the decade (1996-2000), rising to US$13 billion for 2001-05 and to US$24 billion for 2006-10 (Table 1.9). These projections are likely to overestimate investment needs since they are based on historical price, production, consumption, and trade patterns; less than realistic economic assumptions; and less stringent programs designed to maintain environmental integrity in the forest sectors. Government officials and private experts expect that the bulk of the investment (over 80 percent) will come from the private sector, though it is unclear whether the remaining amounts are justifiable public expenditures. The Russian Government is making substantial efforts to mobilize private investment, but policy and institutional issues must be clarified first to create conditions that are conducive to facilitate sustainable private investment. At this time, most of the private and state-owned forest enterprises are not profitable and therefore will also not be in a position to finance large capital investments out of their retained earnings.

Table 1.9: Roslesprom's Projected Investment Requirements for the Russian Forest Sector (billions of 1993 US dollars)

Potential source of investment	*1996-2000*	*2001-2005*	*2006-2010*
Retained earnings of enterprises	5.27	7.67	13.46
Bank credits	0.55	1.92	3.84
Federal and local budgets	1.59	2.38	4.81
Foreign investments	0.48	0.72	1.92
Total investment required	**7.89**	**12.69**	**24.03**

Source: Roslesprom.

Wages and Employment

While employment has declined in most sectors of the Russian economy since the breakup of the former Soviet Union, the forest sector has been especially hard hit, with Siberia and the Far East bearing the brunt. Under central planning, every production unit was assigned employment and output targets, so both were predictable. Once state subsidies were phased out and market forces started to influence production levels, both output and employment fell. Between 1990 and 1995, log production in the Russian Federation declined by 60 percent. Employment statistics for Krasnoyarsk Kray show a 19 percent drop in employment in the forest industry from 1990 to 1994 (23 percent in logging, 11 percent in wood processing, and 21 percent in pulp and paper); by comparison, employment fell 14 percent in the machine industry and rose 3 percent in the electrical power generation industry.

The employment situation is probably worse than these figures indicate, however, because there is high underemployment throughout the forest sector, and production has stopped completely in many logging communities, though employees remain employed on paper. Many enterprises have shorter hours or are idle for long periods, and by the beginning of 1994 36 percent of forest sector enterprises were operating at a loss (*Izvestia* 1995). The logging sector was in the worst shape, with 45 percent of enterprises reported operating at a loss. Employment in the wood processing sector, which is affected by the level of log production, declined as well, as did economic performance in such wood-dependent sectors such as housing and railways.

Salaries in the forest sector vary considerably. A World Bank survey in the Krasnoyarsk region in February 1995 found that workers engaged in forest management activities received the lowest salaries (110,000 rubles per month, which was just slightly above the national official subsistence level of 105,300 rubles per month or about US$20). The average salary was 312,000 rubles for workers in pulp and paper production and 315,000 rubles in wood processing. By comparison, workers in the metal industry received 330,000 rubles per month and those in electrical power production, 728,000 rubles. Wages also vary widely across timber enterprises. Timber enterprises with foreign partners tend to pay much more than others. For example, in Khabarovsk Kray, one joint venture company paid an average monthly salary of 400,000 rubles, whereas an all-Russian company in the same town paid an average of about 110,000 rubles a month.

D. Social Significance

In the former USSR, forests provided employment to more than 7 percent of Russia's workforce and directly affected the lives of 10 million or so people. Some 18 percent of them live in remote logging communities that have been hit hard by the decline in wood production and the attendant decline in social services. Poverty has increased substantially since 1991.[9]

Much of the responsibility for financing social services has been shifted from the federal Government to the regional governments. That shift was reflected in the 1994 federal budget, which assigned joint federal-regional responsibility for financing such programs as health care and education

---

9 *An assessment of poverty in Russia, particularly in the context of overall economic reform, is provided in World Bank 1995a. The socio-economic assessment in the context of Russian boreal forest is available in Pisarenko and Strakhov (1996).*

and social insurance benefits, from child allowance and maternity leave to old age pensions. A severe weakness of the current arrangement is the failure to specify clearly the assignment of responsibilities among various levels of government and the absence of a mechanism for ensuring adequate financing. Thus, the services actually provided vary from place to place, depending on the funding resources available locally.

Forest Communities and the Social Safety Net

When enterprises were still under state control, they provided their employees with health services, housing, transportation, and subsidized utilities. With privatization and the elimination of subsidies, responsibility for providing these services was transferred to local administrations, which finance the services in part through payroll taxes collected from enterprises. In many of the remote communities where forest enterprises are located, however, enterprises have shut down operations or are operating at a loss and so are unable to pay salaries to their employees or taxes to local administrations. The impact on these forest communities has been severe. Their isolation and low population density raise the cost of providing social services, and in the past these communities relied on heavy Government subsidies (transportation, food, salary premiums for qualified health and education professionals). With the phasing out of subsidies, many of these remote communities have been left even more isolated from the outside world and lacking in basic supplies and services.

Aboriginal communities (also known as "small-in-numbers peoples of the North") are the first to be affected by the decline in services. Communication and transportation lines have stopped operating. As forestry operations slowed or stopped, demand for the reindeer meat, fish, and other forest-based goods that the aboriginal populations used to supply to these communities contracted sharply. For most of these communities, maintaining their traditional activities (hunting, fishing, reindeer breeding) is critical to their economic survival and to the preservation of their cultural identities. They have resisted periodic efforts to force their linguistic and ethnic assimilation. Unemployment among indigenous peoples is extremely high, and many families survive mainly on government pensions. The rising rates of unemployment and poverty have intensified social problems among these groups, including alcoholism and child and spouse abuse (for further details, see Annex G).

Some thirty aboriginal ethnic groups, direct descendants of the first known inhabitants of Siberia and the Far East, live within Krasnoyarsk and Khabarovsk Krays and the Sakha Republic (Yakutia). At the time of collectivization in the late 1920s, these native groups were granted special land use privileges. In Khabarovsk Kray, the delineation of "territories for [the] traditional use of natural resources by aboriginal people" has recently been agreed to in principle. The areas have been designated Group I forests, a status that bans commercial harvesting. This reclassification of the land has led to serious land use conflicts between logging enterprises and aboriginal peoples. Conflicts have also arisen among the aboriginal peoples, between those who want to lease out portions of their land to logging enterprises and those who are opposed to such leases.

Unlike the aboriginal ethnic groups, other indigenous peoples, including Russian "old settlers," do not suffer from problems associated with assimilation. These people practice nomadic pastoralism or mixed farming and have adopted fishing, hunting, and reindeer-breeding as secondary sources of income. This cultural and social adaptability sets them apart from the aboriginal ethnic group, whose cultural identity is more closely tied to the forests.

A third broad group consists of migrants -- ethnic Russians, Ukrainians, Tatars, and other Europeans -- who moved to Siberia and the Far East in the 1930s to work in the modern sectors of the economy, and who since the World War II have worked mainly in mining and transportation. For these groups hunting and fishing are mainly recreational activities. These migrant populations were key players in the implementation of early government policies for the development of the industries and the forests of Siberia and the Far East.

NGO Linkages and Cooperation

Nongovernmental organizations (NGOs) have emerged as important new stakeholders during the process of social liberalization in Russia, and they are likely to play an important role in the future development and conservation of Russia's forests and natural resources. Under the umbrella of the Socio-Ecological Union (SEU), over 200 Russian NGOs maintain close links with each other and with the international NGO community. They have joined forces with groups representing aboriginal concerns about developments that could harm their traditional way of life. The NGO community will be an essential partner in any forest development program in Russia, along with the government and other stakeholders.

The SEU has been involved in the development of this forest policy review report from the beginning and has been informed about the scope, objectives, and methodology of the World Bank initiatives in the forest sector. The SEU was also instrumental in bringing to the World Bank's early attention the facts of a major forest pest outbreak in Siberia, to which the Bank responded with an emergency forest protection program in Krasnoyarsk Kray in the summer of 1996. With social liberalization, there has also been a surge toward organization among indigenous peoples, including the establishment of regional and national indigenous organizations and new links with international agencies and groups dealing with issues of indigenous population groups.

E. Forest Management

About 95 percent of Russia's forest land is under federal management. The remainder is owned by communities, state and private farm enterprises, and other enterprises. The Federal Forest Service of Russia administers most of the publicly controlled forest land (89 percent of Russia's forest land) and has a mandate to develop national policies for fire control, reforestation, and research on this land. Other publicly owned forest land is administered by the Ministry of Agriculture and Food (4 percent), the State Committee for Environmental Protection (1 percent), and other institutions (1 percent).

The three-group classification of State Forest Fund land forms the basis for forest resource planning in Russia (see Box 1.6 and Annex A). In practice, however, the system falls short of ensuring sustainable forest management, environmental protection, and conservation of biodiversity. In addition, policies and regulations are not being enforced, and illegal logging and overhunting are taking place even where wildlife populations and biodiversity are in jeopardy.[10]

---

10 *Various western analyses and interpretations of the official Russian forest statistics give different views on the quantitative status and dynamics of Russia's forest resources (see, for example, Barr and Braden, 1988; Shvidenko and Nilsson, 1996). However, it is widely acknowledged that both the quantity and the quality of forest growing stock have declined over the last three decades, particularly in Asian Russia.*

Financing Forest Management

Inadequate funding is one source of the weakness of forest management. Forest management activities are funded through budget allocations from the Federal Forest Service, local administrative budgets, and revenues generated locally from timber sales from sanitary harvesting and thinning operations. Until 1994 (except in 1992), federal allocations for forest management were maintained at a fairly constant level, but they declined by almost half in 1995 and 1996 (in constant 1991 rubles). Since 1991 inflation has severely cut the amount of money (in real terms) available for such field management activities as inventorying, planting, and stand tending, and at the same time the share of the budget that goes to salaries, benefits, and overhead costs has risen (Tables 1.10 and 1.11). The resulting financing gaps have been met partly through arrears and partly through subsidies and revenues generated by nonforest activities.

The largest share of forest management expenses is financed through the federal budget allocation to the Federal Forest Service. The share of federal funding has declined sharply, however, from 70 percent of all expenses in 1985 to 67 percent in 1992 and 45 percent in 1995. Forest districts (*leskhoz*) generate some revenues from forest fees (stumpage, leases), fines, and (sometimes significant) from the sale of wood from thinning and sanitary cutting. Sanitary cutting appears to be used more to maximize current revenue than to maximize the future value of the forest, contrary to its intended objective. The typical flow of funds in the Russian forest sector in 1993-95 is summarized in Figure 1.6 and as it would be following the draft Forest Code of July 1996 in Figure 1.7. (Additional information on operating costs, funding sources, and the flow of funds is provided in Annex B; details of the July 1996 draft Forest Code are presented in Annex C).

Forest Management Planning

Forest management planning for the 70 percent of forest land in Siberia and the Far East that is classified as commercial (Group III) is based on information collected and compiled by thirteen forest planning and inventory enterprises (see map IBRD 28354). These enterprises conduct the entire forest inventory, determine the annual allowable cut, and prepare management plans for all forest districts. Each forest management plan covers a forest district (*leskhoz)* or a forest range (*lesnichestvo*).

The forest management plan (which includes detailed maps) summarizes ecological, climatic, and soil conditions; estimates characteristics of each stand (species, composition, yield class, standing volume); calculates the annual allowable cut for the next ten-year period; and suggests activities for the next ten years (for more detail on maps, see Annex A). The management plan also contains economic projections and an assessment of the forest sector's importance at the rayon, oblast, kray, and republic levels. Each forest management plan must be approved by the Federal Forest Service.

Figure 1.6: Typical Flow of Funds in the Russian Forest Sector in 1993-95

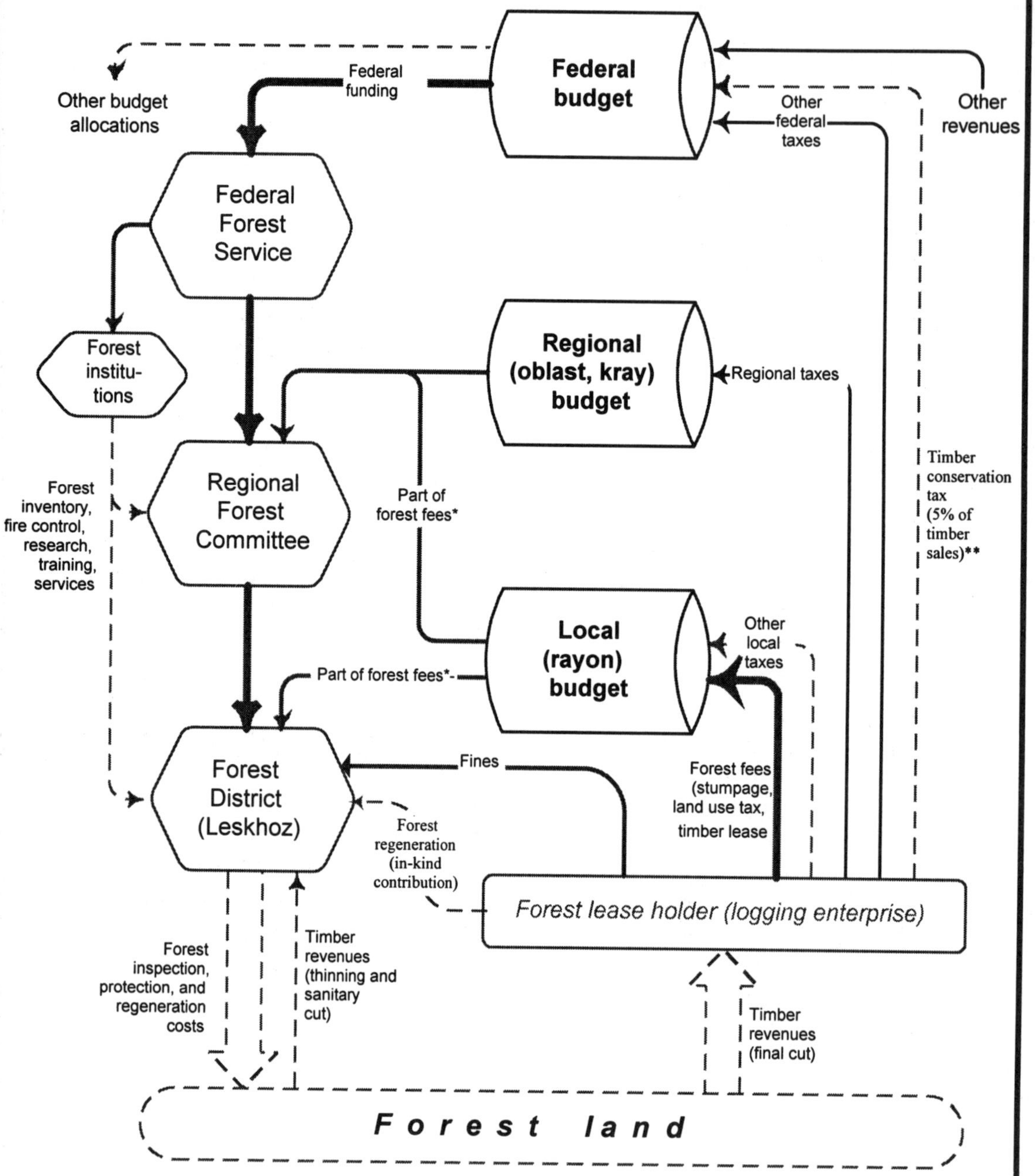

* Funded at the discretion of the rayon administration at a level ranging from 0 to 100% of forest fees.

** Cancelled by the 1995 Federal Budget Law.

Source: The Federal Forest Service of Russia, 1996.

Figure 1.7: Flow of Funds in the Russian Forest Sector as Envisioned in the Draft Forest Code of July 1996

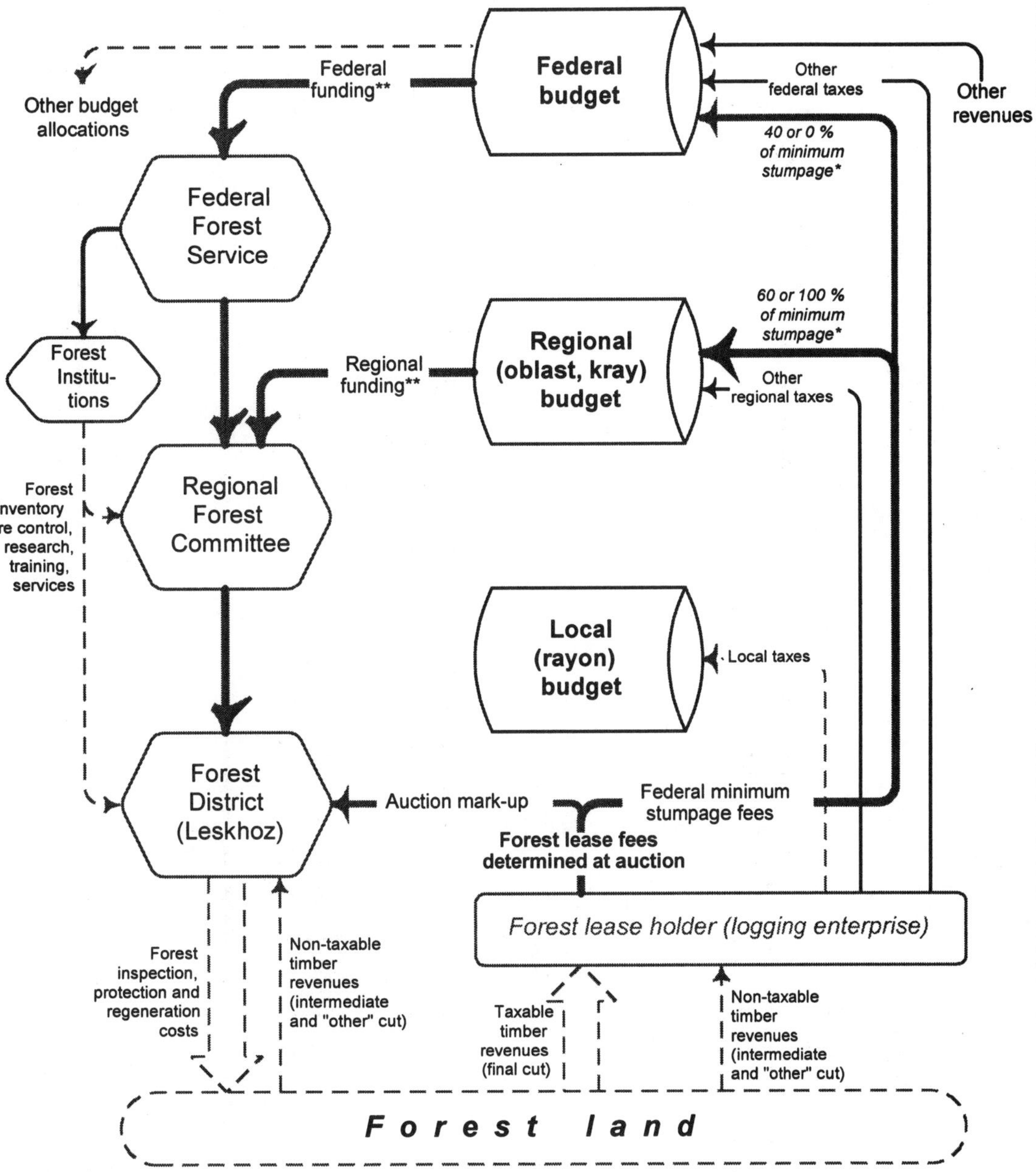

* In major forest-producing regions, 40 % of minimum stumpage fees is proposed to go to the Federal budget; elsewhere 100 % of minimum stumpage fees is proposed to be retained in the regional budget.

** Regional funding earmarked predominantly for forest regeneration and federal funding mostly for forest administration, management, and research.

Source: The Federal Forest Service of Russia, 1996.

Table 1.10: Forest Management Operations Budget, 1991-96 (millions of constant 1991 rubles)

Expenditures and revenues	*1991*	*1992*	*1993*	*1994*	*1995*	*1996 (plan)*
Forest inventory	55.7	43.5	49.6	60.0	30.5	31.9
Aerial forest fire control	129.1	157.4	150.9	181.0	141.2	167.6
Project development	23.1	12.0	17.6	17.1	15.0	12.5
Forest management[a]	292.6	220.4	298.1	156.6	159.5	140.7
Forest pest control	6.8	4.4	4.7	7.3	11.8	12.9
Forest amelioration/drainage	8.5	5.0	7.5	16.9	2.3	2.0
Forest regeneration	170.0	125.2	135.0	128.4	82.3	74.3
Ground forest fire control	73.4	71.2	146.9	59.1	50.9	63.5
Agricultural afforestation	10.4	4.6	7.3	15.5	10.5	5.2
Transport services (customers)	6.5	3.4	3.1	0.6	4.8	4.5
Overhead (safety/training)	109.6	299.9	167.3	179.9	142.2	135.1
Forest management staff	509.8	374.9	694.1	652.7	476.8	400.6
Total expenditures	**1,399.0**	**1,331.8**	**1,557.2**	**1,538.1**	**1,171.3**	**1,058.9**
Federal budget	1,080.0	892.6	1,082.5	1,127.8	522.5	510.4
Retained earnings of leskhozes	305.0	247.2	240.6	248.8	387.5	334.0
Timber sales	3.0	1.2	0.0	3.7	2.8	2.3
Regional budget	11.0	107.6	168.1	95.3	116.0	79.7
Total budget	**1,399.0**	**1,248.5**	**1,491.2**	**1,475.6**	**1,028.8**	**926.4**
Operating losses	-	(83.4)	(66.1)	(62.5)	(142.5)	(132.5)
Memo:						
Cumulative aggregate CPI--consumer price index (%)[b]	**100**	**1,454**	**14,472**	**58,350**	**168,747**	**248,733**

[a] Activities such as forest tending, sanitary cutting, and road construction.

[b] Derived from aggregate average annual CPI estimates made by the IMF/World Bank based on the Russian Goskomstat data. The average annual CPI (net) estimates were 1,354.0 percent in 1992, 895.3 percent in 1993, 303.2 percent in 1994 and 189.2 percent in 1995. For 1996, the 47.7 percent estimate of the Russian Ministry of Economy was used.

Note: Constant 1991 rubles were calculated using the cumulative CPI, as the deflator.

Source: The Federal Forest Service of Russia, 1996.

Despite the sophisticated inventory system and the abundance of information collected for the management plans, the data are rarely used effectively. Little computer technology is employed in their preparation, and most regions have no geographic information system (GIS) capability to assist in resource analysis and planning. Consequently, such analyses are not a significant part of forest management planning. Only with satellite and GIS technology can the management and analysis of inventory data provide accurate and detailed information for making decisions on forest land use, conservation, and utilization. These new technologies also provide excellent opportunities for mapping areas of aboriginal land claims and traditional use, as well as for facilitating the participation of indigenous and other local populations in forest management and planning.

Table 1.11: Relative Shares of Categories in Forest Management Operations Budget, 1991-96 (percentage; based on constant 1991 rubles)

Expenditures and revenues	1991	1992	1993	1994	1995	1996 (plan)
Forest inventory	4.0	3.3	3.2	3.9	2.6	3.0
Aerial forest fire control	9.2	11.8	9.7	11.8	12.1	15.8
Project development	1.7	0.9	1.1	1.1	1.3	1.2
Forest management	20.9	16.6	13.4	10.2	13.6	13.3
Forest pest control	0.5	0.3	0.3	0.5	1.0	1.2
Forest amelioration/drainage	0.6	0.4	0.5	1.1	0.2	0.2
Forest regeneration	12.2	9.4	8.7	8.3	7.0	7.0
Ground forest fire control	5.2	5.3	9.4	3.8	4.3	6.0
Agricultural afforestation	0.7	0.3	0.5	1.0	0.9	0.5
Transport services (customers)	0.5	0.3	0.2	0.0	0.4	0.4
Overhead (safety/training)	7.8	22.5	10.7	11.7	12.1	12.8
Forest management staff	36.4	28.1	44.6	42.4	40.7	37.8
Total expenditures	**100.0**	**100.0**	**100.0**	**100.0**	**100.0**	**100.0**
As percent of total budget:						
Federal budget	77.2	71.5	72.6	76.4	50.8	55.1
Retained earnings of leskhozes	21.8	91.8	16.1	16.9	37.7	36.1
Timber sales	0.2	0.1	0.0	0.3	0.3	0.2
Regional budget	0.8	8.6	11.3	6.5	11.3	8.6
Total budget	**100.0**	**100.0**	**100.0**	**100.0**	**100.0**	**100.0**
Operating losses	-	**(6.7)**	**(4.4)**	**(4.2)**	**(13.8)**	**(14.3)**

Note: This table is based on information provided in Table 1.10.

Forest Resource Allocation

After 1993, forest legislation transfers significant rights and responsibilities of forest management to the regions, including the establishment of leasing arrangements and the determination of stumpage charges and the location and size of harvesting areas. The new leasing arrangements are designed to replace the old system of resource allocation. Leasehold agreements define the rights and responsibilities of each party according to government regulations. The size and location of leaseholds are to be determined by the Federal Forest Service, in cooperation with regional counterparts. A forty-nine-year lease is now available for forest processing enterprises, and it is expected that foreign companies or enterprises with foreign partners will be eligible for these leases.

The Federal Forest Service has introduced competitive bidding in certain areas as a means of establishing timber prices. The bidding is open to domestic and foreign buyers. Prices have gone as high as 45,000 rubles per cubic meter compared with an expected average stumpage price for 1995 of 5,000 rubles per cubic meter. The difference in actual net revenues may be much smaller, however, depending on whether the buyer or the seller assumes responsibilities for reforestation and protection.

Harvesting, Reforestation, and Stand Tending

Harvesting practices in Siberia still follow the mining model: once an area of mature forest is harvested, the logging operation pushes its frontier out to other areas of mature forest. Because of inefficient practices the annual harvested area is larger than need be, forcing operations further into primary forests. Production losses can be as high as 40 to 60 percent of the standing timber volume. Such practices also increase harvesting pressures on easily accessible areas and on Group I and II (protected and noncommercial) forests.

Silvicultural and other harvesting norms are frequently ignored. The concentration of harvesting, the application of large-scale clearcutting without regard for ecosystem characteristics, and inadequate provision for regeneration have seriously affected extensive areas and resulted in unbalanced stand structures. Resource shortages will eventually force improvements, but before that happens, forest policies should be amended to encourage the forest industry to adopt more suitable harvesting and processing methods that allow better timber utilization and conservation of primary forests.

Clearcutting is used in about 90 percent of harvesting in Group III forests, and selective and gradual felling methods are employed in the remaining areas. Clearcutting has created extensive areas of continuous-cut blocks of a thousand hectares or more, which have drastically altered wildlife habitat and biodiversity and resulted in soil degradation and other harmful environmental effects.

Mechanical harvesting equipment (feller-bunchers and feller-skidders) are used for about a third of wood production; manual felling with chain saws accounts for the rest. In most areas, harvesting is confined to the winter months (up to about seven months a year), when the frozen ground allows the use of heavy equipment with minimal impact on the soil and below-freezing temperatures create ice bridges that allow logging trucks to cross immense rivers (some more than 2 kilometers wide). To maximize production during the winter months, many machines are equipped with floodlights and operate twenty-four hours a day.

New regulations limit the size of harvesting blocks to 50 hectares (for example, 500 meters by 1000 meters) on the plains and 25 hectares in mountainous areas. For intermediate felling the limits are 100 hectares, and 50 hectares. In Karabula, in Krasnoyarsk Kray, harvesting operations have included 500-meter-wide strips separated by a 50-meter strip of standing timber left as a source of seed for natural regeneration. While this method seems to conform to the new regulations, it will result in large areas with very little undisturbed forest left. New regulations have to redefine all harvesting parameters —not just the size of blocks—to conform to strict environmental standards from block size and leave areas to harvesting methods, timing, and road access.

Reforestation has proved to be a special challenge in Siberia and the Far East, despite the use of all four regeneration methods: natural regeneration, fill-in planting, artificial seeding, and planting. There are large areas with little or no regeneration or that are dominated by low-value species. Reforestation through natural regeneration requires a rotation period of at least 100 years, and if current trends are indicative, such forests are likely to contain less-valuable species than the original cover. These second-generation forests are dominated by hard-wood species like birch and aspen, while conifers such as pine and spruce are suppressed because of their significantly slower growth during the first forty to fifty years. Later, as succession progresses, the conifers once again become the dominant species.

Reliance on natural regeneration has increased sharply since 1992, suggesting that natural regeneration is motivated more by a lack of funding for new planting than by any well-considered management plan. As much as 80 percent of the reforestation in the Khabarovsk and Krasnoyarsk regions is classified as natural regeneration (Figure 1.8), yet many of these areas are nonproductive or inappropriately stocked because the harvesting practices used were incompatible with natural regeneration (for example, no seed trees of valuable species are left at the harvest). (Annex A provides more detail on silvicultural practices and requirements).

In some large stands in Krasnoyarsk and Khabarovsk regions that were successfully established through natural regeneration, overstocking is common. With thousands of trees per hectare, the intense competition for light and nutrients results in the growth of small stems with little commercial value. That there has been no thinning of many of these stands suggests a lack of analysis of the potential costs and benefits when selecting areas for treatment. Furthermore, revenue pressures lead to the removal of high-value trees during sanitary cutting rather than the unhealthy low-value ones. The result is a gradual decline in stand quality and value that is contrary to the goal of sanitary cutting.

Protection against Fire, Insects, and Disease

Naturally occurring fires often help ensure forest renewal and the evolution of forest ecosystems. In the northern areas, naturally occurring fires are largely low-intensity ground fires that consume the accumulated organic debris, allowing seeds to germinate on the exposed mineral soil. But fires can cause enormous damage as well. High-intensity fires can develop on large clear-cut areas and spread to adjacent standing forests. Controlled burning is rarely used for postharvest treatment, so heavy loads of harvesting debris remain, providing an ideal fuel source, especially in the dry conditions common in large parts of Siberia and the Far East. There is also a very strong relationship between forest fires and the presence of roads and rivers, which attract human activity.

According to the Federal Forest Service, up to 34,000 wild fires are recorded in Russian forests every year. More than 70 percent of forest fires are estimated to be caused by human activity. Many Russian foresters consider fires to be the main problem affecting the condition of forests and the environment. The immense size of forest resources and the lack of adequate equipment and financing restrict fire protection activities to the most severely affected areas. In the southern areas of Siberia and the Far East that are covered by fire protection programs, an average of 10,000 to 15,000 fires annually, affect 100 hectares of forest per fire -- some 1.0 to 1.5 million hectares overall -- resulting in tremendous economic, social, and environmental losses. (The demarcation of Russian forests based on fire potential and the location of fire control bases is shown on map IBRD 28353).

Insects and disease also play an important natural role in the evolution of forest ecosystems, but as is the case with fires, inappropriate human activity can greatly increase the intensity and frequency of pest and disease outbreaks. Effective control and management of insect populations and diseases are thwarted by inadequate planning and funding. Pests and diseases affect an average forest area of 1.5 to 2.0 million hectares annually. Among the most prevalent insects are the Siberian moth, the Gypsy moth, the Nun moth, the Geometric moth, the Prime Beauty moth, and the Pine sawfly. Total forest losses due to pest or disease outbreaks could be as high as the estimated losses due to forest fires. In addition to fire, insects, and diseases, antropogenic disturbances like air pollution and

Figure 1.8: Area under Different Regeneration Methods in Krasnoyarsk Kray, 1985-96

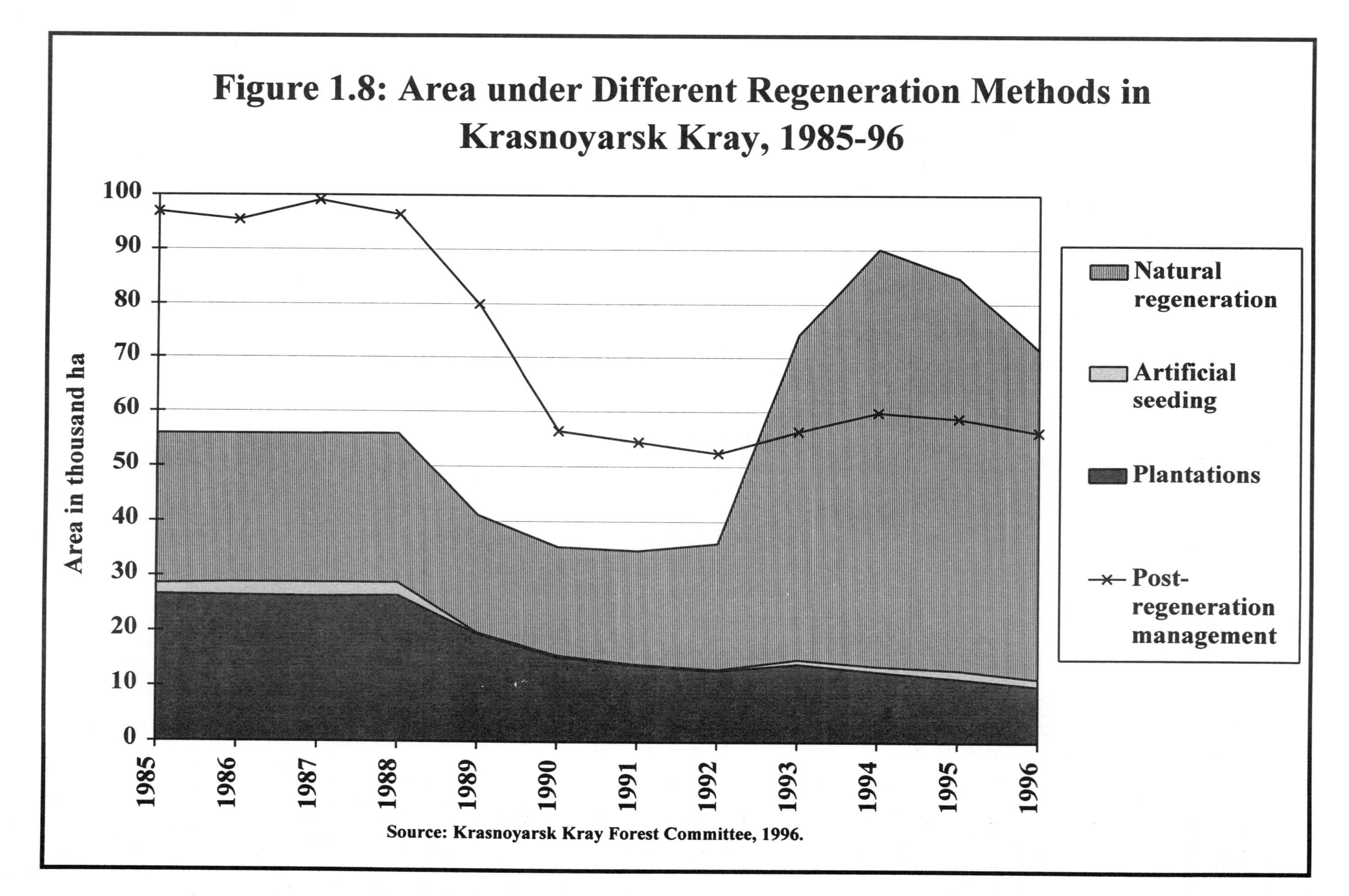

Source: Krasnoyarsk Kray Forest Committee, 1996.

radio nuclide contamination have affected forest growth and wood quality in some areas (Kharuk 1993). The severity of these disturbances and the forest area actually destroyed (as opposed to affected) by different calamities varies from year to year (Figure 1.9).

F. Impact of Transition to Market Economy

Russia has made major strides in its overall economic policy reforms since 1992. It has implemented the largest privatization program in history; substantially liberalized prices, foreign exchange, and foreign trade; and greatly improved the economic and financial stability. Nevertheless, difficult political choices remain. Fiscal revenues and expenditures still need substantial adjustment, and key structural reforms yet to be implemented will severely test the Government's ability to hold the course on economic reform.

The economic and social dislocation that has accompanied the transition has been severe.[11] GDP has contracted by about one-third since 1991, lowering average living standards and worsening income distribution. Fiscal revenues at the federal level shrank from about 16 percent of GDP in 1992 to 10 percent in 1995. The authorities have grappled with ways to cut expenditures, but with only partial success.

While the economic situation continues to be fragile, three factors of fundamental importance to the future of the Russian economy are becoming increasingly clear. First, the shift to a more market-based economy has become irreversible, and the private sector is developing much more rapidly than was thought possible. Second, the volatility in prices -- bordering on hyperinflation during late 1992 -- appears to be over, and inflation has slowed. Third, while the economy continued to contract into 1996, the decline in output seems to be bottoming out, and the recovery is being led by services and other activities that are likely to play an increasing role in Russia's long-term economic development.

The radical economic changes Russia is experiencing will have both short-and long-term consequences for the forest sector. The reform has resulted in dramatic increases in once heavily subsidized energy and transport prices and a decline in demand for wood in the construction and pulp and paper industries. The decline in government expenditures has also resulted in lower federal budgetary allocations (in real terms) for the forest sector. Cutbacks in such forest management activities as forest protection, regeneration, and stand tending and in allocations for forest research have potentially severe long-term implications for sustainable development of the sector. Adjustment has also contributed to disruptions in the lives of some 10 million people who depend directly on forest resources for their livelihoods. As employment in the forest sector has contracted, hunting and other extractive activities have intensified, especially in remote areas that offer few economic alternatives. Such uncontrolled pressure on wildlife populations will likely have long-term consequences for biodiversity, especially for the rare and endangered species in Siberia and the Far East (see Annex I).

---

11 *Additional details on the economic situation are provided in World Bank's most recent Country Economic Memorandum (CEM) for Russia (World Bank 1995e).*

Figure 1.9: Area of Forest Killed by Different Calamities in Russia, 1984-95

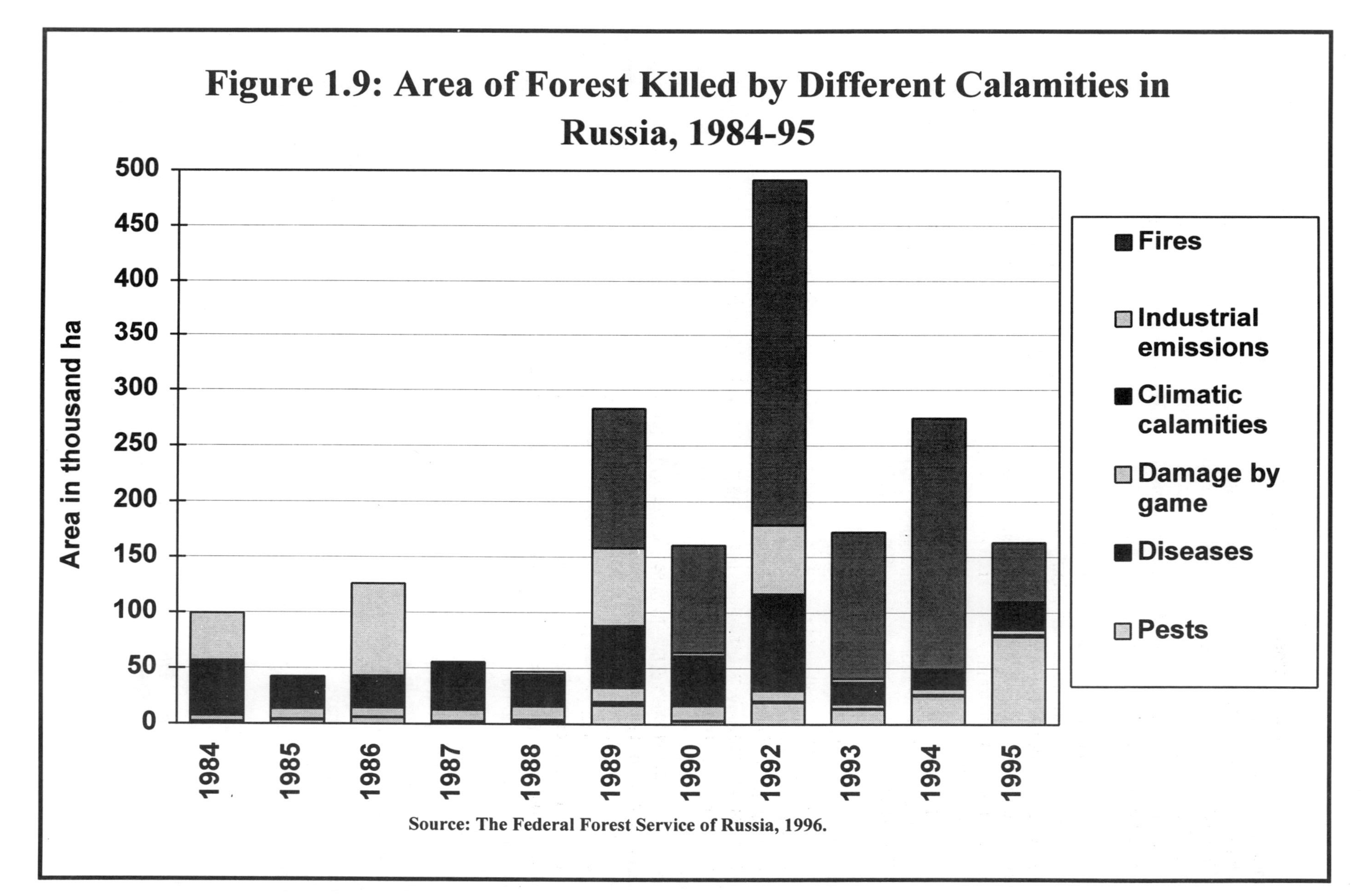

Source: The Federal Forest Service of Russia, 1996.

Successful macroeconomic reform and appropriate forest policy adjustments can ease the burden of transition and provide the basis for a balanced, *long-term* restructuring of Russia's wood-based industries. Only then will the necessary resources and incentives emerge to sustain and protect Russia's unique forest resources. The concept of sustainability needs to be firmly established at every level of government, to make long-term planning for management, training, research, and viable industrial development possible. Better resource management and sustainable industrial activities will result in a more stable employment base in forest communities.

The incentives emerging from the transition will lead to greater opportunities for investment in the development of wood-based industries in areas with a comparative advantage in these activities, such as Northern European Russia and the Far East, and the shutting down of obsolete plants and equipment in wood-deficit areas. The wood harvesting and processing industries will face stiff competition on world markets, and government will need to resist industry pressures to resume transport subsidies. Realistic energy and transport prices will result in significant changes in the geographic distribution of wood processing activities. As these activities move closer to the forests, prospects for the development of a competitive industry in areas such as European Russia and the Far East will be greatly enhanced (see Annex D).

With the need for tough macroeconomic discipline in the *near term*, forest policy-makers should focus on several key tasks with the largest payoffs. That includes setting clear priorities at both federal and local levels, to promote sustainable sector development, maximizing foreign exchange earnings by easing any remaining restrictions on exports of forest products, ensuring that reductions in budgetary support do not endanger the long-term sustainability of the sector, and establishing a social safety net for forest communities in remote areas.

In the *medium term* increases in disposable income and some easing of fiscal constraints will lead to a recovery in domestic demand for wood-based building materials and pulp and paper products. The increase in demand for wood will lead to an increase in prices, allowing some enterprises in the more remote areas of Siberia and the Far East to resume production and to develop value-added processing capacity. Improving economic conditions should also increase the market prospects and profits of locally produced forest and nontimber forest products.

II. Key Challenges: Forest Sector Issues during Transition

The transition to a market economy has exposed many hidden problems in Russia's forest sector. Reforms are urgently needed if the sector is to be placed on an environmentally, economically, and socially sound basis that will allow it to make a sustainable contribution to the country's economic development. Ownership and management responsibility for forests in nearly half the territory of the Russian Federation are unclear, a condition that left unresolved may lead to even more severe and widespread environmental degradation. Timber shortages are occurring in some areas despite considerable idle processing capacity. Forest enterprises are struggling with the same high tax levels and uncertain business climate as other enterprises, but their remote location and special cost structures constitute an additional burden. At the same time forest enterprises are not paying an adequate rate of return to resource owners (in the form of stumpage charges, land use taxes, and timber lease charges) under the current cost structure.

The following four challenges define the nature of the fundamental changes that are needed in forest resources management in Russia. These are:

- Jurisdictional prerequisites for sustainable management, or straightening out the ***legal*** basis for forest land ownership and management across the country, including clarification and enforcement of aboriginal land and resource claims.

- Resource sustainability and ***environmental*** integrity, or adopting policies and institutional arrangements that ensure conservation and sustainable use of forest resources and clearly establish the roles of government, the private sector, and indigenous people.

- Proper resource pricing for sustainable and ***economic*** use of forest resources, or ensuring that commercial users of forest resources are sensitive to the sector's true costs and benefits by extracting a fair share of resource value for the government and placing the full cost of timber processing on commercial users.

- ***Social*** welfare in the forest sector, or ensuring that socially and economically vulnerable groups, particularly the indigenous people, do not suffer during the transition.

A. Jurisdictional Prerequisites for Sustainable Management

Some conflict among federal, regional, and local interests and challenges of fiscal federalism during the transition period are inevitable.[12] But these conflicts must not be allowed to obscure the fundamental task of defining jurisdictional responsibilities and obligations for sustainable management of the forest sector.

---

12 *Much of the discussion in this section draws on Wallich 1994.*

In a market economy, optimal resource allocation is enhanced by transferable forest tenure rights that allow resources to be employed by the most efficient managers through competitive sales, leasing and other contractual arrangements. Such systems increase the incentives for forest owners and lessees to maintain the capital value of the forest through sustainable management. However, international experience has also indicated that such efficient market systems rarely develop in the absence of strong enabling government regulations and appropriate enforcement mechanisms to protect the public goods value of forests and reduce monopolistic market power. Such governance system should be:

- ***Transparent***, providing clear and consistent expectations about the rights and obligations of potential stakeholders based on long-term environmental, economic, and social objectives.

- ***Equitable*** and consistent with national income-distribution goals, so as to be broadly viewed as legitimate.

- ***Accountable***, with resource users subject to monitoring and evaluation, especially with regard to actions that may affect other resource users and resource values.

- ***Balanced***, so that there is a correspondence between resource management needs and anticipated expenditures, at federal, regional, and local levels.

The federal Government cannot develop the sector alone. However, only the Government can ensure that these conditions are met through an appropriate legal and regulatory framework. That framework should also support the Government's broader objective of market-oriented reform as the basis for the development, protection, and utilization of forest resources by instilling confidence in potential investors in the stability of the new system and policies. Without this sense of security, development in the sector is likely to be slow and biased toward short-term exploitation at the cost of long-term concern for forest protection, regeneration, and sustainable development.

Private or Public Ownership

There are no indications of any intention to privatize forest lands in Russia, except for land strictly associated with agricultural enterprises. A presidential decree of December 24, 1993, classifies federal forests as "not eligible for privatization," suggesting that forest land will remain under Federal public ownership. The regions are challenging this interpretation and seeking more autonomy in managing their forests, and negotiations on this issue are under way. Any change in ownership or management responsibilities will necessitate a realignment of institutional functions and objectives for all stakeholders (see Annex C).

Ownership of forest land is a controversial subject everywhere. In countries with limited public administrative capacity, attempts by the central government to strictly control forest resources, management, and marketing have often been unsuccessful -- and have ultimately been abandoned. Countries with well functioning local systems of control and management that later moved to nationalize forests have experienced rapid breakdowns in all aspects of management. Even countries with strong administrative capacity at the center, such as Canada, have decentralized forest control, some of it to aboriginal communities and forest enterprises. In the United States, debate over the role of the federal Government in land management and about the possibility of devolving management of national parks to state control remains unresolved. Equally important, as demonstrated in Western Europe, private ownership of forest land has to be accompanied by considerable legislative control to ensure that long-term national resource management objectives are met.

The choice of tenure strategy for forests is not an all-or-nothing proposition. Indeed, it is not the choice of ownership pattern that matters most but rather that the ownership pattern chosen be applied fairly and consistently and with transparency and legal recourse. Under such conditions management will determine the pace and direction of forest sector development. In the United States, for example, forest land is owned by the federal Government, state governments, native tribes, forest industries, and the so-called nonindustrial private forest owners (owners of small areas that may or may not be under active management for timber or other products). Nonindustrial private forest ownership is a major category internationally and includes both productive and nonproductive forests (Table 2.1). The public ownership share varies considerably; it is 94 percent in Canada, 95 percent in Russia, and 35 percent in the Pacific Northwest of the United States.

Table 2.1: Area of Nonindustrial Private Forest Land in Selected Countries, 1983

Country	*Private forest land (millions of hectares)*			*Percentage of total forest area*	*Number of owners (millions)*	*Average size holding (hectares)*
	Productive	*Unproductive*	*Total*			
Austria	2.465	0.160	2.624	68	n.a.	n.a.
Canada	14.227	0.724	14.951	6	0.500	29.9
European Union	15.636	2.677	18.312	59	n.a.	n.a.
Japan	n.a.	n.a.	14.706	58	5.650	2.6
Nordic countries	29.509	2.601	32.111	57	1.365	23.5
Spain	7.944	10.765	18.709	73	0.826	22.6
Switzerland	0.301	n.a.	n.a.	26	0.252	1.2
United States	112.550	n.a.	n.a.	58	7.558	14.9

n.a. means not available.
Source: Plochmann 1983.

There can be economic as well as political reasons limiting the viability of large-scale privatization of forest land, such as the long production cycles for growing timber in Russia (100 to 120 years). Nevertheless, many management functions that are now in public hands could be carried out by the private sector, from collecting and analyzing inventory data to harvesting operations, resource protection, regeneration, and stand tending.

Redefining the Public Role in the Forest Sector

A much more focused and coordinated strategy is needed for planning and managing forest resources in Russia. There is very little interaction or coordination of strategies among the three principal institutions responsible for forest resource management. The Federal Forest Service is responsible for forest management, the State Committee for Environmental Protection (successor to the Ministry of Environmental Protection and Natural Resources) is responsible for resource conservation and environmental protection, and the State Committee of Forest Industry (Goskomlesprom) holds shares in most forest sector joint-stock enterprises and monitors resource utilization (described in more detail in Annex B). Industrial interests have historically dominated in the decision process to the neglect of forest management and environmental concerns. There can be little real progress toward sustainable forest resource use until these three institutions establish a cooperative mode of action.

Where a multiplicity of forest resources suggests multiple-use management options, a primary objective (say, preservation of biodiversity, watershed protection, or commercial timber production) may be chosen for a particular parcel of forest land. This primary management objective would then determine the kind of organizational structure needed, as well as the financing requirements. An entity responsible for preservation of a national park or other protective reserve, for example, will typically have limited opportunities for cost recovery. Sustainable forest management is possibly only in a land use context that ensures environmentally sound, economically viable, and socially acceptable resource allocation.

Entities charged with forest protection must thus be linked to a predictable source of budgetary support, provided by the level of government committed to the particular management objective. The difficulties facing Russia's Zapovedniks (areas designated for the conservation of biodiversity and the maintenance of protected ecosystems) illustrate the need for an overall planning and budgeting approach. The Zapovedniks are federally funded, but budgetary problems stemming from the current fiscal difficulties of the federal Government are threatening to reverse the gains achieved in conservation and protection of natural resources, including forests.

Where industrial timber production is likely to be the primary objective, the public sector could retain land ownership while transferring operational activities, including planning and management, to private enterprises. Determining who will manage, and at what level of intensity, will require considerable public investment in the land allocation process. Once land allocation objectives have been determined, the Government must make pragmatic judgments about the levels of budgetary support that the federal Government and regions are likely to be able to provide in pursuit of various objectives. Public ownership of land can ensure that the tenure system and regulatory structure make enterprises fully accountable for their performance. Thus government outlays (at various levels) could be mainly for the design and enforcement of forestry regulations.

Russia's responsibilities as a signatory to international environmental biodiversity conventions will also have some impact on this decision process. Regional governments and private firms have little incentive to voluntarily adopt management practices that are in compliance with these obligations. To satisfy international obligations, the federal Government will have to be directly involved in management, adopt an effective regulatory enforcement system for land management activities, establish a clearly defined system of intergovernmental transfers, or choose a combination of these approaches.

Following decisions on the form of ownership and management, the next large issue is the assignment of revenues and expenditures within and among different levels of government, from federal to oblast and rayon. Generally, expenditure assignment should be based on the geographic dimension of benefits, with each jurisdiction providing and financing the services whose benefits accrue within its boundaries. Thus public services, whose benefits do not accrue beyond local boundaries, should be provided by local governments, services that benefit several communities should be provided at the regional level, and services that benefit the whole country should be provided by the federal Government.

The process is complicated, however, by the rapidly changing nature of enterprises and government. Some of the social assets that have been divested from state enterprises to local governments could now be privatized, although many are public goods and should be financed by government. All of these functions must be identified and assigned to the proper level of government. A system of tax assignments, shared revenues, and intergovernmental transfers needs to be set up to provide each level with sufficient revenues to meet these expenditure assignments.

For the forest sector, there is currently no effective mechanism for matching fiscal responsibilities and available financial resources at local or national levels. A first step is to decide how revenues from natural resources should be used and how taxes and rents on natural resources should be structured, who will collect them, and to which jurisdiction they should go to.

Proceeds from the sale of natural resources often exceed the costs of exploitation. Part of these economic rents should go into the public coffers. Exploitation of natural resources often generates significant social costs as well, from the costs of providing public infrastructure to those of environmental degradation, including cleanup and restoration costs. Ultimately, the resource owners (in most cases the public sector) should be compensated by the users not only for the resources extracted but also for externalities associated with harvesting and for the costs of getting a new crop established. And that generally means that private enterprises will be passing higher prices on to the consumer, including the full costs of license fees, stumpage charges, penalties, and economic rents.

Once mechanisms are in place to allow the government to capture the rents from forest exploitation, decisions need to be made about how this money will be distributed. The revenues could be allocated to indigenous peoples residing on or near the productive lands or to municipalities, rayons, or autonomous okrugs. The establishment of a more equitable and transparent system of intergovernmental fiscal arrangements will make it easier to reach consensus on the politically divisive issue of sharing natural resource revenues.

B. Promoting Resource Sustainability and Environmental Integrity

Ensuring the environmentally sustainable management of nearly half the country's land area is a daunting task. At the policy level, the most important considerations are to define the resource base for sustainable production and the management strategy and practices for achieving sustainability and environmental integrity. Russia has participated in various international initiatives to develop criteria and indicators for sustainable forest management (see Annex J). These could be used in developing a comprehensive policy framework and implementation program for resource sustainability. Russia can also seek assistance from the international community, including the World Bank, in this process (Box 2.1).

Box 2.1: World Bank Requirements for Sustainable Forest Management

World Bank involvement in the forest sector aims to reduce deforestation, enhance the environmental contribution of forested areas, promote afforestation, reduce poverty, and encourage sustainable economic development (World Bank 1991). The Bank's lending operations in the forestry sector in all forests and in all countries are conditional on government commitment to undertake sustainable and conservation-oriented forest management. That means:

- Adopting policies and an institutional framework to ensure conservation and sustainable use of existing forests and, with proper incentives, to promote more active participation of local people and the private sector in the long-term management of natural forests.
- Adopting a comprehensive and environmentally sound forest conservation and development plan that clearly defines the roles and rights of the government, the private sector, and local inhabitants.
- Undertaking social, economic, and environmental assessments of the forests being considered for commercial utilization.
- Setting aside adequate preservation forests to maintain biodiversity and safeguard the interests of forest dwellers, specifically their ownership rights and access to designated forest areas.

Clarifying the Resource Base for Sustainable Production

While Russia's forests cover vast areas, many of them are in environments with severe climatic limitations that result in low growth potential, and many are in remote regions that are unlikely to be economically accessible. Other areas are inherently sensitive to disturbance or contain significant nonwood values and should not be harvested for environmental reasons. Many easily accessible forests (close to processing centers and transport corridors) have been overexploited, leaving their associated forestry enterprises without a suitable forest resource base. In many of the more accessible areas, it will be decades before overharvested forests recover sufficiently to support new harvesting. Closure or relocation of processing plants may be the only feasible option for enterprises without a secure timber supply.

Countrywide assessments of the annual allowable cut mask these problems by not explicitly considering economic accessibility or the forest land capability issues that affect ecosystem management. And these assessments provide little information that is useful for planning. If sustainable private sector investment is to be forthcoming, investors need to know which enterprises will still have a viable resource base for the foreseeable future, and where the development of new sustainable enterprises is possible.

What is needed is a comprehensive planning process that encompasses the problems associated with closures and relocations of production capacity and identifies areas where timber production can be both economically and environmentally viable and where opportunities for sustainable and conservation-oriented timber production are most favorable. Fundamental changes to harvest planning and practices are needed to avoid further degradation of the forest resource base and the environment.

Such a comprehensive approach to forest land use planning is an essential prerequisite for sustainable development of the sector. This approach can be introduced only gradually, however, and meanwhile many decisions have to be made about the future of specific enterprises and their forest-dependent communities. Thus, there is an urgent need to evaluate the resource base for existing enterprises both to protect accessible resources from continued overexploitation and to identify areas where immediate investment in sustainable management systems could yield positive net economic, social, and environmental benefits.

For managing the transition to a sustainable market-based forest economy, it is important to identify both enterprises and communities that have a viable future in the forest sector and those whose resource base has been overexploited and for which the only option is to close the enterprise and seek alternative opportunities for its workforce. Identifying these two groups will help in defining the scale of the social adjustment measures needed to assist communities in finding alternatives to nonsustainable forest-based production that will maintain or improve current levels of employment and output. It will also help in defining longer-term planning requirements for rehabilitating overexploited forests and eventually bringing them back into production under a sustainable management regime. Within this framework, there also needs to be appropriate recognition of and conditions for the sustainability of traditional communities, land, and resource-use systems and economies.

Maintaining Biodiversity

Russia, like most countries, needs to systematically identify core areas of biodiversity protection covering a representative range of ecosystems and to bring these areas under effective management. Its capability for doing so has been severely weakened in recent years because of the disruption in scientific activities and the dramatic loss of management control in the protected areas. To address urgent environmental and economic challenges, Russia will need more targeted scientific research input from its research institutes, both for developing appropriate resource management practices and for defining criteria and indicators to monitor biodiversity and general ecosystem health.

The economic hardship experienced by many people in remote forest areas has increased the pressure on fish and wildlife resources. Poaching has increased dramatically with the breakdown in management and control, and many game animal populations are being overhunted (Table 2.2). Protected areas will provide few long-term benefits for biodiversity conservation and resource sustainability unless their ecological, economic, and social systems remain intact (Box 2.2). This requires attention at the planning stage to appropriate forest sector policies and practices, the spatial and temporal relationships between different land uses, and the costs and benefits of resource exploitation compared with resource conservation and, most importantly, systematic stakeholder identification, consultation, and participation.

Table 2.2: Hunting in Krasnoyarsk Kray, 1993-94

Species	*1993 reported harvest*	*1994*			
		Legal quota	*Reported harvest*	*Estimated harvest*	*Estimated harvesting over (+) or under (-) legal quota (%)*
Muskdeer	91	Protected	0	2,000	Protected[a]
Beaver	53	258	54	2,000	+775
Roedeer	1,200	2,000	1,132	10,000	+500
Reddeer	375	800	362	1,000	+25
Moose	1,255	3,00	1,091	4,000	+14
Sable	22,504	63,960	16,072	50,000	-22
Reindeer	251	1,000	183	500	-50
Brown bear	130	500	75	300	-40
Wild boar	60	400	72	240	-40

[a] All hunting was illegal.

Source: Krasnoyarsk Kray Forest Committee, 1995.

Box 2.2: Conserving Biodiversity

Biodiversity--or the total diversity of plants, animals, and other living organisms in all their forms and levels of organization--encompasses the genetic diversity of genes, species, ecosystems, and the evolutionary and functional processes that link them. Biodiversity conservation aims to safeguard the future of all habitats, species, and their genetic components to the extent that this is biophysically, economically, and politically possible. Because biodiversity is not evenly distributed across the earth's surface, representative ecosystems and ecosystems that are particularly rich in biodiversity have to be identified and integrated into a viable protected area system. While the establishment and maintenance of large protected areas is a cornerstone of any systematic conservation program, effective conservation of biological diversity depends on sympathetic management of the total landscape in which the protected areas are situated.

With the support of the Global Environment Facility (GEF), Russia is developing an integrated framework for biodiversity management as part of the Biodiversity Conservation Project (World Bank 1996a). The framework aims to provide an immediate safety net for the protection of biodiversity during the current period of economic difficulty. It is also intended to assist the government in developing biodiversity strategies at national and regional levels and action plans that incorporate economic as well as biological assessments. The project will provide a support program for key protected areas that are critically affected by current economic conditions and develop a significant demonstration program in the Lake Baikal Region for biodiversity conservation.

Promoting Sustainability through Land Allocation

A land allocation process that employs a land use planning procedure is needed to identify sites with particular characteristics or known vulnerability to disturbance and to avoid mutually exclusive land use activities. A formal land use allocation and planning process provides the policy framework and management criteria resource managers need to systematically determine the optimal use of a given parcel of forest land. These processes are designed to classify forest tracts according to environmental sensitivity and conservation value, social and cultural value, and economic potential for commercial utilization in order to optimize the benefits resulting from sustainable use of forest resources (Box 2.3).

Box 2.3: Russia's Experience with Land Use Allocation and Planning

The concept of land use allocation and planning is not a new one for Russia. It has been employed to some extent in determining the present protected area network and the allocation to different forest management groups. Land use planning programs have also been carried out on a trial basis in the Lake Baikal region and the Far East, in cooperation with the nonprofit Ecologically Sustainable Development, Inc. The Federal Forest Service is expanding the Russian Model Forest network (based on the Canadian Model Forest concept, described in Annexes J and K), following a systematic land use allocation and planning approach by applying sustainable resource management criteria. The Gassinski Model Forest has already been established as part of the international model forest network, and a site near Moscow has been selected by the Federal Forest Service for a second model forest.

Often, land use allocation and planning include considerations of multiple uses for a particular area. Multiple-use management introduces important managerial challenges and opportunities, perhaps the greatest being to ensure sensitivity to underpriced but economically and socially important values for land in all categories. Also, biodiversity conservation and sustainable resource management cannot be achieved by focusing efforts solely on the areas to be protected. Ensuring effective environmental protection requires an overall land use planning approach encompassing the total landscape.

For Russia the full application of this concept means a significant expansion and intensification of the current planning approach and the integration of multidisciplinary criteria in the allocation and planning process. Field observations suggest that Russia's current forest classification system (see Box 1.6 in Chapter I) does not give adequate consideration to environmental and biodiversity concerns in Group III forests and to environmentally sensitive and valuable areas that should be protected or managed for multiple values. Furthermore, Group I and II forests are coming under increasing pressure for uses that are incompatible with their environmental and social objectives. The management system needs to be guided by concerns for sustaining the functionality of the total forest ecosystem.

Russia needs a more comprehensive planning and management approach that encourages participatory land use allocation and planning encompassing all forest lands. A schematic presentation, illustrating the systematic assignment of land use priorities, is shown in Figure 2.1. The selection criteria for prioritizing land use allocations need to be defined by the Federal Forest Service

Figure 2.1: A Proposed Forested Land Allocation and Planning Process

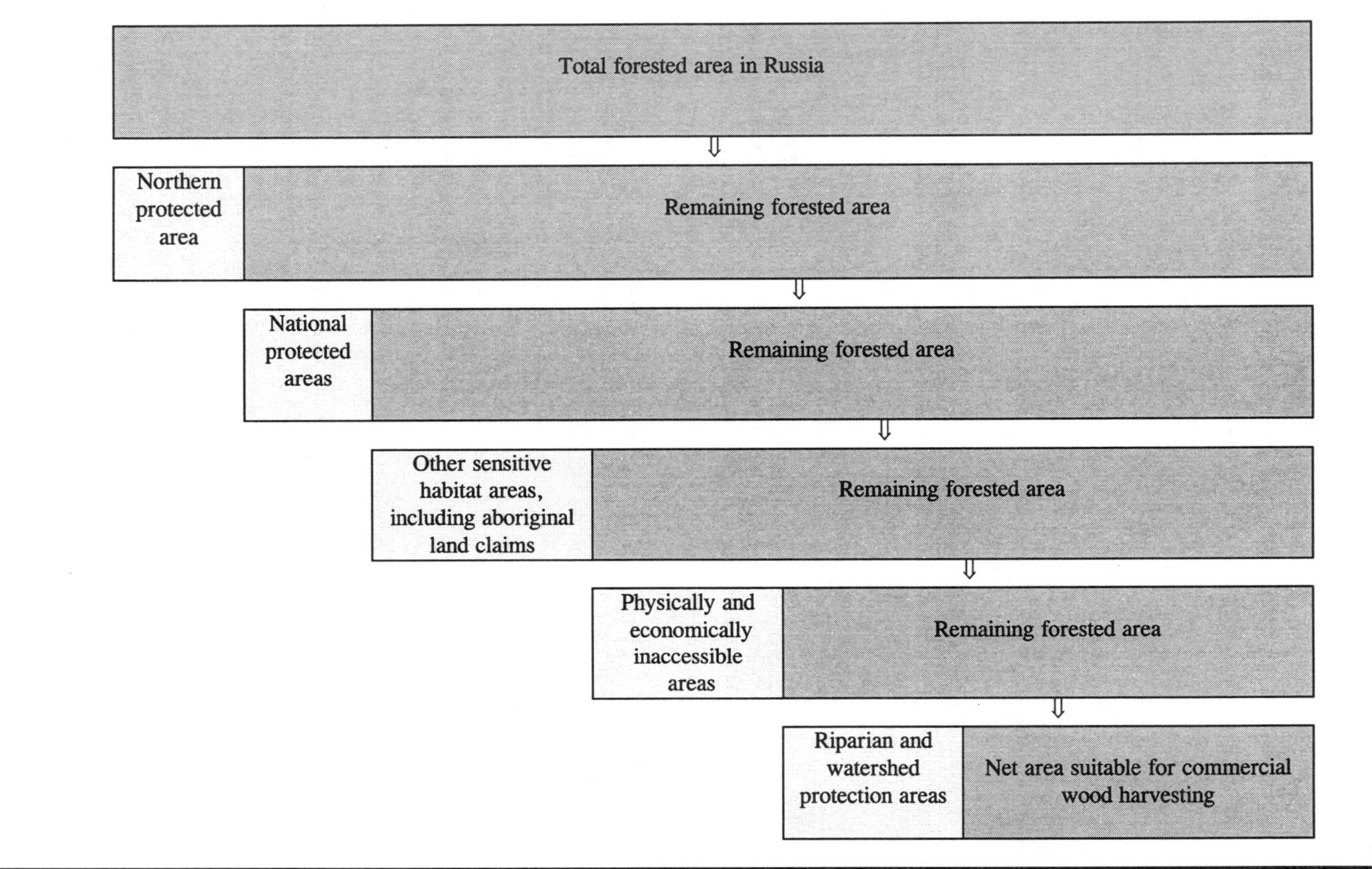

in collaboration with the State Committee for Environmental Protection, the regional authorities, aboriginal communities, scientific research institutes, and other stakeholders in forest resource management. An example is the resource management strategy on biodiversity that is currently being developed in cooperation with the GEF (see Box 2.2).

In this process, the area suitable for forest production or wood supply is the area remaining after the systematic classification and delineation of protected areas, sensitive habitats (including aboriginal land claims), physically and economically inaccessible areas, and riparian and watershed protection areas. Site-specific knowledge and accurate resource inventory data are prerequisites for this approach, necessitating a long planning horizon for both strategic and operational purposes. If sustainability is to be the guiding criterion, environmental protection, recognition of aboriginal claims, and maintenance of biodiversity must be clear and enforceable management objectives in areas where harvesting is the primary objective of resource use. Variations of this planning process are in use in many countries with boreal forests, and their experience could be useful to the Russian authorities in developing an effective land use and decision-making process.

Classifying the northern areas of Siberia and the Far East as unsuitable for harvesting may not create much controversy because of their protected status since 1959, their remote location, and the relatively low commercial value for wood production in these pre-tundra and northern taiga forests. Thus, the real economic impact of moving the boundary of protected areas further to the south, as proposed by the Sukachev Forest Institute, is likely to be minimal. The protected status would not limit subsistence timber use by the aboriginal population. More controversy is likely to attend efforts to exclude from the productive forest sensitive habitat and permafrost areas that are not currently part of the national protected area network, physically and economically inaccessible areas, and riparian and watershed protection areas within a specific wood supply area.

Setting aside such areas would reduce the land base used in calculating the annual allowable cut, thereby reducing wood production potential. Currently, the annual allowable cut is set by the Federal Forest Service at less than the total new volume naturally produced by the forests each year, and about 60 percent or less of that amount has actually been cut annually. But localized overcutting will remain a problem unless calculations of annual allowable cut are tied more closely to the effective wood supply in specific regions. The data available for this review were not adequate for a conclusive judgment about the real potential for wood production, although it is certain that the method currently used does not consider all the relevant environmental issues. A realistic annual allowable cut should be based solely on the net area suitable for commercial wood harvest, as shown in Figure 2.1.

Land managers need to be fully aware of cost-benefit relationships to succeed in a market-based economy. Sensitivity to markets for forest products must not be at the expense of the nonmarket environmental and social functions of forest. Market-based instruments and environmental regulations are needed to establish proper incentives for protecting undervalued aspects of forest ecosystems. Without government subsidies to reduce costs of access, forest areas with only marginal economic accessibility would be unlikely to be developed unless the costs could be passed on to consumers. Thus economic forces could play an important role in the conservation of environmental values, by requiring investors to fully internalize development costs. That would leave large portions of the most sensitive northern forests, which are not attractive to commercial development, free for other uses. Ensuring resource sustainability in forests that are economically accessible will require government regulation of a wide range of commercial activities. An important incentive will be to use regeneration efforts and intensive forest management to increase productivity in easily accessible areas.

Rationalizing Regeneration Strategies

Achieving resource sustainability depends on establishing appropriate harvest levels and establishing a systematic regeneration program. Continuous forest renewal is essential for ensuring an even flow of harvestable timber from a finite production area and, therefore, must occupy a central position in resource development planning and management. Under a land use planning process similar to that presented in Figure 2.1 of this Chapter, large areas of potentially productive forest would be withdrawn from commercial use for reasons of environmental conservation, habitat protection, nonwood resource value, and concerns for the global climate. And once economically unsuitable areas are no longer included in calculating the annual allowable cut, the need for forest regeneration activities will become more apparent.

Russia's seemingly inexhaustible forest resources and generous state subsidies have long determined wood production parameters and pushed forest renewal efforts to the background. The difficulties of the forest sector during the transition have been greatly intensified by the absence of a consistently enforced forest renewal program. With severe wood shortages in the vicinity of processing centers and large areas of degraded and nonproductive forest land, the need for an appropriate forest renewal strategy is evident. All four of the basic methods of regeneration -- natural regeneration, direct aerial seeding, planting, and fill-in planting -- are applied in Russia, though natural regeneration is by far the most common. Each method has its own technical, biophysical, and economic requirements.

One of the main advantages of ***natural regeneration*** is that new seedlings are of the right provenance, naturally suited to the environmental and climatic conditions of the area. If high-quality parent trees are selected, the seed could have an optimal genetic make-up, and germination and survival rates can be high if the seed source is sufficient and appropriately spaced. Natural regeneration requires selecting a harvesting block of a size and shape that reflect the seed dissemination patterns and distances of the desired species. The timing of harvesting has to coincide with the seed production cycle, and seed germination requirements will determine the silvicultural system (clear-cut, selection, seed-tree, and shelter-wood) and site preparation activities (scarification, burning).

Periodic stand treatments are needed to reduce competition from low-value species (such as birch and aspen) that grow faster than conifers and so can easily invade the area. If these less vulnerable species are allowed to spread, they can delay the production of a high-value crop for several decades. Though the direct costs of natural regeneration are minimal, indirect costs can be high. These include stand treatment, delays in establishing the commercial crop because of competition from low-value species, and higher costs of logging operations because seed trees can limit the use of certain equipment or because new roads are required to accommodate smaller settings and larger leave strips.

Direct aerial seeding imitates natural regeneration, but provenance and genetic selection are more difficult to control. An advantage is that direct seeding can cover larger areas and can be applied beyond the seed dissemination range of standing trees. Since one of the objectives of sustainable forestry is to avoid large-scale clearcutting, direct seeding should not be used as the regeneration method of choice in commercial harvesting areas. However, direct seeding is suitable for exceptional use under specific conditions such as large areas cleared by fire or past logging activities.

Planting, although the most expensive regeneration method, is commonly used in North America and Europe. Canada, for example, annually plants an estimated 450,000 hectares, roughly half the harvested area. Planting has important advantages for forest management. It allows for the selection of the most desirable species at the desired spacing for a given area. Because seedlings are already at least two years old when planted, they have an advantage over competing vegetation, reducing the time required for the stand to become fully productive. Under boreal conditions, planting could easily speed up the overall rotation by ten to twenty years, translating into real gains in forest productivity. Proper management and planning can reduce some difficulties associated with planting. The provenance of the planting stock has to be appropriate for the specific site, and tree planters have to be properly trained to plant carefully. As with natural regeneration, periodic stand treatments may have to be carried out to reduce competition from undesirable species.

Reducing Losses Due to Fire, Insects, and Diseases

While it is logistically impossible and economically and ecologically undesirable to respond to all forest fires, the high incidence and severity of human-caused fires and the extensive loss of timber and of social, economic, and environmental values amply justify increased efforts in effective fire management. Over 1 million hectares of forest are affected annually by fire, almost double the area cleared by logging. Entire communities have been economically devastated as fire consumed the timber base around them. Some districts in Russia now use up to 29 percent of their operating budget for forest fire control activities. In bilateral discussions with Canada, the United States, and other countries and international organizations such as FAO, Russia's Federal Forest Service is seeking to exchange technical know-how in fire detection, monitoring, suppression, and management in ways that will benefit all partners (ECE/FAO/ILO 1996).

The risk of fire is a concern for many forest communities and for every private investor thinking about investing in the forest sector. Because the authorities are unable to provide effective fire protection and control, any private investor has to include the costs for developing and maintaining these services into estimates of operating costs. In less accessible areas, these additional costs could make the difference between investing and not investing in an operation. A successful example of World Bank-financed forest fire rehabilitation project in China is described in Box 2.4.

Detection and control of insects and diseases pose similar problems. As in the case of fire protection, cooperative agreements are in place between Russia and several countries for the exchange of chemical, biological, and technical control methods and equipment and the supply of proven chemical and biological control agents. Access to state-of-the-art application methods (such as ultra-low-volume application with a global positioning system) would be a significant improvement over the crude application methods currently used in Russia. Effective employment of new control techniques will require public funding at least initially; over the medium term, as the benefits from these control strategies are realized, such efforts should become self-financing.

Box 2.4: A World Bank-Financed Forest Fire Rehabilitation Project in China

Fire was always a major hazard for the boreal forest in Da Xing An Ling at the Armur river in China, accounting for losses of 135,000 hectares annually in the 22 million hectare forest. In May 1987, the most disastrous forest fire in China's history burned about 1 million hectares in Da Xing An Ling, killing 193 people and destroying the homes of 67,000 people and a large part of the infrastructure.

The fire killed trees with some 30 million cubic meters, of timber, half of it estimated to be commercial quality larch and pine logs. To salvage the timber before it was destroyed by insects and fungi and to establish a fire protection and management system, the Ministry of Forestry, with World Bank support, developed an emergency program. Over a three-year period, 12 million cubic meters of timber was salvaged (the largest operation of its kind ever undertaken) yielding US$1.2 billion in sales revenues, and a fire protection and management system was estimated for the entire region, reducing fire damage from 135,000 hectares a year to several hundred hectares.

The success of the project was based on the following three factors:

- Organization and implementation of the project were managed by a joint effort of all forest enterprises in the region and China Railways and the mobilization of 25,000 workers for the salvage operations.

- The establishment of a multilayered fire protection and management system, including an integrated communication network, satellite and aerial reconnaissance, rapid fire suppression squads equipped with helicopters, paramilitary fire suppression teams equipped with multiterrain amphibious vehicles for personnel transport, and fire engines. The professional fire fighting teams were supported by the communities, which mobilized all available adult workers to fight the fires.

- The provision of specialized expertise and funds through the World Bank.

The effectiveness of modern technology and application methods was demonstrated in the integrated pest management program in the Krasnoyarsk Kray in the summer of 1996, funded by the World Bank in response to a request by the Russian Government and NGOs. There had been reports of serious pest (*Dendrolimus sibiricus*) outbreaks in Siberia's forest requiring an emergency response to contain the problem before it spread. The project also included targeted pest control, monitoring of pest populations and treatment, and training programs.

Enforcing Environmental Standards in Other Sectors

All activities that can affect forest resources need to be thoroughly and systematically assessed before permission is granted to proceed with the activity. Roads built for oil fields, mining, and public transportation are of special concern, since they provide convenient access for timber harvesting in areas that might not otherwise have been developed. They also have substantial potential for causing irreversible damage to the forests and the environment through agents such as fire.

The system for safeguarding against harmful environmental impacts requires modification. Environmental impact assessments focus predominately on technical specifications and standards, which are unrealistically high in some cases, making compliance difficult. Broader issues of institutional strengthening, socioeconomic dynamics, cross-sectoral relationships, and financing for environmental protection receive only minimal attention. Monitoring and enforcement procedures are weak, with a system of inappropriately structured fines doing little to encourage compliance. What is needed is a clearly articulated land use plan based on ecological and environmental criteria that provides an integrated framework for environmental impact assessments. The framework should enable fire protection, biodiversity conservation, and timber production to receive proper attention individually and jointly and will strengthen the policymaking capability of industry managers, local and regional authorities, and federal agencies.

C. Restructuring the Sector for Sustainability and Economic Viability

Policymakers can help to position the forest sector to respond to the changes brought about by economic and structural adjustment in a way that improves long-term performance. Measures are needed to improve natural resource rent recovery, further liberalize international trade, and reduce monopoly and monopsony powers in the sector through strong antimonopoly regulations. This would require measures to improve the efficiency of the forest sector, including effective restructuring of the timber industry (see Chapter I and Annex D for more details). Policy reforms are needed in resource pricing to ensure that timber producers and timber users bear the full costs of timber production. A major impediment to reform is the tax structure, which is distorting timber pricing and reducing scope for additional resource-related charges.

Rationalizing Resource Pricing

International experience shows clearly that a competitive forest industry requires a resource pricing system that makes processors bear the full cost of timber production.[13] Many forest-rich countries, including Russia, have subsidized their industrial sectors by keeping the costs of timber artificially low, whether through energy or transportation subsidies to the timber industry or through trade barriers. Inevitably, the results have been large inefficiencies in processing, uneconomic location of processing capacity, excessive industrial capacity, and low investment in resource management.

Stumpage. The most significant source of inefficiency is the stumpage system (see earlier footnote 7). Stumpage charges are too low, nontransparent, levied only on timber removed from the forest rather than on all timber cut, and favor enterprises with lower operating costs or better-quality wood. A properly designed stumpage system can provide powerful operational incentives for improved efficiency and sustainable forest management. Resource pricing can be designed to motivate resource users to optimize resource utilization on a sustainable basis. Stumpage revenues are also relatively easy to target for specific forest management functions, as the Canadian province of British Columbia has done in funding a forest renewal program entirely through stumpage revenues ($2 billion over a five-year period).

In most stumpage systems, the rent accruing to the resource owner is the residual amount after operating costs and enterprise profits have been deducted from the selling price. In Russia, applying such a system could eliminate most rent-seeking, especially if the system reflected regional variations in

---

13 *For a fuller discussion of the forest rent capture methods discussed here, see M. Gillis, "Forest Concession Management and Revenue Policies" in N. Sharma, ed., 1992.*

resource value and operating costs, including transportation costs. But because the forest resource is undervalued, Russia relies instead on an enterprise profit tax to capture a portion of the resource value. Other countries that use profit taxation for this purpose have developed more complex rent recovery systems based on the actual market value of the resource.

Timber Sales. Countries use a wide variety of sales techniques (auction sales, bidding, area sales, volumetric sales, sales based on appraised values) to extract a reasonable share of the economic rent from timber sales. Russia has had limited experience with such practices, but its experiment in auctioning harvest rights in the Far East is showing good results (prices were as high as 45,000 rubles per cubic meter). Competitive bidding for timber sales under fair conditions maximizes the returns to the resource owner, but it may not always take into account other economic, social, and environmental values. Furthermore, where feasible and appropriate, nonwood products should also be considered in the valuation system to improve the integration of various forest resources into overall forest management.

Separating Resource Rent Capture from Enterprise Taxation

Concession Policy. As much as 90 percent of industrial wood harvested from publicly held lands worldwide is harvested under concession agreements granting an enterprise exclusive rights to exploit or manage a specific area. Concessions are usually awarded on the basis of administrative discretion or competitive auction -- or a combination of the two.

Because conditions for auction generally cannot be met for large parcels of forest land with long-term concessions, concession rights are usually determined by administrative discretion, following negotiations between government officials and eligible applicants. Competitive auction of concession rights is feasible only when there is an adequate inventory of timber resources, when the auction market is sufficiently competitive, when the costs of gathering and evaluating information on stand quality are relatively low, and when the auctioning agency is appropriately staffed. This method is usually limited to small parcels granted for relatively short periods. Canada, Malaysia, and Venezuela have used competitive auctions for short-term licenses. In some cases, features of an auction system can be combined with limited administrative discretion to improve competitive participation by a variety of concessionaires.

Most countries started out with perfunctory or vague concession agreements, moving on to agreements with stronger incentives for sustainable forest use only after their forest resources were severely degraded. Russia, with its large, undeveloped forest areas in Siberia and the Far East, still has the opportunity to avoid this degradation. It can write sustainable forest policy provisions into new concession agreements and revoke the unexpired concessions of companies that fail to comply with forest management obligations for improving performance. It can accompany these efforts with well-structured monitoring and enforcement activities. A few countries allow concession holders to transfer concession rights, which creates a strong incentive for efficient resource use. With transferability, concessioners can reap the benefits of their efforts to maintain long-term productivity, such as avoiding early re-entry on logged-over stands or adopting low-impact logging methods, making such practices more likely.

Timber Taxation. Various levels of government collect revenue from the timber sector through requited and unrequited payments. Requited payments are made by logging enterprises to the resource owner as compensation for taking the resource. Unrequited payments are made by logging enterprises to the government, based on the government's exercise of sovereign power; export taxes and income taxes are the two most common forms.

Requited payments consist of timber royalties, license fees, and reforestation fees. Royalties were traditionally applied to roundwood values, but as countries have increasingly turned to processing their own timber resources, royalties have been assessed on the volume of processed products. This has resulted in some stagnation in processing industries in wood-producing countries. Royalties can be based on volume extracted, number of trees (according to species composition), or value extracted. License fees (one time or annual) are based on total area and can be adjusted for accessibility and the quality of the stand.

Revenues from unrequited payments may be used in support of general government programs. With increased investment in domestic processing capacity, most countries have moved from a reliance on export taxes on logs to a reliance on income (or profit) taxes as a major source of government revenue from the forestry sector. Taxes on roundwood exports, easy to collect because logs were exported through a small number of ports, were once the principal incentive for the rapid development of forest-based industrialization. But the practice entailed high economic costs overall. Also, the government experienced large revenue losses from the sector because of the very high rates of effective protection of the processing industries as a result of the tax differentials between raw and processed materials.

Which method is best for collecting government revenues from the sector depends on the level of ecological diversity in the forest, the forest's health and calculated fire risk, the public sector's capability to monitor forest management, the availability of detailed inventories, the condition of infrastructure, and many other considerations. A key variable in collecting taxes is the administrative capacity of the government. With the history of forest waste in Russia, it may be worth considering to set resource rental charges as fixed annual area fees based on estimated stumpage values for a particular region. This would be relatively simple to administer and would encourage processors to reduce waste. Unrequited taxation policy and payments by forest enterprises should be same as those for commercial enterprises in other sectors.

Reducing the Power of Monopolies

There are very few market economies in which the government retains any significant ownership of assets in the wood processing industry. Public authorities are often active in designing policies to attract industrial investment, as in the United States and Canada, but private firms always make their own investment and management decisions within a defined regulatory framework. And while the government retains regulatory powers in certain instances (for example, regarding the water pollution associated with pulp and paper industries), industry bears the cost of designing and implementing corrective actions. Fees, licenses, and fines are the government's means of recovering compensation for the externalities in the industry, and they can be a strong incentive for bringing about desired changes in management practices.

In the Russian forest sector, corporatization and privatization of industrial enterprises has been proceeding rapidly, as compared to other sectors. The number of state-owned forest enterprises has nominally decreased to a mere 10 percent of the total number since 1991. However, the role of regional and local governments remains critical both in terms of their formal and informal involvement in the management of the newly corporatized enterprises, and through operational subsidies which they continue to allocate to local monopolistic, and uneconomic, timber enterprises in order to keep them afloat "for social reasons".

The organizational structure of the forest industry in Russia has been undergoing continuous changes in the recent years of economic transition (see Annex B for details). However, their impact on regional timber monopolies has been only marginal. Large regional joint-stock companies such as Dallesprom and Dalles in Khabarovsk Kray (similar to the other former regional subsidiaries to the publicly-owned national holding company Roslesprom) used to dominate the forest industry and appeared to be able to influence both stumpage and output prices in the regions. New companies have been attempting to set themselves apart from these monopolies, but their independence continues to be significantly jeopardized by the controlling directors who, in many cases, are also directors in the regional holding companies and in the former Roslesprom.

Although "barriers to entry" for new forest enterprises are expected to be lower as proposed in the draft Forest Code, they are not completely eliminated. Moreover, the draft Forest Code fails to stipulate any explicit antimonopoly provisions that would prohibit any action of a governmental body aimed at restricting access to acquiring rights to forest use or discrimination against certain forest enterprises (see Annex C for details). Similarly, efficiency in the wood-processing sector would improve only through breakup of such monopolies, more rigorous application of antimonopoly regulations and increased competition. This would, in most cases, involve restructuring of the timber concession arrangements linked to the holding companies.

It may be that the Russian federal Government, facing overwhelming responsibilities in so many areas, may simply be unable at this time to address the distortions (market, price, and distribution) that result from monopoly control. It can, however, breakup the monopolies or eliminate some of their more blatant attributes through more specific legislation and an effective regulatory presence in the regions. The many types of antimonopoly measures employed in the forest sector in other industrial countries can provide working models.

D. Social Welfare in the Forest Sector

In addition to conflicts over aboriginal people's land rights, there is a broad range of social welfare considerations related to the forest sector that require immediate attention. The welfare of the approximately 10 million people who depend on forest resources for their livelihoods is at risk since responsibility for social infrastructure and services has been shifted from enterprises to the public sector. These people are made particularly vulnerable by the remoteness of their forest communities and the absence of alternative employment opportunities.

Defining Aboriginal Land Claims in Set-Aside Areas

A deliberate effort is needed to ensure fair and effective representation of native people through the formalization of aboriginal land rights. Delays in formal recognition prevent the authorities from intervening in illegal logging activities on aboriginal land, activities that may irreversibly diminish the potential of the forests to support the traditional lifestyle of these people (see Annex G).[14] It is essential to clarify who will develop and implement forest management policies, allocate resources, and establish resource pricing systems in areas set aside for aboriginal communities.

The regional legislature of Khabarovsk has adopted comprehensive regulations that are fair to the aboriginal communities. The regulations provide territories for traditional and communal uses and give communities virtual autonomy in deciding on nontimber harvesting and approving nonclan users (see below). The reality, however, has not lived up to the intentions of the law, especially with regard to harvesting activities by private logging enterprises on territories designated for traditional use only. There are several federal documents and a draft federal law addressing the land rights and traditional occupations of aboriginal people, but they have not yet been adopted. Forest enterprises are taking advantage of the legal vacuum and harvesting portions of protected (Group I) forests. Most aboriginal groups are turning a blind eye to or even facilitating these violations because the enterprises provide jobs, transport links to district centers, and supplies of basic goods for local shops.

These issues need to be clarified and a new law adopted soon, so that aboriginal people can profit from forest development and receive compensation from nonaboriginal users of communal territories and resources. Clear definitions of clans or "families" need to be established so that territories to be used solely for the pursuit of traditional occupations can be distinguished from those that are communally owned but harvested for industrial timber production. Targeted assistance to aboriginal people, possibly channeled through NGOs, could be especially helpful in developing industries related to traditional occupations (such as berry processing or leather tanning) and in training community members in forestry, game, and fish management.

Small-scale loans and the establishment of cooperatives, social funds, and similar community-based development schemes should be promoted to take advantage of investment opportunities that can strengthen traditional trades and indigenous communities. These investment opportunities include small-scale reindeer herding, wood working, and the production of traditional wood products, fishing, fur processing, and the production of handicrafts. Investments opportunities also exist in modern mobile meat processing and storage facilities. Appropriate training of indigenous people in traditional trades can improve the marketability of their products.

Providing Adequate Social Services in Forest Areas

Along with wages, a job in a forest sector enterprise (as in any other state enterprise) in Russia used to bring with it a house, pension, medical care, sports, paid vacations, preschool education, daycare, loans, subsidized transportation, and more to the people living in these remote forest-dependent communities. Over the past two years, these services have been turned over to local administrations, which have been able to sustain only the most minimal basic services. These services

---

14 *However, according to a Presidential decree (No. 397,1992), expropriation of lands of the indigenous people for nontraditional activities without a local referendum is forbidden (see Fondahl 1995). The social and cultural impact on indigenous peoples of expanded use of the Northern Sea Route is examined by Osherenko 1995.*

have become one of the most serious casualties of the economic transformation in Russia.[15] The government may use certain policy tools to ease the current situation, but social services are a national issue that cannot be resolved by isolated reforms in a single sector. The long-term goal should be policies that improve the investment climate and promote sustainable forest management thereby improving the standard of living for inhabitants of forest communities.

Policies governing the transfer of responsibility for social services from enterprises to local governments are not yet fully developed, and there is uncertainty about the assignment of responsibilities among various levels of government. As these are being sorted out, the problem is compounded by a shrinking tax base for all levels of governments. Enterprises that are still producing often underpay their employees, if they pay them at all. Many enterprises that have ceased production have nevertheless kept their doors open, so that their employees can remain eligible for the few benefits still provided in their community.

A comprehensive, state-financed social services program is not financially feasible for Russia today or in the foreseeable future. All that seems realistically possible is the provision of a basic social safety net for the affected population. Some social services will have to be provided by the emerging private sector. In some enterprises, performance has deteriorated so severely following elimination of social services that the enterprises have restored some basic services in order to boost job performance. However, since the resources to provide these services had to be diverted from production, the result in some cases has been continued employment at enterprises that are producing little or nothing.

For many of the 1.5 to 2 million people who live in the most severely affected remote northern logging communities, possible improvements over the long-term are of little comfort now. Migration from these communities is increasing, and current estimates are that more than 30 percent of the population in the northern area of the Far East will eventually move south. How local governments will deal with this migration and voluntary resettlement is difficult to predict. But the problem affects not only the migrants, but also the people who stay behind and those living in the communities that must absorb more people.

Setting Up Employment Programs for Affected Populations

Market economies generally provide employment assistance of various kinds to areas suffering from major restructuring, either through the national government or through specialized labor assistance and training agencies or regional and local authorities. The programs are generally funded from general tax revenues. Job retraining and public works programs are the two options available in Russia for addressing the unemployment resulting from restructuring. Public works schemes are an effective short-term solution for temporary unemployment and are generally self-targeting. Job retraining programs address medium- and long-term unemployment issues by providing the new skills and expertise needed in the restructured climate--such as in land use planning, environmental and biodiversity protection, and sustainable forest management in the case of forest enterprises.

There is not enough information available about labor prospects in areas affected by job losses in the forest sector to make recommendations about the appropriate scale of government assistance.

---

15 *Many social service aspects of the adjustment process are common across sectors. For a more complete treatment of these issues in the coal sector and of federal employment funds and services in general, see World Bank, 1994.*

Information needs to be collected on diversified employment possibilities in local and neighboring areas, geographical location and transport links, opportunities for new businesses, and housing markets. This information is critical for determining development strategies and setting up employment programs for affected populations. There is also a need to resolve issues related to the assignment of responsibility for expenditure to finance these programs among different levels of government and the establishment of an adequate revenue base to meet these expenditures needs.

The most effective policies for helping people are those that promote long-term growth and economic development. Economic development policies should aim at building local capacity, thereby providing a range of new jobs and activities that will be needed for implementing national and regional strategies. The employment prospects that would accompany the growth of the forest industry and the development of markets for nontimber forest products would have a powerful and positive impact on economic development, especially in Siberia and the Far East, where fewer options are available than in European Russia. Most important, this development will reduce the reliance of remote forest communities on the social services system.

Meeting the Social Welfare Needs of Indigenous People

The aboriginal groups and other indigenous peoples of the forest area of the north are among the most vulnerable groups in Russia today. Many wish to be left alone to follow their traditional way of life. The mass migrations out of these areas have resulted in weakened transportation links to the outside, limited access to supplies and markets, and the loss of jobs, teachers, hospital personnel, and other public service workers. Most able-bodied men and women in the aboriginal communities receive very low salaries. Pensioners are the main bread-winners in many families.

For inhabitants of Russian ethnic background, who constitute a majority of the population that is dependent on forest resources for their employment and livelihood, the adjustments taking place in the sector put the welfare of their families at risk while providing no viable alternatives. Market-based responses will alleviate the unemployment problem over time, but in the meantime the social costs would be unacceptably high. Labor, housing, and financial markets are underdeveloped, allowing little labor mobility or access to medium- or long-term credit for relocation or business start-up capital.

III. SOME SOLUTIONS: TOWARD AN AGENDA FOR FOREST SECTOR REFORM

As Russia continues its transition to a market economy, forest sector policies must change if the resource base is to be sustained and if the people who depend on these resources are to contribute to sustainable economic development. While the ongoing economic reform has strongly affected the sector, the fundamental source of the sector's problems is the legacy of economic and environmental mismanagement inherited from central planning, which sought to convert the sector's natural capital into industrial development without regard for the sustainability of forest resources or natural resources in other sectors. One result is an industrial structure fundamentally mismatched to the distribution of resources, and an economically inefficient flow of wood to obsolete and noncompetitive industries. This situation has been exacerbated by inadequate funding for the most basic resource management activities.

The previous chapter presented a conceptual framework for forest sector reform. The process of developing that framework has already begun, through the introduction of new forest legislation (the 1993 Forest Legislation and the 1996 draft Forest Code) and the partial privatization and restructuring of forest industries. As the reform continues, it should involve a broader range of stakeholders and draw on new sources of external financial and technical assistance. This chapter presents key recommendations and priorities for forest policy reform and public expenditure that flow from the conceptual framework.[16]

A. Integrating the Forest Sector in Overall Economic Reform

Forest sector policies need to be consistent with the overall environmental, economic, and social objectives of the government and the economic reform already under way. Thus, indirect protective measures such as trade barriers and price subsidies should be avoided. The state should stay out of commercial activities in the sector, allowing market forces to allocate resources efficiently. Some temporary measures are needed, however, to ease the impact of adjustment in some remote areas, including job training to assist people in finding new jobs. Key recommendations for integrating the forest sector in overall economic reform are summarized in Table 3.1.

Liberalization of most domestic prices and international trade at the federal level has already occurred. Price controls were lifted on most commodities in 1992, and subsidies have been substantially reduced. However, some now-privatized enterprises are calling for an increase or a resumption of energy and transport subsidies. The Government is wise to resist these efforts and should seek further policy measures to ensure that managers are held to the rigors of market prices. Russia launched one of the largest programs ever to privatize land, property and enterprises.

---

16 *The World Bank's Country Assistance Strategy (CAS) has identified agriculture as a priority sector for Russia and the proposed recommendations for the forest sector are consistent with that strategy (World Bank 1995b). The respective roles of agriculture and the forest sector are under discussion with the Russian Government as part of the World Bank's ongoing dialogue related to the Country Assistance Strategy for Russia.*

Table 3.1: Integrating the Forest Sector in Overall Economic Reform

Issue	*Status*	*Proposed policy objectives*	*Proposed strategy*
Liberalization of key prices (in particular, energy and transport)	Adjustment toward world prices has led to significant curtailment of output and employment	Incorporation of real fuel costs and benefits in decisionmaking; efficiency improvements in industrial utilization of forest resource	• Continue to further liberalize input prices and provide market discipline • Continue to further liberalize forest product prices • Remove inter-regional trade barriers
Rent capture of forest resources	Only a small share of the value of commercial forest resource harvests are captured for resource renewal and public purposes, leading to overharvesting and excessive and poorly located industrial capacity	Collection of a significant portion of the value of harvests from users to ensure resource renewal and a fair return to forest owners.	• Introduce market-based mechanisms (auctions, bidding) to increase rent capture • Incorporate enhanced rent- capture provisions in agreements with foreign-owned and joint ventures • Properly enforce rent capture mechanisms and tax laws to improve recovery of tax revenues
Antimonopoly measures and privatization	Reform has had limited impact on industrial structure in the processing sector; this sector is still dominated by inefficient, interrelated, and monopsonistic holding companies	Efficient and sustainable resource use by competitive enterprises	• Break-up monopolies and monopsonies, including the holding companies • Apply antimonopoly regulations and privatization measures more effectively to increase competitiveness of forest industry • Ease restrictions on joint ventures and forest investment • Increase efficiency in use of timber and other resources in processing sector • Competitive bidding for forest utilization rights
Budgetary stringency on forest management agencies	Reduced budgets have adversely affected forest management and protection; low rent capture from forest utilization	Meeting environmental and forest protection needs	• Scrutinize budgetary process to increase rent capture and maximize efficiency to achieve environmental and forest protection • Increase budget to ensure sustainability, private sector participation, and protection
Social welfare needs of remote forest communities	Significant populations are at risk due to unemployment and declining sectoral output	A minimum social safety net for populations at risk; long- term adjustment in labor markets; development of markets for nontimber forest products; strengthened indigenous communities and traditional economies.	• Target assistance to neediest populations, using local government structures to channel resources • Ease constraints on migration • Clarify land rights to enhance aboriginal welfare through benefits from the management of aboriginal land by aboriginal people • Restructure unemployment compensation, adjusting levels and duration of benefits • Design employment service systems to meet local needs • Organize skill transfer and training programs • Promote community-based credit and development schemes for traditional trades

Much larger share of the economic value of commercially exploited forest resources should be channeled into public expenditure programs. The immediate prospects for any substantial increase in ***rent capture*** are limited, in part because the resource rent is collected primarily as a tax on enterprises instead of a stumpage charge on resource levels. As economic recovery progresses, the Government should experiment more aggressively with a range of rent capture instruments, including more realistic royalty charges based on stumpage estimates.

More economic and business analysis is needed to identify ways to promote competition in the processing sector and to reduce the monopolistic influence of a few large firms on forest allocation, timber sales, processing, and exports. Monopolies should be broken up, and ***anti-monopoly regulations*** should be enforced. An easing of foreign exchange restrictions on foreign firms would complement domestic antimonopoly measures and promote efficiency. These measures will also help integrate forest sector reform into the overall economic reform.

In this period of severe budgetary crisis throughout the economy, the ***budget allocation*** process must consider the financial needs of each sector on their merits. Budget priorities need to be established across and within sectors, with expenditures ranked according to management objectives. While the forest sector should not be exempt from needed budget cuts, it should not be achieved at the cost of reducing sustainable sector development, sacrificing its environmental integrity, and increasing the suffering of the inhabitants of remote forest communities.

Vulnerable populations in remote communities need assistance in providing education, health, and other social services. The deterioration of social services has pushed many people below the poverty line. Responsibility for providing social services may need to be assigned to local administrations to ensure that programs meet the needs of the populations they are intended to serve. An effective human resource development program would also reduce migration from the northern areas into already overburdened areas in the south. A range of new activities are needed to implement the new forest sector policies, and thus job creation should have top priority. These new jobs will reduce the reliance of communities on the social services system. For the long-term, technical assistance to local NGOs will strengthen their institutional capacity for taking on responsibility for many of these services. The provision of needed social services should be accompanied by measures to strengthen traditional economies by making them more efficient and profitable.

B. Making Forest Management Sustainable

Several actions need to be taken to improve the efficiency of forest management. Other forest-rich countries offer many models for land ownership, jurisdiction, public participation, and sectoral policies. For sustainable development of the forest sector to become a reality, accountable and transparent public land management is needed, along with a policy framework that recognizes scarcity. Forest inventories and land registration procedures need to be revised within the context of land use planning, multiple-use management, and the development of forest-related sectors. The promotion of sustainable sector development not only requires strict enforcement of forest policies, laws, and regulations but also regular monitoring of critical forest indicators, both lagging indicators (of events that have already occurred) and leading indicators (signals of likely future problems). Key recommendations for making forest management sustainable are summarized in Table 3.2.

Table 3.2: Making Forest Management Sustainable

Issue	*Status*	*Proposed policy objectives*	*Proposed strategy*
Knowledge of resource base	Inadequate national and regional diagnosis of forest resources and their real potential for various uses, including wood production and conservation of biodiversity	Framework and guidelines for sustainable forest resource management in place, with the necessary allocations, for carrying out broad-scale appraisal; participatory resource appraisal system for sustainable forest resource management	• Promote the use of modern information management techniques for efficient resource assessment and planning • Obtain reliable information on forest resources suitable for planning purposes at different planning levels • Analyze data and stratify total forest land according to land allocation procedures • Undertake a rapid appraisal of the resource base of existing enterprises to clarify investment opportunities and restructuring needs
Land use planning	The three-group classification system used to designate forests for protection and commercial uses is not specific enough	A rational system of land allocation that protects environmental values and facilitates sustainable management for multiple objectives	• Ensure compatibility of land allocation criteria with the interests and capabilities of proposed management structure and governance • Incorporate logical wood supply zone concept into design of commercial forest management areas • Identify key areas needed to close gaps in existing protected area system • Include environmental protection criteria in designating forests for commercial utilization • Formalize aboriginal land allocations and ensure protection of these land rights • Incorporate local participation at all levels of planning process
Management of intersectoral environmental impacts	A significant source of fire risk and other damage to forest resources arises from poor environmental practices in the energy, mining, and infrastructure sectors	Planning process that includes appropriate environmental assessments and enforcement of measures to minimize deleterious effects of various activities	• Review and improve on environmental impact assessment procedures • Revise jurisdictional responsibilities for enforcement of regulations on forest land to reflect decentralized responsibilities and capabilities
Ecosystem management to promote multiple forest values	Timber extraction and impacts from other sectors are excessively destructive and impede satisfactory regeneration	Careful management of forest lands, especially commercial areas, to provide a high level of protection to environmental values; environmentally, economically, and socially sustainable forest utilization and management practices	• Revise and enforce implementation of management guidelines that incorporate ecosystem management and multiple-use concepts • Impose a regulatory and incentive framework to monitor, assess, and motivate concern for effective regeneration

Table continued on the next page

Table 3.2: Making Forest Management Sustainable (Contd.)

Issue	*Status*	*Proposed policy objectives*	*Proposed strategy*
Forest regeneration	Large logged-over and fire-damaged areas remain without sufficient regeneration; harvesting practices are inconsistent with heavy reliance on natural regeneration	Productivity of degraded forest land restored to satisfy economic and environmental objectives; harvesting practices regulated so that they are consistent with desired regeneration methods	• Prioritize degraded areas in relation to environmental costs and future economic potential • Allocate public funding for regeneration of existing degraded land on a priority basis • Restrict and enforce the size of clearcutting and monitor regeneration efforts to prevent continued degradation • Update guidelines on regeneration and sustainable management to incorporate ecosystem management concepts
Resource protection	About 1.6 million ha of forest is being damaged annually by fire, insects and diseases	Improved efficiency and effectiveness of forest resource protection through the use of appropriate technology, methodology, and funding	• Develop comprehensive forest health monitoring and management strategies • Expand cooperation with other countries in technology transfer • Increase protection area according to specified economic, social, and environmental criteria

The first step toward sustainable development of the forest sector is ***to clarify the status of resource base*** to set priorities for comprehensive land use planning. Russian professionals with a knowledge of broad resource potentials and past exploitation patterns should conduct this appraisal, identifying regions where the opportunities for sustainable conservation-oriented forest management are most favorable. Detailed land management plans should then be developed for these areas on a prioritized basis to help target resource conservation efforts and sustainable investment in forest sector development.

This detailed planning exercise will take a long time to complete for Russian's vast forest areas. Many decisions about the future of particular enterprises will have to be made before this information is available, so a rapid appraisal of the status of the resource base for existing enterprises will be needed as well. This analysis will help define the necessary scale of adjustment to the realities of a market economy, will make it possible to assess viable investment opportunities, and will help in the design of the social safety net to assist forest-dependent communities during the difficult period of economic transition. Social assessment methodologies should be used to identify stakeholders, elicit information, and seek their recommendations on environmental protection, land use planning, and sustainable forest management.

Timber production now dominates ***land use management strategies.*** However, even for lands that are to be managed primarily for industrial wood production, there are strong economic and environmental reasons for a management strategy that incorporates protection of wildlife populations, soil and water conservation, and the preservation of biodiversity. Any revision of forest management guidelines should take into consideration local demands for wildlife and other nontimber forest products and should provide for the systematic inclusion of local opinion on the timing and execution of forest management operations.

What is needed is a ***comprehensive land use planning*** approach that identifies protected areas, areas of aboriginal use and claims, areas with special biodiversity values, and areas sensitive to disturbance from commercial logging activities as well as areas suitable for sustainable timber production. This kind of land use planning process is the key to maximizing the social and economic returns to forest resources on a sustainable basis while protecting the environmental and biological heritage of Siberia and the Far East. All stakeholders should be involved in this planning exercise--the Federal Forest Service, the newly established State Committee for Environmental Protection and the Ministry of Natural Resources (successors to the former Ministry of Environmental Protection and Natural Resources), the regional authorities, native communities, the scientific research establishment, NGOs, and others.

Harvesting, postharvest land treatment, and natural regeneration practices need to be examined with an eye to meeting established standards and ensuring better compliance. Areas in which reforestation can meet economic or environmental objectives (wood production, enhancement of biodiversity, or carbon sequestration) need to be identified and prioritized. Harvesting practices should be strictly regulated to encourage the desired regeneration methods, as determined by the land use management plan. The appropriateness of forest regeneration method varies from one region to another, and each has its own technical, biophysical, and environmental requirements. However, natural regeneration is the most common method used in Russia.

Russia should expand its cooperative efforts with other countries to improve the effectiveness of ***resource protection***. Such exchanges in technology and know-how benefit all partners and could have a strong positive impact on Russia by reducing the staggering annual losses due to forest fires, insects, and diseases. Development of integrated approaches to fire management and pest management is the highest priority, with an emphasis on the early detection and rapid mobilization of resources to ameliorate these problems. Advance identification of areas to receive special attention, according to economic, social, and environmental priorities, will greatly improve the effectiveness and efficiency of protection efforts.

Some of the greatest threats to forest ecosystems come from ***operations in other sectors***, especially oil and gas, mining, and infrastructure. While current environmental legislation is adequate for protecting the resource base, enforcement is weak, leaving forest resources at considerable risk of fire, fragmentation, and depletion. There is a need to clarify jurisdiction over land and resources, so that development and enforcement of appropriate environmental standards can proceed.

C. Rationalizing Public Investment and Expenditures

Given an appropriate policy framework, the private sector can be expected to take the lead in developing the wood-processing sector, including modernizing mills or building new ones, increasing harvesting capacity, and improving or extending the transport infrastructure. To ensure that commercial interests do not compromise environmental sustainability, public sector investments are needed as well to supply crucial public goods and services in the forest sector. Private sector firms can often be contracted to provide management services.

A successful public investment program in the forest sector will require significant changes in the way public expenditures on forests are targeted and managed. Budgetary procedures need to distinguish clearly between recurrent costs and investment and should incorporate periodic evaluation of spending performance. In reviewing public expenditure in the sector, the federal Government should explore opportunities for improved management and identify and reorder priorities to emphasize investment in forest fire protection, targeted research, and the development of regulatory and strategic planning capabilities at national and local levels (Table 3.3).

Table 3.3: Rationalizing Public Investment and Expenditures

Issue	*Status*	*Proposed policy objectives*	*Proposed strategy*
Planning for resource sustainability	Little sectoral capacity for long-term strategic planning in the context of a market economy; budget process does not correctly distinguish between investment and current expenditure, leading to chronic misallocation of resources to activities that do not promote sector sustainability	Sectoral capability to assess consequences of policy changes and to disseminate findings to stakeholders and policymakers; economically rational levels and patterns of sectoral reinvestment and resource flows	• Decentralize institutional planning capacity and involve stakeholders, including indigenous people, in an integrated resource planning process
Forest health and protection	Fire, insects, and disease annually cause substantial economic and environmental losses	An integrated management process for forest protection	• Invest in fire, insect, and disease monitoring, management, and control systems and technology to minimize losses of economic and environmental values
Research and technology	Budgetary restrictions have reduced the rate of investment in forest research and slowed implementation of results of new findings	Targeted scientific research support to properly manage forest resources	• Rationalize the allocation of resources to targeted forest research according to forest management objectives • Support research on ways to strengthen traditional economies, technologies, and resource use practices

Public investment in forest protection, particularly the upgrading of fire detection and control capabilities, can yield substantial and immediate benefits by saving old-growth forests from destruction by fire, insects, and diseases and by protecting habitats that harbor unique ecological diversity. Minimizing the losses due to these destructive agents may have the most direct impact on long-term resource sustainability, provided that other resource management objectives are in line with such control efforts.

At the field level, government regulations must aim at reducing excessive logging waste, which increases the fuel load and intensifies the destructive force once a fire takes hold. Controlled burning in areas with a heavy load of logging debris should be considered as a management option. Many countries use training programs and education campaigns to increase public awareness of the dangers and effects of forest fire. Satellite surveillance and computer technology can be engaged to detect and monitor forest fires. Initiatives such as the joint Russia U.S. National Aeronautics and

Space Administration (NASA) project to study the use of satellite imagery for detecting and monitoring large fires, and other international efforts to coordinate the development and exchange of fire control technology, should be continued and expanded. The State Program of Forest Fire Control for 1993-97 could form the basis for an appropriate investment program.

The land use planning capabilities of ***forest research*** institutes have been seriously weakened by the dramatic loss of staff. Resources should be provided to keep the best staff, to fund targeted research in support of resource management objectives, and to continue information collection and the recording of baseline information (forest inventories, remote sensing data, and environmental assessments). These data systems should emphasize public dissemination to help stimulate private sector activity and community involvement. Information management technologies can be used to give decisionmakers and stakeholders better access to information and to improve management efficiency. The model forest network initiated by the Federal Forest Service could serve as a source of relevant environmental and economic forest management information.

Government ought to incur the initial costs of integrated planning for resource sustainability. Such planning is a public good necessary to prepare for and facilitate sustainable forest sector development. Development of planning capacity within the regions and local governments is a critical first step and should be determined by the ownership pattern and administrative and managerial responsibilities assumed by each level. The necessary technical and managerial skills should be matched to site-specific information on wood and nonwood resources, biodiversity, and other environmental values. A scarcity of such expertise could well be a limiting factor. Finally, broad input by local stakeholders, including NGOs, indigenous people, and resource users, should be solicited in every stage of the planning process.

D. Involving the International Community

The work needed in Russia's forest sector clearly exceeds the country's immediate ability to finance it. Because of its importance to global environment and biodiversity, the forest sector in Russia commands a substantial degree of international interest and some funding (Table 3.4). The main focus of these international initiatives is consistent with the needs and priorities outlined in this report, but there is little coordination or interaction among them. The effectiveness of these efforts could be substantially enhanced by greater cooperation within the international community.

The international community has a tremendous stake in the future health and sustainability of Russia's forests and forest enterprises (Table 3.5). The time is opportune for a joint national-international approach that focuses on key forest sector priorities, including the planning and financing of actions to meet Russia's ***international environmental commitments.*** The aim should be to develop menu of options that the government can consider for meeting its international obligations and promoting sustainable forest sector development during transition.

Technical and financial assistance should be provided to accelerate the integration of forest sector policies into the overall economic reform process, make forest management sustainable, rationalize public expenditures, and create an enabling environment for private sector investment in sustainable forest enterprises. Human resources development needs close attention in order to mitigate the negative social effects of the transition and to facilitate future development of the sector.

Table 3.4: Forestry Projects Undertaken by the International Community

Project focus	*Project objective*	*International partner*
Forest resource assessment • Rational use of forest resources in Siberia • Use of satellite technology and geographic information system (GIS)	• Analysis of forest conditions in Siberia • Use of satellite information for resource inventory and mapping	• International Institute of Applied Systems Analysis • French Research Institute of Agriculture and Forestry (CEMAGREF)
Sustainable forest management • Gassinski Model Forest • Sustainable natural resource management • Sustainable development of Lake Baikal Region • GEF Biodiversity Conservation Project-Lake Baikal component	• A working model of sustainable forest management • Sustainable resource management framework in place • Partnership between Russian and U.S. private sector to promote sustainable resource development • Sustainable natural resource management and forest restoration in 3 selected watersheds.	• Canadian Forest Service • USAID and TACIS • USAID • Global Environment Facility (GEF) and the World Bank; and TACIS
Reforestation	• Identification and development of high-quality seedlings for artificial regeneration	• Ministry of Agriculture and Forestry of Finland Weyerhaeuser, Ltd.
Resource protection • Fire management and protection • Satellite imagery • Insects monitoring and control • Forest Emergency Response Program	• Exchange of knowledge and technology about fire management and protection • Use of high-resolution pictures and GIS to study and monitor forest conditions • Contain massive forest pest infestation through the provision of environmentally safe biological control agent in Krasnoyarsk Kray	• Canada, United States • NASA (US) • Canada, United States • The World Bank
Assessment of biodiversity and carbon balance • Management and protection of biodiversity • Protection of biodiversity • Sikhote-Alin project	• Information on sustainable land use and other natural resource utilization • Assessments of current trends in biodiversity in Russia and their links to carbon balance • Inventory	• GEF and the World Bank • USAID • USAID
Ecotourism and recreation • Lake Baikal Ecotourism • Recreational Resources and Ecotourism in Khabarovsk Kray •	• Assessment of the potential ecotourism, and the benefits • Conceptual model of ecotourism, using GIS	• The World Bank and Japan • Canadian Forest Service

Table 3.5: Role of the International Community

Issue	*Status*	*Proposed policy objectives*	*Proposed strategy*
Global environmental sustainability	International interest in the application of sustainable management principles is not matched by adequate financial or technical support	Meeting financial and other obligations for management of nationally owned resources in ways consistent with international environmental commitments	• Adapt international framework on criteria and indicators for sustainable forest management to produce nationally and regionally relevant policies, procedures, and performance indicators • Identify specific policies, investments, and management practices with international environmental consequences that go beyond national economic priorities • Convene donor meetings to mobilize resources for priority activities
Technical assistance	International technical assistance covers wide range of topics and geographic areas but is uncoordinated and of limited impact	International technical assistance focused on key national priorities with the potential to produce systemic change in resource management policy and practice	• In consultation with sectoral stakeholders, donors and financiers, prepare assessment of technical assistance needs and prospective sources of assistance • Promote cooperative agreements between indigenous associations of Russian Federation and other countries of the North for strengthening traditional communities and economies • Develop multidonor partnership agreements to provide systematic targeted assistance
Financial assistance	Financial needs for restoring and maintaining resource sustainability extend beyond the current ability and willingness of the private sector to invest and of the domestic public sector to pay	Adequate financial resources to pursue long-term resource management objectives	• Finance economically, environmentally, and socially viable projects and activities in a coordinated manner to promote sustainability and efficiency in areas that are key to protecting resources, protecting the standards of living of the remote forest population, and attracting private investment

The Forest Advisors Group of multilateral and bilateral donors is developing a new country-driven approach to rationalize assistance for sustainable forest sector development. In consultation with national stakeholders, international and bilateral institutions, and NGOs, Russia should assess its needs and coordinate international resources for technical and financial assistance, using this report to guide its efforts. The consultative process could lead to consensus on sectoral polices and development priorities. This partnership agreement concept is currently being discussed by a number of countries for consideration by the Intergovernmental Panel on Forests appointed by the U.N. Commission on Sustainable Development in April 1995.

The idea of partnership is also vital to the U.N. *Decade of the World's Indigenous People*, to which the Russian Federation has made a strong commitment. Many of the issues confronting the indigenous peoples of Siberia and the Far East can be fruitfully approached through cooperative agreements between the Russian Federation and indigenous associations and governments of other countries of the North (e.g. Canada and the United States).

As a basis for future dialogue on support for reforming the forest sector, the following priority areas have been identified for promoting sustainable sector development during transition and for providing technical and financial assistance:

Short-Term Support (over the next two years)

(a) ***Ongoing policy reform***: Short-term support for policy reform would accelerate the economic transition and help to ensure the sustainability and integration of the forest sector into the overall economic reform framework. This would consist of carrying out the proposed follow-up studies to close information gaps and develop specific options for reform. These options could then be discussed in a series of regional and national forestry conferences in Russia to work out the details of sectoral reform for consideration by the Government. Priorities are to:

- Examine the rent generation capacity of the major forest producing regions and the mechanisms for ensuring sufficient rent capture to support sustainable forest management. This is a high priority activity since the preliminary analysis indicates large potential for generating tax revenues (from both the stumpage charges and taxes on enterprise profits). This activity needs to be integrated with proposed activities for clarifying the status of the resource base for existing enterprises and determining the market prospects for the Russian forest sector. It should also identify essential tasks for achieving sustainable management in each region in order to determine and prioritize forest management budgets.

- Examine antimonopoly measures employed by other countries with large forest resources in order to develop appropriate measures for the forest sector in Russia (as well as for the other related sectors such as transport and energy).

- Examine the influence of transport and energy monopolies on the sustainable management of the forest sector.

- Develop environmental, economic, and social criteria and indicators that will allow analysis of available information to identify status and quality of forest resources and their division into logical supply zones.

(b) ***Clarifying the status of resource base and market prospects***: The first step would be a rapid appraisal of the status of the resource base serving all existing forest-based enterprises in order to identify enterprises with viable resource base that is capable of supporting future investment and sustainable employment. Nonviable enterprises also need to be identified to determine the magnitude of social adjustment needed as the sector moves from a nonsustainable, command-driven, resource-mining approach to environmentally, economically, and socially sustainable production. A rapid appraisal of domestic and international market prospects for products from the major forest regions in Russia would also need to be undertaken. Overall this consists of four steps:

- Strengthen the national strategic planning capacity with expertise in environment, economics, social anthropology, community-based development, forest resource management, and forest planning.

- Develop regionally appropriate rapid resource assessment processes. (remote sensing, mapping, enterprise questionnaires) to synthesize information and close information gaps on the status, distribution, and quality of forest resources in the logical supply zones for existing enterprises. There is also a need to clarify land and resource rights in the various forest zones, particularly in terms of aboriginal land claims and areas to be set aside for biodiversity conservation.

- Provide guidance for undertaking international market studies to identify areas of comparative advantage and disadvantage in relation to potential domestic and international markets. These studies should define the limits to economic resource utilization under a range of price scenarios for both inputs (forest resources, energy, transport, labor) and outputs. Particular attention should be paid to the implications of the emergence of sustainable timber buyers groups in Europe and elsewhere and the growing demand for timber from forests whose sustainability has been certified by independent third parties. These studies should examine both the opportunities and obstacles these trends will create for enhanced market access in the future.

- Prepare status reports for each enterprise and region.

(c) ***Forest health and protection***: Proper management of fire, pests, and other injurious agents has been identified as a high priority in protecting the environmental and economic values of Russia's forest resources. Urgent steps are needed to address immediate problems and to set the stage for longer-term strategic responses to these problems, including financing. In the immediate future:

- Strengthen the ability of forest management authorities to determine the magnitude, temporal distribution, and spatial distribution of fire, pest, and disease management problems.

- Identify the remote sensing, resource monitoring, and direct management requirements for effective forest protection planning and management, particularly for high risk and vulnerable areas to facilitate targeted intervention.

- Establish at least three regional pilot forest projects to develop forest protection regimes and to determine long-term investment needs for forest protection.

- Accelerate the implementation of appropriate regeneration mechanisms on disturbed forest lands.

Medium-Term Support (over the next two to five years)

- Establish institutional arrangements for a new national-regional forest management system that clearly defines rights and responsibilities for resource planning, resource allocation, revenue collection, and field management.

- Initiate detailed resource assessment and land use planning for the national forest system.

- Develop modern resource information management systems at all levels (national, regional, local) of forest management responsibility.

- Develop strategic planning capacity at the national, regional, and local levels, including among indigenous communities.

- Develop an improved operational management and planning capacity for local forest management units that is consistent with modern ecosystem-based concepts of sustainable forest management.

- Establish regional systems to provide information to private and community investors on markets and investment opportunities in sustainable forest production and processing.

- Establish and promote independent environmental certification (based on the criteria of sustainable management of forests) of timber and timber products to comply with international market requirements.

Long-Term Support (over the next decade)

- Develop a comprehensive system of rent capture mechanisms that increases tax revenue generation, improves efficiency, and promotes sustainable sector development.

- Develop comprehensive ecosystem-based forest management systems for all forest production areas, including transparent planning systems, trained personnel, environmentally appropriate equipment, and environmentally and economically sound regeneration of large disturbed areas.

- Develop human resources at all levels, from appropriate short-term technical training programs to long-term university undergraduate and post-graduate programs. Ensure that indigenous and other traditional communities have access to such programs.

- Rationalize the forest research system to establish and maintain a world class capacity for targeted forest ecosystem research and provide information for policy formulation in all the ecological, social, and economic aspects of forest resource management.

- Establish a comprehensive system for achieving a sustainable socioeconomic development in forest based communities.

Activities that would promote transition to sustainable forest management and sectoral development will require considerable technical and financial assistance. Financial requirements for these activities alone could reach US$700 million over the next decade (about US$70 million per year). Investment at this level is necessary to achieve sustainable resource management and to create an enabling environment for private investment in the sector. Within a decade, such investment should be able to transform the sector from a net drain on the national budget to a net contributor to the economy through self-financing forest protection and renewal programs, capture of resource rentals, taxation of forest enterprises, and generation of employment and income. In a worst case scenario of a further reduction in national wood production to 75 million cubic meters, investment in these activities can be supported by resource rental capture of about US$1 per cubic meter over the next decade, a level that is well within the capability of the sector and consistent with the global experience.

The potential for a pilot forestry project, as an initial phase of Bank assistance, was discussed between the Government and the World Bank during the review of this report. During subsequent discussions related to the Country Assistance Strategy (CAS), the Government has requested the Bank to assist it in preparing a forestry project. Once formally included in the Bank's lending program, this pilot project would support a range of targeted activities at the federal level and in two or three regions. It would address strategic planning and selected reform issues by testing reform models in representative forest management solutions. These would include the development and testing of new management and governance arrangements designed to link the capture of resource rentals with management responsibility. A comprehensive forest protection strategy and forest information system would be developed in each pilot region to facilitate management and investment planning in the sector. Preparatory activities, mainly in the pilot areas, will cover analysis of the forest health and protection system, the forest information system, and market prospects; development of national and regional guidelines for sustainable forestry; and identification of ways to strengthen the regulatory and enforcement systems, including options for establishing a certification process.

E. Proposed Follow-Up Studies

There are many aspects of the forest sector that cannot be properly addressed with the information currently available. Information on forest resource is particularly deficient. Additional studies are needed for a better understanding of Russia's forest resources, so that decision-makers at all levels of government and the private sector can make informed decisions. These selected studies should be carried out as soon as possible and should address the following topics:

- **Clarifying the resource base for sustainable production.** A rapid appraisal of the region's forest resources is required to set priorities for comprehensive land use planning and to enable accurate determination of viable wood production areas and a sustainable annual allowable cut. To ensure consistency with contemporary resource management principles, a study should first be carried out on determining the appropriate methodology and criteria for the inventory work, delineation of supply areas, and compilation of the data for determining the annual allowable cut.

- **Aboriginal land tenure and resource rights.** Further studies are needed on the nature and status of aboriginal land and resource claims in Siberia and the Far East. These should include legal, anthropological, and socioeconomic analyses as well as a consideration of international norms and laws, including lessons from the experience of Canada, Greenland, and the United States (Alaska).

- **Assessing forest management systems.** Fires cause unacceptably large losses of forest resources. Current methods and funding of fire detection and suppression should be reexamined from the perspective of overall forest management objectives. The same should be done for protection systems for losses from pests and diseases.

- **Improving information management systems.** There is a wealth of forest management and market analysis data, but much of it is inaccessible to policy-makers and private sector managers. A study is needed to evaluate data collection, analysis, and dissemination techniques and to outline changes in methodology and technology to improve forest management decisionmaking. Socioeconomic information is needed for improved decisionmaking on policies to promote sustainable sector development.

- **Improving transportation and infrastructure.** A study is needed of transportation and infrastructure-related constraints in the forest sector and of the criteria to use in infrastructure planning and management in the forest sector.

- **Identifying markets.** With the forest sector, like the rest of the economy, undergoing massive restructuring, identifying opportunities and constraints in likely markets (such as Western Europe and East Asia) would provide an important guide to industrial restructuring in Siberia and the Far East. The study should identify problems, market opportunities, and investment needs based on resource availability and accessibility, with a particular focus on options for establishing a certification process.

- **Understanding carbon dynamics.** Not enough is known about the effects of boreal forest management on the planet's carbon cycle. Russia's ongoing study of carbon dynamics should be expanded and accelerated to provide information to policymakers about how forest fires and timber utilization affect carbon dynamics, taking into consideration various silvicultural systems and forest regeneration rates.

- **Identifying vulnerability of key species.** Many of Russia's forest-dependent plant and animal species are vulnerable or endangered. A study should be carried out to determine the minimum habitat requirements and requisite management practices for species whose habitat is specific to old-growth or primary forest. The study should be coordinated with work on the national biodiversity strategy, where possible. The results of both studies will feed into the process of identifying sustainable wood production areas.

This report is an initial effort to address selected but critical challenges facing the forest sector in Russia. Despite the size, complexity, and national and international importance of Russia's forests, there is a serious lack of information for making informed management and policy decisions. The findings and recommendations of this report and the conclusions of follow-up studies should be widely disseminated to all the stakeholders who deal with the sustainability of forest resources in Russia, particularly regional and local governments. One way to accomplish this objective is to organize regular regional, national, and international conferences that focus on addressing forest policy reforms necessary for promoting sustainable sector development during transition.

REFERENCES

Backman, C.A. 1995. "The Russian Forest Sector: Production, Consumption, and Export Prospects." *Post-Soviet Geography*, vol. 36(5), pp. 310-322.

Backman, C.A. 1996. "The Russian Forest Sector: Prospects for Trade with the Former Soviet Republics". *Post-Soviet Geography and Economics,* vol. 37 (1), pp. 16-59.

Barr, B.M., and K.E. Braden. 1988. *The Disappearing Russian Forest: A Dilemma in Soviet Resource Management.* London: Rowman and Littlefield.

Bemmann, A. 1995. "Der Boreale Wald als C2-Senke". AFZ6.

Charkiewicz, Z. 1993. "The Actual Far-Easter-Siberian-European Relationships (Vascular Plants)."*Fragment Floristica et Geobotanica,* Supplement 2, no 1, pp. 355-384.

ECE (Economic Commission for Europe)/FAO (Food and Agriculture Organization)/ILO (International Labor Organization). 1996. "Proceedings of a Seminar on Forest Fires and Global Change". European Forestry Commission, Joint Committee on Forest Technology, Management and Training, August 4-10, Shushenskoe, Russian Federation.

Isayev, A.S. (ed.). 1991. *Prognosis of Forest Utilization and Management of Forest Resources by Economic Regions of the U.S.S.R. to 2010.* Two volumes, Goskomles, Moscow (in Russian).

FIRESCAN. 1994. "Fire in Boreal Ecosystems of Eurasia: First Results of the BOR Forest Island Fire Experiment, Fire Research Campaign Asia-North (FIRESCAN)." *World Resource Review*, vol. 6(4), pp. 499-523.

Fondahl, Gail A. 1995. "The Status of Indigenous Peoples in the Russian North." *Post-Soviet Geography,* vol. 36 (4), pp. 215-224.

Gillis, M. 1992. "Forest Concession Management and Review Policies." In N. Sharma, ed., *Managing the World's Forests*. Dubuque, Iowa: Kendall/Hunt.

Holt, Jane. 1993. *Transport Strategies for the Russian Federation.* Studies of Economies in Transformation, No. 9, Washington, D.C.: The World Bank.

IIASA (International Institute for Applied Systems Analysis). 1995. *Siberian Forest Study*. Laxenburg, Austria: IIASA.

Kharuk, V.I. 1993. "Forest Decline in the Siberian North". *World Resources Review,* vol. 5 (1), pp. 72-76.

Kolchugina, T.P., and T.S. Vinson. 1993. "Equilibrium Analysis of Carbon Pools and Fluxes of Forest Biomes in the Former Soviet Union." *Canadian Journal of Forest Research*, vol. 23 (1), pp. 81-88.

Krankina, O.N., and M.E. Harmon. 1994. "The Impact of Intensive Forest Management on Carbon Stores in Forest Ecosystems." *World Resource Review*, vol. 6(1), pp. 161-177.

Krankina, O.N., and R.K. Dixon. 1994. "Forest Management Options to Conserve and Sequester Terrestrial Carbon in the Russian Federation". *World Resource Review,* vol. 6(1), pp. 88-101.

Krever, V., E. Dinerstein, D. Olson, and L. Williams. 1994. *Conserving Russia's Biological Diversity: An Analytical Framework and Initial Investment Portfolio.* Washington, D.C.: World Wildlife Fund.

Newell, J. and E. Wilson. 1996. *The Russian Far East: Forests, Biodiversity Hotspots, and Industrial Developments*. Friends of the Earth - Japan, Tokyo.

Nichols, H. 1993. "Stability of the Boreal Forest-Tundra Ecotone: A Test for the Greenhouse Effect." *World Resource Review*, vol. 5(3), pp. 360-371.

Nilsson, S. 1996. "Do we Have Enough Forests?" International Union of Forestry Research Organization (IUFRO) Occassional Paper No. 5, Austria.

Osherenko, Gail. 1995. "Social and Cultural Impact on Indigenous Peoples of Expanded Use of the Northern Sea Route." In *Northern Sea Route: Future and Perspective: The Proceedings of INSROP Symposium Tokyo 1995.* Tokyo: Ship and Ocean Foundation.

Pisarenko, A.I. and V.V. Strakhov. 1996. "Socio-Economic Assessment of the Russian Boreal Forests". Working Paper WP-96-58. International Institute of Applied Systems Analysis, Laxenburg, Austria.

Plochmann, R. 1983. "Nonindustrial Private Forestry: An International Perspective." In J. P. Royer and C. D. Risbrudt, eds,. *Nonindustrial Private Forest.* Durham, N.C.: Duke University School of Forestry and Environmental Studies.

Simons, H.A. 1992. *Russian Pulp and Paper Industry: An Opportunity Assessment and Analysis Prepared for Canadians*. Vancouver, British Columbia.

Sheingauz, A., S. Nilsson, and A. Shvidenko. 1995. "Russian Forest Legislation". Working Paper WP-95-45. International Institute for Applied Systems Analysis, Laxenburg, Austria.

Shvidenko, A., S. Nilsson, V.A. Roshkov, and V. V. Strakhov. 1996. "Carbon Budget of the Russian Boreal Forests: A Systems Analysis Approach to Uncertainty". In M.J. Apps and D.T. Price, eds. *Forestry Ecosystems, Forest Management and the Global Carbon Cycle.* NATO ASI Series, vol. I 40. Berlin: Springer-Verlag.

Shvidenko, A. and S. Nilsson. 1996. "Expanding Forests but Declining Mature Coniferous Forests in Russia". Working Paper No. WP-96-59. International Institute for Applied Systems Analysis, Laxenburg, Austria.

Shvidenko, A. S. Nilsson, and V. Roshkov. 1995. "Possibilities for Increased Sequestration through Improved Protection of Russian Forests". Working Paper No. WP-95-86. International Institute for Applied Systems Analysis, Laxenburg, Austria.

Shubin, Valery. 1994. *Russian Forests.* Moscow. Federal Forest Service of Russia.

Strakhov, V.V. and A.I. Pisarenko. 1996. "Development and Utilization of Russian Forest Resources." *Silva Fennica,* vol. 30(2-3), pp. 361-371 (review article).

Sunley, Emile, ed. 1995. *Russian Federation: Tax Reform and Revenue Enhancement.* Washington, D.C.: International Monetary Fund.

Wallich, Christine, ed. 1994. *Russia and the Challenge of Fiscal Federalism.* C.I. Wallich. (ed.): The World Bank: Washington, D.C.

World Bank. 1991. *The Forest Sector.* A World Bank Policy Paper, Washington, D.C.

_________. 1994. "Russian Federation: Restructuring the Coal Industry: Putting People First". Report No. 13187-RU (two volumes), The World Bank, Europe and Central Asia Region, Washington, D.C.

_________. 1995a. "Poverty in Russia: An Assessment". The World Bank, Europe and Central Asia Region, Washington, D.C.

_________. 1995b. "Russian Federation: Country Assistance Strategy". The World Bank, Europe and Central Asia Region, Washington, D.C.

_________. 1995c. "Russian Federation: Tax Administration Modernization Project". The World Bank, Europe and Central Asia Region, Washington, D.C.

_________. 1995d. "Russian Federation: Housing Project". Report No. 13022-RU, Europe and Central Asia Region, The World Bank, Washington, D.C.

_________. 1995e. "Russian Federation: Towards Medium-Term Viability". Report No. 14472-RU, The World Bank, Europe and Central Asia Region, Washington, D.C. (was published as a World Bank Country Study in April 1996)

_________ . 1996a. "Russian Federation: Biodiversity Conservation Project". Report no. 15064-RU. The Global Environment Facility (GEF)/The World Bank, Europe and Central Asia Region, Washington, D.C.

_________. 1996b. *Fiscal Management in Russia.* A World Bank Country Study, Washington, D.C.

World Resources Institute. 1994. *World Resources 1994-95.* New York: Oxford University Press.

GLOSSARY OF FOREST TERMS

Annual allowable cut

The average volume of wood that may be harvested annually under sustained yield management. It equals roughly the amount of new growth produced by the forest each year minus deductions for losses due to fire, insects, and diseases.

Biodiversity

The diversity of plants, animals, and other living organisms in all their forms and levels of organization -- including genes, species, and ecosystems -- and the evolutionary and functional processes that link them.

Boreal forest

Forests that form the dominant vegetation zone in the northern hemisphere, extending circumpolar over Russia, the United States (Alaska), Canada, Greenland, Norway, Sweden, and Finland. The boreal zone has a low mean temperature, a short growing season, and a relatively small number of tree species, predominantly conifers. Boreal forests cover about 40 percent of the global forest area and contain about 45 percent of the estimated global wood volume.

Carbon sequestration

Carbon sequestration is the removal and storage of carbon dioxide from the atmosphere. Sequestration occurs through the process of photosynthesis by which green plants take carbon dioxide from the atmosphere and combine it with water to form carbohydrates that can be stored in plant tissues. The energy driving this process is the radiant energy from the sun.

Carbon storage

The carbon store is the pool of carbon held in a forest ecosystem at any one time. A forest carbon is stored in both living and dead plant materials (above and below ground level) and in the forest soil. In Russian forests, it has been estimated that the phytomas (living material) contains 47.1 billion tons of carbon, while the forest floor contains 26.0 billion tons of carbon and the forest soil contains 106.1 billion tons of carbon (Krankina and Dixon 1994).

Carbon sink

A forest is a carbon sink if over the period being considered there is a net increase in carbon storage after the balance of carbon sequestration and emissions have been considered.

Carbon source

A forest is a carbon source if over the period being considered, there is a net decrease in carbon storage after the balance of sequestration and emissions have been considered. Sources of carbon emissions include respiration by forest plants, animals, and micro-organisms; removals of forest products; the decay of dead material; and, in some cases combustion in forest fires. Disturbance by agents such as fire, pests, and logging can increase temperatures at the forest floor and increase the rates of respiration and decay in the forest soil. Depending on their management, forests can be either a sink, a store or a source of carbon.

Clearcutting silvicultural system

A system in which the entire crop is cleared from an area at one time, and an even-aged replacement stand is established. Clearcutting allows full light exposure to the new stand and produces an open area climate. The minimum size of a clear-cut opening is generally considered to be one hectare.

Climax species

A tree species capable of regenerating under prevailing climatic and soil conditions in the late successional stage (shade-tolerant species).

Ecosystem

A functional unit consisting of all the living organisms (plants, animals, and microbes) in a given area and all the nonliving physical and chemical factors of their environment, linked through nutrient cycling and energy flow.

Ecosystem management

A comprehensive approach to management of forested lands to promote multiple resource values. Ecosystem management must be applied in space and time at a variety of levels. At the macro level, it involves maintenance of regional balance between resource protection and resource utilization to maintain biodiversity, productivity, and ecological functionality. At the micro level, it involves detailed management planning and control to maintain structural and biotic diversity through time and site productivity, ecological functionality, and essential environmental protection service.

Endemism

Endemic species are those whose distribution is restricted to a particular area or a region.

Forest health

A condition of forests that are naturally resilient to damage; characterized by biodiversity, a healthy forest contains sustained habitat for timber, fish, wildlife, and humans, and meets present and future resource management objectives.

Forest practices

Any activity on forest land that facilitate uses of forest resources, including timber harvesting, road construction, silviculture, hunting, collection of berries and mushrooms, recreation, pest control, and forest fire suppression.

Forest resources Resources or values associated with forest land, including water, wildlife, fisheries, recreation, timber, nontimber forest products, range and pastures, and heritage.

Forest sector All stakeholders in the forest resource and all activities carried out by them or on their behalf. This includes government ministries and agencies, regional and local administrations, and indigenous people, communities, and enterprises and individuals with ownership title, authority to utilize the resources, and responsibilities to manage and protect forests. It also includes the activities carried out by the research and scientific community in its own interest or that of any stakeholder.

Harvesting pattern The spatial distribution of cutblocks and reserve areas across the forest landscape.

Immature forests Stands of timber whose leading species is younger than a specific cutting age. Cutting ages are established to meet forest management objectives.

Integrated resource management The identification and consideration of all resource values, including social, economic, and environmental needs, in land use and forest management decisionmaking.

Operational plans Within the context of area-specific management guidelines, operational plans detail the logistics for development.

Pioneer species A tree species that first invades a bare area shade-intolerant species).

Primary forest An old growth forest in a mature succession phase whose structure and composition have resulted from unrestrained ecological processes rather than human influences focused on particular management objectives.

Protected areas Areas set aside as parks, wilderness areas, ecological reserves, areas of national or regional interest, and recreation.

Red Book A document describing and listing rare and endangered species of the flora and fauna in a given territory and prepared by an international organization such as IUCN or a national or local environmental group.

Regeneration The renewal of a tree crop through either natural means (seeded on-site from adjacent stands or deposited by wind or animals) or artificial means (planting of seedlings or direct seeding).

Resource sustainability — Production of a biological resource under management practices that ensure replacement of the harvested part by regrowth or reproduction before another harvest occurs.

Resource values — Products, commodities, and services associated with forest lands and largely dependent on ecological processes. These include biodiversity, carbon sequestration, water, wildlife, fisheries, recreation, timber, nontimber forest products, range, and heritage.

Rotation — The planned number of years between the formation or regeneration of a tree crop or stand and its final cutting at a specified stage of maturity.

Sanitary harvesting — Harvesting of aged, unhealthy, deformed, diseased or otherwise undesirable trees to induce regeneration or improve the health and value of the remaining stand. In Russia, this has frequently been interpreted to mean cutting trees that are 50 years older than their optimum cutting age.

Seed tree silvicultural system — An even-aged silvicultural system that leaves selected standing trees scattered throughout the cutblock to provide seed sources for natural regeneration.

Selection silvicultural system — A silvicultural system that removes mature timber either as single scattered individuals or in small groups at relatively short intervals, repeated indefinitely, where the continual establishment of regeneration is encouraged and an uneven-aged stand is maintained.

Shelterwood silvicultural system — A silvicultural system that removes the old stand in a series of cuttings to promote the establishment of an essentially even-aged new stand under the overhead or side shelter of the old one.

Stand — A community of trees sufficiently uniform in species composition, age, arrangement, and condition to be distinguishable as a group from the forest or other growth on the adjacent area and thus forming a silviculture or management entity.

Stumpage — The stumpage value is the difference between the timber's market value and the operating cost necessary to get the wood to a designated market.

Timber license — An agreement that provides for the establishment of harvesting rights and, in some cases, management responsibilities in a described forest area.

Timber supply area — The area from which a primary timber-processing facility extracts its wood resources. Such areas should be identified by taking into account the resource capacity to support sustainable timber production, competing land uses, and the costs of resource extraction and transport.

Timber utilization — The dimensions and quality of wood that are actually cut and removed from an area. Low utilization generally implies high wastage of timber resources, and vice versa.

Utilization standards — The dimensions (stump height, top diameter, base diameter, and length) and quality of trees that must be cut and removed from the land during harvesting operations.

ANNEXES

Annex A

Forest Resources and Forest Management

Russia has been developing its state forest fund over the past 200 years. The fund -- similar in meaning to the English expressions "forest lands" or "forest estate" -- includes all land that is suitable for forest production or relevant to forest management. Russia's forest fund incorporates a spatial mosaic of vegetation, water bodies, the road network, human settlements, and the like that has been shaped by human activities and natural processes within the forest zone. This mosaic consists of different habitats, ecological niches, and conditions for the migration and dispersion of plants and animals. The structure and health of the forest fund determines the levels of biological diversity and stability of Russian ecosystems.

Forestry at the National Level

Management of the forest fund is delegated by the Federal Forest Service to the forest management districts *(leskhoz)*. The forest legislation of the Russian Federation provides the legal framework for forest management. The 1993 Principles of Forest Legislation stipulate that the federal government has the responsibility to control the condition, use, reproduction, conservation and protection of forests to ensure compliance by all forest-users with the established rules governing the use of the forest stock, the rules of forestry, the reproduction, conservation and protection of forests, the rules of state records and reporting, and other norms and rules established by forest legislation. A detailed dicussion of the current and proposed forest laws is provided in Annex C.

General Description

Forest fund lands are subdivided into forest and nonforest lands (see Figure 1.4 in the main report). Forest lands include areas where forests (naturally, historically, or industrially) grow and land that lies between forests, as a natural component of the landscape, and that may someday be forested. Forest land is designated as either "stocked" or "unstocked" at the moment of account. Stocked area is equivalent to "forests" as defined globally. Unstocked covers temporarily unproductive forest areas, such as burns, cuts, dead trees, and treeless areas and woodlands, such as glades, open lands, and sparse woodland. Nonforest lands consist of arable fields, hay fields, pastures, water bodies (lakes, creeks, rivers, pools, dams), gardens (vegetable, orchards, mulberry and other berry producing lands), roads, houses, yards, swamps, sands, ice, and other lands (including nonforest land dedicated for natural, historic, or economic reasons). According to the State Forest Account of January 1, 1993, the stocked area of Russian forest lands is 764 million hectares and total area of forest fund is 1181 million hectares.

The forest fund occupies about 69 percent of Russia's land area (including inland bodies of water). Closed canopy forests cover 43 percent of the country, with 78 percent of them in Siberia and the Far East. More than half of all forests in Russia are growing on low-productivity permafrost soils in Siberia and the Far East. Some 247 million hectares are low-density sparse wood and scrubs, and about 122 million hectares are short stands (height class V). Timber harvesting (and oil and gas extraction) may significantly change plant and animal habitats. In the northern and middle taiga (see below), much of the developed or cleared land has been turned to nonproductive swamp land.

In Russia's forest fund, the average timber volume per hectare is 170 cubic meters for coniferous stands, 130 cubic meters for deciduous hardwoods and 80 cubic meters for deciduous softwoods. The average age of coniferous timber species is more than 150 years, of deciduous hardwoods 100 years, and of deciduous softwoods 40 years. Extending along latitudinal belts from north to south, forests are: pretundra (a transitional zone from tundra to taiga or coniferous forests), taiga (subdivided into northern, middle, and southern zones), broad-leaved forest zone, and forest-steppes (transition from forests to steppes). Estimated areas under these forest zones are given in Table A.1.

Table A.1: Estimated Pre-Tundra and Taiga Forest Areas (Percent Shares)

Forest zone	*Share of total forest fund area*	*Share of total forest land area*	*Share of total forested land area*
Pretundra	14.2	17.0	13.5
Northern taiga	10.0	9.0	8.6
Middle taiga	33.5	37.8	41.5
Southern taiga	18.1	20.0	20.4

Source: The Federal Forest Service of Russia.

Pretundra forests are part of the Group I forests (see below), with boundaries that define a conventional management unit. These boundaries do not coincide with those of the forest-tundra zone, which is a unit of geographical division of the territory. Work is currently under way to mark out the boundaries of the boreal zone. Pretundra forests encompass a 100-150 kilometer-wide belt of vegetation that forms a latitudinal transition from taiga forests to tundra..

Pretundra forests are rich in reserves of fresh water and serve as a habitat for many animal and bird species. All the reindeer pastures in the Russian north are found in these forests, along with rich fishing grounds and considerable reserves of valuable nonwood forest products. These forest lands are also rich in oil, gas, coal, iron and polymetallic ores, and other minerals. Pretundra forests represent the only soil-forming factor in the extreme northern regions.

These forests are rarely dense. Single-storied stands of simple structure prevail, with few tree species (one- and two-species stands are most common). In general, as one moves north and east, forest lands become more scarce, species composition is less diverse, stands have a more open canopy, diameters of trees decrease, and trees often have stem deformities. The dominant species are larch (*Larix Gmelinii, L. Sukaczewii*), spruce (*Picea obovata Ledeb.*), birch (*Betula cajanderi Sukacz.*), and dwarf Siberian pine (*Pinus pumila Rgl.*).

In these northern areas, ground cover is comparatively more important than the trees, which develop proportionally more extensive root systems and less stem wood than in more southern areas. The productivity of stands and growing stock can vary considerably, but the pretundra forests are generally of little or no commercial value, and felling amounts to only 43,000 hectares annually. Most of these forests are inaccessible, and many sites adjoin river valleys where they serve an important protective function.

Northern taiga forests have a species composition that changes considerably across the continent. The main species in the eastern part of the country are larch, dwarf Siberian pine, and Siberian spruce. Common pine and white birch are found almost everywhere in the area. The average growing stock in forest stands in the northern taiga rarely exceeds 50 cubic meters per hectare. The most productive sites are in river valleys and terraces. The forests are used mainly by the local population for their own consumption. Like the pretundra forests, these stands are most valuable for their protective function.

Middle taiga forests consist mainly of larch, Siberian spruce, and some Siberian fir (*Abies sibirica Ledeb.*). Deciduous species include birch and aspen *(Populus tremula)*. Productivity is about 80-150 cubic meters per hectare (corresponding to an average height class III), though there are more productive areas (height classes II and I) with rich, well-drained soils. The middle taiga forests are subject to intense exploitation, with the bulk of clear-cut logging concentrated here.

Southern taiga forests are composed of high-quality stands of common spruce, Siberian spruce, pine, white birch, weeping birch *(Betula pendula)*, and aspen. These species achieve height classes I and Ia under favorable conditions. Productivity in these stands is characterized by an increase in stock volume of 200-250 cubic meters or more per hectare.

Forest Classification

Management objectives are directed to achieve a combination of protection, production, and conservation values. All forest activities must be effected by methods that do not harm the environment, animal life, or human health. Forest management must ensure:

- Preservation and enhancement of ecological, catchment, protective, sanitary, hygienic, and other useful properties of forests for safeguarding human health.
- Multipurpose, sustainable use of the forest stock to satisfy timber and other forest product requirements of the national economy and of citizens.
- Reproduction and improvement of the species structure, improvement of the quality and productivity of forests, and the conservation and protection of forests.
- Application of sustainable sector development policies and the use of advances in science, technology, and leading-edge experience to improve the efficiency of forest management.
- Preservation of the biological, historical, cultural, and natural heritage.

The forest fund is divided into three broad groups (I, II and III) of forests and seven categories according to the biodiversity, ecological, and social functions of forests and their location. Forest management documents establish the criteria for classification of the forest stock by forest groups and protection categories and for the transfer of forests from one group or category to another. This classification determines the general guidelines according to which the forests must be managed, including the types of cutting allowed (sanitary cutting, intermediate cutting, or final cutting).

Group I Forest: Protected Forests. Group I forests are protected for ecological reasons. Group I includes noncommercial forests with mainly environmental functions, including water preservation and recreational functions. Only sanitary harvesting is allowed, including the felling of trees that are 50 years older than their optimum cutting age. There are five categories of Group I forests:

- Hydrological (catchment) protection forests along river banks, lakes, and reservoirs and near spawning areas.
- Anti-erosion forests and shelterbelts to protect steep slopes, agricultural land, roads, and deserts.
- Health and municipal forests around cities and industrial complexes to protect people from pollution.
- Special protected forests such as valuable forest massifs, forests with scientific or historical values, nut-gathering zones, pretundra zone, and the like.
- Forests of the nature protection fund (nature reserves, protected forest plots, and national parks).

Group II Forest: Protected Forests with Limited Commercial Value. Group II forests are protected for industrial and recreational reasons. These forests are located in sparsely forested and densely populated areas. They consist mostly of forests with a limited exploitable value, in which final harvesting is allowed based on the principle of sustainable yield. They may contain areas of sensitive forests (river banks) where no clear felling is allowed.

Group III Forest: Commercial Forests. Group III forests are designated for industrial use. These forests are subdivided into reserved forests and industrial forests. Reserved forests are not developed industrially because of their remoteness and inaccessibility. Group III forests, which are in densely forested regions, may have several functions, the major one being the production of industrial wood. Final harvesting is allowed. Cutting is usually based on demand from forest-based industries. These forest may contain sensitive areas (river banks) where no clear felling is allowed.

Apart from this division into three broad groups, the primary basis for description, analysis, and management of the Siberian and Far Eastern forests is the district. Forest regionalization is based on a classification of hierarchical units that are homogeneous by forest vegetation conditions, ecological and environmental properties, topological structure, productivity and composition, and commercial and social importance. The basic types of regionalization are forest vegetation, forest economics, and forest management. The forest management regionalization does not follow administrative boundaries and is subdivided as follows (IIASA 1995):

Siberia	*Far East*
5 regions (oblast)	8 regions (oblast)
17 groups of districts (okrug)	22 groups of districts (okrug)
49 management districts	44 management districts.

The scientific descriptions of forest systems and their ecological roles, as well as classification schemes for Siberia and the Far East, are well developed and provide the theoretical and scientific basis for forest management.

The Forest Accounts System

The forest accounts system comprises forest inventory and planning units, forest inventories, and the Forest State Account.

Thirteen state ***forest inventory and planning units*** nationwide collect and analyze the data from forest inventories. Each forest inventory and planning unit covers an area of about 37 million hectares. Depending on the type of management applied to the area, forest inventory and planning are to be conducted within the bounds of each forest unit every 10 to 20 years. These inventory and planning exercises feed into the development of the management plans for each territory that are the basis for any forest utilization activity (Federal Forest Service 1994).

Forest inventories are carried out to provide statistical information on forest area, timber volumes, species and age composition, and other dimensions of the forest fund. Inventory data also provide information about changes in the status of the forest fund, including assessments of the impacts of management practices and of fires, floods, pests, and diseases. This information is passed on to the regional and federal forest administration levels in tabular form, with little or no cartographic support or analysis.

Unlike most other countries with large forest resources, Russia does not have an inventory that covers the entire forest area. Rather, its ***Forest State Account*** is based on periodic extrapolations of the data obtained during management planning and, for forests with no recorded inventory and planning exercise or documented changes, on data obtained from aerial evaluation and satellite images by regional forest inventory and planing units. Evaluations of forest conditions and inventories are done visually and are thus more prone to systematic errors, especially in evaluating the growing stock, than are instrument-based evaluations. Decision on what values to ascribe to various attributes of the stock are made separately by various administrative levels (federal, regional, municipal), resulting in inconsistencies in the database. The current methodology of collecting and extrapolating forest resource data provides unsatisfactory information about the forest fund of Russia, especially about overall growing stock, growth and yield estimates, and forest land productivity.

The inventory of January 1, 1993, identified forest fund under federal management at that time at 729.7 million hectares, or 62 percent of the total area of the forest fund. The remaining 38 percent (451.2 million hectares) was not managed and was therefore undocumented; it was estimated based only on aerial visual observations and interpretations of aerial photographs. The unmanaged forest land includes areas that are difficult to access, especially in Siberia and the Far East (almost half the territories of the Eastern Siberia economic region, and well over half of the Far East economic region).

Forest Management

The 13 state forest inventory and planning units are responsible for conducting forest inventories, monitoring forest activities, and preparing management plans for the leskhozes (see Table A.2). The forest area of each leskhoz is subdivided into blocks that are typically 1 km by 2 km (200 hectares), though they can vary from 0.5 x 0.5 km to 2 x 4 km, according to the class of forest inventory. The aerial photographs are used to make an initial classification of the forest into more or less homogeneous stands. Forest engineers then go in the field to assess each stand. The method is not based on systematic sampling. Instead, the forest engineers note down such parameters as age, basal area, and volume based on their years of training and experience. Their accuracy is claimed to be plus or minus 10 percent. The information is entered into a computerized data base system.

Table A.2: Forest Inventory Enterprises in Russia

No.	*Name of enterprise*	*Location*
1	Central	Moscow City
2	Moscow	Shcherbinka, Moscow Oblast
3	Western	Bryansk, Bryanskaya Oblast
4	Northwestern	St. Petersburg, Leningradskaya Oblast
5	Northern	Vologda, Vologodskaya Oblast
6	Karelian	Petrozavodsk, Republic of Karelia
7	Voronezhlesproject	Voronezh, Voronezhskaya Oblast
8	Volga	Nizhniy Novgorod, Nizhegorodskaya Oblast
9	West-Siberian	Novosibirsk, Novosibirskaya Oblast
10	East-Siberian	Krasnoyarsk, Krasnoyarskiy Kray
11	Pre-Baikalian	Irkutsk, Irkutskaya Oblast
12	Amur	Svobodny, Amurskaya Oblast
13	Far-Eastern	Khabarovsk, Khabarovskiy Kray

Source: The Federal Forest Service of Russia, 1996.

The annual allowable cut is calculated from these inventories and used as the basis of the management plan. The inventory also indicates areas where reforestation activities should be carried out. Other issues such as planning of the road network are also included in the management plan. The main objective of the inventory and the resulting management plan is to determine the standing volume by species and by forest group for calculating the annual allowable cut rather than to provide a holistic management plan for the forest ecosystem as a whole.

The annual allowable cut is calculated for all the biological growth of the forest. In Khabarovsk Kray, for example, the annual allowable cut was calculated as 56 million cubic meters. However, only half of this is economically accessible, and of that only a third (about 10 million cubic meters) is commercially valuable, considering the available harvesting equipment, the harvesting methods, the structure of stands, and markets. As a result, much wood is left as "harvesting waste" on the site. Official estimates on the actual annual cut indicate a total extraction of 6 million cubic meters in Khabarovsk Kray.

The actual cut includes only the timber extracted not the volume of timber actually cut, which may be considerably higher (by 20 to 25 percent in general and up to 100 percent in many cases). In the past, forest users paid only for the timber extracted from the forest and not for timber actually cut; today, they pay stumpage fees that are very low and lead to wasteful logging practices. Thus, despite the fact that the actual cut is only 10 percent of the annual allowable cut (6 out of 56 million cubic meters), there may be serious overcuting locally. In Krasnoyarsk, only about 15 percent of the biological annual allowable cut is used at present.

Management plans are prepared for ten to twenty year periods. In general, there would be only one copy of the management plan available at the leskhoz, one at the kray, and one at the state forests statistics unit. In the former Soviet Union, the management plans were official documents and not accessible to the general public. The forest law of 1993 gives institutions and citizens access to such information. According to the law, management plans should include measures to ensure the rational management and use of the forest stock, effective reproduction, conservation and protection of forests, and pursuit of an integrated scientific and technical policy in forestry, including:

- Demarcation of the boundaries and internal structure of the forest stock territory.
- Performance of topographic and geodetic works and special cartography of forests.
- Forest stock inventories, with determination of the species and age structure of trees, their state, and qualitative and quantitative characteristics of forest resources.
- Projection of cutting and filling areas, including identification of forest stock sectors requiring final felling and intermediate felling, and measures for the regeneration of forests and forest amelioration, conservation, and protection.
- Substantiation of the criteria used to classify forests into forest groups and protection categories, and drafting of proposals for transfer of forests from one group or protection category to another.
- Determination of measures needed in forest regeneration and forest growing; and protection of forests against fires, pests and diseases.
- Determination of the scope of forest stock use for game hunting and cultural, recreation, tourism, and biodiversity conservation purposes.
- Silvibiological and other surveys and studies.
- Supervision of implementation of forest projects and operations.

Forest Maps

Maps of Russian forests are categorized as follows (Forest Inventory Instruction 1994): forest management maps, forest district maps, forest district stand maps, maps of exploitable forest fund, layout maps of the forest management unit, layout maps of the forest management units' fire prevention measures, layout forest maps of the administrative structure of Russia, and the 1990 map of the forests of the former USSR. While a few forest management units are beginning to produce digitized maps, most maps are still produced by traditional methods on paper.

Forest management maps are basic forest maps compiled with the aid of geodesic or topographic data. Scales are 1:10,000 for Group I and II management types and 1:25,000 for Group III management type. Other forest maps are generally compiled through reduction and generalization of larger-scale maps. A completely plotted original management map will contain minor roads and planning compartment boundaries, survey lines, strata boundaries, permanent inventory plots, nurseries, forest seed plots, protected forest sites, waysides near main roads, forest access roads, permanent trails, streams, rivers, land-reclamation canals, lakes, edges of ravines and precipices (as well as lines of watershed ridges in mountainous regions), numbers and areas of planning compartments and strata, names of rivers, lakes and major streams, boundaries of administrative regions, categories of protection forests, and areas transferred to a long-term use, offices of forestry and logging enterprises, forest districts, logging units, bean houses, cordons, winter huts, and barracks and other buildings. Year of harvest or burn, as well as the type of cut-over, must be indicated on the maps. Protected areas that are too small to be plotted on the map are to be shown by means of out-of-scale conventional signs. Thinned-out contour lines derived from topographic maps are to be included.

Forest district maps are compiled by assembling management maps, supplemented with some additions, such as conventional signs of open stands, slashes, cut-over areas, arable lands, bogs, and wetland, as well as a legend that includes age and growth classes, relative density of stand, and exploitable volume groups. The scale must be 1:25,000. These maps are intended for use in compiling forest stand maps, survey schemes of forestry practices and other forest district maps, and layout maps of forestry units. They are also used for planning the allocation (and the graphic representation) of all forestry practices and other work carried out within the forest fund in the district.

Forest district stand maps are compiled from forest district maps. Each mapping unit is color-coded to show dominant species and age gradations; bogs, reservoirs, and boundaries between neighboring land holdings are also differentiated by color. ***Maps of exploitable forest funds*** are compiled from the forest district map by coloring all mature and over-mature productive stands included in the exploitable forest fund. Dominant species and age groups are color coded.

Layout maps of the forest management unit reflect the structure of forestry units and their allocation. These maps show stocked areas, lands covered with closed and free-growing forest plantations, and plantations established under a canopy layer in the process of stand conversion. The maps are color-coded according to the dominant tree species and age group.

Layout forest maps for fire prevention measures are compiled on a scale of 1:25,000, with colors denoting fire units by danger classes and plotting fire belts and coverings, canals, reservoirs, fire-resistant forest borders, fire lines, fire roads, minor roads, fire-chemical stations, points for storing fire-prevention equipment, lookout towers, aerial forest fire control unit staging locations (including mechanized forces and the residential areas of the fire fighting units), helicopter landing grounds, recreation and smoking places, tourist camps, and ground and aerial patrol routes.

Layout forest maps of the administrative structure are compiled on a scale of 1:200,000 or smaller, depending on the size of the area involved. Boundaries of forestry units, wood enterprises, and districts, as well as the road network, are to be plotted. Dominant species and age gradation are color coded. The ***map of the Forests of the USSR,*** published in 1990, has a scale of 1:2,500,000 and provides an overall view of the distribution of the forest fund forests in the former USSR and provides other site-specific information, such as the location of valuable tree species, swamps and large areas destroyed by fire.

Forest Leasing

Licenses to use forests are granted by district authorities, with the participation of the regional Committee of Forestry, through direct negotiations, auctions or contests. Timber harvesting tickets (orders) and forest tickets (for the use of nonwood resources) certify the right to short-term use of a forest, as specified in the documents. A lease grants long-term utilization rights to forest plots, and may be valid for one to forty-nine years. Leases are handled by leskhozes. Forest users are given a timber harvesting ticket or forest ticket each year for which the lease is valid, specifying permitted type of utilization, in concrete volumes and at specific locations.

The responsibilities of the forest user, as specified by the 1993 Principles of Forest Legislation, include:

- Avoiding damage to the remaining forest sotck and natural regeneration, and preventing soil erosion.

- Restoring, at their own expenses, forest stock disturbed as a result of harvesting activities.

- Applying forest regeneration measures in cutting areas and in areas where natural regeneration has been destroyed following harvesting.

- Taking fire prevention measures.

- Removing all timber and harvesting wastes from the felling area.

The new Forest Code (Article 83) proposes to expanding the duties of the forest users to include complying with the forest legislation and with the terms of their lease, concession, or long-term use contract; avoiding harmful effects on public health and on the natural environment; covering the costs of transforming the leased parcel of forest land to a category agreed on in the lease contract; turning back the leased parcels of forest land to the leskhoz upon completion of works; covering silvicultural damages and losses; making timely payments for forest utilization; complying with sanitary rules and other requirements as established by the federal and regional bodies of forest administration; respecting the rights of other forest users; submitting to forest administration and state statistics agencies the information regarding the forest use and information needed to determine lease payments.

Supervision and control of forest users is the responsibility of the leskhozes. The aerial photos of logged-over areas taken by the forest inventory and planning units after the main harvesting period in spring are used to determine whether reforestation is required and whether the forest users have abided by the cutting plan and regulations. Based on such material, the regional Committee on Forestry may take appropriate action, if necessary.

Where violations are found, the forest users may be told to rectify the situation or to pay a fine. Disputed cases may be brought to trial. In practice, fines are rarely imposed, because the leskhozes are poorly equipped and lack control capacity. On the occasions when fines are assessed, forest users often try to delay payments for a year or longer, and high inflation rates wipe out the value of the fine. But because fines have been so low, violators have chosen to pay the fines rather than work according to the prescribed silvicultural principles. For example, the fine per cubic meter of waste left on the logging site was only 1,000 rubles (equivalent to about twenty cents in 1995).

Forest Regeneration

As a general rule, the mix between natural regeneration and artificial reforestation is 70:30 for northern and middle taiga, 50:50 for southern taiga, and 30:70 for mixed forests, while the steppe and forest steppe rely almost entirely on plantations. For the whole of Siberia and the Far East, annual reforestation (both planting and seeding) amounted to about 215,000 hectares during the 1980s (Pisarenko, Redko, and Merzlenko 1992), but this has dropped even further during the transition period.

In Krasnoyarsk Kray, total replanting during 1990-94 covered an area of 79,000 hectares, an average of almost 16,000 hectares a year, while natural regeneration occurred on 222,500 hectares, an average of almost 45,000 hectares per year. No information was available on survival rates, but Obydennikov (1995) reports that when reforestation takes place after harvesting, the results are poor because of soil compaction and erosion resulting from the use of heavy logging machinery. Survival rates for coniferous plantations are reported to be only 20 to 40 percent. The most recent inventory in Krasnoyarsk Kray in January 1993 found some 2 million hectares of forest land is bare and in need of reforestation. A reforestation program prepared for 1996-2000 assumes that 1.4 million hectares would be able to regenerate naturally, while the remaining 0.6 million hectares would require artificial reforestation (replanting). However, only 170,000 hectares are accessible in the planting season.

In Khabarovsk Kray, replanting averages about 10,000 hectares a year. The emphasis is on planting softwood species, particularly Kedra *(Pinus sibirica)*. These valuable species have been seriously overexploited. In the absence of sufficient seed trees, the species is becoming increasingly scarce and has been declared a protected species. No estimates are available on survival rates. The annual area treated for natural regeneration covers about 90,000 hectares per year. Silvicultural treatments may include scarification, tending, and preservation. The total area requiring artificial reforestation is estimated at 5 million hectares in Khabarovsk Kray.

Artificial Reforestation. Nearly every leskhoz has a big nursery, producing from several hundred thousand to several million seedlings annually. In Krasnoyarsk Leskhoz (147,000 hectares), for example, the nursery produces about 2 million seedlings yearly. The seedlings stay in the nursery three to five years, and the general practice of planting is by naked root. Standards for each species specify the minimum size considered adequate for surviving weed competition. The main species grown in the nurseries are common pine *(Pinus sylvestris)* and cedar *(Pinus sibirica)*.

The planting season starts in March. Plantations are generally single species. Practically all planting activities are carried out in logged-over areas because of access roads, though reforestation or regeneration activities are generally carried out on less than half the harvested area, because much of it is not accessible during the planting season. Other, often vast, areas where forests have been destroyed by fire, insects, diseases, or windfall, are generally not replanted because of inaccessibility. Replanting of permafrost areas is also reported to be difficult (the seedlings are being pushed up), and such areas are therefore designated for natural regeneration.

Natural Regeneration. Assisted natural regeneration is the most widely adopted method of reforestation. According to Federal Forest Service--Cutting Rules for Siberia (1993), certain measures are to be taken during harvesting to protect and promote natural regeneration, such as leaving several seed trees within cutblocks (particularly important for pine regeneration), leaving adjacent cutblocks untouched for some years, preserving undergrowth while harvesting, and cleaning up the site by windrowing or fire. These activities are the responsibility of the logging company and should be checked by the forest enterprises. The department of reforestation in Krasnoyarsk Kray favors the "narrow-band" harvesting system, because natural regeneration is reported to do well after such harvesting.

The department of reforestation of the Federal Forest Service is responsible for promotion of natural regeneration. This is done by prescribed burning, scarification (exposing mineral soils to promote germination of seeds), the tending of young seedlings, and related activities. Natural regeneration is reported to be good in light needled forests (on light soils) but do much less well in dark needled forests (on heavy soils), where tall grasses and herbs appear soon after clear felling and suppress seedlings. These grasses also increase the risk of wild fires, which kill most seedlings and juvenile trees.

There is also widespread concern about the increase of less valuable juvenile and immature stands of hardwood species following the harvesting of the more valuable coniferous species (Pisarenko, Redko, and Merzlenko 1992). This is often the case in large-scale clear-cuts, where pioneer species (such as aspen and birch), started from windblown seeds, quickly colonize the area, particularly after a fire. This is a natural stage in the ecological succession in forests, however, and these pioneer stands will eventually be invaded by conifer species (after ten to thirty years) to form mixed forests.

Access Development

Most of the economic development and population centers are located in the southern parts of Siberia, particularly in the area south of the Trans-Siberian railway up to the border and north of it up to some 150 km. These are also the areas where most logging has taken place. Much logging has also occurred along major rivers. In the past, most of the harvested wood in Siberia and the Far East was removed through floating and rafting (Tatarinov 1992). Floating logs in booms caused major damage and the deposition of organic wastes and is prohibited today. Logs are still transported along the major rivers in Krasnoyarsk (Yenisey and Angara) and Khabarovsk (Amur and Ussuri) on pontoons.

Fire Protection

Over the 1975-88 period, fire, insects, disease, and other causes (such as windfall), excluding clear felling destroyed an average annual forest area of 1.04 million hectares (Isaev 1991 in IIASA 1995), an area equivalent to average annual forest harvesting. Fire alone has destroyed 30 million hectares in Siberia and the Far East. In 1995, 16 percent of the total forest area destroyed in Russia was by adverse climatic conditions (mostly windfall), 33 percent by fire and 46 percent by insects and diseases (up dramatically) from 2 percent in 1991; State Report, 1996. The summer of 1996 was marked by a major increase in forest fires in Russia (1.2 million hectares affected as of July 1, 1996). Harvesting and fires are thought to make forests more susceptible to windfall.

A fire protection zone has been drawn across Russia, designating the northern tundra and transitional forests as unprotected and southern areas as protected forests. In total, 61 percent of the forest fund area is under some form of fire protection; 78 percent in West Siberia, 66 percent in East Siberia, and 52 percent in Far East (see Table A.3). The fire protection zone follows the line of the northern taiga forests. Above that area, preventive or fire fighting measures are taken only in exceptional cases. Scientists at the Siberian and Far Eastern Forest Research Institutes have proposed enlarging the protection zone, forbidding forest exploitation activities in order to protect the fragile ecosystem. The southern border of this fire protection zone coincides roughly with the transition from tundra forest and sparse forest to taiga. The area just north of this zone is also highly sensitive to human disturbances and needs protection and appropriate management prescriptions.

Fire ecology in northern biomes is a complex issue. Fire is considered to be a natural part of the ecosystem, particularly in the northern taiga and the transition area to the forest tundra zone. Days are very long during the short growing season, allowing high biomes production and the accumulation of organic matter (decomposition is slow because of low temperatures). Fires burn the organic matter, allowing seeds to germinate on the exposed mineral soil. Dormant seeds, buried in the permafrost layer for years, finally get a chance to germinate, creating a vegetation cover and drying up wetlands that sometimes form temporarily. In this way, fire plays an important role in the dynamics of the ecosystem, helping create a mosaic of different formations and habitats in a highly diversified ecosystem and creating favorable conditions for different life forms, thereby safeguarding biodiversity. It is in this context that decisions should be made about when and where to fight fires. Large-scale, uncontrolled fires require intervention because of the harm they cause to forest biomes and the atmosphere, but intervention becomes more questionable for small fires.

Many Russian foresters consider large fires to be the main negative factor affecting the condition of forests and the general ecological situation. On large clear-cut areas, fires can grow large and hot, destroying adjacent intact forest stands. Areas with large amounts of harvest residues are especially susceptible. Foresters hesitate to use prescribed burning to clear the site for fear of being blamed for causing other forest fires. There is also confusion about whether such practices are even allowed.

Table A.3: Aerial Forest Fire Control Bases in Russia

No.	*Name of base*	*Location*
1	Central Base	Pushkino, Moscow Oblast
2	Northwestern Base	Petrozavodsk, Republic of Karelia
3	Northern Base	Arkhangelsk, Arkhangelskaya Oblast
4	Syktyvkar Base	Syktyvkar, Komi Republic
5	Western Urals Base	Perm, Permskaya Oblast
6	Urals Base	Yekaterinburg, Sverdlovskaya Oblast
7	Tyumen Base	Tyumen, Tyumen Oblast
8	Khanty-Mansiysk Base	Khanty-Mansiysk, Khanty-Mansi Autonomous Okrug
9	West Siberian Base	Novosibirsk, Novosibirskaya Oblast
10	Tomsk Base	Tomsk, Tomskya Oblast
11	Krasnoyarsk Base	Kransnoyarsk, Krasnoyarskiy Kray
12	Irkutsk Base	Irkutsk, Irkutskaya Oblast
13	Transbaikalian Base	Ulan-Ude, Republic of Buryatia
14	Chita Base	Chita, Chitinskaya Oblast
15	Yakutsk Base	Yakutsk, Republic Sakha (Yakutia)
16	Amur Base	Blagoveshchensk, Amurskaya Oblast
17	Far-Eastern Base	Khabarovsk, Khabarovskiy Kray
18	Maritime Base	Vladivostok, Primorskiy Kray
19	Northeastern Base	Magadan, Magadanskaya Oblast
20	Gorno-Altay Air Wing	Gorno-Altaysk, Republic of Altay
21	Sakhalin Air Wing	Yuzhno-Sakhalinsk, Sakhalinskaya Oblast
22	Kamchatka Air Wing	Petropavlovsk-Kamch., Kamchatskaya Oblast
23	Koryak Air Wing	Ossora, Koryak Autonomous Okrug
24	Chukchi Air Wing	Anadyr, Chukchi Autonomous Okrug

Source: The Federal Forest Service of Russia, 1996.

The Siberian International Center for Ecological Research on Boreal Forests in Krasnoyarsk has a forest fire monitoring program to detect and record large fires and to collect information on climatic conditions, combustible material, and similar details. Remote sensing technology is used to monitor forest fires. Because of lack of fire fighting aircraft and operational budgets, only large fires in the southern (protected) areas are fought. There are 10,000 to 15,000 fires annually in the area protected from forest fires in Siberia and the Far East, with an average loss of about 100 hectares of forest per fire (IIASA 1995). Most large fires occur in the southern and middle taiga. There seems to be a relation between forest density (availability of combustible material) and the occurrence of large fires.

The State Report on the Status of Natural Environment of the Russian Federation (1995) estimated that 90 percent of fires in the forest protection zone in the past five years were of human origin. In Krasnoyarsk, 70 percent of the fires are estimated to be of human origin. The remaining 30 percent are attributed to dry lightening, which is very common in the middle and northern parts of Siberia. The Institute of Forest Research near Moscow has found a strong relationship between fires and the presence of settlements, roads, and major rivers. In addition, the occurrence of fires is reported to be much higher in large clear-cut areas.

A strong fire protection program requires an extensive road network to provide ready access to fire fighters. But access development may also speed up the destruction of now inaccessible areas, actually increasing fire hazards. Also, widespread fire suppression could increase the likelihood of large fires on the large complexes of contiguous forests of the same age class that are expected to develop following the creation of the large clearcuts in Siberia and the Far East. These areas provide ideal conditions for insect and disease outbreaks, which in turn create ideal conditions for large-scale fires, setting in motion a costly vicious cycle.

Water Catchment and Soil Protection

Forests in the upper parts of a watershed are important to water catchment and soil protection. Different types of forest, tree species, and management practices (particularly the methods and frequency of harvesting operations) will affect these functions differently. It is important to distinguish between soil protection and water catchment functions, although they are closely related. Forests in upper watersheds provide a permanent canopy closure protecting the soil. During periods of harvesting and in the first two or three years of planting, however, there may be considerable increase in soil erosion, as well as in runoff and stream flow.

About half the Siberian and Far Eastern forests are in mountainous areas, which have important catchment values, particularly in connection with hydropower reservoirs, drinking water supplies, and fisheries resources. Many of these mountain forests are situated on thin soils, which are prone to erosion once forest cover is removed. Clear-cutting, once practiced over large areas with stands of *Pinus sibirica*, is no longer allowed. Clear-cuts on slopes in the southern part of Krasnoyarsk show severe erosion, and reforestation efforts remain unsuccessful.

A change in forest cover will have a noticeable impact on a smaller watershed, but much less of an impact on large or compound watersheds. Such changes can affect streamflow patterns (more frequent and higher peak flows) and water quality (particularly increases in sediment load and organic matter). In some places spawning areas for salmon have disappeared following the conversion of forests into swamps through large-scale clear-cutting in the long-season frost zone (Institute of Water and Ecology Problems in Khabarovsk).

The major sources of site degradation associated with logging are poor design, construction, and maintenance of roads; skid tracks from the use of the blade on steep slopes; and soil compaction from the use of heavy machinery on intensively used sites (landings). Soil compaction can substantially reduce infiltration rates and increase runoff rates. Several Russian and international studies have shown that some 20 percent of the area harvested is adversely affected by soil disturbance and another 10 percent by roads. Roads were recognized as a major source of runoff and sediment (Federal Forest Service -- Silvicultural Requirements, 1993). Proper planning, road system layout, and conduct of harvesting operations (choice of equipment, training of personnel, climatic conditions) are thus important for reducing soil erosion.

Forestry in the Khabarovsk and Krasnoyarsk Regions

Most of Russia's forest types are represented in Khabarovsk and Krasnoyarsk regions (Figures A.1 and A.2). In Khabarovsk, spruce and larch dominate (Figure A.3). In Krasnoyarsk, the distribution of dominant species (pine, spruce, fir, larch, Siberian pine, aspen and birch) is more even, though birch and aspen are heavily represented. Birch and spruce occupy less than 20 percent of the area of mature forest lands, but they occupy almost half the total forest area in the young age classes (see Figure A.2). This is partly the result of past harvesting conditions, which favored the establishment of low-value aspen and birch over the higher-value coniferous species.

The age of a mature forest varies by species. For instance, birch and aspen forests mature in 40-60 years, while Siberian pine forests require 100-120 years. The average age of forests in Krasnoyarsk is 104 years, though a large proportion of mature forests are in extremely remote areas, while a high proportion of immature forests are in easily accessible areas. The average age of forests in Khabarovsk is 82 years. Forests cover 50.1 million hectares in Krasnoyarsk and 39.4 million hectares in Khabarovsk.

Volumes and Growth

The standing volume in the two regions (4.6 billion cubic meters in Khabarovsk and 7.6 billion cubic meters in Krasnoyarsk) is 28 percent of total standing volume in Siberia and the Far East. Forests in Krasnoyarsk are denser, at 151 cubic meters per hectare, than in Khabarovsk at 116 cubic meters and contain a greater average volume, an indication of more favorable average growing conditions (see Figures A.4 and A.5). Part of the difference is due to the higher proportion of mature forests in Krasnoyarsk.

Several interesting growth patterns are evident from Figures A.4 and A.5. Siberian pine shows the highest stocking of the main species. The growing pattern is more regular in Khabarovsk, possibly indicating more homogeneous conditions in that territory, but overall growing conditions are better in Krasnoyarsk, as evident in the higher stocking levels of individual species at different ages when compared with those in Khabarovsk. Siberian forests grow very slowly, a serious disadvantage in terms of rate of return on capital investment that is partly offset by the high wood quality produced under these conditions. The high-density, even-grained wood commands a high market price.

Forest growth in Russia is estimated by dividing the incremental growth in the standing volume during a certain period of time (e.g., ten years) by the duration of that time period. This method underestimates actual growth. More precise methods are to measure the diameter growth from samples of individual trees as part of a forest inventory or to estimate it from yield tables. The total estimated annual growth of forest is 51 million cubic meters in Khabarovsk or roughly 1.3 cubic meters per hectare per year, and 69 million cubic meters in Krasnoyarsk, or roughly 1.4 cubic meters per hectare per year. This is much lower than in most other forests in the world. It is possible to produce 3-4 cubic meters per hectare per year with intensive management on larger areas.

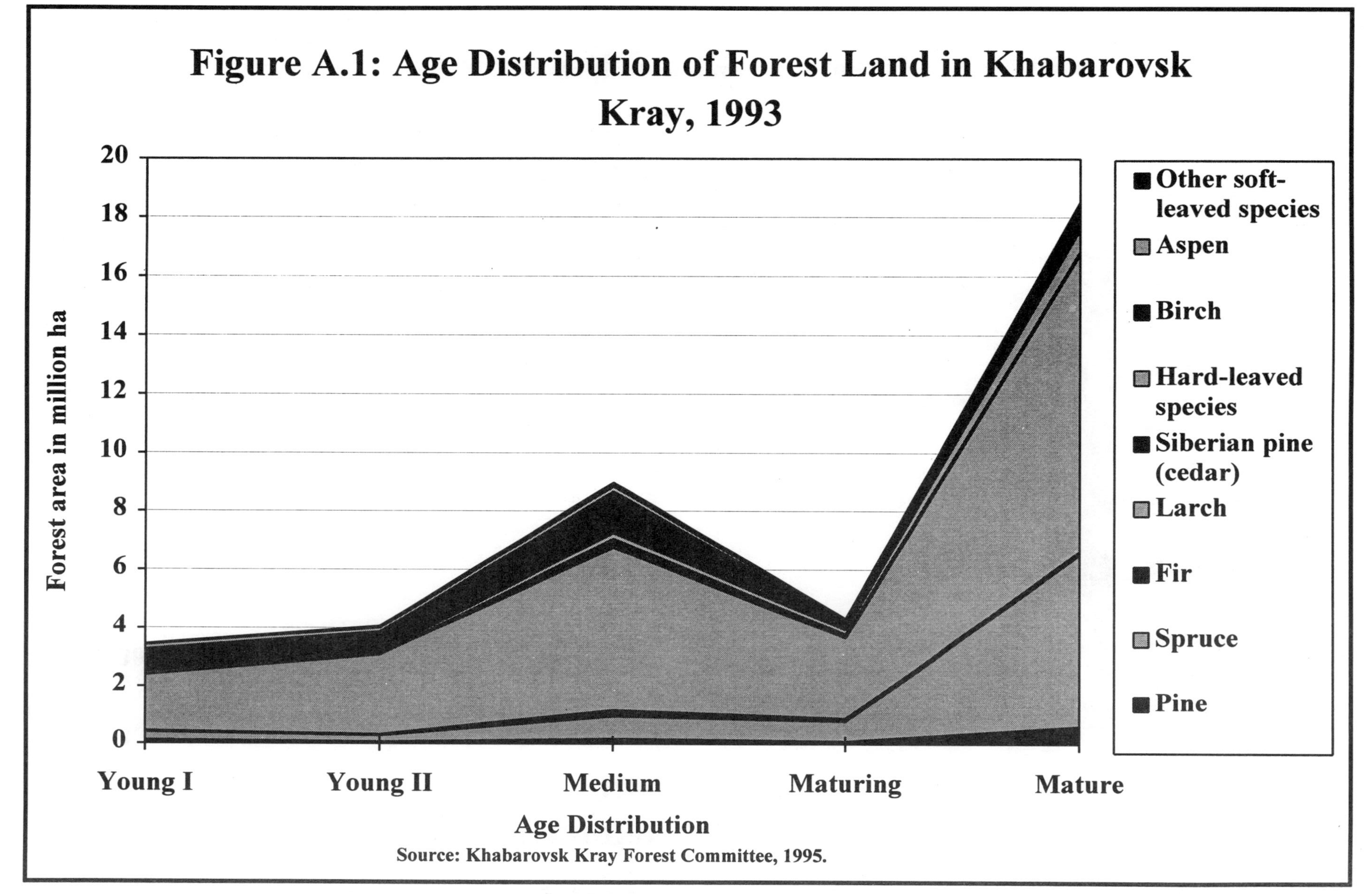
Figure A.1: Age Distribution of Forest Land in Khabarovsk Kray, 1993
Forest area in million ha
20
18
16
14
12
10
8
6
4
2
0
Young I
Young II
Medium
Maturing
Mature
Age Distribution
Other soft-leaved species
Aspen
Birch
Hard-leaved species
Siberian pine (cedar)
Larch
Fir
Spruce
Pine
Source: Khabarovsk Kray Forest Committee, 1995.

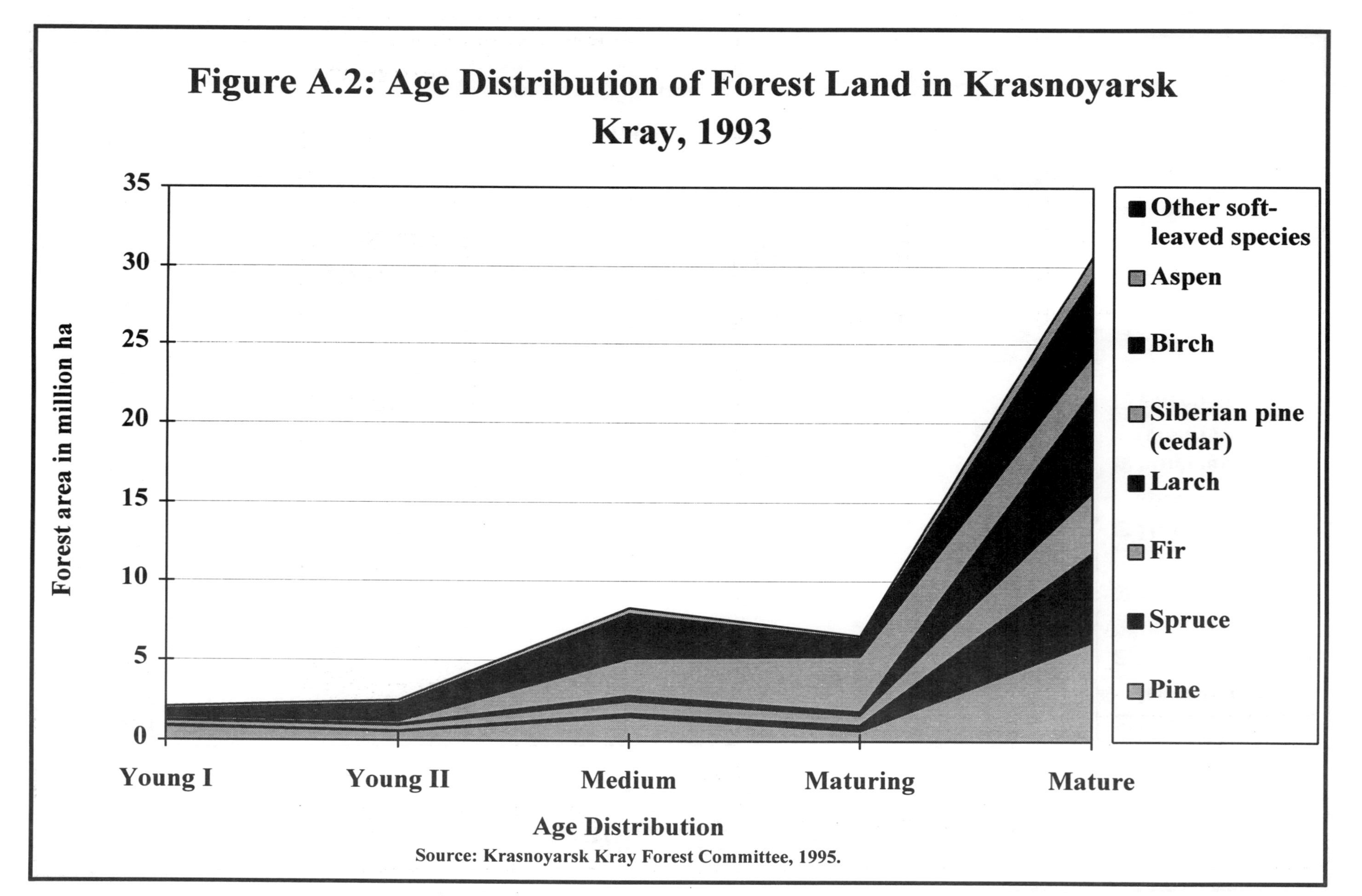
Figure A.2: Age Distribution of Forest Land in Krasnoyarsk Kray, 1993
35
30
25
20
15
10
5
0
Forest area in million ha
Young I
Young II
Medium
Maturing
Mature
Age Distribution
Other soft-leaved species
Aspen
Birch
Siberian pine (cedar)
Larch
Fir
Spruce
Pine
Source: Krasnoyarsk Kray Forest Committee, 1995.

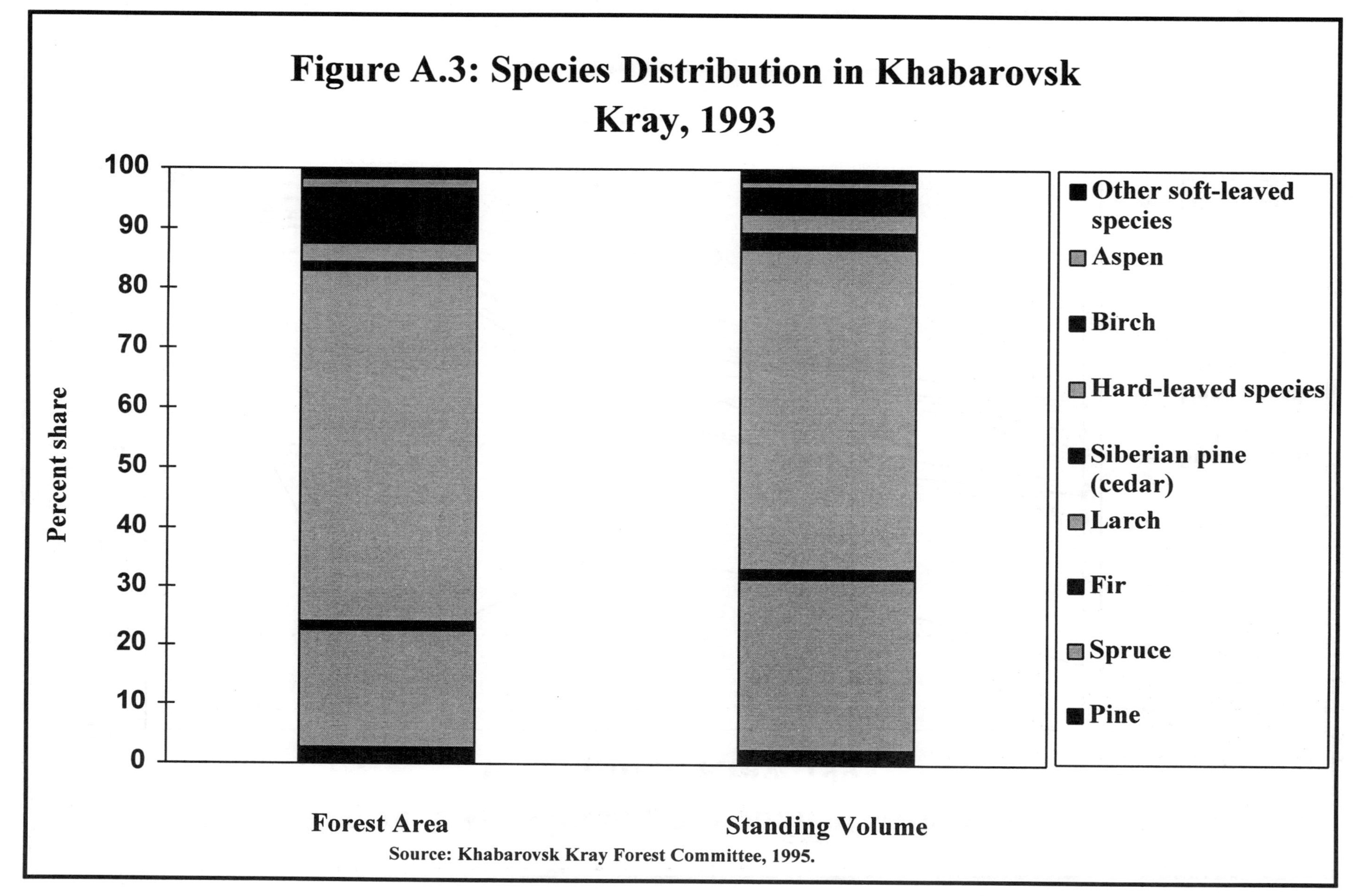
Figure A.3: Species Distribution in Khabarovsk Kray, 1993
100
90
80
70
60
50
40
30
20
10
0
Percent share
Other soft-leaved species
Aspen
Birch
Hard-leaved species
Siberian pine (cedar)
Larch
Fir
Spruce
Pine
Forest Area
Standing Volume
Source: Khabarovsk Kray Forest Committee, 1995.

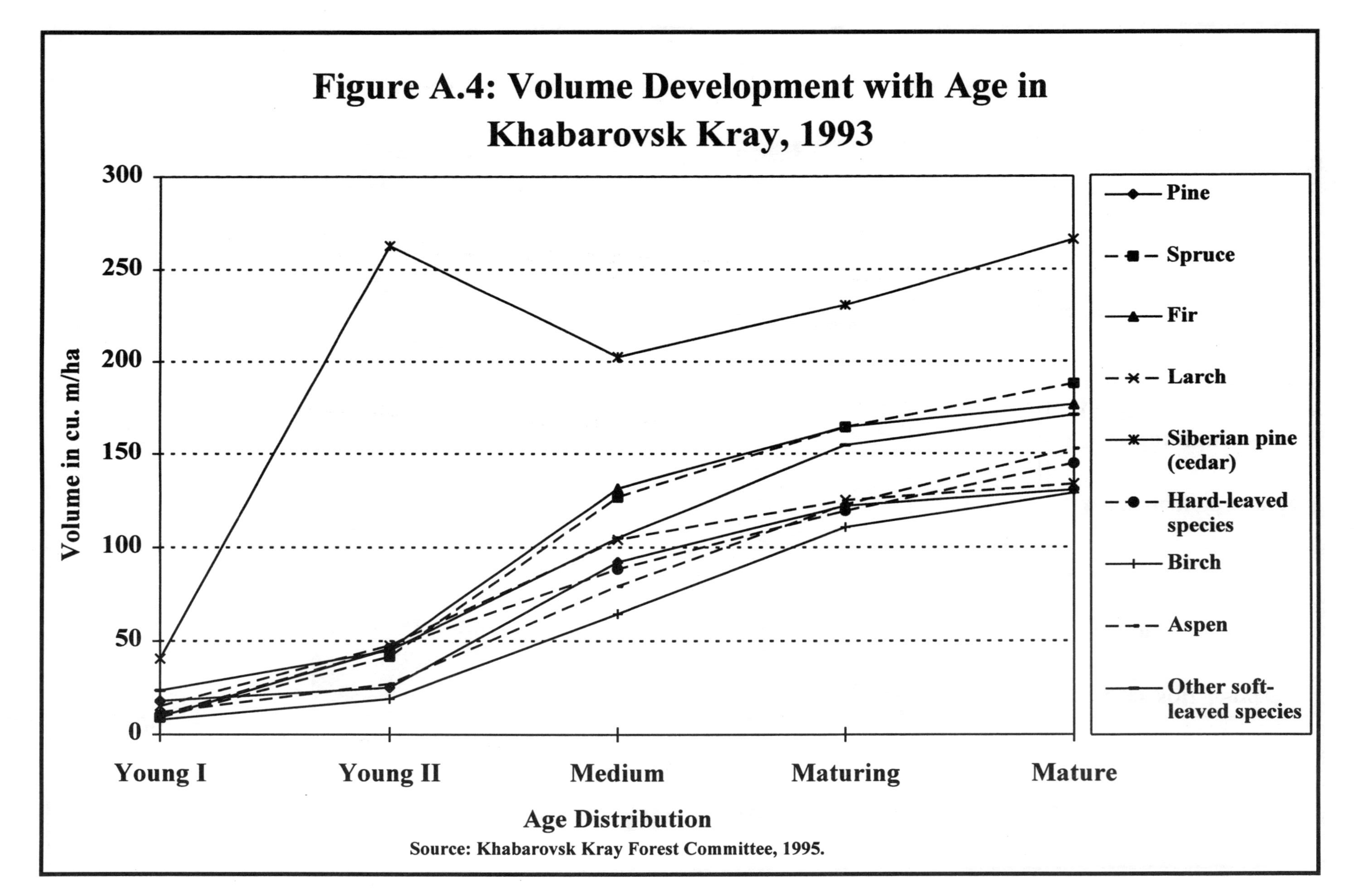
Figure A.4: Volume Development with Age in
Khabarovsk Kray, 1993
300
250
200
150
100
50
0
Volume in cu. m/ha
Young I
Young II
Medium
Maturing
Mature
Age Distribution
Pine
Spruce
Fir
Larch
Siberian pine (cedar)
Hard-leaved species
Birch
Aspen
Other soft-leaved species
Source: Khabarovsk Kray Forest Committee, 1995.

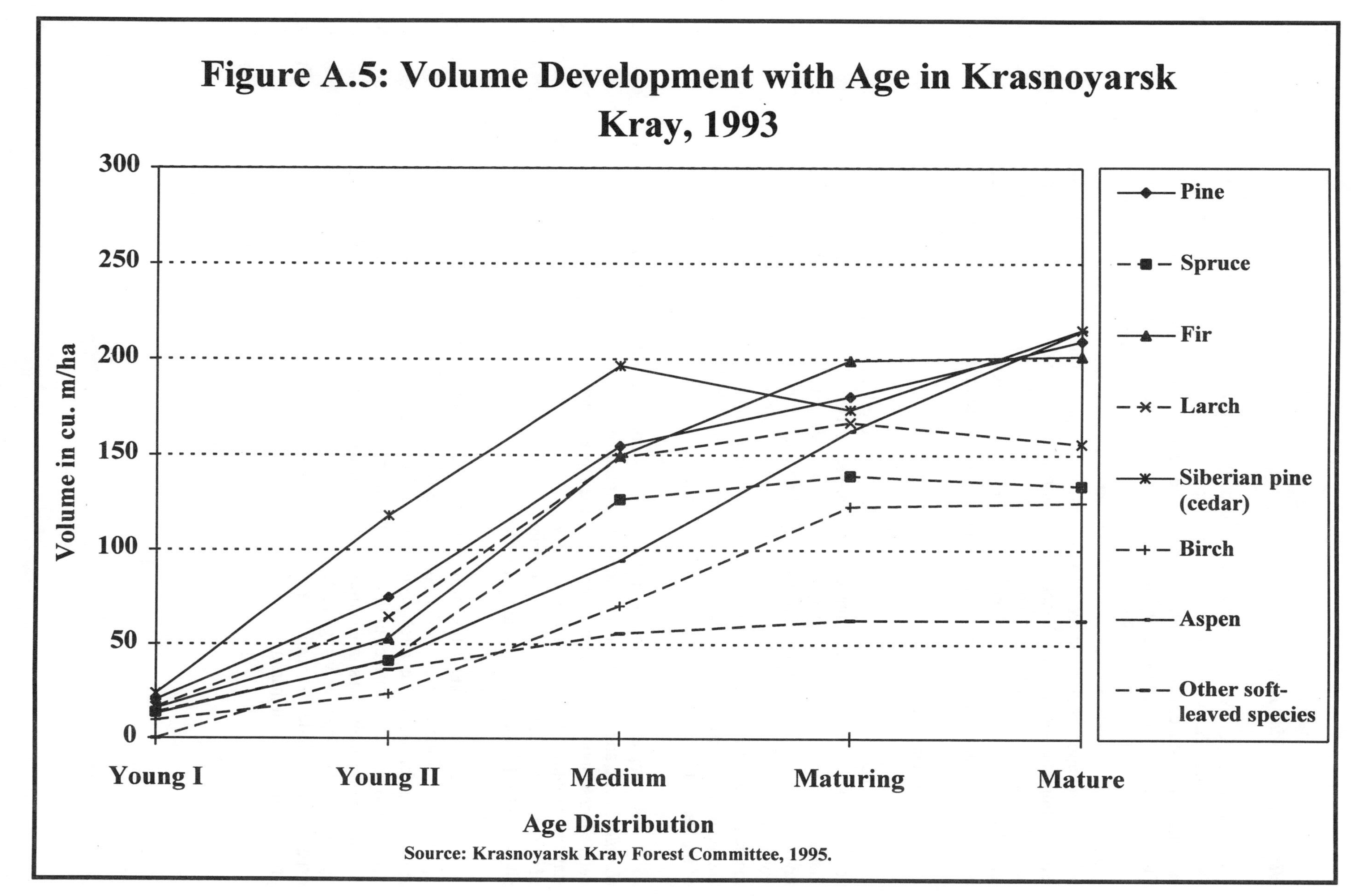
Figure A.5: Volume Development with Age in Krasnoyarsk Kray, 1993
300
250
200
150
100
50
0
Volume in cu. m/ha
Young I
Young II
Medium
Maturing
Mature
Age Distribution
Pine
Spruce
Fir
Larch
Siberian pine (cedar)
Birch
Aspen
Other soft-leaved species
Source: Krasnoyarsk Kray Forest Committee, 1995.

Historical Harvesting Levels

Harvesting levels have declined dramatically since the introduction of a market economy. In 1994, the annual harvest volume in the Khabarovsk region had fallen to one-third its 1987 level and has remained there since. The decline was about the same (in percentage terms) in the Krasnoyarsk region. Final cuts, including clear-cuts and regeneration cuts, are a high proportion of the total harvest (about 95 percent for Khabarovsk and 90 percent in Krasnoyarsk), suggesting an exploitative style of forest management (see Figures A.6 and A.7). That proportion has risen over the past ten years. Under intensive and appropriate resource management, the proportion of final cutting and other types of cutting (such as thinning and sanitation) should be about equal. During the late 1980s, final cuts exceeded annual allowable cuts in the Khabarovsk region, but today the actual cut in both regions is substantially below the annual allowable cut. Estimated annual growth of the forests exceeds by far the annual harvest level in both regions, but the growth estimates include areas that are protected (Group I and II forests).

Forest Management Planning

All economically accessible forests have a forest management plan, detailing the harvesting activities and other operations planned over a ten-year period. These plans are based on a forest inventory that assesses each stand individually every ten years. In principle, about 10 percent of the forest area is inventoried each year over the ten-year cycle, and a corresponding management plan is developed. The inventories aim to estimate the volume of mature stands with a standard error of 10 percent and of medium-aged or maturing forests with a standard error of 20 percent. The inventory, field assessments, and plans are prepared by professional foresters in the regional forestry inventory enterprises that are part of the Federal Forest Service (see Table A.2 earlier).

A complete forest management plan covers one forest district (*Leskhoz)* or forest ranger district (*Lesnichestvo*) and consists of a general description of the ecological, climatic, and soil conditions; a detailed description of each stand with estimated parameters (such as species composition, yield class, standing volume); and suggested activities to be undertaken during the next ten-year period. Summaries of the district's standing stock, age distribution, and average yields are documented, as is the annual allowable cut for the next ten years. A variety of maps are prepared with the plan.

There is no consultation with either the local community or the territorial authorities in the development of these plans. A draft of the plan is sent to the Federal Forest Service in Moscow for final approval, a formality that rarely generates questions or revisions. In the past, the final version was delivered to the local manager in heavy bound volumes. In recent years, Khabarovsk has been storing the information for their plans in electronic form on diskettes, which are distributed to managers to facilitate operational planning. Few regions have computerized their system, however. These efforts should be expanded to include the map data base, preferably using geographical information systems (GIS) to provide a more useful management and planning tool.

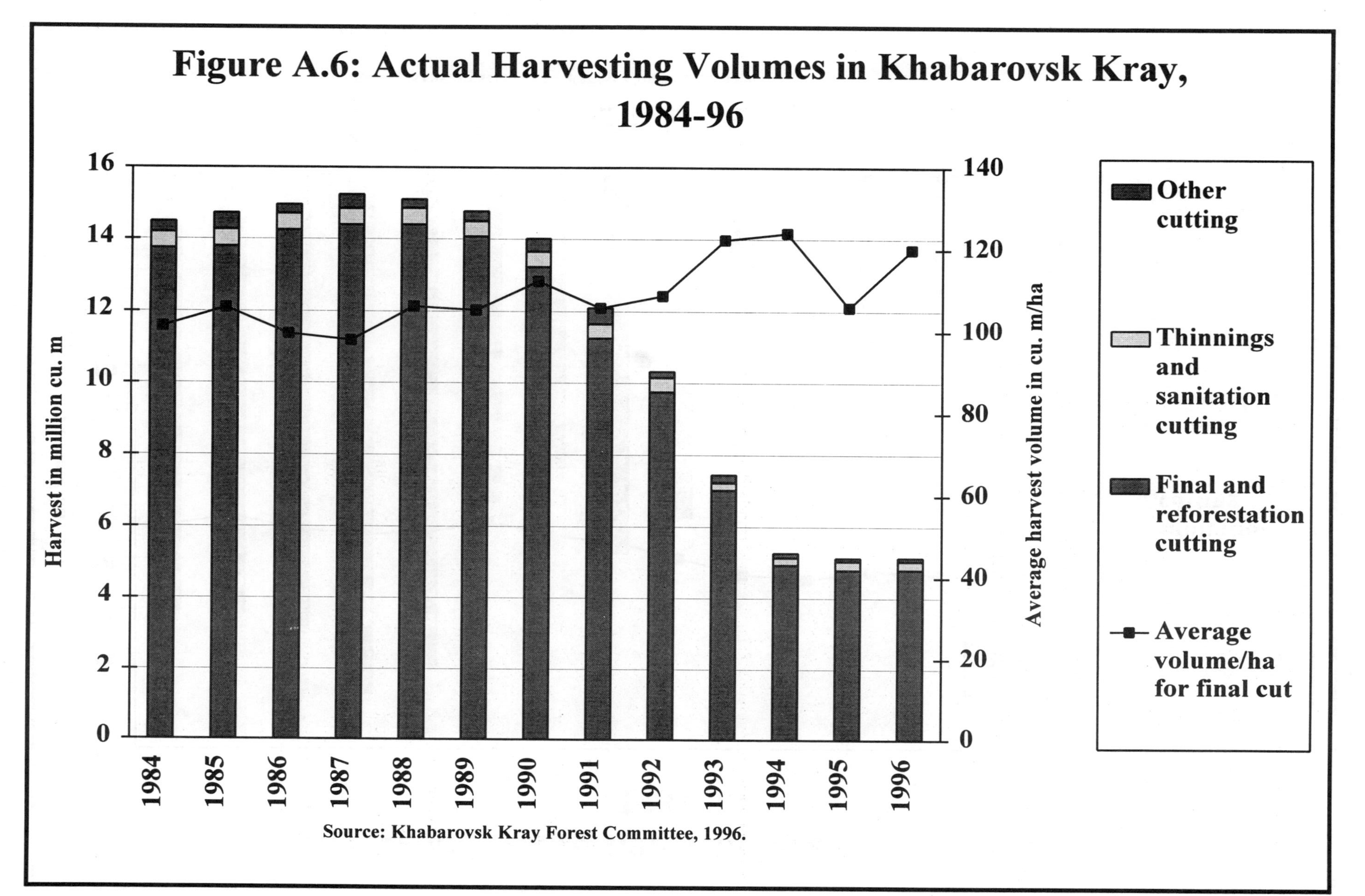
Figure A.6: Actual Harvesting Volumes in Khabarovsk Kray, 1984-96
Harvest in million cu. m
16
14
12
10
8
6
4
2
0
Average harvest volume in cu. m/ha
140
120
100
80
60
40
20
0
1984
1985
1986
1987
1988
1989
1990
1991
1992
1993
1994
1995
1996
Other cutting
Thinnings and sanitation cutting
Final and reforestation cutting
Average volume/ha for final cut
Source: Khabarovsk Kray Forest Committee, 1996.

Figure A.7: Actual Harvesting Volumes in Krasnoyarsk Kray, 1984-96

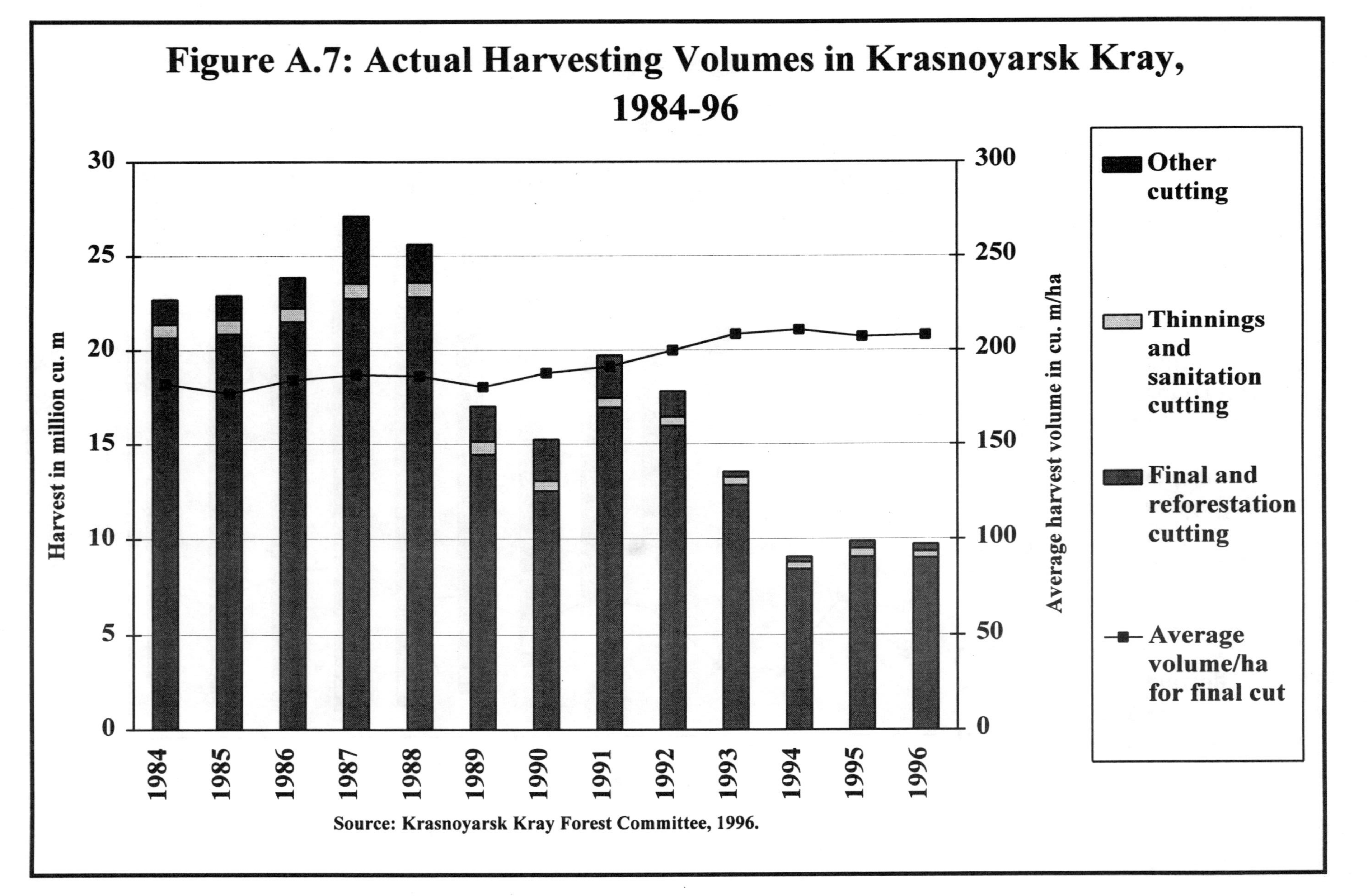

Source: Krasnoyarsk Kray Forest Committee, 1996.

Calculation of the Annual Allowable Cut. The annual allowable cut (AAC) is the maximum annual volume that may be harvested during a ten-year period while maintaining the long-term sustainability of the forest resource. The AAC is calculated at the district or ranger district level and then aggregated to yield the regional AAC. There is an AAC for final cuts and one for thinning and other cuts.

The AAC for final cuts is calculated using four different formulas in which the growing stock of mature and maturing forest and estimated growth are independent variables. The original formula was developed years ago in Germany to obtain a constant and sustainable flow of wood over a twenty-thirty-year period. Only forests that are economically accessible should be included; forests on slopes exceeding 21° and those set aside for conservation or protection should also be excluded from the formula.

The AAC for thinning and other cuts is calculated by foresters during field surveys, according to such biological attributes as stand density and desirable species mix. The recommendations made by foresters are reviewed by the local Forest Service, which decides what will actually be done during the period under particular financial and labor constraints. This type of AAC is rarely mentioned, since it covers such a small percentage of total cuts.

Though the present system for calculating the annual allowable cut is reasonable, in practice it has four defects that can lead to distortions and to long-term adverse consequences for the sustainability of the forest resource:

- The absence of local participation in preparation of the management plan results in a lack of public commitment to the plan and difficulties in implementing it. This is a severe shortcoming especially in areas where the forest is the main source of income or where forests are close to population centers. Consultation is critical for integrating conservation and protection objectives into the plan.

- Despite regulations requiring it, conservation and protected areas are often not appropriately taken into account in calculating the AAC.

- Although each district manager is supposed to follow an AAC for the individual district, there are indications that regionally aggregated AAC are sometimes applied instead, so that some areas have become severely overcut while others (those that are less accessible) are underutilized.

- To maximize production, each stand should be harvested as close as possible to its optimum rotation age. The present methods of estimating the AAC are probably biased downwards, because the sustainable supply is based on a relatively small area (district or ranger's district) by assuming that a normal age distribution should be obtained in the long term. The underestimation of forest growth will also reduce the calculated AAC.

To improve the overall land use allocation process, the following procedures should be applied to the preparation of forest management plans:

- Form a steering committee of local representatives of the Federal Forest Service, forest research institutions, wood processing industries, the State Committee for Environmental Protection, the Ministry of Natural Resources, the local authority, indigenous peoples, and NGOs. This committee should guide development of the plan.

- Define a wood supply area, consisting of a group of forest districts located within the natural catchment area of a wood processing industry center or a planned center. The wood supply areas could be redefined when major new wood processing industries are established.

- Define requirements for forest conservation, protection, and other restrictions on commercial management of the forests that have a direct influence on the wood supply. Requirements for production of nonwood products and the needs of indigenous people should also be considered.

- Simulate different wood supply scenarios, based on the detailed information from the forest inventory and excluding restricted areas. The consequences of each scenario should be discussed by the steering committee, which should eventually achieve consensus on a single scenario that then becomes the wood supply plan for a five to ten-year period.

- Forest operations and the wood processing industry would have to operate within the framework established by the plan. The plan should also provide the framework for the operational planning of harvesting and silviculture at the district level and for strategic planning in the wood processing industry. When the assumptions underlying the plan change, the process should be repeated to revise the plan.

Forest Regeneration. Five methods of forest regeneration are being used in Siberia: natural regeneration, selective felling, artificial seeding, planting, and a combination of natural and artificial regeneration. ***Natural regeneration*** is an efficient method in large areas, especially where pines are dominant. The cost is low, consisting mainly of pre-commercial thinning once the regeneration has been established. The new generation is guaranteed to be of the same genetic material as the previous one, which may be advantageous in areas where primary forest is being harvested and it is desirable to maintain the species that have adapted to the climate and soil.

The selection of seed trees must be made carefully. In some areas, weak and damaged trees have been chosen as seed trees instead of the strongest trees with the more desirable genetic characteristics. Fifty-meter wide strips of the original forest were left uncut as a seeding source on some sites, but the strips were up to 300 meters apart from one another. This technique is unlikely to give satisfactory results since the seeds from a pine tree spread a maximum of one tree length from the source tree, leaving at least 80 percent of the area uncovered. While there will be some viable seeds in the logging debris, the resulting regeneration will likely be patchy and with uneven stocking.

Selective felling is used mainly to regenerate areas where shade-tolerant species, such as fir and spruce, dominate. With skilled foresters marking the trees to be removed, and the harvesting companies observing the marks and taking care not to damage the remaining trees or the surrounding soil, this method can produce high-value uneven-aged forests. From a biodiversity standpoint, this type of regeneration ensures the maintenance of existing ecosystems in a managed forest. The disadvantages are high harvesting costs (low harvest volume per hectare) and the danger that the genetic capital would become depleted if the best trees are consistently harvested.

Artificial seeding can be a complement to natural regeneration that can give excellent results at relatively low cost if done carefully. This method requires a reliable source of large quantities of good quality seed at reasonable cost. The origin and distribution of the seed has to be tightly controlled to ensure proper site matching.

Planting is the preferred method in areas where the existing forest has an unsuitable composition of species for the site or is too weak to regenerate by itself, where a new species should be introduced, or where soil conditions are not suitable for other types of regeneration. This is usually the most costly regeneration method and should be used only when the public nonwood benefits are equal to or greater than the costs.

A combination of artificial and natural regeneration is widely used to accommodate the specific characteristics of a particular site.

Much of the regeneration over the past fifty years has been of low quality, since little attention has been given to tending and silviculture. The use of various regeneration methods over the last ten years is illustrated in Figure A.8 for Khabarovsk and in Figure 1.8 (in the main report) for Krasnoyarsk. No statistics were available on selective felling. The pattern is much the same in the two regions, with the amount of planting decreasing since 1988 and the areas left to natural regeneration increasing dramatically. With much less funding available from the federal budget in recent years, it is easy to understand the increased dependence on natural regeneration as a management tool, particularly because the first few years require little investment. The downward trend in the tending of regenerated areas is a source of concern, however, since natural regeneration must be complemented by adequate tending in order to produce high-value forests and to maintain rich biodiversity.

Natural regeneration is the most suitable form of forest regeneration in most areas of Siberia, both because wood growth rates do not justify the higher costs of other methods and because of the benefits of maintaining biodiversity. To obtain good results, the best trees must be left as seed trees and evenly spaced over the regeneration area (say fifteen to twenty trees per hectare). Exposure to wind should be minimized by selecting the shape and size of the cutting areas. The seed trees should be harvested after the natural regeneration has been established, and when the income can offset the cost for the necessary pre-commercial thinning of the regeneration. Pre-commercial thinning must be carried out within an appropriate period of time (say within five to ten years after harvesting); otherwise, the thinning becomes considerably more expensive and the seed trees will inflict more damage on the regenerated areas when they are felled.

Figure A.8: Area under Different Regeneration Methods in Khabarovsk Kray, 1984-96

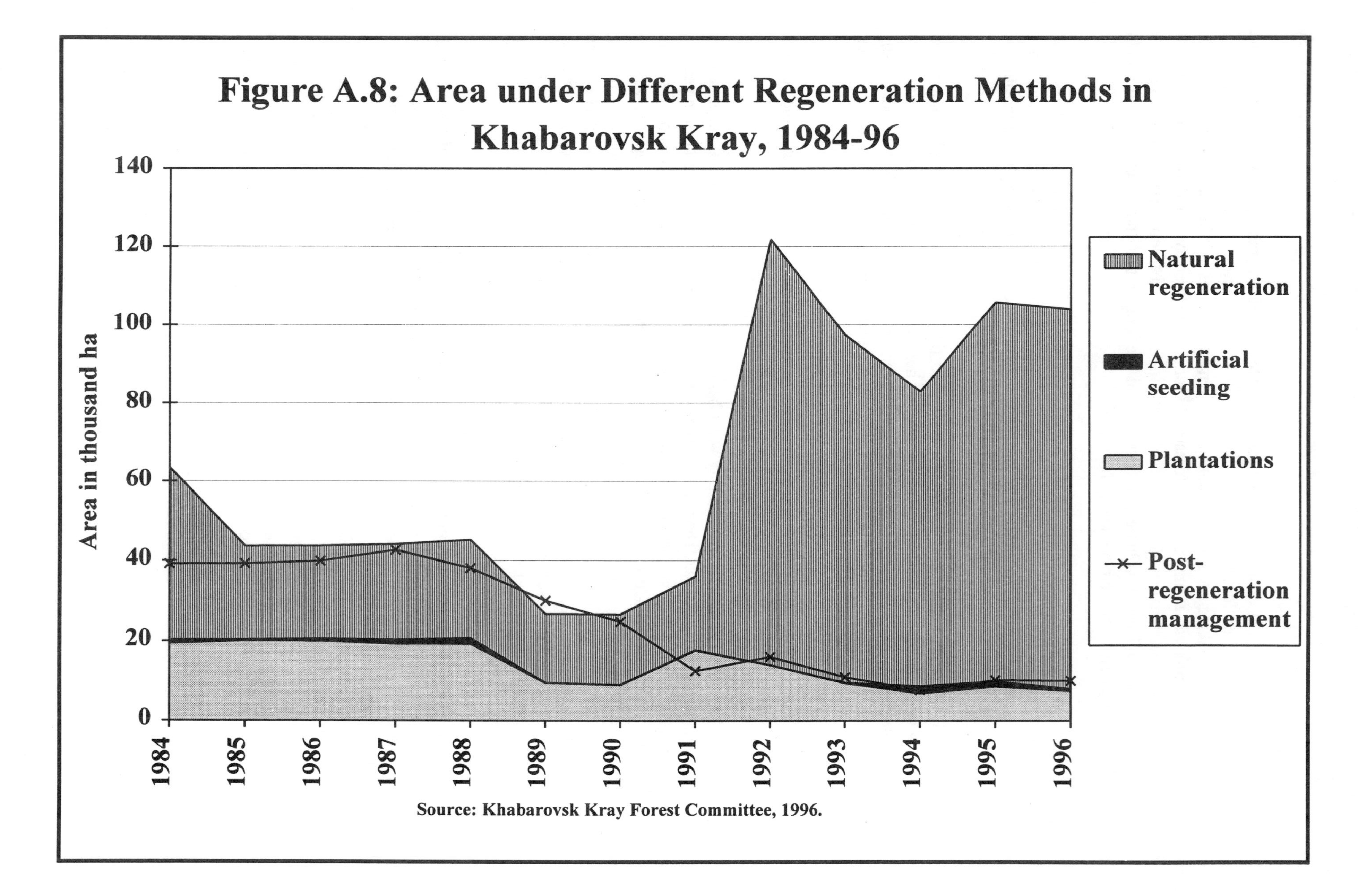

Forest Management

Harvesting practices in Siberia are essentially extractive mining; the resource is exploited until it is depleted and then production moves on to another area. It will take at least a hundred years before forests exploited in this way are ready for harvesting again, and the new forests may contain a smaller share of valuable species. Today, areas close to industrial centers have been stripped of valuable forests, and the wood processing industry has to venture further and further from these centers to find good wood resources.

Second-generation forests in cutover areas are dominated by soft, broad-leaved species like birch (*Betula pubescens*) and aspen (*Populus tremula*). Though these areas have been planted with conifers like pine *(Pinus spp.)* and fir *(Abies sibirica)*, the naturally seeded birch and aspen have grown faster than the conifers. Eventually, the suppressed conifers will replace the pioneer species, but the initial dominance of birch and aspen can delay the succession by as much as sixty years.

Planting pine after birch and aspen have become well-established is costly (three times as expensive as planting in clear-cut areas) and unlikely to yield the desired result. A better solution might be to thin the soft, broadleaf species so that the younger conifers can get enough direct light to flourish. In time, thinning operations could become self-financing, if markets for birch and aspen become established. Birch has become very popular in the wood processing industry in Europe, and it is also an excellent fire wood. Aspen is good for pulping and for wood for specific purposes like saunas.

Damage from Forest Fires, Insects, and Other Causes. Most forest fires are caused by human activities in areas where commercial harvesting has taken place. Large areas around Khabarovsk have been turned into vast waterlogged wastelands because repeated fires have prevented regeneration of the forests. This phenomenon is probably one of the most serious threats to the sustainable management of forests in Siberia.

Although the total area burned is greater in Khabarovsk than in Krasnoyarsk (Figures A.9 and A.10), there are indications that fire prevention through early spotting and aggressive combat has had beneficial effects in Khabarovsk. But the declining trend in fire fighting expenditures in both regions, in real terms, is cause for concern. For example, Figure 1.9 (in the main report) shows a big increase in area destroyed by fire in Russia during 1992. It would be most cost-efficient to concentrate fire rehabilitation efforts in areas close to wood processing industries and populated areas, where the forest is valued for both production and recreation. Russia has the knowledge and skilled workforce to apply up-to-date fire remediation principles and techniques, but funding is extremely low and uncertain.

Figure A.9: Forest Fires in Khabarovsk Kray, 1984-96

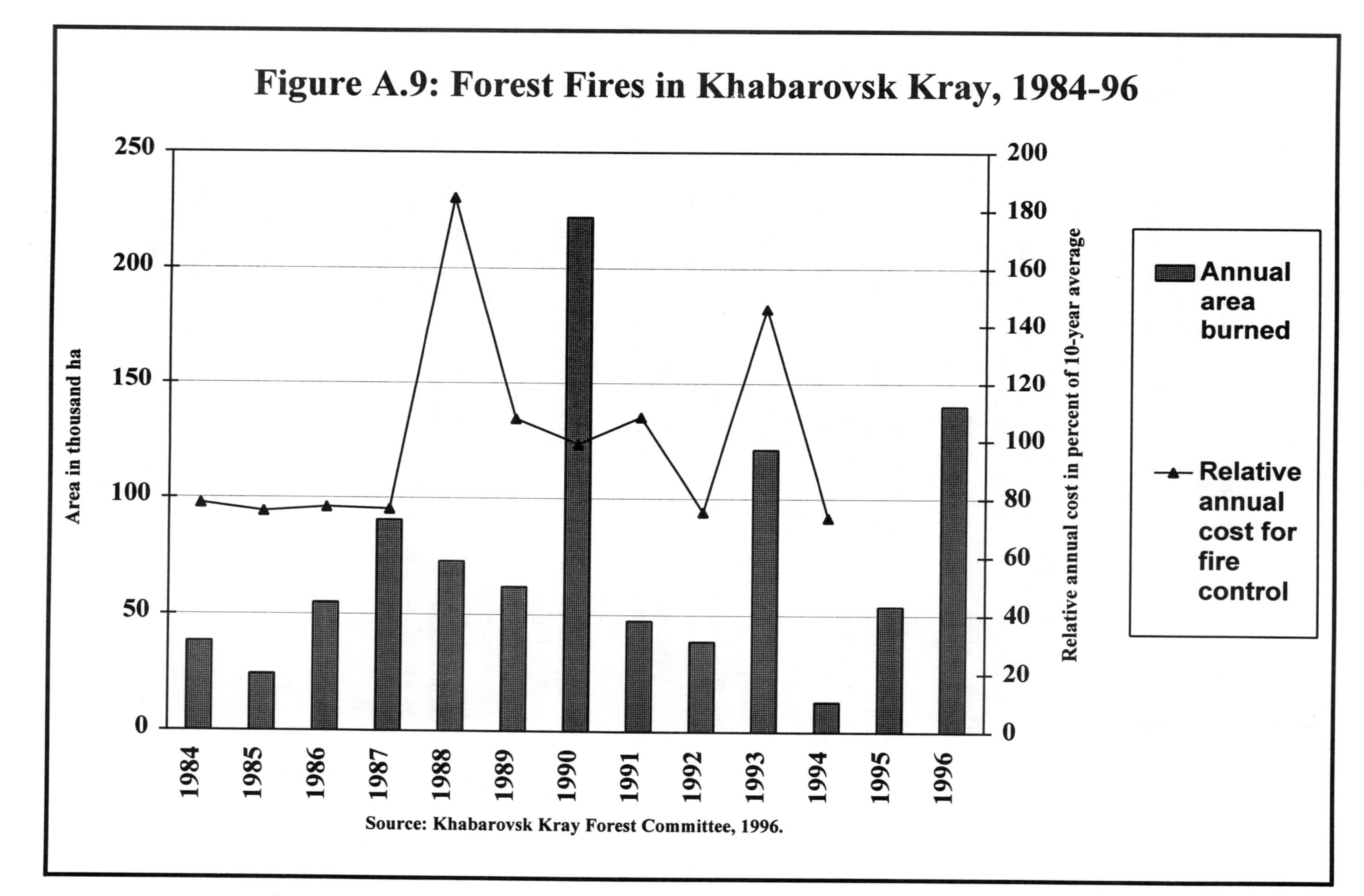

Source: Khabarovsk Kray Forest Committee, 1996.

Figure A.10: Forest Fires in Krasnoyarsk Kray, 1984-96

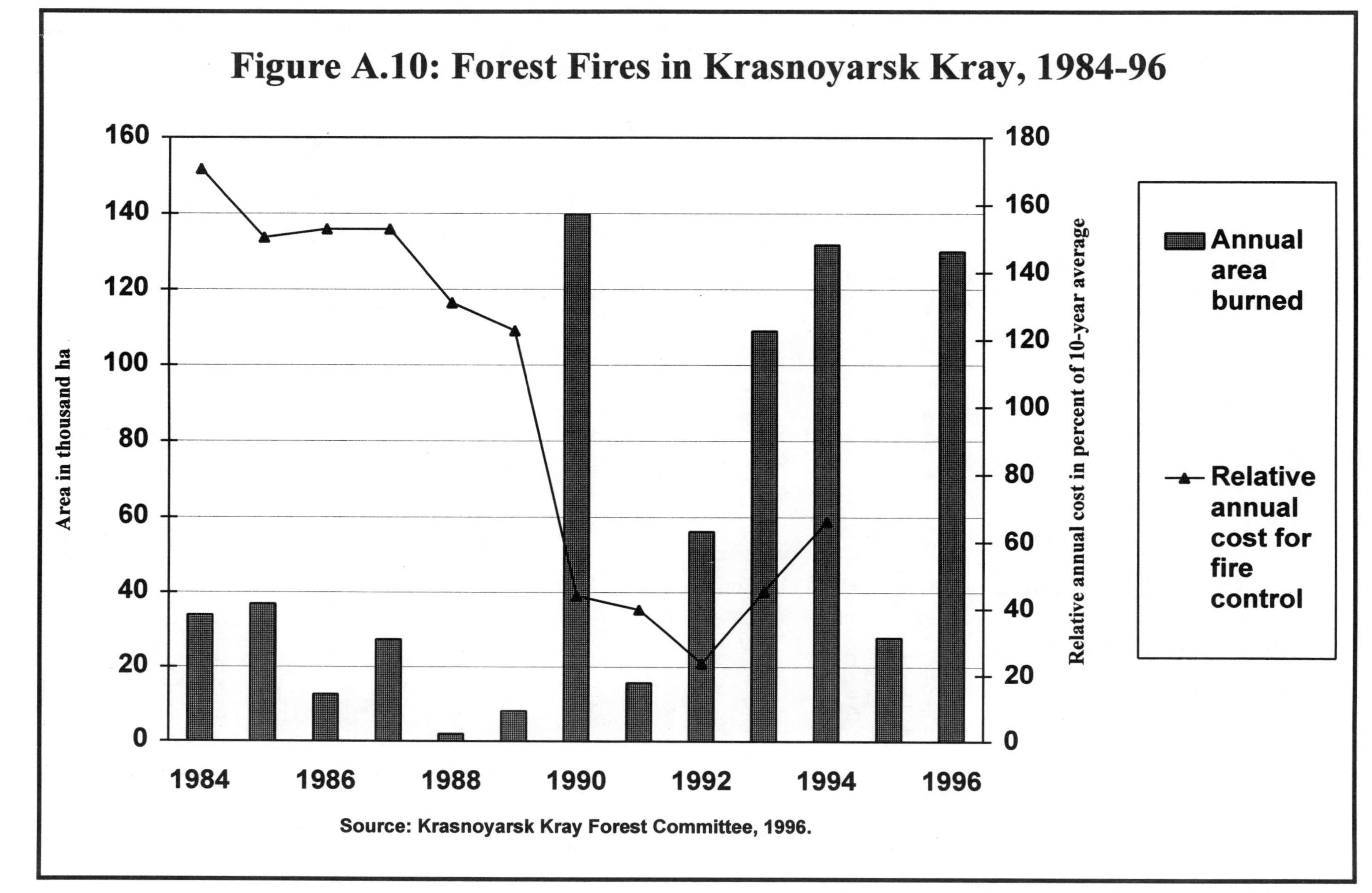

Source: Krasnoyarsk Kray Forest Committee, 1996.

On average, insect attacks appear to be a relatively less significant problem in most areas (Figure 1.9 in the main report), but there are localized insect problems. The potential for serious attacks of bark beetles, for example, is high in harvested areas that contain large amounts of logging waste. An abnormal outbreak of Siberian silkwork in 1995/96, for the second time in the last thirty years, became a major cause of tree mortality in Krasnoyarsk Kray (see main report).

Defoliation from industrial emissions does not seem to be a major problem in Siberia, except in the vicinity of industrial centers, such as the smelter industry in Norilsk in the Krasnoyarsk region. These emissions alone have defoliated some 500,000 hectares annually. The most serious damage due to industrial emissions in a one-year period is reported in the range of 40,000 to 80,000 hectares of dead forest. Oil exploration and exploitation are reported to have also caused serious damage to forests in Siberia.

Nonwood Products. Nonwood products from the forests have long been important to the rural economy. Fruits and berries have traditionally dominated the nonwood products market (roughly 80 percent), but medicinal herbs are gaining rapidly in market share (from 10 percent in 1991 to 24 percent in 1993). Currently, only a fraction of the potential output of these products is being produced, and even this is declining due to the breakdown of the distribution system (Figure A.11). The output and sales of these products are expected to recover as soon as the economy is stabilized.

In Krasnoyarsk, the production of medicines and herbal ointments is taking a potentially profitable turn. Among the products being developed is a deodorant with long-lasting effect and ointments for curing skin blemishes, controlling psoriasis, and revitalizing hair growth. These products could have significant market potential if tests confirm their effectiveness. Hunting is another important source of income from the forests. Some game-rich areas in Siberia and the Far East are of high value not only for the local indigenous populations, but also for tourists (including ecotourists).

Investment Opportunities

The analysis here suggests three areas for public investment: forest protection (fires and pests), intensive silviculture in areas close to wood processing centers, and forest management information systems. Forest protection investments are the highest priority. These should include investments in systems for early fire detection and combat and for the monitoring and control of insect populations. The sustainable development of the forest sector is not possible without such well-functioning systems.

Investments in intensive silviculture should aim to increase the wood flow and value of forests that are close to wood processing centers. These forests are increasingly more valuable not only for their of wood products, but also for environmental and recreational purposes. Investments should include operational costs for early thinning and cleaning of areas undergoing regeneration and the acquisition and maintenance of appropriate harvesting machinery for such operations.

Investments in forest management systems are essential. Flexible and efficient planning is necessary for the sustainable use of the vast forest resources of Siberia. That will require computerized information and distribution systems linked to processing and forest management units at the local (*Lesnichestvo*) level.

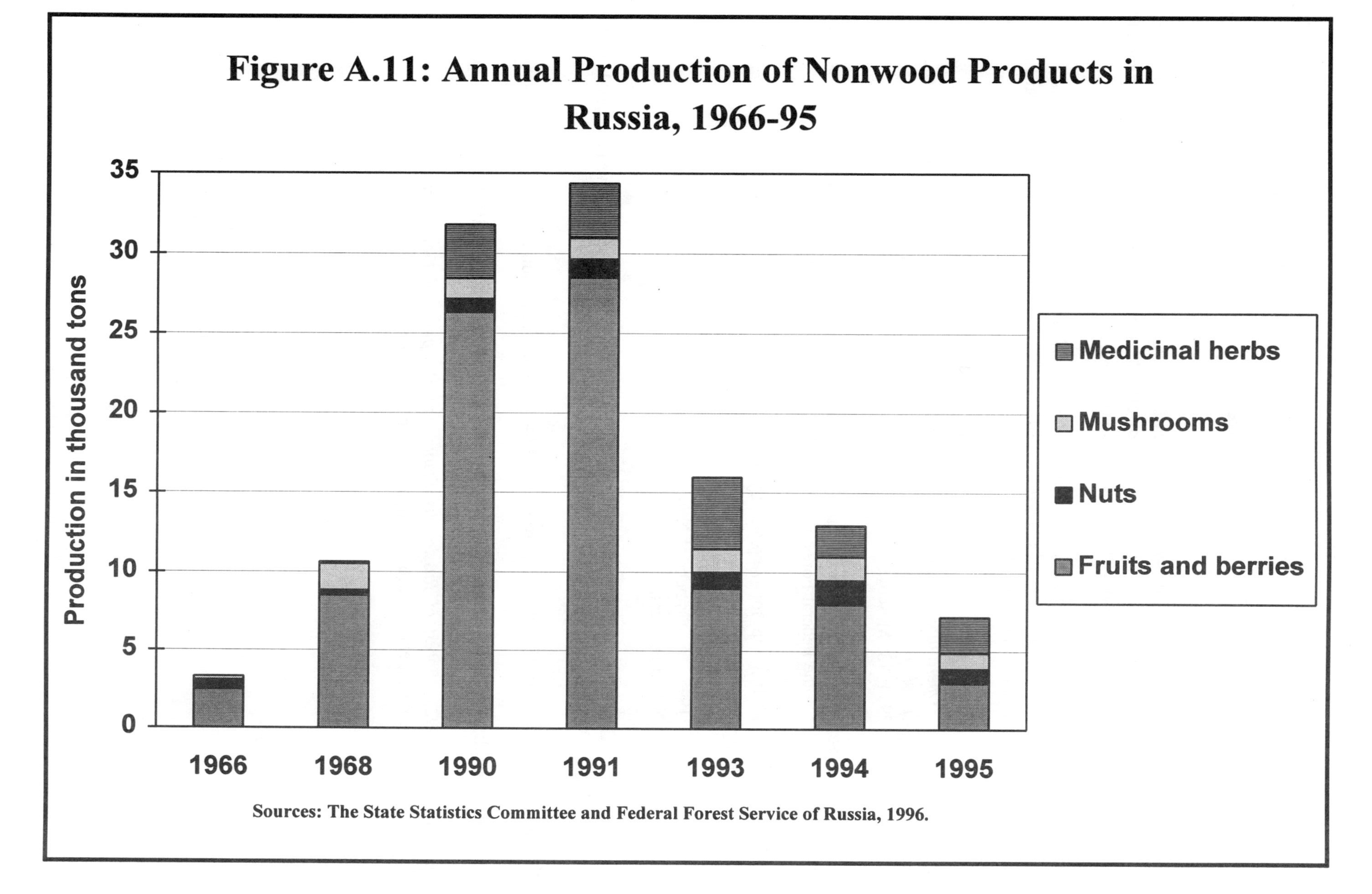

Sources: The State Statistics Committee and Federal Forest Service of Russia, 1996.

References

Federal Forest Service. 1993. *Commercial Cutting Rules in the Forests of Western Siberia (Pravila rubok glavnogo polzovaniya v lesakh Zapadnoy Sibiri).* Approved by the order of the Federal Forest Service of Russia on October 29, 1993, Moscow.

Federal Forest Service. 1993. *Commercial Cutting Rules in the Forests of the Far East (Pravila rubok glavnogo polzovaniya v lesakh Dalnego Vostoka).* Approved by the order of the Federal Forest Service of Russia on July 30, 1993. Moscow.

Federal Forest Service. 1993. *Silvicultural Requirements To Technological Processes in Forest Harvesting Operations (Lesovodstvennye trebovaniya k tekhnologicheskim protsessam lesosechnykh rabot).* Approved by the order of the Federal Forest Service of Russia on November 29, 1993. Moscow.

Federal Forest Service. 1994. *Forest Inventory Instruction (Lesoustroitelnaya instruktsiya).* Approved by the order of the Federal Forest Service of Russia on December 15, 1994. Moscow.

IIASA (International Institute for Applied Systems Analysis). 1995. *Siberian Forest Study.* Laxenburg, Austria: IIASA.

Obydennikov, V.I. 1995. Assessment of Natural Regeneration of Forests After Commercial Cutting. Moscow, VNIITsLesresurs.

Pisarenko, A.I., G.I. Redko, and M.D.Merzlenko. 1992. Artificial Forests (Iskusstvennye Lesa), In 2 volumes. Moscow.

State Report on the Status of Natural Environment of the Russian Federation in 1995. Moscow, 1996.

State Report on the Status of Natural Environment of the Russian Federation in 1994. Moscow, 1995.

Tatarinov, V.P.1992. *Forest of Russia. Its Status and Prospects of Development.* (Les Rossii. Sostoyaniye i perspektivy yego razvitiya.), Moscow, VNIPIEIlesprom.

Annex B

Institutional Framework for the Forest Sector

Institutional Background

In the former Soviet Union, forests were owned and managed by the territorial offices of the federal Ministry of Forestry and the federal Ministry of Wood Processing and Pulp and Paper Industry. Although remnants of the old centralized structures remain, no single agency has emerged as a clear leader capable of restructuring the forest sector to promote sustainable development.

The federal Government of Russia has direct control of forest management and conservation through the Federal Forest Service (FFS) and the newly established State Committee for Environmental Protection (previously the Ministry of Environmental Protection and Natural Resources). As part of the privatization program, the government has divested its operational control over forest industries, setting up Roslesprom, a stated-owned national timber industry holding company. At present, the federal government pursues forest industrial policies and maintains its control over forest enterprises through the management of state-owned shares entrusted in the State Committee for Forest Industry (Goskomlesprom). Responsibility for game and wildlife management, agro-forestry, and shelterbelts is with the Ministry of Agriculture and Food. The Russian Academy of Sciences and several specialized institutions of the State Committee for Science and Technologies and of the Ministry of Education complement the capabilities of the institutes, laboratories, and colleges of the Federal Forest Service and the State Committee for Environmental Protection in fundamental and applied forest research, education, training, and human resource development.

The Ministry of Finance is no longer active in the forest industry since this now privatized sector of the economy receives little federal budget appropriations. However, about half of forest management operations (45 percent in 1995 and 48 percent in 1996 planned) are still funded through the federal budget (see Table B.1 and Figures B.1 and B.2). The Ministry of Economy deals with the forest sector as a whole, through a department that monitors performance and coordinates the development of federal programs and policies for the sector. However, this ministry has no sectorwide executive authority, giving rise to a fundamental gap between top-level political decisionmaking and sectoral line management that leaves many key issues unattended or unresolved.

The Principles of Forest Legislation of the Russian Federation of March 1993 and the draft Forest Code reflect the controversies arising during the transition from the centrally planned and managed system of the former Soviet Union to a loose confederation of subnational constituencies in Russia (republics, krays, oblasts, autonomous oblasts, and okrugs). The unresolved division of responsibilities and poorly defined budgetary authorities of these different levels of government lead to conflict as these subnational entities seek to codify their own forest laws and regulations. In the absence of tight federal control, the subnational entities have largely assumed the leadership role in the development of their forest resources.

Table B.1: Forest Management Operations Budget, 1985-96
(millions of rubles)

Current expenditures and revenues	*1985*	*1986*	*1987*	*1988*	*1989*	*1990*	*1991*	*1992*	*1993*	*1994*	*1995*	*1996*
Forest inventory	33	33	33	34	34	38	56	633	7182	35034	51418	79436
Aerial forest fire control	69	76	75	83	66	74	129	2289	21832	105602	238231	416902
Project development	7	6	6	6	6	10	23	174	2553	10000	25309	31047
Forestry operations	138	133	133	137	131	165	293	3205	30109	91384	269167	350000
Forest pest control	4	4	3	3	3	4	7	63	682	4284	19901	32000
Forest amelioration/drainage	13	9	8	9	6	5	9	73	1080	9880	3810	4953
Forest regeneration	93	86	85	86	78	100	170	1821	19531	74903	138895	184730
Ground forest fire control	34	35	37	41	34	40	73	1036	21257	34467	85913	158000
Agricultural afforestation	7	7	7	8	8	7	10	67	1062	9018	17663	13000
Transport services (to customers)	5	4	5	5	4	4	7	49	449	340	8079	11300
Overhead (safety / training)	45	44	46	46	61	61	110	4361	24208	104968	239946	335924
Forest management staff	204	197	199	206	193	206	510	5451	10044	380831	804509	496304
Total expenditures	**634**	**635**	**636**	**662**	**624**	**714**	**1399**	**19365**	**225363**	**897476**	**1976598**	**2633800**
Federal budget	439	445	446	478	448	521	1080	12978	156661	658060	881640	1269541
Retained earnings of leskhozes	158	155	155	150	143	160	305	3594	34817	145200	653921	830771
Timber sales	37	35	35	34	33	33	3	17	0	2171	4781	5600
Regional budget	-	-	-	-	-	-	11	1564	24326	55592	195801	198285
Total budget	**634**	**635**	**636**	**662**	**624**	**714**	**1399**	**18153**	**215804**	**861023**	**1736143**	**2304197**
Operating losses	**-**	**-**	**-**	**-**	**-**	**-**	**-**	**(1212)**	**(9559)**	**(36453)**	**(240455)**	**(329603)**

Source: The Federal Forest Service of Russia, 1996.

Figure B.1: The Structure of Forestry Funding Sources in Russia, 1985-96

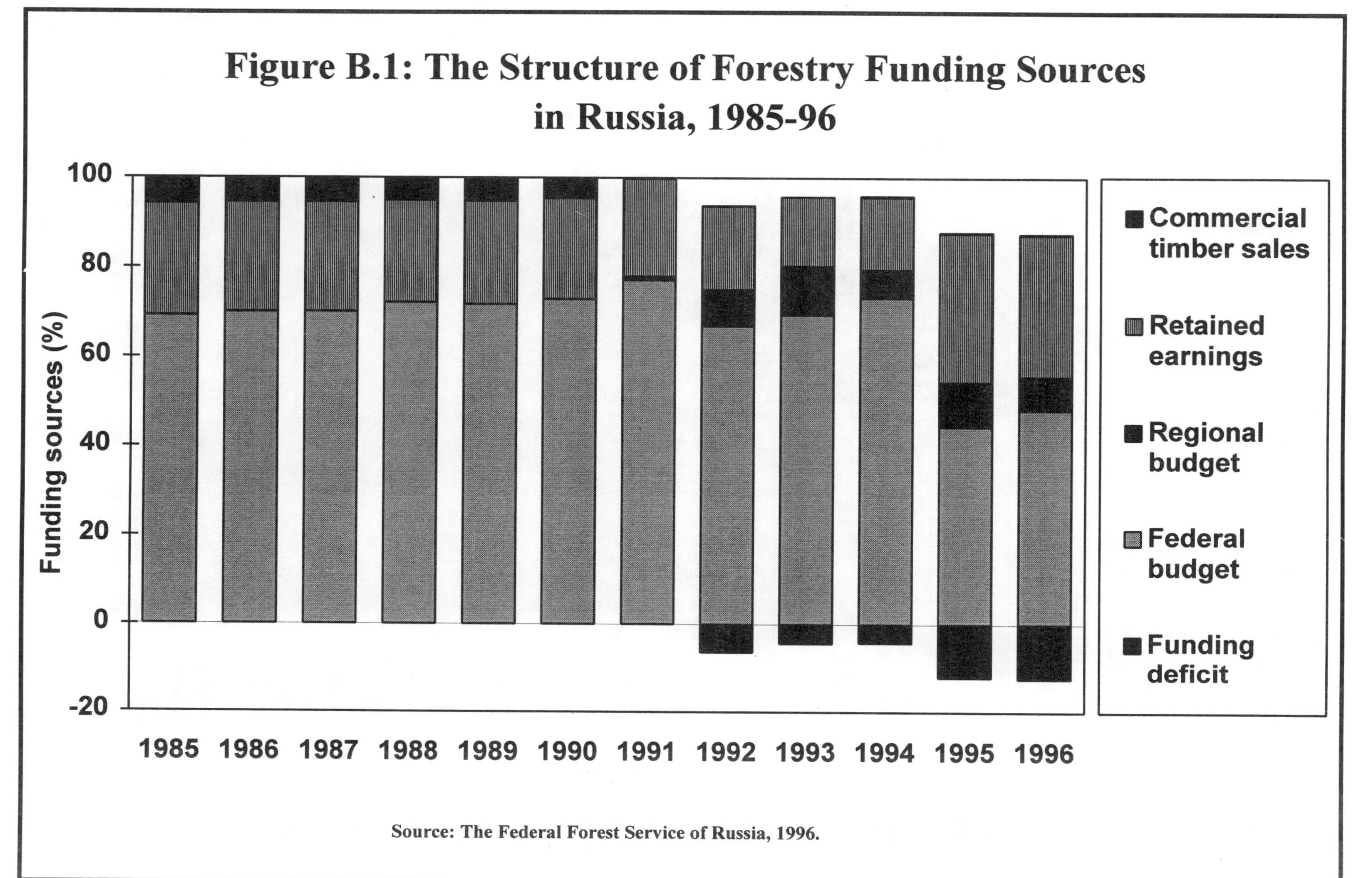

Source: The Federal Forest Service of Russia, 1996.

Figure B.2: The Structure of Forestry Operating Costs in Russia, 1985-96

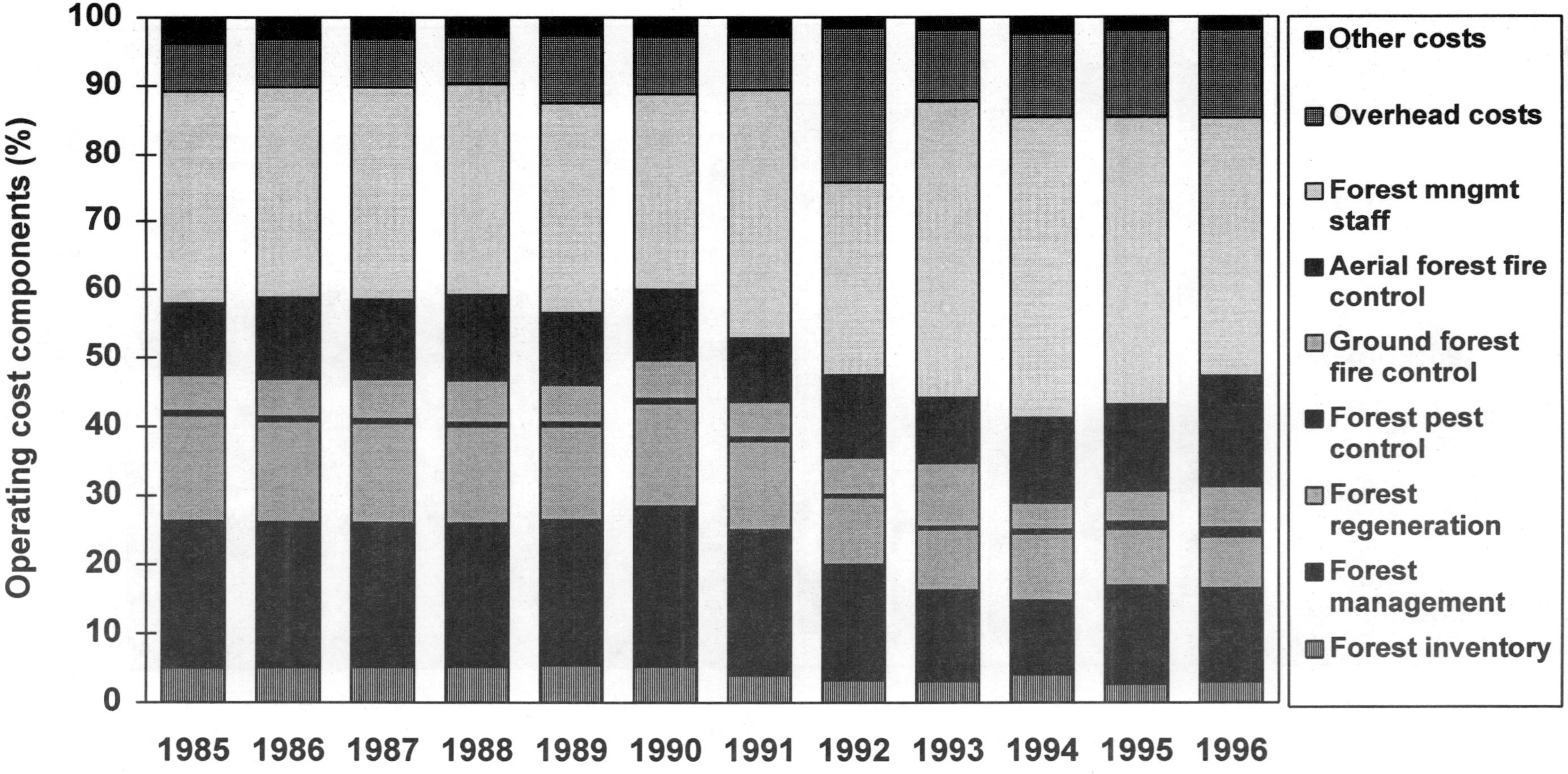

Operating cost components (%)

100
90
80
70
60
50
40
30
20
10
0

1985 1986 1987 1988 1989 1990 1991 1992 1993 1994 1995 1996

Other costs
Overhead costs
Forest mngmt staff
Aerial forest fire control
Ground forest fire control
Forest pest control
Forest regeneration
Forest management
Forest inventory

Source: The Federal Forest Service of Russia, 1996.

These subnational entities have declared sovereignty over the natural resources within their borders, a declaration that is in direct conflict with the "joint management" of "nationally owned" forests, as mandated by the Constitution (see Annex C for details).

Institutional arrangements differ widely among these subnational entities. In export-oriented Khabarovsk Kray, commercial forest users have already become more diversified in their activities and their form of ownership. The Kray Commission on Forest Utilization, created in December 1994 is charged with handling matters related to forest lease allocations. It consists of representatives of the Federal Forest Service, the kray administration, other kray agencies such as the Environmental Protection Committee, the Game Management Department, the Antitrust Department, and the State Property Fund, along with representatives of the timber industry and forest research groups.

Krasnoyarsk Kray (see Figure B.4 later) has also established a Forest Committee, which is charged with making all decisions on forest resources allocation. The committee reports both to the Kray administration and to the Federal Forest Service. Through an advisory board (a collegium), the committee coordinates its activities with the Kray-level agencies for environmental protection, land management, game and fisheries management, and water management. In addition, it assumes responsibility for contracting out certain forest management functions to federally operated forest fire control bases, forest inventory enterprises, forest research institutes, and a technical academy.

Agencies Dealing with the Forest Sector

Under central planning, forest sector management of the former USSR was based on territorial and sectoral principles. At the center of the forest industry structure was the Ministry of Forest, Pulp and Paper, and Woodworking Industries, supported by territorial and production associations at the regional level. The forest management system was headed by the State Forest Committee, regional committees and departments at the territorial level, and Ministries of Forestry at the Republic level.

With the reform of the late 1980s, management of the forest sector changed considerably. The State Forest Committee was reorganized into the Federal Forest Service. In 1991, the Ministry of Forest, Pulp and Paper and Woodworking Industries was abolished. Since then agencies dealing with forest industry have undergone several reorganizations, as described in the following sections.

Federal Forest Service

The Federal Forest Service (FFS) would be 200 years old in 1998. The organizational structure of the Federal Forest Service is shown in Figure B.3. Figure B.4 shows how the Federal Forest Service, regional administrations (with Krasnoyarsk Kray administration, as an example), forest managers, and forest users interact. The FFS has eighty-one regional bodies (ministries, committees, and administrations) representing its interests throughout the Russian Federation. Each regional body has a similar structure and functions; they are referred to as regional committees on forests in this report. These committees are responsible for forest management and protection across the Russian Federation for 1,740 forest management units (*leskhoz*), and 8,000 forest compartments or ranges (*lesnichestvo*). There are also several other forest-related entities that are subordinate to the FFS, including forest planning and inventory enterprises, forest research institutes, and training units.

Figure B.3: Organization of the Federal Forest Service of Russia

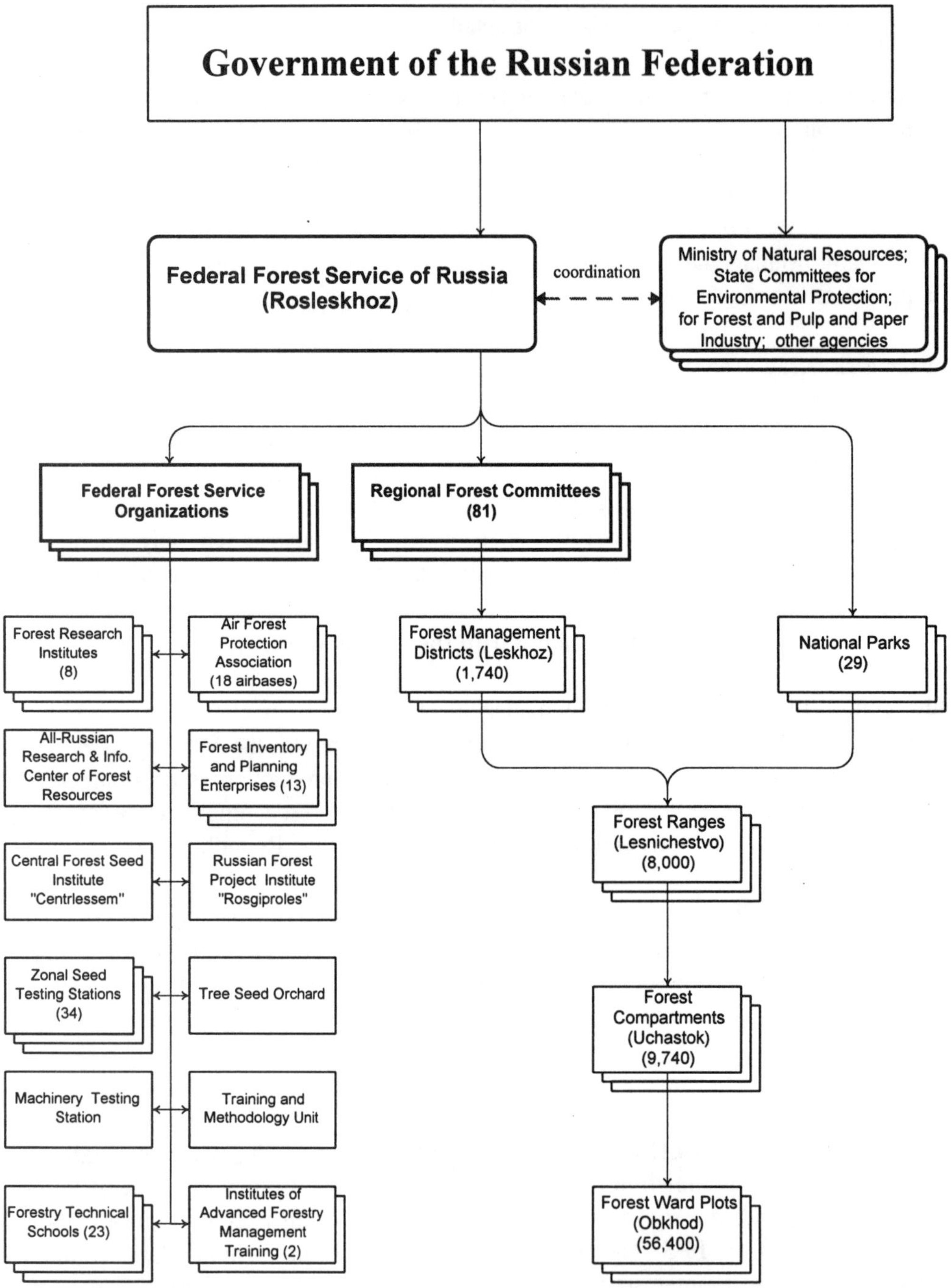

Source: The Federal Forest Service of Russia, 1996.

Figure B.4: Institutional Framework of Forest Management in Krasnoyarsk Kray

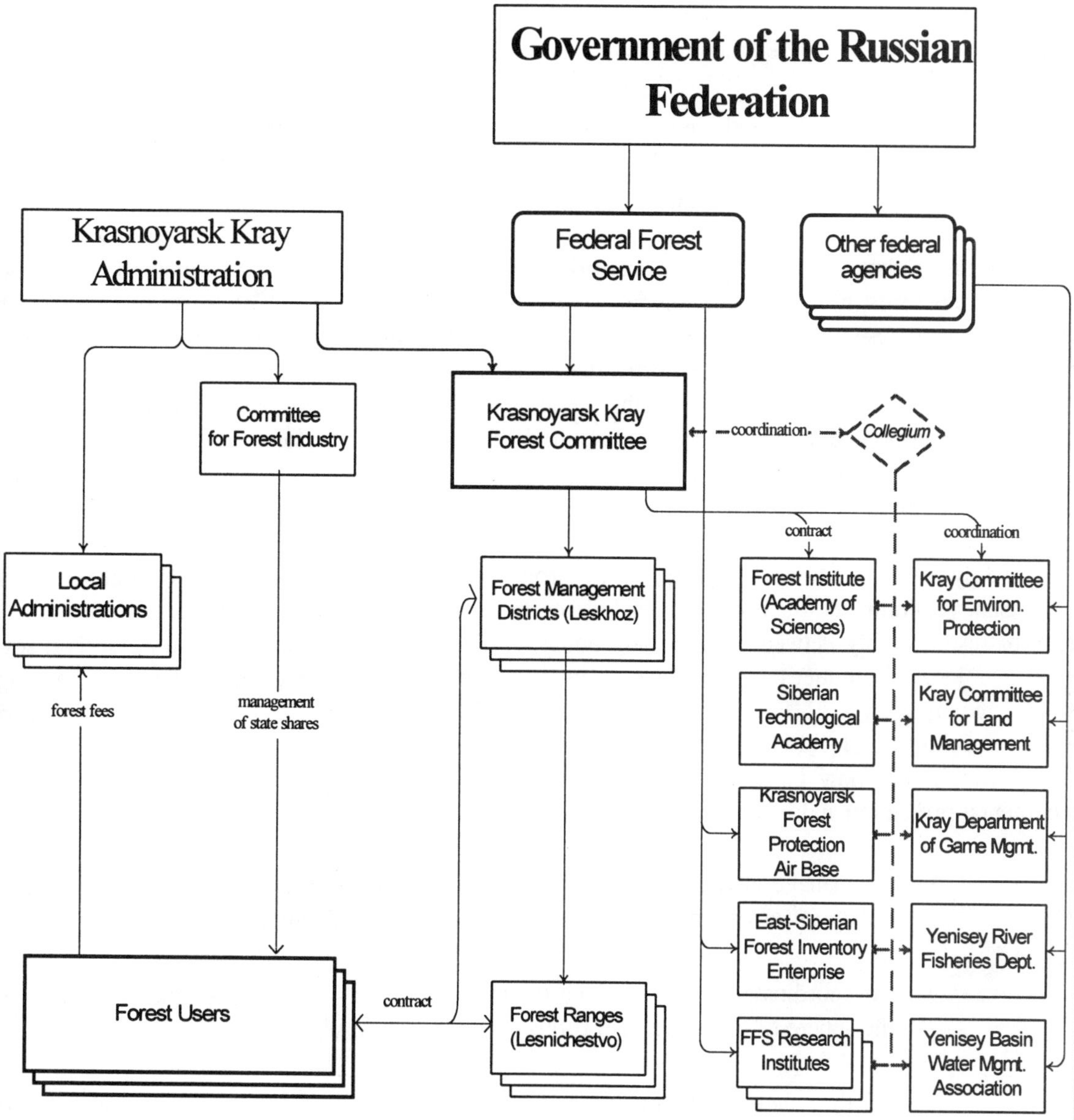

Source: Krasnoyarsk Kray Forest Committee, 1995.

The FFS is responsible for interregional and intersectoral coordination and regulation of forest utilization, international cooperation, and training. Its responsibilities for the planning and management of economic activities are being transferred to the regional and local levels. The principal functions of the FFS in the area of environmental protection and natural resource utilization are:

- To establish federal policy on utilization, regeneration, and protection of forests and forest management development.
- To ensure sustainable forest utilization and the conservation of the forest's wealth and to strengthen the protective, hydrological, recreational, and other functions of forests.
- To develop and improve ecological methods pertaining to forest management.
- To develop and implement state forest management programs.

The forest planning and inventory enterprises (see Table A.2 in Annex A) conduct inventories and produce ten-year forest management plans for each leskhoz (see Annex A). The forest research institutes conduct theoretical research and are involved in direct application of forest management principles. For example, research institutes prepare the norms that forest planning and inventory enterprises are to follow and establish the methodology for determining the annual allowable cut. Research institutes prepare legal forest management-related documents initiated by the FFS or one of its regional committees.

State Committee for Environmental Protection

In July 1996, the former Ministry of Environmental Protection and Natural Resources was split into the State Committee for Environmental Protection and the Ministry of Natural Resources. The division of responsibility between them is still being worked out. The former Ministry also had several regional and local committees representing its interests throughout the Russian Federation (see Figure B.5). Of the ministry's 21,174 employees, as of January 1, 1994, 9,443 were employed in various regional committees and 1,255 in research institutes. The principal functions of the former Ministry (some of which will now be carried out by the State Committee for Environmental Protection) in environmental protection and natural resource utilization were:

- To manage environmental protection and to ensure a unified scientific and technical policy for environmental protection and resource utilization.
- To coordinate ministries, departments, enterprises, institutions, and organizations in the sphere of environmental protection and natural resources.
- To formulate the normative and methodological basis for environmental protection, resource utilization regulation, and ecological security.
- To establish a unified system of ecological monitoring.
- To organize and conduct state environmental impact assessments.

Figure B.5: Organization of the Former Ministry of Environmental Protection and Natural Resources of the Russian Federation

* Note: Following the Government restructuring in August 1996, the MEPNR and the Committees for Geology and Water Management were abolished and replaced by two new federal agencies - the Ministry of Natural Resources and the State Committee for Environmental Protection. As of October 1996, distribution of functions between the two new agencies was not yet announced.

Source: The Former Ministry of Environmental Protection and Natural Resources of the Russian Federation, 1996.

- To organize and implement state control in environmental protection and natural resource utilization and to ensure compliance with environmental safety norms.

- To provide appropriate environmental information to the public.

- To organize and manage the zapovednikis and the Red Book of the Russian Federation.

- To meet Russia's obligations to international organizations, participate in international agreements, and collaborate with international organizations in natural resource protection and environmental management.

- To develop and effectively utilize the material and technical support of the regional committees and other organizations subordinate to the former Ministry of Environmental Protection and Natural Resources.

The regional committees have many of the same functions at the subnational levels. They are also responsible for a network of interdistrict Committees on Nature Protection, which conduct inspections and punish offenders.

State Committee for Forest Industry

The management structure of the forest industry sectors of Russia has been undergoing continuous change. In 1993, the Russian Forest Industry Company (Roslesprom) was established in accordance with the decision of the State Committee for Management of State Property of the Russian Federation to manage the forest industry sector. Later, it was made a state company by Presidential decree. Roslesprom participated in the decisionmaking process of federal bodies on problems relating to the forest industry sectors; worked out measures for the development of forest industry export potential; directed the use of the sector's extrabudgetary fund for financing scientific research; contributed suggestions for differentiating property rights; and helped work out the sector's tariff and other agreements, together with trade unions and other organizations.

Following privatization of nearly 90 percent of logging, woodworking, and pulp and paper enterprises, new holding companies were established to replace the former system of management. Organized as open-end joint stock companies holding blocks of shares of subsidiary enterprises, holding companies have the right to engage in investment activities. Holding companies influence the activity of subsidiary enterprises through their participation in shareholders meetings.

At the beginning of 1996, there were about fifty forest industry holding companies accounting for over one-third of the total volume of unprocessed timber production, one-fourth of sawn timber production, and 61 percent of pulp production. Efficiency has been low in many of the holding companies, and there are few holding companies operating in high chemical wood processing, a sector where demand has been relatively stable. Financial and production groups are being established, combining technological enterprises, commercial banks, investment funds, and other financial organizations.

Roslesprom was not successful as a state managerial body, largely because it was not a true federal body. It remained a commercial organization in many respects and was unable to perform many functions assigned to it. Thus, for example, enterprises stopped transferring resources to the extrabudgetary fund for financing scientific research, so Roslesprom had no funds for working out scientific and technical issues. Its low status kept Roslesprom from being able to protect the interests of the forest and forest industry sectors in such important spheres as taxes and credit. A number of laws and regulations affecting the sector's activity were adopted that ignored the interests of the forest industry.

To improve management of the forest industry sector at the federal level, the State Committee for Forest, Pulp and Paper, and Woodworking Industries (Goskomlesprom) was established in June 1996 by Presidential decree and was vested with functions in conformity with requirements of a market economy (see Figure B.6). All Roslemprom's functions were transferred to Goskomlesprom. Roslesprom will remain a small commercial organization or will be transformed into a joint stock company, with the controlling block of shares owned by the state. Unlike Roslemprom, which had been essentially a commercial organization, Goskomlesprom is a full-fledged federal managerial body within the executive branch. Goskomlesprom has a staff of about 150.

In establishing Goskomlesprom, the Government acknowledged the important role of the forest industry sector in the Russian economy. Its main objective is to promote the efficient operation of the forest industry sector by:

- Resolving the key organizational, economic, and financial problems affecting the operation of forest enterprises, including the protection of their interests in the executive and legislative branches.

- Establishing programs for the structural reform of the forest sector, to increase its efficiency, and ensure the further growth of production of competitive products.

- Establishing a unified scientific and technical policy for developing priority lines of machinery and technological processes and supporting forest machine building plants.

- Promoting domestic and foreign investments in the forest sector.

- Suggesting ways to develop foreign economic activity, including cooperation with the countries of the Commonwealth of Independent States (CIS).

- Working out, together with trade unions, tariff and other agreements related to economic and social protection of the interests of people employed in the forest and forest industry sectors.

- Preparing short- and long-term forecasts for the forest sector.

Figure B.6: Organization of the State Committee for Forest, Pulp and Paper and Woodworking Industry of the Russian Federation

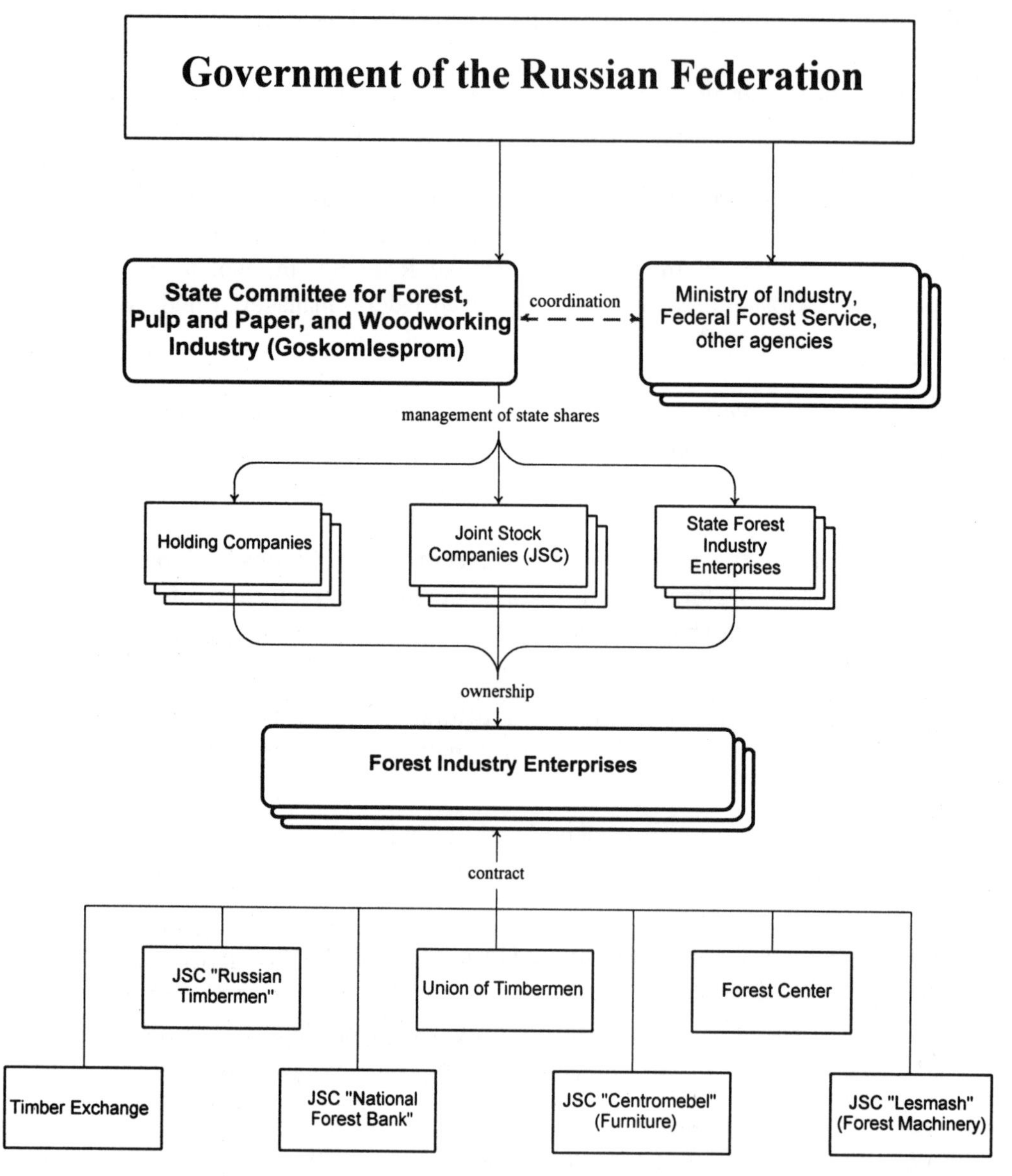

Source: Goskomlesprom of Russia, 1996.

Federal Programs in the Forest Sector

Fire Control

A state Program of Forest Fire Control for 1993-97 was approved in mid-1993, with the following priorities:

- Strengthening aerial and ground fire control services (see Table A.3 in Annex A) and creating new units for the early detection and fighting of forest fires.
- Establishing specialized ground fire-fighting units in forest regions equipped with cross-country fire engines on all-terrain towing vehicles.
- Developing an airborne tanker fleet for aerial fire fighting.
- Developing and implementing a new satellite system of forest fire monitoring and an integrated system of forest fire detection.
- Creating a computerized information and communications network for forest fire control units.

Emphasis will be given to research and development activities and to the conversion of military technologies to civilian applications. Resource will be allocated to various forest regions according to the national significance and valuation of the resources, their ecological functions, the wfrequency of fire occurrence, and the economic development of each region relative to the others. This program anticipates protecting 770 million hectares of forests through land-based divisions and specialized aerial services.

Forest Regeneration

The State Program of Forest Regeneration for 1993-95, endorsed by the government in mid-1993, was intended to establish organizational and financial measures to aid in developing the material and technical requirements for reforestation. These are to include the utilization of genetically improved forest seeds and seedlings and the introduction of progressive technologies for forest plantation. In forest-abundant areas, emphasis is to be given to improving species composition and assisted natural regeneration, including the conservation of undergrowth and seed-generating stands of commercially valuable species. The forest regeneration activities were to take place, on an area of 1.33 million hectares, of which 400,000 hectares are to be directly planted or sown. However, actual funding for the program was significantly delayed and the main activities were later incorporated into another federal program, "Forests of Russia (1996-2000)" which has not yet been approved.

Development of the Forest Industrial Complex

The Forest Industrial Complex Development Program was adopted by the Government in November 1995. This program is intended to integrate the utilization of timber resources, improve the quality and competitiveness of pulp and paper products, and reduce the harmful environmental effects of the logging and wood-processing industries. Priority is to be given to the development of processing facilities within forest-abundant regions, to eliminate the need to transport raw materials over long distances at great expense. Investments in this program will come mainly from industry, with only about 20 percent contributions coming from federal and local budgets. The public sector contribution may come through reduced taxes or temporary tax benefits, the revision of rail tariffs, or soft credits for seasonal logging and wood processing.

The program's objectives for the logging industry include the creation of a sustainable resource base for timber harvesting through intensified silvicultural management, the introduction of modern logging technologies, increased processing of soft deciduous and low-value wood near logging areas, and the construction of new forest roads in areas where operations are hampered by climatic conditions. Objectives for the milling and wood-processing industries include modernization of facilities for the transition to the production of higher-quality, humidity-controlled sawnwood; the technological upgrading of particle-board and furniture manufacturing facilities; and the construction of new facilities for the manufacturing of prefabricated housing units.

State Scientific-Technical Program "Russian Forest"

The most comprehensive environmental program in the Russian Federation is outlined in the National Environmental Action Plan (NEAP), which was developed through the participation of ministries, departments, and subjects of the Russian Federation and reviewed by interdepartmental committees. The plan is a far-reaching proposal to improve the health of the environment in Russia. Among the programs under the NEAP that focus on the forest sector are Forest Regeneration, Protecting Forests from Fires, and the Russian Forest, an environmentally oriented program under the authority of the State Committee of Science and Technologies.

The Russian Forest program, approved in September 1993, has four focus areas: forest rehabilitation and forestation, forest utilization and economics, forest fire protection, and forest monitoring and protection. Its objective is to improve the environmental and economic returns from the Russian forest sector, while giving a boost to research institutions by strengthening them financially.

The Russian Forest program addresses a broad range of interdisciplinary forest issues through institutional collaboration. The lead implementation organizations have already been identified and their roles defined (Table B.2). Among the broad cross-section of institutions targeted for participation in the Russian Forest program are various institutes of the Russian Academy of Sciences, Federal Forest Service institutes, and forest industry associations. This program, which is to be financed largely through the federal budget, reflects priorities for the forest sector as perceived by the Russian authorities.

None of the programs mentioned here has received full funding, and some have received no more than 20 percent. As a result, the programs are not being implemented as intended. Implementation is well behind schedule. It is critical that these programs receive appropriate funding. Research institutes across Russia are also suffering financially whatever their source of funding. Their budgets have been cut back to a minimum, and many have been forced to close or to turn to shorter work weeks. Those that have survived are engaged in a constant struggle to keep their best researchers.

Table B.2: Priority Forest Sector Activities as Articulated in the State Scientific-Technical Program of "Russian Forest"

Project activity	*Lead implementation organizations*
	1. Rehabilitation and Forestation
1.1 Elaboration of long-term programs for improving the genetic and silvicultural state of Russia's forests	- Research Institute of Forest Genetics and Selection - Institute of Ecological Nature complex, Siberian Division, Russian Academy of Sciences (RAS) - Arkhangelsk Institute of Forestry and Forest Chemistry - Institute of Silviculture, RAS - St. Petersburg Forest Technical Academy - International Institute of forestry
1.2 Elaboration of a genetic-selection basis for industrial plantations and forest regeneration	- Moscow State University of Forestry - Scientific-Production Association on Nut Management - St. Petersburg Research Institute of Forest Management - St. Petersburg Forest Technical Academy
1.3 Elaboration of the most efficient measures for natural regeneration	- Arkhangelsk Institute of Forestry and Forest Chemistry - Arkhangelsk Forest Technical Institute - St. Petersburg Forest Technical Academy - Institute of Forestry of Karelian Scientific Centre, RAS - St. Petersburg Research Institute of Forest Management
1.4 Creation of a rational system of regeneration, forestation, and reconstruction of less valuable species on a zonal-topological basis	- St. Petersburg Research Institute of Forest Management - Silversk Scientific Production Forest Trial Station - All-Russian Research Institute of Forest Fire Protection and mechanization of Forest Management. - Moscow State University of Forestry - Far East Forest Research Institute - Voronezh Forest Technical Institute - Central Trial Office of Forest Management Machines - St. Petersburg Forest Technical Academy - All-Russian Research Institute of Forest Management Mechanization - Russian Forest Scientific-Technical Association - Siberian Technological Institute - Karelian Research Institute of Forest Industry

Table continued on the next page

Table B.2: Priority Forest Sector Activities as Articulated in The State Scientific-Technical Program of "Russian Forest" (Contd.)

Project activity	*Lead implementation organizations*
	2. Forest Utilization and Economics
2.1 Elaboration of an integrated forest utilization plan meeting the conservation and nature protection functions of forests	- All-Russian Research Institute of Forest Management and its Mechanization - All-Russian Scientific Production Association of the Forest Industry - Moscow State University of Forestry - All-Russian Research and Planning Institute of Economics, Organization of Production Management, and Information in the Forest, Wood-Processing, and the Pulp and Paper Industry
2.2 Elaboration of an integrated system of forest management for market economy conditions	- All-Russian Research Institute of Forest Management and its Mechanization - Moscow State University of Forestry - Institute of State and Law, RAS - St. Petersburg Research Institute of Forest Management - St. Petersburg Forest Technical Academy - All-Russian Scientific Production Association of the Forest Industry - Institute of State and Law, RAS
2.3 Elaboration of scientific principles and creation of a system of multi-use, rational forest utilization, under the principles of sustainability	- Institute of Forest Management, RAS - Far East Forest Research Institute - All-Russian Research Institute of Forest Management and Mechanization - All-Russian Research Information Center on Forest Resources - Moscow State University of Forestry - Institute of Forestry, Karelian Scientific Centre, RAS - Voronezh Forest Technical Institute - Institute of Ecological Nature Complex, Siberian Division, RAS - Arkhangelsk Institute of Forestry and Forest Chemistry - Kostroma Forest Trial Station - Siberian Technological Institute - All-Russian Scientific Production Association of the Forest Industry - Research Institute of Mountain Forest Management and Forest Ecology
2.4 Elaboration of technology and machines for forest thinnings and logging	- All-Russian Scientific Production Association of the Forest Industry - Dalmatovskii Mill "Start" - Central Trial Office of Forest Management Machines - All-Russian Research Institute of Forest Management and Mechanization

Table continued on the next page

Table B.2: Priority Forest Sector Activities as Articulated in The State Scientific-Technical Program of "Russian Forest" (Contd.)

Project activity	*Lead implementation organizations*
3. Forest Fire Protection	
3.1 Creation of an optimal fire fighting system	- St. Petersburg Research Institute of Forest Management - All-Russian Research Institute of Transportation Vehicles - Siberian Technological Institute - International Institute of Forestry - Centre of Ecological Problems and Productivity of Forests, RAS - Institute of Forestry of the Siberian Division, RAS - All-Russian Research Institute of Forest Fire Protection and Mechanization of Forest Management
4. Monitoring and Protection	
4.1 Elaboration of a scientific, methodological and technological basis for forest monitoring	- International Institute of Forestry - Institute of Forestry of the Siberian Division, RAS - All-Russian Research Institute of Forest Management and Mechanization - Moscow State University of Forestry - St. Petersburg Forest Technical Academy - Urals Forest Technical Institute
4.2 Study of the effects of technical pollution on forests and elaboration of preventative measures to increase forest sustainability	- Institute of Forestry, Karelian Scientific Centre, RAS - Moscow State University of Forestry - St. Petersburg Research Institute of Forest Management - All-Russian Research Institute of Forest Management and Mechanization - All-Russian Research Institute of Chemical Applications in Forest Management - Centre of Ecological Problems and Productivity of Forests, RAS
4.3 Establishment of forest management system for forest utilization in radioactive pollution conditions	- All-Russian Research Institute of Chemical Applications in Forest Management - Tomsk State University "Fire and Ecology" - Briansk Technological Institute
4.4 Elaboration of a methodological basis for evaluating the role of forests in global carbon cycles	- Institute of Forest Management, RAS - Institute of Forestry, Karelian Scientific Centre - St. Petersburg Forest Technical Academy - Institute of Biology, Komi Scientific Centre, RAS - Institute of Botany, Komi Scientific Centre, RAS
4.5 Elaboration of a scientific basis for forecasting and control of forest insect outbreaks	- Centre of Ecological Problems and Problems and Productivity of Forests, RAS - Moscow State University of Forestry - All-Russian Research Institute of Forest Management and Mechanization - Research Institute of Mountain Forest Management and Forest Ecology - St. Petersburg Forest Technical Academy

Source: The Federal Forest Service of Russia.

It is hoped that the Russian Forest program will foster the creation of a permanent network of forest and environmentally oriented institutes. Institutions now tend to work on similar subjects in isolation from one another, so the program would improve institutional synergy. Adding environmental NGOs to the institutional mix could also significantly strengthen the environmental impact of the Russian Forest program.

Forestry Education, Training, and Research

Some 238,000 public sector employees work in the Russian forestry sector (as of January 1, 1996), which is less than 0.4 percent of the labor force in Russia. Of the one-quarter (66,000 people) who hold management-level positions, 37 percent have a university-level education and 51 percent have secondary specialized (college level) education. Among foresters in other positions about 2 percent have higher education and 16 percent have secondary specialized education.

Primary and College Education

The Russian educational system was reorganized during the 1980s. Beginning at age 7 (first grade), children receive 8 years of comprehensive mandatory, mostly state-supported schooling (some children start at zero grade at age six). Students can then choose to go directly into the work force or to continue their education by taking short-term (from several months to 1 year) courses in many businesses or go on to secondary school (3 more years), vocational school or college (3-4 more years). After secondary school, vocational school, or college students may go on to a university (institute, academy). It usually takes from 5 to 7 years to obtain a diploma of engineer or a Master of Science degree, and 3 more years to get a Ph.D. degree.

Before the 1930s, forest regeneration and other work was done by seasonal workers (peasants of nearby villages, mostly women and children). After state forestry enterprises were established, and Russia began to invest in field forest stations (especially beginning 1947), many permanent workers were hired. In 1960, about 57,000 people worked in forestry (planting, pest control, timber management) and were paid through the national budget; another 112,000 people worked for profit (pre-commercial cutting, thinning, logging and other industries). In the 1990s, about 15,000-20,000 people were trained annually as qualified forest workers. Today, only about 2,200 qualified workers are trained annually for forestry. There are 22 consulting locations throughout Russia for this purpose (Teplyakov 1994).

Secondary forestry education was established in 1925-30. By the mid-1950s, there were 16 forestry secondary schools with 1,140 students; today there are only 3 (with 2,950 students). Forestry schools provide basic training in forestry and forest industry field jobs and forestry machines and intensive courses in tree marking, thinning, felling, and other forest-related working skills.

Forestry colleges ("leskhoz-tekhnikum") were established as a part of the reorganization of the forestry education system in the 1920s. Currently, there are 23 forestry colleges in Russia, only three of them east of the Urals (Novosibirsk Oblast, Altay Kray, and Khabarovsk Kray). Eighteen forestry colleges implement pilot forestry projects on about 500,000 hectares of forest lands. In 1996, there were 9,500 full-time students and 5,900 part-time students enrolled in forestry colleges. Enrollment by specialization is as follows:

Specialization	*Enrollment*
Forestry and Urban Forestry	2,910
Forestry Economics and Accounting	700
Felling Technology	30
Wood Processing Technology	150
Forestry Machinery and Equipment	250

Forestry colleges are dependent on diminishing funding from the federal budget. The Federal Program of Secondary Forestry Education for the Federal Forest Service of Russia (1996-2000) was developed to improve the situation for the professional training of foresters. But with major arrears in budget allocations, almost all the funds received go to wages; even regular facility maintenance and utility bills remain unpaid.

Higher Education and Advanced Training

In 1993, Russian ***forestry higher education*** celebrated its 190th anniversary. At present, forestry, timber industry, and pulp and paper industry specialists are trained in about 40 institutes, including forest engineering (technical) schools, polytechnics, technological institutes, universities, and academies. Training is provided in 15 areas of specialization, such as forestry, urban forestry and landscape gardening, forest engineering, wood treatment technology, chemical and mechanical technology of wood and wood materials, forest machinery and logging equipment, and forest economics (Oblivin 1992).

A typical curriculum offers a 5-year training program, with an average of 30 hours of class work per week during a 10-month academic year. Programs used to include up to two months of extensive professional field training throughout the country. However, attendance at such field activities has declined dramatically in recent years because of prohibitively high travel costs and severe economic pressure on students to seek summer jobs instead of unpaid field training activities.

An intensive 3-year university program is available for those who have finished forestry college and have practical experience in forest-related areas. Employers pay the salary of employees attending the program. Graduates usually come back to their institution and are promoted to higher positions (director, manager, or senior specialist).

Advanced training exists in several forms. Teachers and highly qualified researchers are trained through postgraduate and doctorate programs. Nearly every institute has a department in which foresters can update their knowledge and professional skills. There is also a specialized All-Russian Institute for Advanced Training of Forest Managers and Specialists (VIPKLH), located in Pushkino near Moscow. The institute reports directly to the Federal Forest Service. Its highly qualified faculty, also conducts research in forest administration, management, and economics. Another institute was established in Divnogorsk, near Krasnoyarsk, to offer advanced training to forest managers and specialists in Siberia and the Far East.

Forest Research

With over 200 years of forest management experience, Russia is a recognized leader in forest scientific research and development. Scientific institutes of the Federal Forest Service alone conduct research in eleven subject areas, including silviculture and forest ecology (42 percent of the total number of projects), mechanization (18 percent), forestry economics and accounting (8.5 percent), and forest inventory (8 percent).

The system of forest research institutions has always been well developed in Russia. It includes a federally funded system of Federal Forest Service institutes, which comprises five research institutes, one information center, and one joint research-and-development center (see Table B.3). The timber industry, through Goskomlesprom (and the former Roslesprom), controls another twenty-five research institutes, eight of them state-owned, fourteen under mixed ownership (joint stock companies), and three that have been privatized. The Russian Academy of Sciences and its regional branches host six institutes with an internationally recognized record of advanced fundamental research in forest ecology, biology, and related sciences.

Each forest research institute has an area of specialization in a narrow set of sectorial issues in which it takes a lead position. The institutes also have a regional function covering a wide array of forest problems for their region, including the development of regional forest policies. The institutes have sixteen Forest Experimental (Field) Stations across the country and over thirty Experimental Forest Districts (Leskhoz) and Ranges (Lesnichestvo), as well as a number of specialized laboratories, stations, tree nurseries, design bureaus, and experimental factories.

In 1995, the Federal Forest Service research system employed about 1,300 professional staff, including about 35 full professors and more than 300 Ph.D.-level researchers. Between 1990 and 1995, the research staff in the forest sector shrank dramatically-by about 35 percent in the Federal Forest Service system and by as much as 75 to 85 percent in the former Roslesprom system (Teplyakov and Berger 1994).

Forest research has also been traditionally conducted in a number of forest technical and polytechnic institutes, academies and universities of the higher education system, the Russian Academy of Sciences, the Russian Academy of Agricultural Sciences (RAAS), research groups of the Academy of Natural Sciences, State Committees, and institutes and groups under the Ministries of Environmental Protection and Natural Resources, Agriculture and Food, and others. Most of these institutions are in Moscow, St. Petersburg, Bryansk, Voronezh, Yekaterinburg, Yoshkar-Ola, and Krasnoyarsk (see Tables B.3 and B.4 and Map IBRD 28354).

Table B.3: Forest Research Institutes of the Federal Forest Service of Russia

Research institute	***Year established***	***Main research areas***	***Research staff***
St. Petersburg Forestry Research Institute	1928	Forest wildfire protection, drainage problems, chemical means of forest tending, economics, planning and inventory, tree nurseries, forest outdoor recreation management, (especially protected forest areas), labor management problems. Co-ordination of forestry research in the northwestern economic region of Russia	180
All-Russian Research Institute of Silviculture And Forestry Mechanizations, Pushkino, Moscow Oblast	1934	Planning and coordination of forestry research, intermediate cutting, forest restoration, forestry mechanization, forest management and inventory, economics, forest valuation, standards. Coordination of forestry research in the central regions of European Russia and the Urals economic regions	350
Far East Forestry Research Institute, Khabarovsk	1939	Forest restoration, development of new technologies, forest genetics and selection, forest protection, forest valuation, planning and management, ecology, Siberian pine (cedar) problems. Coordination of forestry research in the Far East economic region of Russia	80
Research Institute of Mountain Silviculture and Forest Ecology, Sochi, Krasnodarsky Kray	1944	Mountain forestry, ecology, watershed management, outdoor recreation management, forest restoration, introduction of tree species, breeding, international exchange of seeds. Coordination of forestry research in the Northern Caucasus economic region	45
Arkhangelsk Forest and Forest Chemistry Institute, Arkhangelsk	1958	Forest management in near-tundra forests, utilization of felling debris, resin-tapping. Coordination of forestry research in the northern economic region	110
All-Russian Research Institute of Forest Fire Control And Mechanization, Krasnoyarsk	1968	Development and implementation of means, techniques, and equipment of preventing, discovering, and fighting wildfires; technology of complex mechanization of forestry operations. Coordination of forestry research for Siberia	60

Table continued on the next page

Table B.3: Forest Research Institutes of the Federal Forest Service of Russia (Contd.)

Research institute	*Year established*	*Main research areas*	*Research staff*
Research Institute of Forest Genetics and Tree Species Breeding, Voronezh	1971	Genetics, breeding, seed growing, introduction of tree species, international exchanges of seeds. Coordination of forestry research in the southern regions of Russia	90
All-Russian Research Institute of Silvicultural Chemistry, Ivanteyevka, Moscow Oblast	1973	Protection of forests wildlife from human-induced impacts, selection of ecologically safe pesticides, pesticide side effects, forest protection, biotechnology, forestry in radio-contaminated forests.	120
All-Russian Research and Information Center of Forest Resources, Moscow	1988	Accumulation, analysis and processing of information on forest resources, building up and updating of databases and information systems for forest resources, inventory and mapping, ecological and resource-oriented monitoring, processing of aerial and remote sensing imagery, climate change	190
Research-Industrial Center on Forest Seed Production, Pushkino, Moscow Oblast	1995	Seed testing, breeding, selection, processing, and testing	25

Source: The Federal Forest Service of Russia.

Table B.4: Forest Research Institutes and Graduate Schools Outside the Federal Forest Service of Russia

No	Name of institution	Affiliation	Location
	Forest Research		
1	International Forest Institute & Center for Forest Productivity Studies	Russian Academy of Sciences (RAS)	Moscow
2	Institute of Forest Research	Russian Academy of Sciences (RAS)	Uspenskoye, Moscow Oblast
3	Institute of Parasitology	Russian Academy of Sciences (RAS)	Moscow
4	Sukachev Institute of Forest	Siberian Branch, RAS	Krasnoyarsk
5	Biological Institute	Siberian Branch, RAS	Krasnoyarsk
6	Institute of Forest	Ural Branch, RAS	Yekaterinburg
7	Institute of Forest	Karelian Branch, RAS	Petrozavodsk
8	All-Russian Research Institute of Agricultural and Forest Amelioration (VNIALMI)	Ministry of Agriculture and Food	Volgograd
9	All-Russian Institute of Medicinal Plants (VILAR)	Ministry of Agriculture and Food	Moscow
	Forestry Graduate Programs		
1	Arkhangelsk Forestry Technological Institute	Ministry of Education	Arkhangelsk
2	St. Petersburg Forestry Technological Academy	Ministry of Education	St. Petersburg
3	Timiryazev Agricultural Academy	Ministry of Education	Moscow
4	Moscow State Forest University	Ministry of Education	Mytishchi, Moscow Oblast
5	Mari Politechnical Institute	Ministry of Education	Yoshkar-Ola
6	Voronezh Forestry Technological Academy	Ministry of Education	Voronezh
7	Bryansk Technological Institute	Ministry of Education	Bryansk
8	Ural State Forestry Technological Academy	Ministry of Education	Yekaterinburg
9	Krasnoyarsk Technological Academy	Ministry of Education	Krasnoyarsk
10	Petrozavodsk State University	Ministry of Education	Petrozavodsk
11	Kostroma Technological Institute	Ministry of Education	Kostroma
12	Novocherkassk Institute of Melioration Engineering	Ministry of Education	Novocherkassk, Rostov Oblast
13	Bashkir State Agricultural University	Ministry of Education	Ufa
14	Nizhniy Novgorod Agricultural Academy	Ministry of Education	Nizhniy Novgorod
15	Udmurt Agricultural Academy	Ministry of Education	Izhevsk

Source: The Federal Forest Service of Russia.

Financing Forest Education, and Research

About 85 percent of forest-related research and education costs have been covered in recent years through federal budget appropriations to the State Committee for Science and Technologies and the Ministry of General and Professional Education. This is in dramatic contrast with funding sources for timber and other forest industry-related research and training, for which the federal budget provided only 8 percent of the funding. The money actually received by the forestry sector in 1995 (in contrast to the amount allocated) covered only 40 percent of operating requirements of research institutes and 56 percent of the requirements of forestry colleges (tekhnikums). In 1996, the minimum sustainable operational costs in forestry research were estimated at 21.3 billion rubles, but the federal budget allocated only 13.5 billion rubles. The lower priority for research spending under the severe fiscal constraints resulted in a major decline in the research budget from 3.6 percent of the operational budget in the forest sector in 1989 to about 0.5 percent in 1993. Regional budgets have recently been able to provide only a very limited funding for forest research and training, primarily through the so called "1.5-percent research fund" channeled to certain forest management activities undertaken by the regional authorities.

Wages in the Forest Sector

The dramatic decline in the scope of forest research in Russia has been caused largely by the severe erosion in salaries in federally funded forest institutes. A November 1995 survey of civil service salaries reported a low of 443,000 rubles per month in forestry, 575,000 rubles in the timber industry and a high of 2,075,800 rubles in natural gas production. The national average was 615,700 rubles per month. Within the Federal Forest Service, the average salary of forest research staff was just 85 percent of the agency average. Most of the talented professional researchers left to work in better paid occupations in the private and semi-private sectors (mostly in retail and commerce). The average age of the professional staff in the Federal Forest Service research system is now more than fifty-five years, suggesting the potential "extinction" of the once formidable forest research capacity in Russia.

References

Oblivin, Alexander N. 1992. "Planning and Management of Training Specialists for Forestry and Forest Industry Market Economy". In the Proceedings of the IUFRO International Conference *Integrated Sustainable Multiple-Use Forest Management Under Market System,* September 6-12, 1992, Pushkino, Moscow Oblast, Russia. Copenhagen, Denmark.

Teplyakov, Victor K. 1994. "Forestry Education in Russia". *The Forestry Chronicle,* vol.70 (6), November - December.

Teplyakov, Victor K., and Dimitry S. Berger 1994. "Scientific Support in Forest Management". *Foresters' Manual.* V.D.Novosel'tsev (ed.). 2 volumes, sixth edition. Moscow.

ANNEX C

EVOLUTION OF FOREST LEGISLATION IN THE RUSSIAN FEDERATION

The political and macroeconomic transformations under way in Russia have been accompanied by a series of changes in Russian forest legislation, following the enactment of the Principles of Forest Legislation in March 1993 (hereinafter referred to as the "Principles"). Other legal documents that are of major importance to the country's forest sector include the Constitution (December 1993), the Civil Code (Part I, October 1994 and Part II, December 1995), and the federal laws "On Ecological Expertise" and "On Specially Protected Areas." Presidential decrees "On the Concept of Transition of the Russian Federation towards Sustainable Development" (No. 440, April 1, 1996), "On the Federal Target-Oriented Program of Government Support to State Nature Preserves and National Parks Before the Year 2000" (October 1995), and others are also important to the Russian forest sector.

In December 1995, the Duma (the lower house of Parliament) adopted a new Forest Code. The President sent the Code back to the Duma for reconsideration. The Duma revised the Forest Code, taking into account the President's comments, and passed it again in July 1996. However, the Federation Council (the upper house) rejected the Forest Code on the grounds that it did not comply with the Constitution and other laws of the Russian Federation. In October-November 1996, the draft Forest Code was discussed by a joint committee of both houses of the Parliament and the Government. The discussion was reportedly focused almost entirely on the forest ownership issues and a compromise was reached for Article 19 that allows more flexibility for regional ownership of forests. With this change, the July 1996 draft Forest Code was expected to be passed by the Duma on December 11, 1996. The discussion here is based on the official text of the draft Forest Code dated July 5, 1996 (see Attachment 1 for its table of contents).

The text of the draft Forest Code (July 1996) differs substantially from that of the 1993 Principles. In 20 chapters and 138 articles, it contains a number of new concepts and definitions, as well as essentially revised standards and regulations governing the utilization, protection, conservation, and regeneration of forests. According to the Federal Forest Service, the main objectives of the new Forest Code are to strengthen the state system of forest administration and management and to provide a comprehensive legal framework for sustainable utilization of forest resources under the market economy.

New Concepts and Definitions

The draft Forest Code more clearly specifies the ***sphere of application of the forest legislation*** in the Russian Federation. Regulation proceeds from the concept of the forest as an aggregate of forest vegetation, land, fauna, and other environmental components having major ecological, economic, and social significance. Pursuant to the Code, *all relations involving utilization, protection, conservation, and regeneration of forests shall be governed exclusively by the forest legislation* (Article 5). Other areas of law (civil, administrative, and legislations on land, water, and vegetation) are listed as applicable to specific aspects of forest relations. The use and protection of the State Forest Fund lands are to be regulated jointly by the forest and land legislation. *"Relations involving utilization and* *protection of wildlife, water bodies, mineral resources, atmospheric air shall be governed by the forest legislation to the extent it is required for ensuring rational utilization, protection, conservation and regeneration of forests"* (Article 5, Part 5).

The list of the ***objects of forest relations*** has been extended, and the definition of the State Forest Fund has been revised. Pursuant to Article 6 of the Code, *"the Forest Fund of the Russian Federation (hereinafter referred to as the "Forest Fund"), parcels of the Forest Fund, the rights to their use, and forests that are not part of the Forest Fund, parcels thereof, the rights to their use, and tree- and shrub-type vegetation are objects of forest relations."* The ***notion of the State Forest Fund*** itself, defined by the Principles as comprising all forests and all land allocated for forestry purposes, is narrowed in the new Code: *"All forests except for those located on defense lands and the lands of populated localities (settlements), and also lands of the Forest Fund not covered with vegetation (forest lands and non-forest lands) make up the Forest Fund"* (Article 7). However, the bulk of the Code's provisions deal with both the State Forest Fund and the forests not included in the State Forest Fund, so the newly introduced distinction between the two categories appears to be artificial. However, it does complicate forest management because for the non-forest fund forests the Code does not regulate such important issues as state inventory and monitoring, the system of payments for their use, or sources of funding the costs of public administration and management of these forests.

The draft Code introduces the concept of public and private ***forest easements*** (Article 21), but contains only very general provisions on regulating the establishment of such easements and the procedures for the use of the applicable civil, land, and other legislation.

Forest Ownership and Governance Issues

The draft Forest Code introduces the concept of the ***transferability (availability for turnover) of the objects of forest relations.*** In compliance with the civil legislation of the Russian Federation, land and other natural resources can be alienated or assigned in any way to the extent such transfer is provided for in the land legislation and laws on other natural resources (Civil Code, Article 129). The draft Forest Code, however, outlaws any purchase, sale, lien, or other deal that is conducive to alienation of State Forest Fund or non-forest fund forest parcels. Nevertheless, it allows transactions involving a transfer of rights to the use of State Forest Fund or non-forest fund forest parcels, as well the transfer of tree- and shrub-type vegetation outside the State Forest Fund.

A ban on the purchase, sale, lien, or other deal that results in alienation of State Forest Fund and non-forest fund forest land is tantamount to their removal from "turnover". Transfer of the right to use State Forest Fund and non-forest fund forest parcels is regulated by the Civil Code and land legislation rather than the forest legislation.

The draft Forest Code introduces a concept of ownership. The Constitution provides for the possibility (but does not make it binding) of various forms of ownership related to natural resources, including land and forests, specifically, private, state, municipal and other (Article 90). The civil legislation treats forests as real estate (Civil Code, Article 130). Owners of such property have the right to assign it to other persons, to transfer it to such persons while remaining the owners, to use and manage the property, and to perform other actions that do not violate the law (Civil Code, Article 209). Contrary to these constitutional provisions, the draft Forest Code proposed in July 1996 that all State Forest Fund forests and the forests growing on land allocated for defense purposes be under the federal ownership (Article 19). Subsequent revisions of this Article, which reportedly provided more flexibility and accommodated regional interests, were not available when this report was being finalized. Furthermore, the draft Forest Code defines ownership to include the obligation to bear the costs of protection, conservation, regeneration, and organization of the rational use of the owned objects and the right to earn revenues from the use of the owned objects (Article 18, Part 2).

The Civil Code stipulates that land and other natural resources (including forests) that are not owned by individuals, legal entities, or municipal bodies shall be the property of the state (Article 214, Paragraph 2). Proclaiming state property as the federal property or the property of the subjects of the Federation (subnational governments, including Republics, krays, oblasts, and okrugs) shall be effected in the manner stipulated by the law. Presidential Decree "On the Federal Natural Resources" (December 16, 1993, No. 2144) states that land plots and other natural resources (including forests) can be regarded as federal property by virtue of their location or their purpose, or on the basis of a mutual agreement reached between the federal authorities and subnational authorities.

The Constitution (Article 72, Part 1(c)) interprets the issues relating to ownership, use, and management of land and other natural resources (including the forests) as under the joint jurisdiction of the Federal and subnational governments. For that reason, the Forest Code's provision that all lands of the State Forest Fund and all forests, except municipally owned forests, shall be federal property has evoked objections by a number of subnational governments and the Code has been rejected by the Federation Council. This rejection, however, was not unanimous. According to the Federal Forest Service, many forest-abundant regions are hesitant about claiming State Forest Fund lands because this would mean taking over all the associated costs of forest management and might legitimize claims by forest-abundant districts within the regions for rayon ownership of the best forests. The draft Code does give strong authority to the regions on such issues as forest management and regeneration and the award of forest use contracts.

Forest Regulation and Management Issues

The draft Forest Code stipulates that public administration and regulation of the utilization, protection, conservation, and regeneration of the State Forest Fund forests shall be carried out by the Federal Government directly or by the duly authorized federal executive bodies. The functions of any such federal body shall be defined by the Government.

The draft Forest Code also changes the ***division of responsibilities among different levels of government*** for utilization, conservation, protection, and regeneration of the State Forest Fund forests. The *competence of the Federal Government* (both legislative and executive branches) would include:

- Ownership, use, and disposal of the State Forest Fund, including a common investment policy for forest lands protection, conservation, and forest regeneration.

- Transfer of forest fund lands to non-forest Fund lands for purposes not connected with forest management and use of the State Forest Fund or the reduction of the State Forest Fund in Group I forests.

- Declaration of forest areas as zones of emergency ecological situations and zones of ecological disaster.

The *competence of subnational governments* is proposed to include:

- Taking decisions on leasing, uncompensated use, and short-term use of parcels of the State Forest Fund.

- Establishment of forest tax and lease rates (except minimum stumpage rates), as well as payments for conversion of forest lands to non-stocked ones.

- Conversion of forest lands to non-stocked ones for the purposes unrelated to forest management and utilization of the State Forest Fund and the State Forest Fund conversion in the Group II and III forests.

The competence of substantial governments is being broadened to include most of the rights of bodies of local self-government in the field of the use, protection, and conservation of the forest fund and forest reproduction. The new Code does not specify the terms of reference of bodies of local self-government; it only states that those bodies may be entrusted by the state with powers in the use, protection, conservation, and regeneration of the State Forest Fund in compliance with the legislation of the Russian Federation. Briefly, part of the current competence of the bodies of local self-government is transferred to the subnational governments and, likewise, part of the current competence of the subnational governments is transferred to the Russian Federation.

The draft Forest Code offers a crucial definition of the federal body of forest administration (the Federal Forest Service) as the ***body of state regulation of forest management***, that is, a public administration agency. Effectively, this means that this agency cannot engage in profit-making activities, including industrial logging and timber processing. Similar restrictions would apply to all forest service employees as civil servants. Article 50 of the Code emphasizes *the incompatibility of commercial logging and timber processing with the regulatory functions of the state over the utilization, conservation, protection, and regeneration of forests*. The Code provides explicit definition of the functions of leskhozes and national parks. While they become *de jure* public administration bodies, they remain *de facto* state enterprises engaged in forest management activities. As before, leskhozes are to be engaged mainly in organizational and monitoring rather than administrative functions.

Under to the draft Forest Code, the leskhozes, Federal Forest Service units as part of the public administration, would be entitled to certain ***tax and forest fee exemptions*** on forest management activities (Article 104, Part 3). This is a confusing provision, because it makes no distinction between forest regulation (administrative functions) and forest management (economic functions). Nevertheless, in the view of the Federal Forest Service "forest management activities constitute the essence of the public administration of forests during the current transition period" (Giryayev, personal communication). For example, pursuant to Article 91 of the Code, leskhoze responsibilities would include intermediate cutting to increase forest productivity if there are no other users to perform this cutting. Similarly, intermediate cutting is exempt from forest fees even if it is performed by a commercial forest lease holder (Article 103).

Forest Utilization Issues

The draft Forest Code contains provisions governing the establishment and termination of rights to use State Forest Fund and non-forest fund forest parcels and the legal protection of such rights. It is broadly acknowledged that the draft Code is a major step forward clarifying the ***mechanisms of forest resource allocation and use*** (Articles 31 - 45), which include contracts for the lease, uncompensated use, and concession of parcels of the State Forest Fund (for up to forty-nine years) and contracts for short-term use (up to one year).

Auctions are to be the principal method of awarding lease contracts. Auction commissions are to be chaired by regional (oblast) administrations rather than by district (rayon) administrations, as is currently stipulated in the Principles. These commissions are to include representatives of the regional forestry department (deputy chair), environmental protection agencies and other interested organizations. The enlarged membership of the auction commission would provide for collegiate decision-making relating to the leasing of parcels of the State Forest Fund. Leased parcels shall not be transferred to a lessee's ownership following the expiration of the lease term. The ***obligations and rights of forest users*** are detailed in Articles 23-30, providing additional transparency in their relations with their lessors.

Forest concessions, a new concept in Russian forest legislation, may be awarded by the Federal Government or its duly authorized body (Federal Forest Service) to any person considered by the Russian law as an investor. Concession agreements are to be concluded on the basis of tenders or auctions. The conditions of a forest concession agreement include procedures for sharing the developed forest resources (products) or services; procedures for the earmarking and payment of taxes, fees, and other charges; and investor obligations pertaining to the construction and maintenance of infrastructure facilities and other terms envisaged in the laws of the Russian Federation and defined at the parties' discretion. Forest concession agreements are to be registered in compliance with the civil legislation and the laws of the Russian Federation on concessions.

The draft Forest Code also formalizes the notion of *agreements on uncompensated (free-of-charge) use* of forest fund parcels. Decisions for granting State Forest Fund parcels for such use for up to forty-nine years are to be made by the regional authorities. The right of free-of-charge use is given to agricultural organizations. Hunters associations are also eligible to use forest lands for amateur and sports hunting.

Barriers to entry for new forest users are lowered, but not completely eliminated. Part 3 of Article 34 still provides for nonauction awards of lease contracts (for a period of up to five years) by the regional administration for forest users that have been *"active in a given territory for an extended period of time"* and that *"possess industrial capacities for harvesting and processing of timber and other forest resources."* Moreover, the draft Forest Code has no explicit ***antimonopoly provisions*** prohibiting actions by a governmental body aimed at restricting access to forest use, discriminating against some forest users, or refusing to grant leases to winners at timber tenders and auctions. This leaves considerable uncertainty regarding the scope of state intervention and favoritism in logging industries--all the more important following the recent re-establishment of the State Committee for Forest Industry and the anticipated reorganization of the timber industry.

Forestry Funding Issues

Payments practices for the utilization of the State Forest Fund are also revised in the draft Forest Code. The allocations for reproduction, protection, and conservation of forests specified in the Principles are to be canceled. Taxes collected for short-term utilization of forest areas are extended to all types of forest use. Forest tax rates are to be set by regional, rather than local, administrations, in concurrence with the respective regional forest management authorities, or as defined by timber auction results.

The Forest Code proposes major changes in the flow of funds in the forest sector (see Figures 1.6 and 1.7 in the main report). Under the Principles payments were to be made to district (city) budgets and, at the discretion of the bodies of local self-government, part of the proceeds could be earmarked for protecting and conserving forests. The draft Code establishes a totally ***new mechanism of financing*** the costs of forest administration and management, which the Federal Forest Service believes to be fundamentally sustainable. Forest fees shall be determined for each leased forest tract and for each type of forest use at the forest auctions. These rates shall be no less than the ***minimum stumpage rates*** determined by the Federal Government.

Forty percent of the applicable minimum rate shall go directly to the federal budget, and sixty percent shall go to the regional budget, where these funds shall be earmarked for forest regeneration. This would apply only to forest-abundant regions, where the established annual allowable cut for commercial logging is over 1 million cubic meters. All other regions would receive 100 percent of the minimum rate of forest fees. Local budgets will receive no income from the utilization of forests located in their territories, however. *Forest fees and lease payments in excess of the federally established minimum stumpage rate shall go directly to the leskhozes, shall be tax-exempt as budgetary funds, and shall be used solely for forest management purposes* (Article 106). These procedures for allocating resources recognize the right of the forest owner to receive an income from forest use.

A change is also envisaged in the procedures for covering the costs of forest administration and management. The cost of maintaining state bodies of forest administration and management (except for forest reproduction costs) are expected to be financed from the federal budget, while forest regeneration costs are expected to be financed from the regional budgets. This pattern of financing establishes new economic and financial relationships between the federal Government and subnational governments, forest administration bodies and forest users.

The proposed new system of payments for forest use and financing of forest management provides a better balancing of the interests of the federal and subnational governments in the protection, use, and regeneration of forest resources. The costs of forest management that were covered by the federal budget would be distributed between the federal and regional budgets; federal and regional budgets would also share in the payments for forest utilization (as described above).

Issues of Environmental Sustainability and Public Participation

In a significant departure from the 1993 Principles, the draft Forest Code of July 1996 substantially reduces the influence of environmental protection agencies in decisionmaking on forest management. All issues related to the utilization, protection, conservation, and regeneration of forests are to be *governed exclusively by the forest legislation* (Article 5). Environmental legislation is referred to only in the context of specially protected territories -- the zapovedniks, national parks and nature parks (Articles 125-127). The Code has no direct references to the role of federal legislation on state ecological expertise, though ***state ecological expertise*** itself is mentioned in several articles of the Code.

The draft Forest Code provides for the introduction of the state expertise of construction sites that affect the state and reproduction of forests (Article 65). The Federal Law "On Ecological Expertise" lists areas of state ecological expertise that affect forests, including land and forest resource use (including forest management projects); materials substantiating conversion of forest land to nonstocked ones; agreements on production sharing and concessions that envisage the use of natural resources. Despite discrepancies between these statutory acts, they mention a large number of areas that are subject to mandatory state ecological expertise at the federal and regional levels. The rights granted to citizens and public organizations with respect to ecological concerns offers considerable ground for preventing negative effects of economic and other activities on forests.

The draft Forest Code introduces mandatory ***certification*** of timber stands and subsidiary forest resources. Certification responsibility is vested in the Federal Forest Service. Certification procedure are to be established by the Federal Government.

Information on the State Forest Fund, including data on state forest inventories, cadastres, management, monitoring, and other information obtained at the federal expense are declared federal property (Article 75). The procedures for providing access to this information by citizens and legal entities shall be established by the federal Government.

A number of uncertainties remain with respect to ***forest utilization, in particular in protected territories.*** The draft Forest Code introduces procedures for removing forest lands that follows the procedures for converting forest lands to nonstocked areas for purposes unrelated to forest management. The right to alienate federal forest lands is given to the federal Government (forests of Group I) and to regional authorities (forests of Group II and Group III), but the procedures are in opposition with laws granting property owners rights in the disposal of land (including alienation of land areas) and with environmental protection laws that forbid removing areas from nature preserves, game refuges and national parks. Thus the draft Forest Code is more liberal than the forest, land, and environmental legislations now in force.

The draft Code leaves unsettled the issue of state control of forest protection, use, and regeneration in the territories of forest management districts (leskhozes) and national parks that are not part of the Federal Forest Service. A sizable part of protected territories is identified within the boundaries of forest lands and falls under the jurisdiction of both the Forest Code and the federal law "On Specially Protected Natural Territories" which contain different norms and rules.

Relation to Pending Changes in Other Legislation

The proposed Forest Code contains a number of important provisions enabling and regularizing multiple forms of forest use during the transition to market economy. The new forest governance structure also provides for flexibility in the distribution of responsibility between federal and regional levels of authority. However, all such provisions are enabling, rather than mandatory in character, leaving considerable room for the old and inefficient system to continue in force. The Code is not in full harmony with a number of Federal laws on environmental protection. Many of these shortcomings could have been avoided had there been greater public participation and more open discussion at the preparation stage. Nevertheless, there are no legal obstacles to amending the Forest Code once it is enacted.

The upcoming adoption of the new Land Code of the Russian Federation and entry into force of the Civil Code's Chapter 17 on Property Right and Other Proprietary Rights to Land will inevitably require changes in the forest legislation. Changes will also be warranted by the introduction of municipal and private ownership of land, the distribution of state-owned lands among federal and subnational levels, and extension of ownership rights to a parcel of land to include the forest and plants growing within its boundaries (Civil Code, Article 261). Various types of ownership of forests will call for new norms and regulations to govern forest relations based on the specific characteristics of each type of property right.

Changes in state forest administration and management need to be closely tied to the development of a market economy by streamlining economic and financial relations between forest owners and users. Changes in the system of forest use payments and in the financing of forest management will also be required.

Changes in forest legislation may also be needed to accommodate the major reorganization of the federal Government structure and functions initiated by the Presidential Decrees No. 1176 and 1177 of August 14, 1996. These decrees outline a new distribution of policy, regulatory, and administrative functions among different federal executive bodies (ministries, state committees, and federal services). The ongoing redefining of the responsibilities of agencies in charge of environmental protection (the new State Committee for Environmental Protection) and natural resource utilization (the new Ministry of Natural Resources, and State Committee on Forest, Wood-Working and Pulp and Paper Industry) might also require some revisions in forest laws.

ATTACHMENT 1

FOREST CODE OF THE RUSSIAN FEDERATION

(Adopted by the State Duma on July 5, 1996)

Table of Contents

Chapter 9. Fundamentals of the Organization of Forest Management

Section IV. Use, Conservation, Protection and Reproduction of Forests (Both Included and Not Included in the Forest Fund) and of Lands of the Forest Fund Not Covered by Forest Vegetation.

Chapter 10. Use of the Forest Fund and of Forests Not Included in the Forest Fund

Chapter 11. Reproduction of Forests and Reforestation

Chapter 12. Conservation and Protection of the Forest Fund and of Forests Not Included in the Forest Fund

Chapter 17. Particulars of Use of the Forest Fund

Chapter 18. Particulars of Use, Conservation, Protection and Reproduction of Forests Not Included in the Forest Fund

Chapter 19. Particulars of Use, Conservation, Protection and Reproduction of Tree- and Shrub-Type Vegetation

CLOSING PART

ANNEX D

STATUS OF FOREST INDUSTRY, TRADE, PRICES, AND TAX REVENUES

Forest Industry

Under central planning in the former Soviet Union, the forest industry had a low priority, usually receiving only residual funding. The forest industry's share in capital investment was only about one-third to one-half its share in gross industrial output. Though that share increased between 1980 and 1990, it has declined since then to less than half its 1980 level.

From 1980 to 1995, the share of centralized capital investment from federal or subnational governments in the sector declined, and the share of internal enterprise funds devoted to capital investment rose. For the economy as a whole centralized capital investment dropped from 90 percent in 1980 to 23 percent in 1995; in the forest sector it declined from 80 percent to 5 percent. Internally financed investment shrank too, so that by 1995 it was at just one-fifth of its 1990 level in real terms.

Federal and subnational governments provide a small amount of funding on a grant basis and allocate the rest as preferential credits. Logging has typically been given priority in capital investments, with much less investment in the pulp and paper industry and the wood industry. Internal funds continue to provide the lion's share of capital investment, through depreciation deductions, operating profits, or, recently, through privatization and the capitalization of assets. Few private investors, domestic or foreign, are making any long-term investments in industrial development at this time because of high inflation, economic uncertainty, and the lack of regulation.

In 1996, there were 3348 forest industry enterprises; and, by January 1996, 3194 had been privatized. At present, only half of the capacity is utilized and, in many cases, the technology is old and inefficient. The key issues that need to be addressed in the forest industry, both privatized and state owned, include:

- Low productivity in harvesting and wood processing.
- Insufficient depth in value-added wood products manufacturing.
- The economic and logistical challenges of long transport distances to domestic and international markets.
- Slow progress in adopting environmentally sound and sustainable forest resources harvesting practices.
- Excessive levels of waste in the harvesting and production processes.

Resolving these problems will require:

- Adjustments in policies and regulations, governing enterprise ownership, foreign investments, and pricing in order to eliminate constraints and to promote sustainable development of the forest sector.

- Promotion of small producer groups through international assistance, technology transfers, technical assistance, and some financial seed capital.

- Restriction of the size of clear-cuts in natural forest stands and the introduction of silvicultural systems that promote natural regeneration.

- Retirement of the heaviest logging machinery in order to improve the soil and water conditions of forested areas.

- More rational, intensive, and efficient use of sanitary harvesting and of by-products at all stages of forest industry.

Types and Uses of Lumber Products

The timber from Siberian conifers is generally regarded as of high quality.[1] Slow growth results in close rings and fine-textured wood. Knots are generally small and widely dispersed because the narrow crowns of high-latitude boreal conifers are exaggerated under the stress of harsh climatic conditions. These trees have relatively narrow sapwood (rarely 3 centimeters wide), so logs generally remain straight even under prolonged storage or delays between felling and sawing.

Whitewood species (spruce and fir) have had traditionally good markets, and in regions around the Japan Sea these species account for some 90 percent of the timber used in housing. Experts consider this wood the equal to American hemlock and Japanese cedar (*sugi*), with smaller knots, better finish, and greater strength.[2] Whitewood is widely used in laminated columns and in a broad range of construction elements. In Europe, where Siberian spruce is regarded as one of the best timbers available (stronger than European spruce), it is increasingly used in joinery.

At the beginning of the 1970s, Siberian larch was considered merely as a secondary species and marketed as piling material. However, because it is relatively stable, has good damp-resistance properties, and has low distortion in squares or beams, Siberian larch is widely accepted and even preferred for a range of specialty end-uses by foreign markets. Siberian larch is in the Douglas fir/larch

---

1 *The Bank mission visited a modern circular sawmill (Swedish-made ARI), that is to be combined with a massive edge-glued wood boards (MEWB) manufacturing plant under construction, in joint venture with the international IKEA group. Conifers, mainly pine and spruce, are utilized and boards are to be exported (17,000 m³ per year) to IKEA-owned furniture factories in western Europe for manufacturing high-value furniture.*

2 *Spruce and fir, woods that are relatively low in resin content, are used almost exclusively in making pulp because of the lack of technology and equipment needed to handle raw material that has a high resin content.*

group according to Japanese conventional strength tests. Domestic pulp and paper mills in Bratsk, Baikalks, and Selenga in the Lake Baikal basin use a fairly high percentage of larch in their manufacturing process.

Red pine (*Pinus sylvestris*) is also well regarded in foreign markets. It grows slowly and has smaller knots than Japanese red pine. In the United Kingdom, East-Siberian red pine, particularly from the Krasnoyarsk region, is generally classified as the finest available anywhere. Red pine logs from the Central Siberian Plateau are valued for their close grain and beautiful texture and their competitive price compared with Canadian-grown redwood sawn timber.[3]

Korean pine from Siberia is valued for its even-textured surface and stability in woodworking, although its valued characteristics are found only in the footlog; the upper parts of the stem are knotty and unsuitable for carving. In Japan, imports and end-uses of Korean pine from Siberia compete with timber from Southeast Asia. It is used not only in carving and pattern making but also for high-quality construction material. In general, while there are some "hard" hardwoods (oak, ash, elm, walnut) in the Asian part of Russia, most hardwoods are soft, mainly birch and aspen. These species are widely neglected except in pulp and plywood industries.

Harvesting and Transport

The primary harvesting methods are *stemwood methods*, which involve the harvesting and transporting of roundwood (delimbed stems), and *tree-length methods* which involve the harvesting and transporting of whole trees, including tops and branches. The delimbed stems from final cuttings are transported by truck from upper landings at roadside to mechanized log yards at lower landings, where the logs are cross-cut and sorted by size. Some processing is done at small mills near the mechanized wood yard, but the mills have a very limited capacity and produce generally for local consumption only. Most logs are transported to sawmills, veneer and plywood mills, or particle and fiberboard mills, or they are exported. Much less common in Russia is the *assortment method*, in which logs are sorted and cross-cut in the forest, so that loading is done only once and transport costs are reduced and are essentially paid for by purchasers of the logs. Logs are priced according to end-use value.

Chainsaws of Russian and Russian-Swedish origin are commonly used in thinning and final cuttings.[4] In fully mechanized final cuttings, Russian feller-skidders are used, along with feller-bunchers, some of them with extra-wide tracks and some of them self-loading. A wide-tire forwarder is used when the assortment method is applied. Some heavy logging equipment has recently been declared illegal for use in harvesting operations because of the excessive soil damage it can cause. Finnish harvesters, feller-skidders, and forwarders are being used on an experimental basis.

---

3 *The mission visited a sliced veneer (Japanese Marunaka brand of equipment) factory at Boguchany area (Angara River) where veneers of red pine are produced for export to the Japanese market.*

4 *The traditional high-handle Druzhba (Russian translation of friendship) chainsaw has been redesigned and adapted to international ergonomical, security, and noise standards, in joint venture with the Swedish Husqvarna company.*

Nearly all extraction is based on the skidding of stemwood or whole-length trees. The butt end of the trees is lifted off the ground and placed on the vehicle; the tree crown rests on the ground, and the load is pulled to the roadside or landing. The standard skidding tractor is a tracked, heavy vehicle, equipped with a winch and a hydraulically operated load table. Clam-bank skidders are also used. In sanitary thinning delimbing is normally done using chainsaw in the forest, while in final cuttings logs are normally delimbed at roadside using heavy Logma-type delimbers equipped with tracks.

In final cuttings, where large volumes of wood are collected at roadside, bundles of stems are loaded by a heavy tracked Russian-made loader that picks up the load and hauls it back over itself and onto the truck; no turning of the loader is required. A few cable-elevator type loaders are still used. They are less damaging to the environment but provide less flexibility with lower production. The most common transport truck is a cab and truck with a semi-trailer. The butt end of the stems rest on the truck and the tops are suspended by the trailer. The payload is normally 25 cubic meters per truck.

Most lower landings or mechanized logyards are equipped with a gantry-crane on rails to unload logs. The lifting capacity of 20 to 30 tons is adequate to move the whole truckload off the truck at one time. Stems are separated from each other by cross conveyors, hydraulic cranes, and manually. The bucking of stems is done one by one, by manually operated circular saws, electric chainsaws, or standard petrol chainsaws.

The logs are transported by chain conveyors and sorted to cradles or boxes arranged in storage piles. In some cases chains are used to bundles the contents of each cradle. The selection of bucking points along the stem is made by trained personnel, but in modern mechanized logyards, computers are being used for this and other functions, for optimization and accounts purposes. In the boreal regions, where trees are small and logs relatively easy to assess, log quality sorting may be done at the felling site by skilled staff. Relatively small logs are harvested during thinning and other early intermediate cuttings, and since only the butt log is of certain quality, bucking can be done in the forest, and the forwarding method can be applied.

Harvesting losses are typically large in Siberia and the Far East. This is the combined result of the use of heavy felling and extraction machinery that cannot accommodate selective or environmentally careful harvesting techniques, and the employment of the stemwood method, which reduces the amount of roundwood for sale at roadside. Although no official statistics are available, gross estimates of total felling volumes and harvesting losses in the 1980s indicate that an average of 10 to 15 percent of commercially logged timber volume is lost at harvesting sites (a high of 50 percent was estimated for Primorsky Kray). Overall, nearly half the potential harvested resource is lost each year (Table D.1). Since harvesting volume has come down in recent years, harvesting losses have also declined at least in physical volume. The logical conclusion is that the resource is undervalued by current management practices.

Timber Processing and Marketing

In 1988 the forest industry contributed 5 percent of industrial production and 7 percent of industrial employment to the economy of the former Soviet Union, most of it from what is today the Russian Federation. However, the output of forest products declined since 1988 and were dramatically since 1992 (see Table D.2).

Table D.1: Felling Volumes and Harvesting Losses in the Former Soviet Union in the 1980s

Category	*Volume*	
	Million cubic meters	*Percentage share in total*
Total drain from productive forest	775	100
Clearcutting	329	42
Thinning	16	2
Sanitary cutting	43	6
Cutting for roads and other	24	3
Total felling	**412**	**53**
Harvesting losses	50[a]	7
Losses due to forest fires[b]	50	7
Losses due to rot and death	263	34
Total estimated losses	**363**	**47**

[a] Unofficial sources estimate harvesting losses to be 175 million cubic meters.
[b] Excludes losses from forest fires on closed forest areas.

Source: The Federal Forest Service of Russia.

Table D.2: Output of Forest Products in Russia, 1980-95

Product	*Unit*	*Former Soviet Union 1988*	*Russia*							
			1980	*1988*	*1990*	*1991*	*1992*	*1993*	*1994*	*1995*
Wood	mill. m^3	389	328	354	304	269	238	175	119	115
Sawnwood	mill. m^3	103	80	84	75	66	53	41	31	27
Plywood	mill. m^3	2.3	1.5	1.7	1.6	1.5	1.3	1.0	0.9	0.9
Particleboard	mill. m^3	8.1	3.5	5.5	5.6	5.4	4.5	3.9	2.6	2.2
Fiberboard	mill. m^3	2.1	n.a.	1.6[a]	n.a.	1.5	n.a.	n.a.	0.8	0.7
Wood pulp	mill. ton	10.9	n.a	10.4[b]	n.a.	8.4	n.a.	n.a.	4.2	5.4
Cellulose	mill. ton	n.a.	6.8	n.a.	7.5	6.4	5.7	4.4	3.3	4.2
Paper	mill. ton	6.3	4.5	5.3	5.2	4.8	3.6	2.9	2.2	2.8
Cardboard	mill. ton	4.5	2.5	3.2	3.1	2.6	2.2	1.6	1.2	1.3

n.a. means not available.
[a] Converted from square meters to cubic meters by assuming an average thickness of 3.2 millimeters.
[b] Includes 2.1 million tons of groundwood.

Source: The State Statistics Committee of Russia.

Construction activities declined 43 percent between 1990 and 1993, and new housing 32 percent.[5] Consumption of paper and paperboard declined to 14 kilograms per person, one of the lowest rates of consumption in the more-developed world. Investment in the sector declined 87 percent, employment in the production sector 25 percent, and output per employee 48 percent. Most of the 3,025 officially registered log production enterprises, especially those with high cost structures and obsolete equipment (such as the pulp and paper industry), are bankrupt.

Roundwood and sawnwood exports are increasingly restricted and have declined to about 20 percent of their previous levels. The Government intends to replace these exports with exports of value-added wood products. While some of the decline may be state-directed, some is due to soaring transport costs and other effects of the economic transition. Transport is currently economically viable for a distance of up to about 1,000 km for logs, and 2,500 km for sawnwood, while the distances from many wood supply areas to the nearest seaport exceed 5000 km.

Wood processing plants are poorly equipped, and recovery is significantly lower than in countries in Northern and Western Europe with similar natural resources. Recovery could likely be raised significantly through the introduction of modern technology and management practices.

A recently established woodworking plant at Bratsk, financed by the German government, is designed to mill smallwood using modern canter/chipper technology that allows the milling of wood as small as 8 to 18 cm in diameter.[6] This mill makes it possible to use wood from thinning and sanitary cuttings that were previously wasted because of technological limitations and the disincentives resulting from the distorted pricing structure. The largest Russian wood industry complex, also at Bratsk, has been allowed to reinvest its export revenues. It has received a 10 billion ruble loan for modernizing its equipment to allow it to produce better quality products at competitive prices. Such improvements can be seriously undermined, however, by raw material supply problems.

The pulp and paper industry and other fast-growing major end-use industries are likely to have a strong impact on the development of production and processing in the timber industry. As public demand for newspapers and books increases, publishers and other paper consuming industries will demand paper at competitive prices and of a consistent quality. Similarly, the demand for packaging and paperboard will increase as the production of consumer products rises. These types of processing industries are likely to offer some of the best joint venture opportunities for national and foreign investors in the near term.

---

5 *Average living space area in Russia is about 18 square meters per person in comparison with 30-35 square meters in Europe and 50 square meters in the United States.*

6 *For the purpose of providing housing for returning personnel of the former Soviet Army from Eastern Germany. Massive and edge-glued wood boards (MEWB) are produced for prefabricated flooring panels, and other woodworking plants have been established at Sokol/Vologda Kray (producing windows) and at Maikop/Krasnodar Oblast (producing doors).*

At Boguchany, IKEA has invested in a sawmill that can manufacture large, edge-glued wood boards to be used in high-quality furniture making at IKEA's factories in Western Europe.[7] Reports of IKEA's success in its joint venture furniture-making enterprise in Poland suggest the potential for a similar value-added based production capability in Russia.

Another recent joint venture investment was undertaken in a pulp and paper plant (AO Volga, Balakhna, Nizhny Novgorod Oblast) by Herlitz International Trading (HIT) AG/München,[8] the International Finance Corporation (IFC), other investors, and employees. The president of this joint venture is a commercial director from HIT, and the directors of both finance and marketing have experience in other international private sector firms. Production in 1994 totaled 270,000 tons. Some 60 percent of the projected production of 520,000 tons will be exported, and the rest will be sold on the Russian market.[9] An interesting aspect of this enterprise is that it provides its own raw material supply, mainly on contract with the forest administration of Nizhny Novgorod Oblast. The logging operation is being subcontracted to foreign firms, but the plan is for the local leskhoz to take over this job once it has acquired the modern equipment needed to do the job cost effectively. The labor costs are a fraction of those in Western Europe, and energy and water, at least for the time being, are also much cheaper. Once the older paper machines are replaced, emissions of chemicals will be dramatically reduced.

Mechanical Wood Processing

Milled softwoods and hardwoods, plywood, particleboard, and fiberboard are to some degree substitutes for each other in various end-uses. When the raw material base for milled products and plywood becomes more scarce (and therefore more expensive), production of reconstituted wood rises. The construction industry is the primary end-user of these products. The manufacturing and mechanical engineering industry uses milled wood and wood-based panels, the packaging industry mainly milled or sawnwood, and the furniture industry plywood, particleboard, and manufactured wood-based panels.

Primary wood processing in the former Soviet Union was based in sawmills, using Russian-made framesaw lines without edgers or kiln-drying facilities. Most sawnwood was shipped green or incompletely air-dried, undressed or dressed by special export sawmills, and delivered unsorted. This rudimentary technology is obsolete, and primary processors (loggers) are effectively subsidizing end-

---

7 *The original investment of US$10 million made by IKEA has probably increased to at lest US$30 million, due to the serious financial and managerial problems of the Russian partner, extremely high relative to IKEA's other investment. Usually, IKEA finances such foreign investments through its subsidiary SWEEDWOOD INTERNATIONAL (Sweden), and SWEEDWOOD puts their own management personnel on-site to assist in managing the foreign operation.*

8 *HIT is a paper and paper products trader, belonging to the HERLITZ AG/Berlin enterprise. In 1993 and 1994, HIT sold 300,000 metric tons of paper at a value of about US$120 million. They have negotiated their marketing rights for the next six years, at 2.7 million metric tons, at an average price of US$560 per metric ton.*

9 *The 4,800 employees of AO Volga are currently producing more than 500,000 ton of newsprint a year. Paper machine No. 9 was put into production in late 1994, and is one of the biggest and most modern paper machines in the world.*

processors with supplies of raw material at below-market prices. To maintain a share in this market, these enterprises will have to convert to high-value processing closer to the site of the raw material processing.

During 1994, industrial capacity increased slightly for filing board, cellulose and paper; declined for unprocessed timber and sawn timber; and remained about the same for plywood, fiber board and card board (Table D.3). The capacity utilization rate varied between 36 percent (lowest) for card board and 58 percent (highest) for unprocessed timber. The capacity utilization rate for the forest industries remained low in 1995 and even in 1996. The capacity utilization rate has fallen along with the demand for final products and the supply of raw materials and other critical inputs. In addition to being underutilized existing capacity is not very modern or efficient.

Table D.3: Capacity Utilization in Forest Industry in Russia, 1994

Item	*Unprocessed timber (mill. cu.m.)*	*Sawn timber (mill. cu.m.)*	*Plywood (mill. cu.m.)*	*Filing board (mill. cu.m.)*	*Fiber board (mill. cu.m.)*	*Cellulose (mill. ton)*	*Paper (mill. ton)*	*Cardboard (mill. ton)*
Capacity								
Jan 1, 1994	205.7	56.3	1.76	6.11	0.48	8.66	6.01	3.40
Jan 1, 1995	184.0	52.5	1.76	6.25	0.48	8.78	6.17	3.40
Output	118.9	30.7	0.89	2.63	0.23	3.33	2.38	1.22
Capacity Utilization (%)[a]	58	55	51	43	48	39	40	36

[a] Output divided by capacity on January 1, 1994 times 100.

Source: The State Statistics Committee of Russia.

Wood-Based Panel Industry

Only about 14 percent of the plywood produced in Russia comes from Siberia and the Far East. Plywood production has increased much more slowly in the past twenty years than other wood-based panel industries such as particleboard and fiberboards. However, the Russian plywood industry has always been a strong international competitor, and despite the 40 percent reduction in production between 1985 and 1993, its exports increased 100 percent. The export grades are mostly standard and sold at low prices. The main trends in the development of this industry are toward large-dimension plywood sheets and an increase in the share of softwood in plywood production.

Russia produced 68 percent of the particleboard output of the former Soviet Union. Because of the high priority given to the particleboard industry, fairly modern Western technology was installed in factories throughout the country between 1986 and 1990, although obsolete peeling and slicing equipment is still used in the processing plants. Particleboard production suffered disproportionately less than other wood processing industries, in part because the raw material was readily available. Cement-bound particleboard is the most commonly produced, but particleboard for special construction applications (roofing, load-bearing walls) is planned to come on-line in the near future. Some 8 percent of total production was exported in 1995, primarily to former trade partners in the Soviet bloc and to France.

Pulp and Paper Mills

At the time of the dissolution of the former Soviet Union, the pulp and paper industry was facing serious difficulties. Sixty-five percent of the machinery and equipment was old and badly worn. The industry caused severe environmental damage, and most of the sulfite pulp mills have been closed or are forced to operate at severely reduced production levels. Russian production of pulp declined by 50 percent, but the share of production exported has almost doubled in the last few years, suggesting great potential for the industry in the future (this boom occurred as a result of a doubling of world prices). Recession and inflation at home cut domestic demand for paper products more than 55 percent in 1995.

Forty percent of pulp production is market pulp (not integrated in the paper and paperboard manufacturing process). Market pulp plants are usually found in remote areas in Eastern Siberia and the Far East, relatively close to export markets that offer lucrative prices. The average size of pulp mills has been increasing slowly. At a time when an efficient modern mill produces a minimum of 500,000 metric tons a year, the average pulp mill in Russia in 1990 was producing 130,000 metric tons a year. Russia has few of the large-capacity mills. Russia has always been a leader in the production of dissolving pulp, used in the production of rayon wool (280,000 mt), viscose silk (78,000 mt), and acetate filaments (300,000 mt) for tire cords, cellophane, plastics, and special papers. However, the production of dissolving pulp has declined substantially since 1990.

Taxation of Forest Enterprises

The tax burden on Russia's timber industry is considered one of the greatest obstacles to restoring production and profitability -- as it is for other commercial enterprises. Tax legislation is complex and poorly documented. Follow-up documents providing detailed instructions and interpretations of tax legislation are rarely provided to outlying regions. Tax collection is very poor, however.

As of early 1995, the four most important of the more than twenty taxes were:

- ***Enterprise profit tax,*** levied at the beginning of each quarter, based on estimated gross profits for the coming quarter. Currently, this tax is 13 percent (federal) plus up to 22 percent (territorial).

- ***A value-added tax (VAT)*** of 20 percent is levied on fuel, spare parts, and equipment.

- ***Timber conservation tax,*** originally levied at the territorial level at 7 percent, has been superseded by a federal tax of 20 percent, which was reduced to 5 percent after aggressive lobbying by the timber industry and then revoked in April 1995.

- ***Payroll taxes,*** assessments for social and medical insurance, unemployment, and pension reserves amount to 40 percent of payroll costs.

Other taxes include:

- ***Territorial taxes,*** including stumpage fees (differ by species), an additional 20 percent VAT levied on stumpage, a timber lease fee based on the primary species and length of the lease, and a land use tax.
- ***Municipal taxes*** of up to 3 percent of an enterprise's gross revenues may be levied for a variety of purposes (education, police, housing maintenance, sanitation, business licensing, highways). Local managers complain that the 3 percent limit is not always observed.
- ***Miscellaneous taxes,*** an expanding category of taxes that sometimes accounts for a major portion of the total tax liability of enterprises. Enterprises often find it cheaper to pay the fines for logging and environmental violations rather than investing in compliance measures; in 1993 such fines exceeded total stumpage payments by 1,000 percent in Khabarovsk region. A "voluntary" fee of 1.5 percent is collected on the total sales contract, to support science and research in the industry. In practice, these fees are often higher, and hidden as consulting fees or service charges.

In Khabarovsk, the tax burden seems to be disproportionately borne by inland companies involved in processing and by limited export enterprises. Many taxes are based on gross payroll and value-added, which penalizes labor-intensive production for the domestic market. There is some anecdotal evidence that a very large portion of timber industry earnings, and therefore tax liability, remains out of reach of the federal Government. Logging companies with access to export markets are exempt from VAT on export production. Through intentional downgrading and underscaling, log exporters are able to underreport revenues from sales. Mills producing for the domestic market have fewer means of concealing their earnings.

Legislative and Regulatory Principles of Investment

The law "On Investment Activities in the Russian Federation" defines the rights and obligations of investors. The federal Government is expected to continue to invest in forest management and to provide a more comprehensive legal framework for dealing with issues such as taxation, antitrust measures, economic incentives, and sustainable forest resource management.

Private investment can also be attracted through the development of the securities market. The most common type of securities exchanged in Russia today are shares of privatized enterprises and of financial credit institutions. There are no federal laws regulating this activity, though a presidential decree governs the licensing of certain activities of banks, insurance, credit, and other financial institutions. This decree also established the Federal Commission for Securities and Share Market, the body responsible for the regulation of securities markets and stock exchange operations.

Investment Priorities. Chemical and chemical-mechanical wood processing (paper, paperboard, plywood, wood-based panels) and the manufacturing of finished wood products (furniture and cabinetry) offer attractive prospects for investment. Ample raw material, water and energy resources, a developed transportation network, skilled labor force, and potential local and international markets provide a good economic base. Investment opportunities in Krasnoyarsk include pulp and paper mills, plywood and panel mills, and the upgrading or expansion of sawmilling and woodworking enterprises. In Khabarovsk, opportunities exist for developing value-added facilities to make better use of the valuable hardwood species for furniture, veneer, parquet, and specialty plywoods.

Development and investment priorities by various branches of forest industry include:

- ***Logging:*** the creation of a sustainable and rationalized resource base, rapid rehabilitation of productive forests, improved management of forest resources, improved harvesting methods (including thinning), and infrastructure to extend the logging season.

- ***Sawmilling and woodworking industries:*** requirement, modernization, and reconstruction of enterprises, with an emphasis on quality manufacture and environmental impacts, and the establishment of new capacity for the manufacturing of high-value products.

- ***Pulp and paper production:*** upgrading and modernization of pulp and paper production facilities to increase efficiency and to reduce negative environmental impacts.

Exporters and Foreign Investment. In the late 1980s, exports of logs and other forest products were virtually monopolized by the centrally controlled firm Exportles, with branches in Khabarovsk, Sakhalin, and Primorye. In 1990, the semi-private shareholders company Dallesprom was established to conduct export and import operations for the Russian timber industry. Over the next two years, Dallesprom became the conduit for log exports from its shadow companies, some of which were particularly aggressive in pursuing their own private interests. As a result, Dallesprom's official sales lagged, leading to a shareholders revolt against management. Under new management since late 1992, Dallesprom has solidified its position as the primary exporter to Asia and has used its wealth and position to establish a host of subsidiary companies to handle insurance, banking, and import operations. It has also fostered close ties with several new private operators that have grown out of Dallesprom.

The joint stock company Far Eastern Forest Complex (A/O DVLK) was established in 1992 as a vehicle for the privatization of Russia's timber industry. Initial shareholders included the major enterprises in Dallesprom, but following the Dallesprom shareholders revolt in late 1992, the Far Eastern Forest Complex has become in essence a private development company. It is currently building and operating a log export facility in Primorskii Kray and promoting construction of a new logging road linking the southern interior of the Khabarovsk Kray with the coast.

Until April 1996, export taxes in Russia were such a burden that falsified invoicing was rampant. Exports of forest products from Russia were substantial before 1990, dropped in 1992, and then recovered to US$4.2 billion in 1995. In 1995, foreign economic activities (mainly exports) are expected to provide 20 percent of federal budget revenues. The share of forest and paper products in these earnings was roughly 5.8 percent in 1995, mainly from roundwood and lumber.

Foreign investments are regulated by the law "On Foreign Investment in the Russian Federation" which specifies the foreign entities that are allowed to invest in Russia. These range from foreign persons and legal corporations to foreign nations and international organizations. They may establish a wholly foreign-owned enterprise; share in an enterprise with Russian owners; purchase Russian enterprises, shares, bonds, security, or property; or give loans, credits, or property as investment in certain defined activities. This law also provides for state guarantees of protection, legal settlement of disputes or liquidation, and unimpeded transfers of payments (after taxes) abroad.

The State Investment Corporation was established in early 1993 as a formal guarantor for foreign investors. Foreign investors may be exempted from duties on imports brought in as part of an investment, and wholly foreign-owned firms may export without a license. Tax rates for foreign investors cannot be less than 50 percent of the tax rate assessed to an all-Russian enterprise, however.

According to the State Committee of Statistics, foreign investment in Russian industry in 1995 was US$1.2 billion, or roughly 3 percent of total investment. Preferred ventures are in fuel and energy (22 percent), food (24 percent), and forest and forest products (13 percent). Options include establishment of joint ventures or financing through the government with government guarantees, including through the International Finance Corporation (IFC). Joint ventures appear to be the most popular form of foreign capital investment, with over 200 joint ventures operating in the forest and forest products sector. Most are in intermediate trade operations, but some are involved in industrial development. The increase in joint ventures since 1992 indicates the interest of foreign investors. But many of the ventures are paper agreements only, with investors waiting for improvements in legal and administrative conditions and in management infrastructures before implementing them.

Forecasting Forest Sector Development. Federal and regional development programs for the forest sector are based on forecasts by JSC Nipieilesprom. The forecasts rely on a database that includes information on macroeconomic forecasts, the condition and utilization of raw materials (wood), the technical level and availability of production capacities in the main types of forest industry activities, demand for forest and paper products, the condition of related machine-building facilities, and the quantitative effects of various legislative and regulatory acts.

The objectives of current government development programs for the forest sector include quantitative and qualitative improvements in output, development of regional capacities in forest resource development and utilization, improvement of scientific and technical support, environmental improvements, sustainable forest resource management, and stimulation of private investment.

In a stable economy with steady growth, government forecasts call for the development program to result in a threefold increase in commercial output of forest and forest products sectors by the year 2010: 550 percent for paperboard, 450 percent for wood-based panels, and 370 percent for chemical and chemical-and-mechanical wood processing. The share of rough wood in export volumes will decline from 29 percent today to 6 percent in 2010. Currency earnings would rise 400 percent. To achieve these goals, 80 percent of the required investment will have to be raised in the private sector since only about 20 percent will be allocated through federal and local budgets.

International Forest Trade

Before 1992, international trade in forest products was highly centralized and dominated by intergovernmental transactions carried out by specialized foreign trade organizations. Trade policies were designed to support distorted domestic price structures, and barter arrangements were the primary mode of transactions. There was no uniformity or transparency in trade regulations.

According to customs statistics, total exports from Russia increased from $54 billion in 1992 to $78 billion in 1995, while total imports increased from $43 billion in 1992 (an $11 billion trade surplus) to $47 billion in 1995 (a $31 billion trade surplus). The share of trade with countries outside the Commonwealth of Independent States (CIS) has been increasing. However, trade with the CIS countries is likely to be under estimated due to unreported barter deals.

International trade in forest products made up 5.4 percent of exports ($4.2 billion) and 1.7 percent of imports ($0.8 billion) in 1995 (see Tables D.4 and D5.), well up from trade values and volumes in 1994 (see Tables D.6 and D.7). The share of non-CIS countries in Russian exports of forest products increased from 83 percent in 1994 to 90 percent in 1995 (Japan has become a major importer of Russian logs); their share in Russian imports of forest products increased from 85 percent to 92 percent. The main exports are timber (unprocessed and sawn), paper-pulp (insoluble cellulose sulphate), and newsprint, which together in 1995 accounted for 74 percent of total exports of forest products. The main import items are construction wood products, paper and cardboard (saturated), paper hygiene products, and wallpaper which together accounted for 51 percent of total imports of forest products in 1995.

Efforts to liberalize trade policies began in 1992. The exchange rate has been unified, is determined by market, and is convertible for most current account transactions. Most domestic prices, particularly at the federal level, have been liberalized. The role of centralized intergovernmental trade has been reduced, most foreign trade organizations have been abolished or privatized, and enterprise to enterprise trade is allowed. Export taxes have been phased out (they had been 8 percent on unsawn and sawn timber and 10 percent on cellulose), and export quotas have been abolished. Import subsidies have been eliminated and import tariffs reduced. Lists of registered exporters and importers and obligatory lists of commodities for trade have been eliminated. Import tariff and export tax exemptions have been virtually eliminated, and a customs law has been adopted.

These trade policy reforms are significant achievements. They have led to a rising volume of trade, a gradual convergence of prices to world levels; and a more realistic exchange rate. In response to policies designed to achieve macroeconomic stability, the ruble has been gradually appreciating in value. As the ruble appreciates, imports will become relatively less expensive and exports more expensive, which is likely to increase demand for protection.

As of August 13, 1996, the tariff rate on imports of forest products ranged between 5 percent and 30 percent (Table D.8). The number of products subject to import tariffs increased from 1994 to 1996. The system of special exporters, export licenses, and quotas was abolished in April 1995, but voluntary preshipment monitoring of the quantity, quality and price of exports and preshipment registration of export contracts still continue.

Russia should joint the World Trade Organization (WTO) as soon as possible and adopt a trade regime consistent with the WTO guidelines. Overall, Russia should endeavour to substitute exports of high-value processed timber products for exports of low-value unprocessed timber. Such a strategy would allow Russia (both at the national and regional levels) to reduce timber harvests and exports, while maintaining a given level of export earnings. More involvement in high-value timber processing is also likely to benefit the local economies through potentially higher income and employment.

Forest Product Prices

Prior to price liberalization, forest product prices were controlled by the government and remained relatively stable throughout the 1970s and 1980s. These official prices were highly distorted and led to misallocation of resources, heavy losses and waste, low profitability, and sub-standard product quality. Presidential Decree No. 297 "On Measures of Price Liberalization" was issued on December 3, 1991 to liberalize prices (including prices for a large number of forest products) effective January 2, 1992. Price liberalization was followed by the liberalization of domestic marketing and foreign trade regimes. The price and trade liberalization led to sudden increase in prices and reduction in demand for forest products. Wages, particularly wages in forest communities, did not keep up with price increases and, as a result, household incomes declined. While the prices have been substantially liberalized at the federal level, the oblast governments continue implicit controls on prices and trade through inter-regional trade barriers and control of marketing margins.

The most important primary forest products are roundtimber (unprocessed logs) and sawntimber. The prices for these products vary by species of wood, location (transportation and handling costs are generally high) and the quality of wood. Domestic prices (from January 1994 to December 1995) paid by wholesale buyers for round timber and sawn timber are reported in Table D.9. Prices for both products have increased, but roundtimber prices have increased faster in ruble terms than sawn timber prices; almost ten times for round timber and six times for sawntimber from January 1994 to December 1995. The main reason for this increase is gradual price adjustment to the market economy and higher transport costs which comprise a large share of prices for unprocessed timber. Stumpage charges, on the other hand, did not increase and remain extremely low.

The export unit value for selected forest products is reported in Table D.10 for 1994 and 1995. As far as unprocessed timber is concerned, average export prices were almost four times the domestic wholesale prices (US$52 per cubic meter as compared to US$14 per cubic meter) in 1994 and twice (US$58 per cubic meter as compared to US$30 per cubic meter) in 1995. Clearly the domestic wholesale prices for unprocessed timber are converging to the corresponding export prices. The transport costs to seaports, however, are generally higher than the transport costs to wood processing plants in Russia.

The c.i.f. prices in Japan for unprocessed timber logs for three Russian forest species vary a great deal, with larch prices being the lowest and prices for whitewood and red pine about the same (Table D.11). However, the c.i.f. prices in Japan for Russian logs are less than half the c.i.f. prices for logs of comparable wood from North America. The c.i.f. prices for Radiata Pine from New Zealand to Japan are generally higher (once f.o.b. prices are adjusted for freight) as compared to prices for red pine from Russia.[10] Similarly, the annual average c.i.f. prices for Russian coniferous sawnwood in the United Kingdom were about two-third the corresponding prices from Canada from 1993 to 1995 (Table D.12). While these differences may be partly due to differences in wood quality and transport costs, they also reflect the low stumpage charges paid in Russia.

---

10 *In the context of international trade, the acronym c.i.f. refers to cost, insurance and freight and f.o.b. refers to free-on-board prices.*

The price data clearly indicate that while timber prices in Russia (for both domestic and export markets) remain lower than the comparable world prices, they are gradually converging. Domestic costs for factors such as labor, energy and transport continue to increase and the exchange rate continues to appreciate. This will result in higher domestic and export prices. However, the main reason for low timber prices (now and likely to remain in the future) is the low resource prices i.e. low stumpage charges. Clearly, there is a potential to increase stumpage charges to remove any market distortions which keep timber prices low and secure the necessary investment in forest management for sustainable production. Furthermore, there is a need to improve quality of both unprocessed and processed timber as well as quality of other forest products. Given large price differences in unprocessed timber and finished forest products, increased emphasis must also be given to exports of value-added forest products. This has important implications for policy reforms needed to facilitate private investment in order to rehabilitate and modernize the forest industry in Russia.

Potential Forest Tax Revenues

The potential for tax revenue from the forest sector in Russia is substantial. There are at least three main sources of tax revenue: stumpage charges, taxes on harvesting companies and taxes on wood processing activities. Because of the high level of uncertainty about sustainable levels of wood production and future costs and prices, the potential tax revenue is estimated in 1996 U.S. dollars at two levels of wood production and three levels of costs and prices. The domestic prices at present are lower than the assumed international prices. However, with the continuing liberalization of prices and trade, the domestic prices are expected to converge to international prices. Since the underlying assumptions are conservative, the potential tax revenue estimates are on the conservative side. For example, at present, the average stumpage charges in Russia are less than US$1 per cubic meter whereas under auction the stumpage charges in Russia and some neighboring countries are over US$10 per cubic meter. In Scandinavia, the stumpage charges may be as high as US$30 per cubic meter.

The potential tax revenues from the forest sector in Russia, under the most conservative assumptitons, are estimated to be at least US$0.9 billion per year. They could be as high as US$5.5 billion depending on assumptions about wood production and profitability of harvesting companies and wood processors (see Annex Table D.13). Unless the government is able to reform the forest sector policy, increase stumpage charges and improve tax recovery, they will not be able to recover the potential tax revnues. The potential tax revenue is adequate not only to finance all the expenditures related to forest management, regeneration, protection and sustainability (the forest management operations budget in 1996 is approximately US$425 million) but also make a major fiscal contribution to the treasury. Furthermore, higher stumpage charges will discourage over-exploitation of the forest resources and waste of harvested wood, thereby, promoting efficiency and sustainable sector development. The reforms suggested in this report are essential to realize the potential tax revenues through sustainable sector development which is consistent with maintaining the environmental integrity of country's forest resources.

Table D.4: Russian Exports of Forest Products 1995

Product	Total		Non-CIS		CIS	
	Quantity (thousand tons)	Value (million dollars)	Quantity (thousand tons)	Value (million dollars)	Quantity (thousand tons)	Value (million dollars)
Timber and timber products	--	2,107.9	--	1,940.3	--	167.6
Fuel wood	737.8	27.8	701.4	27.0	36.4	0.8
Timber unprocessed (m^3)	18,446.0	1,064.5	17,948.8	1,040.8	497.1	23.6
Sleepers	168.6	25.3	4.9	0.7	163.7	24.6
Timber sawed	--	709.4	--	640.1	--	69.2
Wood filing panels	--	21.5	--	3.6	--	18.0
Wood fiber panels	--	32.0	--	21.1	--	10.9
Plywood (m^3)	670.5	193.2	657.0	188.9	13.5	4.3
Wood containers	102.8	12.8	44.0	6.6	58.9	6.2
Construction wood products	8.8	5.6	3.4	2.0	5.4	3.6
Paper-pulp	--	951.3	--	919.0	--	32.3
Cellulose sulfate, soluble	79.5	85.8	76.7	82.5	2.8	3.3
Cellulose sulfate, insoluble	1,092.7	762.7	1,062.6	743.5	30.1	19.2
Cellulose sulfite, insoluble	159.6	96.4	151.5	90.7	8.1	5.8
Paper, cardboard, and their products	--	1,175.9	--	950.1	--	225.8
Newsprint paper	1,005.1	598.3	916.4	542.3	88.7	56.0
Paper and cardboard, nonchalked	219.2	153.4	150.2	108.2	69.0	45.1
Craft-paper and cardboard, nonchalked	251.7	143.3	233.9	130.0	17.8	13.4
Other paper and cardboard, nonchalked	296.5	166.0	241.0	128.3	55.6	37.7
Paper and cardboard, chalked	8.5	7.9	5.7	3.4	2.8	4.5
Paper and cardboard, saturated	34.1	22.9	29.7	17.3	4.4	5.6
Wallpaper	4.9	7.2	1.1	1.0	3.8	6.2
Paper hygiene products	3.6	4.8	1.5	2.2	2.1	2.6
Paper and cardboard containers	34.8	33.5	9.4	8.0	25.4	25.5
Paper and cardboard labels	--	4.5	--	0.1	--	4.4
Other paper and cardboard products	4.2	6.9	1.1	0.8	3.1	6.1
Total	--	**4,235.1**	--	**3,809.4**	--	**425.7**

Source: Customs Statistics of Foreign Trade of the Russian Federation, 1995.

Table D.5: Russian Imports of Forest Products, 1995

Product	*Total*		*Non-CIS*		*CIS*	
	Quantity (thousand tons)	*Value (million dollars)*	*Quantity (thousand tons)*	*Value (million dollars)*	*Quantity (thousand tons)*	*Value (million dollars)*
Timber and timber products	--	186.7	--	179.0	--	7.7
Fuel wood	5.4	0.2	2.9	0.2	2.5	0.1
Timber unprocessed (m^3)	975.6	25.6	970.7	25.3	4.9	0.3
Sleepers	0.3	0.0	0.3	0.0	0.0	0.0
Timber sawed	--	7.7	--	6.3	--	1.4
Wood filing panels	--	8.7	--	8.4	--	0.3
Wood fiber panels	--	6.9	--	6.6	--	0.3
Plywood (m^3)	54.2	2.7	52.3	2.3	1.9	0.4
Wood containers	6.5	1.8	3.9	1.0	2.6	0.8
Construction wood products	30.5	111.7	28.5	109.6	2.0	2.0
Cork and cork products	--	2.2	--	2.2	--	0.0
Paper-pulp	--	23.0	--	19.0	--	4.0
Cellulose sulfate, soluble	10.3	9.9	6.7	6.4	3.6	3.6
Cellulose sulfate, insoluble	5.8	5.0	5.8	5.0	0.0	0.0
Cellulose sulfite, insoluble	6.1	6.5	6.1	6.5	0.0	0.0
Paper, cardboard, and their products	--	598.3	--	542.8	--	55.5
Newsprint paper	1.0	1.0	0.7	0.8	0.2	0.1
Paper and cardboard, nonchalked	11.2	13.1	6.9	8.6	4.3	4.5
Craft-paper and cardboard, nonchalked	6.6	4.6	1.3	1.8	5.3	2.7
Other paper and cardboard, nonchalked	26.5	20.8	12.3	11.7	14.2	9.1
Paper and cardboard, chalked	11.8	8.4	7.2	5.9	4.6	2.4
Paper and cardboard, saturated	57.2	127.4	51.8	119.3	5.4	8.0
Wallpaper	26.0	57.2	23.3	49.6	2.6	7.6
Paper hygiene products	37.5	120.0	33.3	117.0	4.2	3.0
Paper and cardboard containers	52.4	95.2	43.1	87.8	9.3	7.3
Paper and cardboard labels	--	42.1	--	41.7	--	0.3
Other paper and cardboard products	18.9	31.8	14.7	25.4	4.2	6.4
Total	**--**	**810.2**	**--**	**743.0**	**--**	**67.2**

Source: Customs Statistics of Foreign Trade of the Russian Federation, 1995.

Table D.6: Russian Exports of Forest Products, 1994

Product	Total		Non-CIS		CIS	
	Quantity (thousand tons)	Value (million dollars)	Quantity (thousand tons)	Value (million dollars)	Quantity (thousand tons)	Value (million dollars)
Timber and timber products	--	1,664.8	--	1,468.0	--	196.8
Fuel wood	778.9	24.3	694.8	21.5	84.1	2.7
Timber unprocessed (m^3)	14,850.3	765.3	13,509.8	716.2	1,340.6	49.1
Sleepers	69.5	11.2	2.8	0.3	66.7	10.9
Timber sawed	--	623.7	--	549.4	--	74.3
Wood filing panels	--	23.0	--	4.4	--	18.7
Wood fiber panels	--	32.4	--	19.6	--	12.8
Plywood (m^3)	631.9	147.1	591.0	140.5	40.9	6.6
Wood containers	164.0	14.8	40.7	5.4	123.3	9.4
Construction wood products	18.7	9.3	2.9	1.5	15.7	7.7
Paper-pulp	--	384.6	--	347.7	--	36.9
Cellulose sulfate, soluble	68.4	37.9	40.7	22.3	27.8	15.6
Cellulose sulfate, insoluble	774.6	309.3	729.5	293.2	45.1	16.1
Cellulose sulfite, insoluble	91.3	32.8	80.3	30.1	11.0	2.8
Paper, cardboard, and their products	--	521.5	--	321.9	--	199.6
Newsprint paper	680.4	196.9	574.1	164.8	106.3	32.1
Paper and cardboard, nonchalked	230.8	91.7	85.3	32.3	145.5	59.4
Craft-paper and cardboard, nonchalked	215.0	62.0	176.9	51.4	38.1	10.6
Other paper and cardboard, nonchalked	244.3	69.4	168.1	45.4	76.2	24.0
Paper and cardboard, saturated	31.4	13.4	24.4	9.2	7.0	4.2
Wallpaper	12.1	7.8	4.4	2.5	7.7	5.3
Paper hygiene products	8.4	5.1	3.7	2.0	4.8	3.1
Paper and cardboard containers	73.1	43.6	14.6	5.3	58.5	38.3
Paper and cardboard labels	1.6	3.0	0.1	0.1	1.4	2.9
Other paper and cardboard products	5.7	4.0	1.4	0.9	4.4	3.1
Total	--	**2,571.0**	--	**2,137.7**	--	**433.4**

Source: Customs Statistics of Foreign Trade of the Russian Federation, 1995.

Table D.7: Russian Imports of Forest Products, 1994

Product	*Total*		*Non-CIS*		*CIS*	
	Quantity (thousand tons)	*Value (million dollars)*	*Quantity (thousand tons)*	*Value (million dollars)*	*Quantity (thousand tons)*	*Value (million dollars)*
Timber and timber products	--	88.5	--	77.7	--	10.8
Fuel wood	0.3	0.1	0.2	0.1	0.0	0.0
Timber unprocessed (m^3)	328.9	5.2	310.7	4.7	18.2	0.5
Sleepers	1.6	0.3	0.9	0.1	0.7	0.2
Timber sawed	--	5.2	--	3.7	--	1.5
Wood filing panels	--	4.8	--	3.5	--	1.4
Wood fiber panels	--	2.8	--	2.0	--	0.8
Plywood (m^3)	66.6	3.4	49.5	2.7	17.0	0.8
Wood containers	10.2	2.7	1.1	1.7	9.1	1.0
Construction wood products	23.2	51.4	16.9	48.6	6.3	2.7
Cork and cork products	--	2.0	--	1.9	--	0.1
Paper-pulp	--	2.2	--	0.3	--	1.9
Cellulose sulfate, soluble	0.0	0.1	0.0	0.1	0.0	0.0
Cellulose sulfate, insoluble	0.0	0.0	0.0	0.0	0.0	0.0
Cellulose sulfite, insoluble	0.0	0.0	0.0	0.0	0.0	0.0
Paper, cardboard, and their products	--	289.3	--	245.6	--	43.7
Newsprint paper	0.4	0.4	0.3	0.3	0.1	0.0
Paper and cardboard, nonchalked	10.1	7.0	3.9	4.6	6.2	2.4
Craft-paper and cardboard, nonchalked	2.4	0.9	0.4	0.4	2.0	0.5
Other paper and cardboard, nonchalked	14.0	6.3	2.9	2.5	11.0	3.8
Paper and cardboard saturated	22.4	42.0	15.9	36.2	6.4	5.8
Wallpaper	58.3	51.2	16.0	39.8	42.3	11.4
Paper hygiene products	15.4	52.4	13.1	51.3	2.3	1.1
Paper and cardboard containers	30.6	38.2	18.5	33.4	12.1	4.8
Paper and cardboard labels	3.7	17.1	3.0	16.6	0.7	0.5
Other paper and cardboard products	16.1	20.3	8.8	14.1	7.3	6.2
Total	**--**	**382.0**	**--**	**325.5**	**--**	**56.5**

Source: Customs Statistics of Foreign Trade of the Russian Federation, 1995.

Table D.8: Russian Import Tariff Rates on Forest Products, 1994-95

Product	*Ad valorem rates as of (percent)*		
	July 1, 1994	*July 1, 1995*	*August 13, 1996*
Timber and timber products	--	20	20
Fuel wood	20	20	20
Unprocessed timber	20	20	20
Other tropical timber	5	5	5
Sleepers	20	20	20
Sawn timber	20	20	20
Plywood from tropical timber	5	5	5
Other plywood	--	5	5
Wood for pencil production	15	15	15
Wood filing board	20	20	20
Wood filing board, unfinished	--	20	30
Wood fiberboard	20	20	20
Plywood	20	20	20
Wood container	20	20	20
Construction wood products	20	20	20
Mosaic parquet	--	20	30
Other parquet	--	20	30
Other products from fiberboard	--	20	20
Other wooden products	--	20	20
Cork and cork products	--	0	5
Paperpulp	--	15	15
Cellulose sulfate, soluble	15	15	15
Cellulose sulfate, insoluble	15	15	15
Cellulose sulfite, insoluble	15	15	15
Paper, cardboard, and their products	--	15	15
Newsprint	15	15	15
Paper and cardboard, nonchalked	15	15	15
Paper for wallpaper	10	10	10
Craftpaper and cardboard, nonchalked	15	15	15
Craftpaper for insulation	1	5	5

Table continued on the next page

Table D.8: Russian Import Tariff Rates on Forest Products, 1994-95 (Contd.)

Product	*Ad valorem rates as of (percent)*		
	July 1, 1994	*July 1, 1995*	*August 13, 1996*
Other paper and cardboard, nonchalked	15	15	15
Paper for goffering from semicellulose	--	5	5
Sulfite wrapping paper	5	5	5
Parchment, tracing paper	--	5	5
Multilayered paper and cardboard	5	5	5
Paper and cardboard goffered	20	20	20
Paper and cardboard, saturated[a]	15	15	15
Paper and cardboard	--	--	5
Paper and cardboard from cellulose fibers, other	--	--	5
Paper, cardboard, and canvas[b]	1	5	5
Ricepaper	1	5	5
Wallpaper	15	15	15
Paper hygiene products	15	15	15
Bathroom paper products	20	20	20
Paper towels	--	--	5
Products for surgery, medicine, and hygiene	--	--	5
Other paper hygiene products	--	--	5
Containers from paper or cardboard	10	10	10
Boxes from nongoffered paper or cardboard	--	10	10
Stationary	15	10	10
Paper and cardboard labels	1	5	5
Reels, bobbins, spools	2	5	5
Other paper and cardboard products	15	10	10
Paper and cardboard for filters	1	5	5
Cards for perforators	5	5	5
Lined paper for registration equipment	1	5	5
Paper for machines	2	5	5
Condenser paper, other	1	5	5
Wood-processing equipment	5	10	10
Boring machine	--	5	5
Chopping machines	--	5	5

[a] Paper and cardboard from cellulose fibers bleached, less than 150 g.
[b] Paper, cardboard, and canvas from cellulose fibers and other.

Source: Customs Statistics of Foreign Trade of the Russian Federation, 1995.

Table D.9: Nominal Monthly Sale Prices for Selected Forest Commodities in Russia, 1994 and 1995

Year/month	*Price in rubles per cu. m*		*Exchange rate (rub./U.S. $)*	*Price in U.S. dollars per cu. m*	
	Unprocessed timber	*Sawn timber*		*Unprocessed timber*	*Sawn timber*
1994					
January	18,473	69,495	1,444	13	48
February	22,004	77,307	1,583	14	49
March	23,494	47,091	1,719	14	27
April	26,030	84,101	1,794	15	47
May	29,180	105,808	1,880	16	56
June	30,086	89,668	1,958	15	46
July	30,134	99,314	2,026	15	49
August	30,787	92,264	2,122	15	43
September	30,875	106,187	2,347	13	45
October	31,217	115,845	3,044	10	38
November	42,341	127,352	3,151	13	40
December	52,726	187,812	3,388	16	55
Jan.-Dec. Ave.	**30,612**	**100,187**	**2,212**	**14**	**45**
1995					
January	71,249	249,859	3,858	18	65
February	62,559	293,591	4,259	15	69
March	99,623	210,840	4,749	21	44
April	116,330	186,332	5,030	23	37
May	127,827	203,476	5,060	25	40
June	155,567	222,359	4,709	33	47
July	159,935	254,977	4,518	35	56
August	164,442	263,872	4,416	37	60
September	173,163	276,384	4,472	39	62
October	164,516	456,322	4,501	37	101
November	173,659	457,222	4,544	38	101
December	175,651	412,332	4,622	38	89
Jan.-Dec. Ave.	**137,043**	**290,631**	**4,566**	**30**	**64**

Notes:

1. The data in the table refer to prices paid by wholesale buyers.
2. Exchange rate is the monthly average auction rate at the Moscow Inter-Bank Foreign Currency Exchange.
3. Average annual wholesale prices (in thousand rubles) in 1993 and 1995, respectively, were as follows: round wood, 7.4 and 89 per cu. m; sawn timber, 22.6 and 284 per cu. m; plywood, 116 and 1,260 per cu.m; chipboard, 42 and 446 per cu. m; fiberboard, 0.2 and 2.5 per sq. m; cellulose; 165 and 3,253 per ton; paper, 167 and 2,847 per ton; and cardboard, 110 and 2,353 per ton. Source: NIPIEPI Lesprom of Russia.

Source: The State Statistics Committee of Russia, Prices in Russia 1996.

Table D.10: Export Unit Value of Forest Products from Russia, 1994 and 1995 (U.S. dollars per ton)

Product	*1994*			*1995*		
	Total	*Non-CIS*	*CIS*	*Total*	*Non-CIS*	*CIS*
Timber and timber products						
Fuel wood	31	31	32	38	38	23
Timber unprocessed (per m^3)	52	53	37	58	58	47
Sleepers	161	107	163	150	149	150
Plywood (per m^3)	233	238	162	288	287	321
Wood containers	90	134	76	124	150	105
Wood construction products	497	517	493	637	589	667
Paper-pulp						
Cellulose sulfate, soluble	553	548	561	1,079	1,076	1,148
Cellulose sulfate, insoluble	399	402	357	698	700	637
Cellulose sulfite, insoluble	360	374	251	604	599	709
Paper, cardboard, and products						
Newsprint	289	287	302	595	592	631
Paper and cardboard, nonchalked	397	379	408	700	720	654
Craft-paper and cardboard, nonchalked	288	291	278	569	556	749
Other paper and cardboard, nonchalked	284	270	314	560	532	678
Paper and cardboard, chalked	n.a.	n.a.	n.a.	919	594	1,579
Paper and cardboard, saturated	427	375	608	670	583	1,258
Wallpaper	641	562	686	1,459	848	1,645
Paper hygiene products	601	548	642	1,326	1,469	1,223
Paper and cardboard containers	597	366	654	962	851	1,003
Paper and cardboard labels	1,922	1,015	1,995	n.a.	n.a.	n.a.
Other paper and cardboard products	689	649	701	1,633	724	1,956

Note: The export unit values are derived by dividing export value by export volume for each product.

Source: Customs Statistics of the Foreign Trade of the Russian Federation, 1994 and 1995.

Table D.11: Export Price Trends of Russian and New Zealand Origin Unprocessed Timber Logs in Japan, 1993-95 (U.S. dollars per cu. m)

Year/month	*Russian logs (c.i.f.)*			*New Zealand logs*
	Whitewood	*Larch*	*Red Pine*	*Radiata Pine (f.o.b.)*
1993				
October	112	92	110	85 ~ 90
November	112	90	114	85 ~ 90
December	112	90	114	85 ~ 90
1994				
January	116	91	114	110
February	125	91	120	110
March	130	95	127	110
April	131	96	127	120
May	131	96	127	120
June	131	96	120	120
July	131	96	118	113
August	137	100	128	113
September	143	106	134	113
October	143	106	134	110
November	144	108	142	110
December	144	108	142	110
1995				
January	145	113	145	112
February	145	117	147	112
March	145	124	147	112
April	138	128	140	124
May	138	128	140	124
June	128	124	127	124
July	122	117	127	125
August	119	115	127	125
September	100	110	127	125

Notes:
1. Russian whitewood, 22 ~ 30 cm, 3.65, 3.7, 3.8 m, c.i.f. Japan Sea Ports.
2. Russian larch, 22 ~ 30 cm, 3.8, 4 m, c.i.f. Japan Sea Ports.
3. Russian red pine, 22 ~ 30 cm, 3.8, 4 m, c.i.f. Japan Sea Ports.
4. New Zealand radiata pine, a sort, f.o.b.

Source: Japan Lumber Reports, October 27, 1995.

Table D.12: United Kingdom Import Prices (c.i.f.) of Coniferous Sawnwood from Russia and Canada, 1993-95 (U.S. dollars per cu. m)

Year/month	*C.i.f. Prices*		Russia as percent of Canada
	From Russia	From Canada	
1993			
January	155	185	84
February	147	181	81
March	124	240	52
April	155	239	65
May	165	200	82
June	154	210	73
July	160	288	55
August	151	343	44
September	162	285	57
October	152	152	100
November	162	173	94
December	162	243	67
Jan.-Dec. Ave.	**154**	**228**	**67**
1994			
January	163	259	63
February	158	234	67
March	100	230	43
April	178	321	55
May	181	255	71
June	193	307	63
July	201	262	77
August	197	233	84
September	207	261	79
October	171	268	64
November	218	322	67
December	222	295	75
Jan.-Dec. Ave.	**182**	**270**	**67**
1995			
January	200	249	81
February	212	286	74
March	210	288	73
April	202	296	68
May	204	308	66
June	203	278	73
July	208	228	91
August	194	292	66
September	207	305	68
October	173	326	53
November	171	323	53
December	173	260	67
Jan.-Dec. Ave.	**196**	**287**	**68**

Sources: Timber Bulletin. Vol. XLVIII (1995), No. 1 and Vol. XLIX (1996), No. 1, Forest Product Prices.

Annex Table D.13: Alternative Scenarios for Potential Annual Tax Revenues from the Forest Sector in Russia
(million 1996 U.S. dollars)

Tax scenarios	*Under wood production of*	
	110 mill. cu. m (current level)	*300 mill. cu. m (possible muximum sustainable level)*
1. Stumpage charges		
Scenario 1: $ 3 per cu. m	330	900
Scenario 2: $ 6 per cu. m	660	1,800
Scenario 3: $ 10 per cu. m	1,100	3,000
2. Taxes on harvesting companies		
A. Cost		
Scenario 1: $ 20 per cu. m	2,200	6,000
Scenario 2: $ 15 per cu. m	1,650	4,500
Scenario 3: $ 10 per cu. m	1,100	3,000
B. Gross profit		
Scenario 1: $ 2 per cu. m	220	600
Scenario 2: $ 4 per cu. m	440	1,200
Scenario 3: $ 5 per cu. m	550	1,500
C. Tax (at 35% rate)		
Scenario 1	77	210
Scenario 2	154	420
Scenario 3	193	525
3. Taxes on wood processing activities		
A. Paper-pulp (50% of wood output)		
a. Value of output		
Scenario 1: at $ 500 per ton	4,583	12,500
Scenario 2: at $ 600 per ton	5,500	15,000
Scenario 3: at $ 700 per ton	6,417	17,500
b. Gross profit (at 20% margin)		
Scenario 1	917	2,500
Scenario 2	1,100	3,000
Scenario 3	1,283	3,500
c. Tax (at 35% rate)		
Scenario 1	321	875
Scenario 2	385	1,050
Scenario 3	449	1,225
B. Sawn wood (50% of wood output)		
a. Value of output		
Scenario 1: at $ 125 per cu. m	2,750	7,500
Scenario 2: at $ 150 per cu. m	3,300	9,000
Scenario 3: at $ 175 per cu. m	3,850	10,500

Table continued on the next page

Annex Table D.13: Alternative Scenarios for Potential Annual Tax Revenues from the Forest Sector in Russia (Contd.)
(million 1996 U.S. dollars)

Tax scenarios	*Under wood production of*	
	110 mill. cu. m (current level)	*300 mill. cu. m (possible maximum sustainable level)*
b. Gross profit (at 20% margin)		
Scenario 1	550	1,500
Scenario 2	660	1,800
Scenario 3	770	2,100
c. Tax (at 35% rate)		
Scenario 1	193	525
Scenario 2	231	630
Scenario 3	270	735
Total tax revenue		
Scenario 1	**921**	**2,510**
Scenario 2	**1,430**	**3,900**
Scenario 3	**2,012**	**5,485**

Notes:
1. Export parity price for unprocessed wood is assumed to be U.S. $ 55 per cubic meter.
2. Average internal transport cost is assumed to be U.S. $ 30 per cubic meter of round timber (average weighted haul distance by rail is about 1,000 km).
3. The balance (difference between the export parity price and transport cost) is comprised of stumpage charges, harvesting cost, and gross profit.
4. Total profit tax paid is assumed to be 35 percent of gross profit. Other major taxes such as payroll taxes, and value-added tax (VAT), which together are of the same magnitude as the profit tax, are not included in the estimate.
5. Gross profit is assumed to be 20 percent of assumed prices for paper-pulp and sawn wood.
6. One ton of paper-pulp output requires six cubic meters of wood input.
7. One cubic meter of unprocessed wood yields 0.4 cubic meter of sawntimber.

Source: World Bank staff estimates, 1996.

ANNEX E

TRANSPORT AND PORT FACILITIES FOR SUSTAINABLE FOREST DEVELOPMENT

The reform and restructuring of the forest sector is likely to influence transport demand, especially in Siberia and the Far East. Transport operations under central planning resulted in a highly subsidized system that is entirely unsuited for the needs of a market economy. Along with most other sectors of the economy, transport suffers from the effects of the current fiscal and administrative chaos. Inflationary pressures on wages and fuel prices, combined with declining demand and reduced output levels, are creating pressure on government funds to finance costs that cannot be funded from operating revenues.

Historically, east-west rail transport and roads along the southern borders of Siberia and the Far East were built to connect the western territories with the resource rich regions of Siberia and the Far East, to facilitate commercial expansion and satisfy military needs. The main flows of timber were from north to south in the western part of Russia to the northern ports for export, and from eastern Siberia to the Pacific ports. Significant volumes of timber also moved on rivers and lakes. Demand for rail transport is expected to grow as timber production and transportation distances increase.

Transport Modes

Forest products are transported by rail (60 percent of total), inland water (24 percent), road (11 percent), and merchant ship (4 percent). Much of the timber volume is floated on rafts, and is likely not counted in port statistics. The Federal Forest Service controls its own river and seaport terminals, which are distinct from the areas controlled by the river and seaport authorities. The most notable of these is in St. Petersburg; it handles both domestic and international timber traffic.

Railway tariffs account for much of the cost of delivered logs. Russia has a fixed tariff scale for all regions of the country that is based on the profitability of the cargo to be shipped and the expenses incurred during transit (loading and unloading) rather than on the actual costs of transporting the goods to market. Because the tariffs are uniform across regions, some regions are effectively subsidizing others. Actual transport costs (on per ton basis) vary from US$7.65-11.50 (from Khabarovsk) to as high as US$45.80 from Krasnoyarsk to Port Nahodka and US$43.70 from Krasnoyarsk to European ports. It is not difficult to see that it is uneconomic to export unprocessed forest products or products that have little value-added to either Europe or the Pacific Rim and will become even more so as railway transport tariffs approach real costs.

The Tumen River Area Development Project proposes establishing a railway corridor across Choybalsan, Mongolia-Manzhouli, and the Harbin-Tumen River Delta to the Pacific Ocean. The system will serve an estimated 150 million customers in Siberia and the Far East, Mongolia, China, and the Democratic People's Republic of Korea and will facilitate the transport of an expected annual cargo of 3 million metric tons by the year 2000 (Kehr 1994). This line would reduce by 2,000 km the distance that Russian cargo must travel for export to the Pacific Rim countries.

River transport is strongly affected by freezing temperatures, which limit ship traffic while providing frozen waterways that can be used as truck transport routes. River transport is unlikely to be further developed, because the economically accessible timber resources in the vicinity of navigable rivers have been largely depleted.

Road transport is still underdeveloped in Siberia and the Far East, in part because it received little attention from former governments. Also, strong seasonal effects dictate road transport movements in both summer and winter in different parts of the region. The continued use of inappropriate, heavy log-moving equipment rather than lighter equipment that can overcome some of these terrestrial problems is another bottleneck. Further limiting the use of road transport are breakdowns of capital equipment as spare parts cannot be purchased readily due to foreign exchange constraint and the long distance between processing facilities and harvesting operations.

A summary of main ports and port capacity in Russia is provided in Table E.1 The federal Government still owns most of the main ports in the Far East, although some of the terminals have become private joint-stock companies. Where privatization has resulted in competition, as in Sovetskaya Gaven, a former military terminal, prices for port services have risen some 800 to 1000 fold in the past three years; by comparison railway service charges increaseed 4,000 percent.

Trade Routes and Sea Carriers

Trade in forest products through different trade routes is summarized in Table E.2 for 1995 and the pre-1991 period. Forecasts of maritime timber exports from Russia, by port basin, are provided in Table E.3. Russia's principal sea carriers (not all are involved in timber or wood products trade) include the following:

- The Arctic Shipping Company (previously the Yakutsk Production Organization), headquartered in the Lena river estuary in East Siberia, with a fleet consisting mainly of general cargo ships, many of them "ice-class."

- The Baltic Shipping Company, Russia's most sophisticated and diversified carrier, headquartered in St. Petersburg. Involved in bilateral trade it, has 34 registered timber carriers at 4,350 deadweight tons (dwt) of more than 150 total ships in service.

- The Far Eastern Shipping Company (Pacific coast trade) is well-diversified and second in size to the Baltic Shipping Company. Operating out of Vladivostok, it has thirty-nine timber carriers (4,000 to 6,000 dwt).

- The Kamchatka Shipping Company, headquartered in Petropavlovsk-Kamchatsky, has a fleet consisting mainly of small, ice-strengthened hull general cargo ships.

- The Murmansk Shipping Company, headquartered in Murmansk, has a sizable fleet of ice-class vessels and a diversified service network to Western Europe and the Mediterranean.

Table E.1: Port Capacity by Region in Russia
(millions of tons)

Port basin and ports	*Soyuzmor NIIProekt capacity*	*Alternative estimates*				
		Bank estimate	*Projects underway*	*Other berths*	*Minor ports*	*Total capacity*
Northern						
Arkhangelsk	3.61	5.70	0	0	0	5.70
Murmansk	9.33	11.15	3.80	1.24	0	16.19
Others	0	0	0	0	6.15	6.15
Subtotal	12.94	16.85	3.80	1.24	6.15	28.04
Baltic						
St. Petersburg	12.48	19.3	4.80	3.53	0	27.63
Kaliningrad	4.90	6.90	0	0	0	6.90
Others	0	0	0	0	2.31	2.31
Subtotal	17.38	26.2	4.80	3.53	2.31	36.84
Black Sea/Azov						
Novorossiysk	47.19	47.83	0	2.90	0	50.73
Tuapse	17.50	18.50	0	0	0	18.50
Others	0	0	0	0	0.69	0.69
Subtotal	64.69	66.33	0	2.90	0.69	69.92
Far East						
Vanino	8.45	12.47	0	0	0	12.47
Vostochniy	10.30	14.3	0.40	0	0	14.70
Nakhodka	5.18	8.85	0.24	6.30	0	15.39
Vladivostok	4.32	7.69	0.24	2.00	0	9.93
Others	0	0	0	0	4.56	4.56
Subtotal	28.25	43.31	0.88	8.30	4.56	57.05
All Basins	**123.26**	**152.69**	**9.48**	**15.97**	**13.71**	**191.85**

Source: World Bank 1996.

Table E.2: Forest Products Trade and Trade Routes in Russia
(million of tons)

Trade routes and products	*Before 1991*	*1995*
Through the Baltic and White Seas		
Sawn and veneer logs	0.81	0.90
pulpwood	3.95	0.80
Sawn wood	2.54	1.40
Wood chips	0.04	-
Wood pulp	0.22	0.30
Paper/paperboard	0.05	0.50
Subtotal	**7.52**	**3.90**
Through the Pacific		
Sawn and veneer logs	4.98	4.50
pulpwood	1.38	1.50
Sawn wood	0.34	0.20
Wood chips	0.31	0.20
Wood pulp	0.10	0.10
Subtotal	**7.11**	**6.50**
Through the Black Sea		
Pulpwood	0.34	0.30
Sawn wood	0.85	0.40
Wood pulp	0.26	0.20
Newsprint	0.17	1.00
Paper/paperboard	0.33	0.30
Subtotal	**1.95**	**2.20**
Total	**16.58**	**12.60**

Source: The State Customs Committee of the Russian Federation.

Table E.3: Forecasts of Maritime Timber Exports from Russia by Port Basin, 2000 and 2005 (millions of tons)

Port basin	*2000*		*2005*	
	SoyuzMorNIIProekt	*Alternate*	*SoyuzMorNIIProekt*	*Alternate*
Northern	2.03	1.22	2.82	1.49
Baltic	2.36	1.16	2.40	1.22
Black Sea	0.79	0.43	0.80	0.51
Far East	5.00	3.30	6.20	4.07
Total	**10.18**	**6.12**	**12.22**	**7.29**

Source: World Bank 1996.

- The Northern Shipping Company, involved mainly in the transport of sawn timber, cardboard, and pulpwood from the northern latitudes to Western Europe, the Mediterranean, Africa, and the United States. It has a fleet of over 100 general cargo ships in the 2,500 to 6,000 dwt range.

- The Novorossijsk Shipping Company, headquartered in Novorossijsk, has successfully teamed up with Scandinavian interests in establishing an off-shore shipping business. Its fleet consists largely of oil and petroleum product tankers with an average 50,000 dwt capacity.

- The Primorsk Shipping Company, based in Nakhodka carries mainly oil and petroleum products, vegetable oils, molasses and other similar products to Asia, Europe, and Africa. Its fleet consists mainly of oil and petroleum product tankers.

- The Sakhalin Shipping Company, based in Holmsa on the Sakhalin Peninsula, provides mainly sea-rail ferry services and general cargo cabotage (coastal trade).

Need to Strengthen the Transport Sector

While wood and timber products constitute a relatively small proportion of the materials transported within and from the Russian Federation (agriculture and energy-related products are by far the largest in both volume and value), the prospects for the transport sector are nevertheless inextricably linked with the prospects of the forest sector, especially in Siberia and the Far East. Whether development of the forest sector will drive development of the transport sector, or vise versa, remains to be seen.

Several factors need to be addressed to strengthen the transport sector. Changes in the economic framework in general, and in how the industry conducts its business, will determine the nature and size of the transport services developed specifically to serve the forest sector:

- The Government needs to move away from direct involvement in operations toward providing a legal and regulatory framework under which privatized operators of transport services can work profitably. To the extent that the Government feels it necessary to soften the impact of price liberalization, especially for fuel, it should link any subsidies to improvements in performance and to successful cost-recovery measures. And where social welfare concerns dictate transport subsidies for particular regions (such as northern regions), the services should be contracted through a competitive bid process.

- The Government needs to invest in essential reconstruction, maintenance, and training in the transport sector, rather than in expansion or modernization. Increased capacity is less urgent than preserving existing capacity. For example, despite substantial evidence of rapid deterioration of the railway infrastructure, the Ministry of Railways is contemplating expensive investments in high-speed rail systems, foreign-made passenger cars, and sophisticated reservation systems (see Holt 1993 for other examples of investments being made with inappropriate assessments of their true costs and benefits).

- The implicit subsidy of energy consumption is the main reason why transport is over used in the Russian economy compared with practice in other industrial economies. Raising energy prices to world levels will accelerate the shift to more rational, cost-effective operations in the transport sector, while reducing fiscal expenditures and increasing revenues.

A detailed World Bank (1996) analysis of Russia's national ports found that the lack of competition to be costly to the economy, leading to higher costs, poor services, and limited investment to improve port efficiency. Government should ensure that the monopolistic joint stock companies now operating the ports not be permitted to do so in perpetuity. Major shippers should be encouraged to lease dedicated facilities for their own operations to isolate them from the inefficiencies of other operating company. To promote competition between ports, it may be desirable to form an independent port authority at each port. Implementation of these recommendations is likely to result in a suitable framework for investment in port services and facilities, lower port charges, higher productivity, and more efficient port operations for Russia's seatrade. These recommendations apply to all ports, including those that deal primarily with trade in forest products.

References

Holt, Jane. 1993, *Transport Strategies for the Russia Federation.* Studies of Economies in Transformation, No. 9. Washington, D.C.: The World Bank.

Kehr, K.H. 1994, Working Paper for Project Completion Report of China: Daxinganling Forest Fire Rehabilitation Project. World Bank, Washington, D.C.

World Bank. 1996. Russian Federation: Restructuring Russia's National Ports. Report No. 1500-RU, Europe and Central Asia Region, The World Bank, Washington, D.C.

Annex F

Status of Privatization and Enterprise Reform in the Forest Sector

Joint Ventures and Other Investments

Joint ventures in the forest industry are emerging throughout the country and in all types of activity, including forest harvesting, wood milling, pulp and paper production, and particleboard and plywood production. European Russia and the Far East have experienced for greater foreign investment and related activity than the Urals and Siberia. Many companies are investigating investment opportunities and spending substantial time and resources negotiating terms and conditions of cooperation.

Several bilateral agreements have important implications for the development of the commercial forest industry in Russia. An agreement by the Russian-Japanese Committee for Economic Cooperation in 1994 ensures the development of mutually beneficial relations through the exchange of forest products from Russia and equipment, spares, and materials from Japan. A memorandum of understanding between the governments of Russia and the United States in 1994 provides the foundation for a cooperative relationship in forest and pulp and paper industries, ensuring protection through negotiations with the U.S. Export-Import (Exim) Bank and the Overseas Private Investment Corporation (OPIC), both semi-autonomous U.S. government agencies.

Foreign ventures first took hold in the forest sector when Bulgarian and Korean firms received contracts for forest harvesting 1968. Harvested wood and resulting products were distributed on a 60 percent (to the USSR) and 40 percent basis. Industries also emerged from this partnership. A new agreement is scheduled to take place between the Russian Federation and the Republic of Korea for continued cooperation in harvesting, processing, and regeneration during 1995-98. The agreement would create five joint forest harvesting enterprises in the Amur and Khabarovsk regions and will employ 7,000 Korean workers. Korea will pay for the shipment of all products out of Russia, which will be exempt from export taxes.

Another type of joint forest enterprise is exemplified by the Russian-Japanese enterprise Igirma-Tairiky, in the Irkutsk region in the basin of the Angara River, a zone of high-quality Angara pine forest. This enterprise specializes in sawnwood for export and has been expanding yearly since its beginning in 1989. The joint Russian-Finnish venture Landenso is involved in a highly diversified forest industry cycle, including nursery, regeneration and protection, intermediate and sanitary cuttings, road building, harvesting, sawing and others. This has been a successful venture not only in industry development but also in addressing the social problems of the forest communities involved.

Various investment inputs (mainly modern harvesting and processing equipment) are being offered on a concessional basis directly by foreign firms or financed by governments or international institutions. Examples include Finnish deliveries of highly efficient forest harvesting and wood processing machines to Karelia, proposed credits on concessional terms to be returned in the form of products supplied by the new enterprises, and deliveries of equipment by the U.S. firm McDermot, on account of credits offered through Citibank.

The Finnish firm Jakko-Poyry assisted in a project in 1991-93 that generated a forest and the forest industry masterplan for European Russia (the main taiga zones of Komi and Karelia Republics and six adjoining regions). Each republic and region developed its own masterplan, with forecasts of wood consumption and production up to 2005. Information on forest management and policy, protection of the environment, and multifunctional utilization was collected, analyzed, and incorporated into the plan. Recommendations were made on intermediate thinning and cutting and the artificial regeneration of forests in cut areas.

A similar project with the U.S. corporation MIDA-USA encompasses cooperation in forest management, sawmill technology, kiln technology, secondary wood processing, use of sawmill and processing waste products, and assistance in marketing products globally and in leasing Russian forests. The task of selecting several enterprises that will receive financing from both the Russian Government and the European Bank for Reconstruction and Development (EBRD) is underway, with one such enterprise, the Ruza Forest Enterprise, already in the planning stage.

The Privatization Program

The Government of the Russian Federation has established a program to privatize federal and municipally owned enterprises (referred to collectively as "state enterprises").[1] The new owner must be a private entity. Ownership may not be transferred to another enterprise or entity that is more than 25 percent owned by federal, regional, or municipal governments.

The main objective of the privatization program is to create private owners who will spur development of a market economy by increasing the efficiency and productivity of state enterprises. Other objectives include contributing to the financial stabilization of the Russian economy, promoting competition, attracting foreign investment, and ensuring a social safety net and needed infrastructure. The program was also designed to establish the institutions and infrastructure needed to expand the scale of privatization in later years.

Approach to Privatization

The two government organizations responsible for the sale of state-owned enterprises are the State Committee for the Management of State Property (GKI) and the Russian Property Funds. While GKI is the principal policy organ for general privatization strategy and for some specific transaction procedures; the Property Funds facilitate the transfer of shares to new private owners.

Small-scale enterprises (those with 200 employees or fewer and a book value of less than 10 million rubles as of January 1992) were typically owned by municipal governments and included

1 *This section briefly describes the privatization program of the Russian Federation. The official statement of the Program can be found in a number of laws and decrees, including the "Law of the RSFSR on Privatization of State and Municipally-Owned Enterprises in the RSFSR" (July 1991), the "State Program of Privatization of State and Municipally-Owned Enterprises of the Russian Federation 1992" (June 1992), the "Decree on Accelerating Privatization of State and Municipally-Owned Enterprises (January 1992), and the "Decree on Organizational Measures for Transforming State Enterprises and Voluntary Associations of State Enterprises into Joint Stock Companies" (July 1992).*

enterprises engaged in wholesale and retail trade, construction, agriculture, food, and trucking. These were privatized through competitive auctions and tenders carried out by local Committees for the Management of State Property and local Property Funds. Early in the process (during 1992) mandatory privatization was required of (among others) all construction and construction materials-producing facilities and enterprises and all enterprises in any sector that operated at a loss unless otherwise exempted.

Most ***medium- and large-scale enterprises*** have been, or will be, transformed into open joint-stock companies (referred to as "corporatization"), with some stock being given or sold to employees on preferential terms. The balance is sold to Russian and foreign bidders in competitive auctions or tenders. There are virtually no restrictions on who may hold these stocks or how often they can be sold (although workers must pay for their shares in full before they can sell them in a secondary market). Transformation into a joint stock company also entails taking on a legal form that is compatible with the emerging market economy and consistent with the legal forms of ownership found in other countries.

The program specifies that ***very large enterprises*** (more than 10,000 employees and a book value of assets greater than 150 million rubles in January 1992) could be privatized only by the GKI in accordance with opinions offered by relevant ministries. In most cases consideration for privatization has required complex analysis and preparation of detailed plans. In the meantime, GKI retains a controlling block of stock in these enterprises that it will hold for a short period of time.

A ***special category of assets and enterprises*** that were not allowed to be privatized was created in 1992. It included all forest resources, territories that are protected or reserved for special use, unique cultural and natural monuments and objects that relate to the historical and cultural heritage of Russia, forest and plant protection services, geological mapping, survey and weather services, and port structures and facilities.[2]

Mechanics of Privatization

The government has set forth a model corporate charter that each new joint-stock company is to follow. The charter specifies how the company is to be organized and managed. Initially, the charter specifies that the council of directors will include the director general of the company, a representative of the appropriate Property Fund or GKI, a representative of the workers collective, and a representative of the local government. After stock has passed into private ownership, the holders of common stock may change the charter to permit a change in the composition of the council of directors. An association or group of enterprises may not be combined and transformed into a single company, but a single enterprise can be separated into independent companies, taking into account current antitrust laws.

Vouchers, or "privatization checks," began to be sold in October 1992. Voucher holders could exchange their vouchers for stock in state enterprise as they undergo privatization. Vouchers were exchanged through competitive auctions organized by regional GKIs and Property Funds and open only to voucher holders. The intention was that a minimum of 50 percent of the stock in each enterprise would

---

2 *For more details, see State Committee of the Russian Federation for the Management of State Property, 1992. Foreign Investment Opportunities in the 1992 Russian Privatization Program: A Guide for Potential and Present Investors. Moscow.*

be sold exclusively to voucher holders and that the remainder would be purchased for a combination of vouchers and cash.

Vouchers can be resold to non-residents, who in turn can also use their vouchers in combination with cash to purchase stock in an enterprise. The development of financial institutions that can assist the public to purchase state property or exchange their vouchers has been encouraged. Investment funds have emerged that own stock on behalf of many individual members.

The proceeds from the sale of state property are earmarked for specific purposes, including the maintenance of a social safety net, environmental protection, industrial restructuring and demonopolization, the maintenance of the social and physical infrastructure, and the covering of budget deficits (see Table F.1 for the division among the various levels of government). The local authorities determine how their share of these proceeds are to be allocated and disbursed.

The workers and managers of all state enterprises have primary responsibility for the corporatization and privatization of their enterprises. In addition to vouchers they also receive other benefits. They can buy unlimited quantities of stock of their own enterprises on a preferential basis. Employees accrue some share of the sale proceeds if their enterprise is sold to an investor, or they can receive discount prices on the purchase of their enterprise. If the enterprise is liquidated, the employees also receive some percentage of the sale proceeds, or employees can lease their enterprise, with an option to purchase it at a later date.

The GKI in Moscow and in each region (oblast) and in many cities, manages and supervises the transformation of medium-size and large firms into joint-stock companies and assists all firms subject to privatization. GKI must also approve the establishment of all forms of joint ventures involving state enterprises, including those established by foreign investors.

The Ministry of Finance registers enterprises that have foreign investment and collects taxes from foreign companies on profits earned from business activities and on interest, rents, and dividends received from sources in Russia. The Ministry has a strong influence on the country's tax structure and can thus affect the decisions that domestic and foreign investors make to ensure maximum profitability.

The Ministry of Foreign Economic Relations, which succeeded the Ministry of Trade, accredits the branch offices of foreign companies doing business in Russia. It issues export licenses and implements Russia's foreign trade policy. It also authorizes Russian entities to invest in foreign countries. Trade missions abroad are directed by the Ministry of Foreign Affairs, which supports foreign investment in Russia as part of its job of strengthening economic relations with other countries.

The Central Bank of Russia regulates the use of foreign currency and rubles in Russia, even by foreigners, including restrictions on the use of foreign currency by residents. It registers commercial banks and is responsible for establishing banking norms such as minimum capitalization ratios, reserve levels, and maximum risk levels.

Table F.1: Allocation of Privatization Proceeds after Payments to Workers' Collectives (percentage)

Recipient	*Municipal property*	*Regional and federal property*
Local budgets	45	10
Republican, territorial, regional budgets; budgets of autonomous districts	25	45
Federal budget	20	35
State privatization authorities, including Property Funds at all levels, committees for management of property, GKI, and Russia Property Fund	10	10
Total	***100***	***100***

Source: GKI.

Legal Framework for Foreign Investment

The privatization program specifies a number of methods for selling the stock in a newly created Russian corporation that is not otherwise given or sold to employees or Russian investors. With few exceptions, foreign investors can participate freely in the sale of stock.

Foreign investors are encouraged to participate in the bidding for stock in open joint-stock companies and may buy vouchers on the secondary market and use them to purchase stock. Foreigners can purchase entire enterprises that have not been created as joint-stock companies, although some enterprises may have certain employment or investment restrictions on their operations. Foreigners can also purchase liquidated assets or purchase the enterprise as a going concern prior to its liquidation. Foreign investors can purchase leased enterprises from workers and management, provided the lease agreement does not preclude this action.

Foreign investment is permitted in all sectors of the economy with two exceptions: foreign investors can purchase small enterprises only with the permission of the appropriate local council, and they may purchase enterprises in the defense, mineral, fuel, and energy industries only with the permission of the federal or republican governments. The following summary provides a general description of the main federal laws or decrees enacted since 1990 to regulate foreign investment in Russia. Many of these documents have been subsequently revised or amended. It is, therefore, essential that potential foreign investors continuously monitor the Russian laws regulating foreign investment in order to remain current with the legal and business environment.

The *Law on Foreign Investment* sets forth basic rules governing the establishment and operation of enterprises with foreign ownership in Russia. The law permits the establishment of a wholly owned subsidiary or a partnership and grants foreign investors some legal protections, their property may not be nationalized or confiscated without compensation, and they are legally entitled to repatriate profits in foreign currency after payment of taxes and fees,. They may also export what they produce without obtaining licenses (although other laws impose licensing restrictions that may apply to them). This law also provides for dispute resolution in either Russian or foreign courts. Issues of compensation for actions of the government are to be resolved in the Supreme Court of the Russian Federation or in the High Arbitration Court unless otherwise provided by treaty. Arbitration is governed by the ***Law on the Arbitration Court and by the Law on the Arbitration Code of Procedure.***

The *Law on Enterprises and Entrepreneurial Activity* outlines the legal forms for organizing businesses, specifies the rights and obligations of businesses, and provides for their registration and liquidation. The ***Law on Joint-Stock Companies*** creates companies with limited liability, general powers, and shareholder management, either open (free trading of stock) or closed (restricted sales of stocks). The law specifies minimum capital requirements for registration.

The *Law on Taxation of Profits of Enterprises and Organizations* outlines policy with respect to tax on profits, generally defined as revenues less expenses. Businesses are entitled to deductions for certain investments in the oil and coal industries and in environmental protection and for contributions to charitable organizations. In addition to the tax on profits, all enterprises must pay a tax on dividends, interest, and income received from an ownership interest in another enterprise if there are no exemption in bilateral tax treaties. And enterprises must pay a value-added tax on the sale price of most items. In addition, the Russian Government imposes a variety of other taxes on businesses, including a tax on securities operations, a tax on the property of business, an excise tax applied to certain luxury items, and a tax on land owned by businesses.

The *Temporary Import Customs Tariff of the Russian Federation* that is usually revised on a semiannual basis subjects imports to various levels of customs duties, usually between 5 and 30 percent of the value of the item. Export quotas and duties, chiefly on raw materials, were provided for by law in 1991. In April 1995, however, export duties on all types of forest products were abolished. Import tariffs on forest products remain and vary from 5 percent to 30 percent.

Foreign currency restrictions require that the purchase or sale of foreign currency be effected only by authorized banks, prohibit Russian entities from establishing bank accounts abroad without permission from the Central Bank, restrict transactions between Russian entities in foreign currency, and restrict the payment of wages or bonuses to Russian citizens in foreign currency.

The *Civil Code* sets forth the general commercial law of Russia and contains standard contract principles. Foreign citizens have equal legal standing with Russian citizens.

The *Law on Ownership* specifically grants citizens and legal entities the right to own property other than land. Property owners are entitled to manage their property at their discretion, to transfer property to third parties, and to use property as collateral. Foreigners may own property in Russia on an equal footing with Russians except where otherwise provided by law.

The ***Land Decrees*** allows rights to private ownership, purchase, sale, lease, and mortgage of agricultural land. A new draft Land Code is under preparation by the Parliament.

The ***Law on Competition and Restricting Monopoly Activity in Consumer Markets*** prohibits agreements among competitors, price setting or other activities to limit competition, and forbids the dissemination of false or distorted information that may damage competitors. An antimonopoly committee is empowered to review and approve or disapprove mergers and acquisitions and to order changes in contracts, to issue fines to market participants, and to split up enterprises occupying a dominating position in the market.

The ***Labor Code, the Foreign Investment Law,*** **the** ***Law on Collective Agreements and Contracts,*** **and the** ***Law on Pensions,*** all regulate labor relations in Russian enterprises. They set standards, minimum salary levels, and circumstances under which an employee may be fired or released; require employers to negotiate collective agreements; and set social insurance contributions by employers as a percentage of payroll costs.

The ***Law on Banks and Banking Activity*** sets forth the basic requirements for establishing and operating a bank. Foreign banks are permitted to operate in Russia provided they are lincenced by the Central Bank of Russia. Russian banks may also be owned by foreign investors.

The ***Law on Protection of the Environment*** assigns responsibilities among the various levels of government in the federation and sets forth the administrative and criminal liability for violations of the law.

The Law on Ecological Expertise requires that a mandatory environmental assessment be conducted by the federal authorities for all joint ventures with foreign investment in excess of $500,000, as well as for concessions and production sharing agreements.

The ***Law on Consumer Protection*** requires that manufacturers reimburse consumers for damages they have suffered due to defective goods and requires that manufacturers disclose certain information on the labels of their goods.

The ***Statute on the Issuance and Circulation of Securities and on Stock Exchanges in Russia*** provides for securities to be registered with the Ministry of Finance and for issuers to provide investors with prospectuses in connection with their investment.

ANNEX G

POVERTY, UNEMPLOYMENT, AND THE SOCIAL SAFETY NET IN FOREST COMMUNITIES

Siberia and the Far East include tundra and forest tundra (much of it mountainous), boreal forests, broad-leaved forests, dry steppes, and forest steppes.[1] Population densities are very low, less than one person per square kilometer throughout the area, with areas of one to ten persons per square kilometer in many of the river valleys, and areas of ten to twenty-five persons per square kilometer near the large cities and in lowland Khakasia. Most of the region is occupied by aboriginal groups, either alone or sharing the area with other indigenous groups.

Sociocultural Groups

Oversimplifying considerably, the population of these regions can be divided into three sociocultural groups: aboriginal, other indigenous, and migrant peoples. These groups differ in history of settlement, occupation and exploitation of land, degree of social modernization and participation in commercial and industrial activities, and dependence on the biological resources of their territory for physical subsistence and survival as a distinct cultural community. Although there are no clear boundaries between these three groups, cultural divides exist in the minds of the people who occupy these lands and are recognized in the regional and federal legislations governing the allocation of natural resources.

Aboriginal groups (also known as "small-in-numbers peoples of the North") were declared "primitive and underdeveloped" in the 1920s and accorded certain privileges by the USSR. These groups are engaged largely in subsistence fishing, hunting, and reindeer breeding, and are the least active in modern sectors of the economy. They view their way of life as the only means of survival for a culture distinct from the larger, multiethnic villages they inhabit Their way of life thus serves to inhibit their acculturation and assimilation into other segments of society.

Other indigenous groups arrived later. The practiced nomadic pastoralism (the Khakas, Yakuts) or mixed farming (Russian "old settlers"). Having learned many of the skills of the aboriginal people and developed more efficient or modern methods of their own, these groups also consider the semitraditional occupations of hunting, fishing and reindeer breeding as an essential part of their cultural heritage. Unlike the aboriginal people, these groups do not view modern practices or occupations and assimilation into modern society as threats to their cultural identity. The Russian conquests of the late seventeenth century

---

1 *This analysis of the social and economic characteristics of population groups in the forest zones of the eastern half of Siberia and the Far East covers the territories of the Khabarovsk and Krasnoyarsk Regions, the Republics of Sakha and Khakasia, the Taymyr (Dolgan-Nenets) and Evenk autonomous Areas, and the Jewish Autonomous Province - an area of 5.5 million square kilometers. Indigenous ethnic groups in other areas (especially those affected by oil, gas, mining and other developments in western Siberia and on the Kola peninsula) are not discussed in the annex. Each of these administrative territories has equal political status in the Federation, and consists of rural districts, towns, and cities, each with its own administrative body. Autonomous areas and regions are generally quite small in population and have often made cooperative economic and administrative arrangements with larger bodies, complicating the interpretation of statistics.*

greatly influenced the future of these indigenous groups. Tribes either evacuated the overrun territories or accepted Russian rule and settled down to farming. The Russian occupiers from the colonization era (then "old settlers,") assimilated into the local populations, creating a genetically mixed population.

The ***migrant groups*** are predominantly post-World War II ethnic Russians. Most came to work in the modern sectors of mining and transportation, and while some have taken jobs in commercial hunting or fishing, most consider these activities pastimes or hobbies.

Ethnic Groups and their Use of Forest Resources

Most of the aboriginal peoples belong to the Mongoloid race, with some cultures (the Khakas in particular) having a distinct Caucasoid mix, and other communities showing Uralic features (Bruk 1994). These people speak languages of the Turkic, Tungus-Manchurian, and Uralic families and the isolated languages of the Kets, Nivkhs, and Yukagirs (Bruk 1981). Many of the aboriginal ethnic groups, except the Udegeys, have been Christianized. However, there has recently been a revival of shamanism, a tradition that was never entirely suppressed (Puchkov 1994).

The ***aboriginal ethnic groups*** comprise the following:

- ***Evenk and Even.*** From Western Siberia to the Pacific Coast, the Evenks and Evens specialize in hunting, subsistence fishing (Gorokhov 1994a), and reindeer breeding (mainly transport animals). Other southern Evenks adopted farming and cattle breeding. The Evens and northern Evenks took on reindeer pastoralism, moving year-round in search of grazing lands (Sirina 1994).

- ***Negidal and Yukagir.*** The Negidals and Yukagirs are either fishermen with some hunters or hunter-fishermen with some reindeer breeding for transportation and some food collection and gardening to supplement their living. The Negidal are known to occasionally hunt seal (Smolyak 1994a). The two groups are settled in permanent villages (Gorokhov 1994b).

- ***Oroch and Udegey.*** These groups are forest hunters who also fish and collect nontimber food products, primarily for preserving. The Orochs and Udegeys live in permanent villages and do not maintain reindeer herds (Smolyak 1994b). The final cutting of forests in some areas forced part of the Udegey community to resettle, and they eventually disappeared. Those who have survived apparently do so because they have resisted final cutting in their territory (Shnirelman 1993).

- ***Nanay and Ulch.*** The Nanays and Ulchs were originally fishermen with some hunting and food collection (forest and seaweed, depending on the location of the village). They are settled in permanent villages. Today, they specialize in fishing or, in limited numbers, have taken jobs in logging or forestry enterprises (Messhtyb 1994; Smolyak 1994c).

- ***Nivkh.*** The Nivkh have long been engaged in fishing. They are settled in permanent or semipermanent villages at the mouths of rivers near the ocean. Food collection from the sea, coast, and forests was important to subsistence. Seal hunting and forest hunting were once practiced, mainly for fur marketing (Taksami 1981).

- ***Ket.*** The Kets are fishermen and forest hunters who also engage in reindeer breeding for transport. Food collection is a relatively unimportant activity. The Kets recently abandoned reindeer-herding and turned to hunting for fur as well as limited fishing and food gathering for subsistence (Vainshtein 1994).

- ***Selkup and Shorts.*** Fishermen, hunters, and reindeer herders, the Selkups were once nomadic but are now settled (Vasiliev 1994c). They collect forest food products and fish for a living. Intermarriage with Russians (the Selkups) and Khakas (the Shorts) have strongly affected the languages and traditional practices of these groups (Vasiliev and Malinovskaya 1993; Butanaev 1993).

- ***Dolgan.*** The Dolgans are a recent ethnic group (end of the nineteenth century) of aboriginal people mixed with Russian old settlers. They practice reindeer herding, hunting of wild reindeer for meat and furs, fishing, and the collection of tundra food products. While most have moved to local urban settlements, they still work in traditional occupations (Vasiliev 1994a).

- ***Nenets, Enets, and Nganasan.*** For these tundra-dwelling ethnic groups, reindeer herding continues to be the chief occupation, supplemented with fishing and reindeer hunting for fur and meat (Vasiliev 1994b).

Unlike these aboriginal groups, the ***other indigenous groups*** in the region (Yakuts, Khakas, and Russian Old Settlers) are ineligible for certain entitlements. While the status of the Yakuts and Khakas as indigenous people creates no problem, the definition of "indigenous Russians" is an issue. The population census of 1926 distinguished between locally born indigenous Russians and migrants (Russkie starozhyly). Ambiguity is introduced by the fact that some "indigenous" Russians may have been descendants of the massive migration of ethnic Russians to Siberia and the Far East that began around 1905. The true indigenous groups have a long history of contact with the aboriginal groups, and both understand each others' motives and behavior -- better than the migrants seem to understand either.

Russian Old Settlers are spread throughout these regions, but they occupy mainly river valleys. They are engaged primarily in fishing, in combination with some farming in the south and hunting in the north. Settlers never adopted reindeer breeding, although they once owned large herds that were pastured by the aboriginal people (Gulevsky and Simchenko 1994). Russian Cossacks also claim to be "indigenous," and in the Khabarovsk Region they are actively pressing for indigenous status, which would make them eligible for free hunting and fishing licenses and land allocation free of rent or tax. The Cossacks are unlikely to succeed since their claim is no more justified than that of many other groups.

The ***Khakas*** are Turkic-speaking, Christianized people and are divided into four tribes. They are among the most urbanized and "Russified" groups of Siberia. Originally these tribes were seminomadic pastoralists, breeding horses and sheep and practicing traditional mountain agriculture. Hunting was once extremely important, and rich and diverse ceremonies evolved around that activity. Collecting nontimber forest products, especially roots and cedar nuts, was also important for preparing traditional foods (Butanaev 1994).

The ***Yakuts,*** also Turkic-speaking and Christianized, were once composed of 35 to 40 tribal subdivisions, but no longer. Their traditional pursuits were similar to those of the Khakas (V. Ivanov 1994), until the eighteenth century, when the group that migrated to the northwest was forced to abandon horse and cattle breeding in tundra and forest-tundra. They adopted reindeer breeding for large-scale commercial production of meat and skins. This new group, called "reindeer Yakuts", emerged during the nineteenth century as probably the most efficient reindeer pastoralists in Eurasia. Many Yakuts continued to practice this occupation during the Soviet period but were absorbed into multiethnic state or collective farms.

Migrant populations are the majority population in many districts. Composed mainly of ethnic Russians, they also include Ukrainians, Byelorussians, and Tatars, and are generally well mixed and culturally similar to "European" Russians, at least in urban areas. The rural population is somewhat more complex, as the people tend to consolidate according to their cultural origins or to abandon the area for the cities after they have earned enough money. Siberian Russians tend to have the strongest cultural identity and behavioral differences, particularly in rural areas. These migrants usually work in mining, transportation, geological surveying, or logging enterprises and only exceptionally take up jobs in forestry or the traditional sector. An interesting side note is that many of the loggers are ex-convicts who, having learned their trade serving time in labor camps, migrate to these camps after their release.

Nongovernmental Organizations

Many nongovernmental organizations (NGOs) have sprung up in recent years to speak on behalf of aboriginal groups. They are engaged in a variety of activities, from collecting information about problems faced by the aboriginal groups and articulating their concerns for mass media, to studying and marketing traditional music and poetry and helping define the concepts for establishing territories of natural resources reserved for traditional use by aboriginal people. Some international NGOs are also active in Siberia and the Far East.

The most active and influential of the NGOs, represented in all administrative territories, districts, and villages, is the Association of Indigenous Small-in-Number Peoples of the North, Siberia and the Far East of the Russian Federation, founded in late 1993. This group is organized on a national level (as are the International Fund for the Development of Small-in-Number Peoples and Ethnic Groups, the Charity Fund for the Development of Culture of the North and of Small-in-Number Peoples of the North, the Fund for Survival and the Development of the Economy and Culture of Small-in-number Peoples of the North, the International League of Small-in-Number Peoples and Ethnic Groups, and the Fund of Small-in-Number Peoples of the North). Other NGOs are organized on a local level or on behalf of particular ethnic groups or linguistically or culturally related groups.

The Association of Indigenous Small-in-Number Peoples (known in different regions by variations on this name), in particular the regional division active in the Turukhansk and Eniseysk districts of the Krasnoyarsk Region and in Evenkia, was directly involved in defining the concept of "territories for traditional use" and the concept of "clan/family/communities." The Association also helped, in cooperation with the district administrations and specialists in the Federal Forestry Service, in organizing the communities and allocating lands.

Social and Cultural Problems

The problems facing the aboriginal groups are similar to the problems facing such groups throughout the world. Declining or increasing populations can become a social problem, as can acculturation (the loss of cultural and behavioral traits and the skills necessary to continue traditional occupations or social rituals) and assimilation, ethnic as well as linguistic, including the irreversible biological intermixing with nonaboriginal groups. These problems are exacerbated by relatively high unemployment, poverty, and alcoholism, a phenomenon linked directly to the dramatic decline in the proportion of men to women, due to the greater incidence of drowning, suicide, fights, and freezing among men (Sokolova 1990).

For most aboriginal groups, except the Selkups and the Ents, populations are rising in both relative and absolute numbers. The mass emigrations of nonaboriginal peoples from the North, which began in the early 1990s, could strengthen this trend and lead to the emergence of significant minorities of the aboriginal people in certain administrative areas.

Acculturation, assimilation, and biological intermixing are serious problems for most groups. Most of the aboriginal groups fall loosely into three population segments. One segment continues to live in nomadic or isolated communities. A second lives in multiethnic villages but continues to pursue traditional occupations. A third lives in large, multiethnic settlements and pursues occupations in the modern, nontraditional sectors. Approximately half the employed population of aboriginal groups falls into the third segment (Sokolova 1990).

Despite these differences in settlement patterns and lifestyle, they share strong linkages and a sense of shared clan, community, or ethnic identity. Links are especially strong between the small settlements and nomadic and isolated populations living in outlying camps. There are also common political, cultural, educational, kinship, economic, and linguistic ties, as well as trade and sharing between various settlements. Children living in the villages or larger towns, for example, spend their vacations with grandparents and other kin in reindeer or fishing camps where they improve their native language competence, learn traditional skills, and reinforce their sense of shared culture and identity.

Linguistic assimilation has occurred mainly through the adoption of the Russian language and, in Yakutia, the Yakut languages. But even when these tribes adopt one of these languages for convenience, the aboriginal groups continue to identify strongly with their ethnic origin (Kuznetsov and Missonova 1993). Ethnic assimilation is occurring mainly among urban aboriginal people who can no longer benefit from their ethnic minority status in the way their rural counterparts can. Genetic mixing (with nonaboriginal groups) is so common that the population increases of the Selkups, Kets, and Nganasans are attributable mainly to the children of mixed marriages. This may lead to ethnic ambiguity and, more important, to a loss of biological adaptation to harsh northern environments (Klokov and Koryukhina 1994).

The partition of lands between neighboring aboriginal and other indigenous communities, including hunting and fishing grounds and reindeer pastures, took place more than a century ago. Whatever its fairness originally, the partition is long-established and accepted, and both parties now view the divisions as "natural." Thus, the demarcation of "communal lands" for clan, family, or community groups has not caused social conflict. In cases where collective and state farming relocated many households, the social memory of the patterns of their elders has been recalled, and a new partition of lands, based on exchanges where necessary, has been carried out. However, when Russian old settlers and Yakuts leave their native areas and settle in new places, they may come into direct competition with aboriginal people for jobs in the traditional sector. The problem does not arise if they are seeking jobs in the modern industrial or transportation sectors. As newcomers, these people may find themselves treated as "migrants" rather than "indigenous peoples," regardless of the ethnic makeup of the community.

The most serious social problems among the migrant groups and between migrant groups and local or aboriginal groups arise because of various industrial enterprises. The problems are usually related to land use, either because the land is being spoiled or destroyed by the ecologically improper management of the enterprises or because the land use pattern upsets the established patterns of land allocation agreed to among the local population prior to the creation of the industrial enterprise. An example is the 4,000-5,000 hectares allocated annually to a geological survey enterprise in Evenkia in the late 1980s. The pollution left behind from oil test wells left the land no longer suitable for hunting, fishing, or as reindeer pastures.

Traditional Occupations and Culture

The concept of traditional occupations of people in these regions appears widely in Russian literature, mass media, and legislative and administrative affairs. It refers to hunting for fur and meat; trapping and hunting seals and small whales; fishing in rivers, lakes, and along seacoasts; reindeer breeding; collecting nontimber forest products such as berries, edible plants, nuts, mushrooms and herbs; and manufacturing ethnic clothes, utensils, and preserved foods. Many of these traditional occupations have undergone dramatic transformations as a result of collectivization and modernization - for example, the introduction of modern nets and mechanized sea vessels and the conversion from reindeer breeding for local transportation to large herding and breeding enterprises for the marketing of meat and skins.

The concept of "neotraditionalism," the development of traditional occupations in combination with modern social and medical services and related technologies, has recently emerged in discussions among Russian experts and aboriginal activists. This concept promotes:

- Dispersal of rural populations from large settlements to small villages centered on established hunting and fishing grounds and reindeer pastures.
- Increase in investment in the traditional sector.
- Increase in subsistence-oriented production for self-sufficiency.
- Establishment of the village community as the central social, cultural, and economic organization responsible to its people (Pika and Prokhorov 1994).

One survey revealed that over 90 percent of the aboriginal population of the Taymyr, Evenkia, and Krasnoyarsk regions believe that their future lies in the development of the traditional sector (Gulevsky and Simchenko 1994). Most Russian ethnologists believe that the survival of aboriginal ethnic groups depends on preserving and developing their traditional culture and occupations (Shnirelman 1994).

There are essentially two sectors of the economy that depend on the use of forest resources for these groups: the forest sector, which includes the management and use of timber resources, and the "traditional" occupations referred to above, including the management and use of nontimber forest resources. The forest sector includes both forestry and the timber industry. The Federal Forest Service oversees forestry activities through smaller administrative bodies (leskhoz) that conduct surveys; monitor the use of the forests; take charge of sanitary cutting, regeneration, leasing, or the allocation of land to different users (for logging, hunting, or fishing); and controls the activities of these users. Employees in this sector include foresters, forest rangers, and permanent or seasonal technical staff. Statistics on the forest industry are reported with agricultural statistics. The timber industry is represented by the Goskomlesprom -- the State Committee for Timber, Pulp and Paper, and Woodworking. The industry includes logging, wood-processing, and pulp and paper companies.

Of the remaining forest territory in these regions, 4 percent is managed by agricultural enterprises under the auspices of Rosagroprom, as state or collective farms or, more recently, joint-stock or cooperative enterprises. Finally, 1 percent of the territory is managed by the State Committee for Environmental Protection, as nature reserves, and 1 percent by other organizations such as the Ministry of Defense (for testing grounds). In theory, at least, this land cannot be used by the timber industry.

While some of agricultural enterprises engage in traditional agriculture such as cattle or horse breeding, hothouse horticulture, or crop farming in the south, many of the workers registered as "agricultural" are in fact professional hunters, fishermen, and reindeer herders. These hunters and fishermen are employed in state enterprises that harvest game and fish (gospromkhoz) and often employ their workers in harvesting other nontimber resources where they are abundant. There are also some aboriginal groups that have left the cooperative or joint stock companies in recent years, to form private clan, family, or community enterprises. There are collective enterprises (called koopzveropromkhoz) for breeding fur animals and for hunting and fishing, transporting and distributing basic supplies to rural areas, and processing and selling nontimber products. There are also fishing collectives, or rybkolkhoz.

Dependence on the Biological Resources of the Forests

The use of biological resources of the forest are important to indigenous groups as a source of direct employment, timber for construction materials and firewood, nontimber products for consumption and local barter and trade, and hunting and fishing as a hobby. These are socially important phenomena. Construction using wood materials and the use of firewood for heating and cooking are not only traditions of the aboriginal and other indigenous groups, but are readily adopted practices of the migrant population as well, whether rural dwellers or urban dwellers with country homes. The Federal Forest Service typically subsidizes (by offering lower rates to) veterans, disabled persons, aboriginal groups, and employees of the forestry and timber industry enterprises.

The gathering of berries, nuts, and mushrooms is pursued partly for economic reasons, especially among aboriginal people procuring traditional food, and partly for recreation. The harvest is almost entirely consumed by the gatherers, with little or no surplus for marketing. Gathering continues today, with complete disregard for licensing and regulations. Few, if any, attempts are made to enforce these regulations.

This is not so with hunting and fishing, however, which are also pursued both for subsistence and recreation. These pursuits are tightly regulated, mainly because of their profitable nature. Most state enterprises employ only about 40-50 percent of their hunters and fishermen full-time. The remainder of their catch comes from so-called amateur hunters, who depend heavily on their "hobby" as a source of income. These hunters often compete directly with the local aboriginal and indigenous hunters. No fisherman in the region can really be called an "amateur," since fish is an important seasonal staple for nearly all the population of these regions. Many "nonfishing" members of rural fishing communities spend weeks catching fish to feed their family for the remainder of the year.

Effects of the Current Economic Processes and Policies

A sociological survey in 1989 of twenty-five settlements covering 102 forestry and logging enterprises with 6,560 employees found that 42 percent of employees were in logging, transport, and wood processing in timber enterprises; 21 percent as forest guards; 12 percent worked each as forestry specialists and office workers in logging enterprises; 4.5 percent as directors and administrators with special education; and 3 percent as forestry workers (Rezultaty 1990).

More recent data (1994) show that of 598,000 workers in Khabarovsk, 5.5 percent were working in the timber industry and 0.7 percent in forestry. In the Krasnoyarsk region, including Evenkia and Taymyr, of 1.46 million workers, 5.8 percent were in the timber industry (logging, wood processing, and pulp and paper) and 0.5 percent in forestry. From 1993 to 1994, employment in the timber industry fell 19.4 percent (employment dropped 13.8 percent in the machine-building industry and rose 3 percent in the electric power producing industry over the same period).

Employment in logging enterprises in Krasnoyarsk Region declined substantially. Eleven of forty three enterprises were unable to pay salaries to their workers. Forest guards have long been among the lowest paid workers. In early 1995, they earned approximately 90,000 rubles a month. During that time, mean monthly salaries were 180,000 rubles in agriculture and 231,000 rubles in industry.

Very little data exist on employment and income in the traditional sector. In Khabarovsk in 1993, 4.3 percent of the employed population was working in agriculture and 0.1 percent in fishing. Of the aboriginal population (141,000), about 47 percent was employed in agriculture and traditional sectors (Sokolova 1994), while roughly 25-30 percent of the able-bodied population was unemployed, surviving through subsistence fishing, hunting, food gathering, and reindeer breeding. The same study claims that some 15 percent are unwilling to work at any job (Klokov and Koryukhina 1994).

In the Krasnoyarsk region (including Evenkia and Taymyr), the number of domestic reindeer on state enterprises fell from 121,000 in 1981 to 78,000 in 1993 (the number of reindeer in private ownership increased from 17,000 in 1981 to 26,000 in 1994). The production of fish declined from 5400 tons in 1980 to 3,300 tons in 1993. The production of sable fur in 1993 was only 15 percent of production in 1985 (based on purchases from hunters) (Narodnoe khoziaystvo Krasnoyarskogo 1994).

The reason for these declines is obvious. The sharp rise in the prices of fuel and declining local demand for meat and fish due to dramatic increases in outmigration magnified the inefficiencies of many of the traditional sector activities once heavily subsidized. As a result, those employed in the traditional sector are becoming more active in subsistence hunting, fishing, and reindeer breeding. These households are finding it increasingly difficult to acquire cash to buy necessary supplies. The primary income-earners in many households are pensioners or those who qualify for child support or who work in village administration, schools, or hospitals.

In 1991, there were twelve state farms in Evenkia, six specializing in reindeer breeding and hunting and six in breeding fur-bearing animals. All twelve were economically inefficient and survived on state subsidies. Only half the 803 people employed in hunting and fishing for salaries were aboriginal people. In 1992, there were fifteen state farms and three collective enterprises engaged in these activities. The number of professional hunters and fishermen employed had dropped to 230, 78 percent of whom belonged to aboriginal groups.

In Taymyr in 1992, there were eighteen state farms, one state enterprise for hunting and fishing, and one collective enterprise for breeding fur animals, hunting, and fishing. These enterprises employed 995 professional hunters and fishermen. Some 430 nomadic households (down from 670 in the early 1980s) and the 18 indigenous households were employed in the traditional sector and operating as part of the state farms. Average annual production of domesticated reindeer meat fell 27 percent from the early 1970s to the late 1980s, fish production remained relatively stable, and fur hunting became virtually unprofitable (Gulevsky and Simchenko 1994).

In Khabarovsk, the total area of hunting grounds, including that used by aboriginal communities, state enterprises, and amateur hunters, diminished from 78.9 million hectares in 1990 to 60.1 million hectares in 1993 (Sostoyanie okruzhayushchey 1994). The region had two state farms and one collective farm, five collective fishing enterprises, one state hunting and fishing enterprise, and one collective enterprise for breeding fur animals (Gulevsky and Simchenko 1994). Average annual production of reindeer meat remained relatively stable over the period 1970-88, fur hunting remained profitable, and fish production increased 500 percent.

The official rate of unemployment among aboriginal people in Khabarovsk was 11 percent in late 1994, but the reality is far worse. Because many workers no longer receive salaries from enterprises that are not operating but have not officially closed, the real number of unemployed is close to 30 percent. Even and Evenk reindeer herders from state farms in the northern districts received no income. They were supplied with free flour and other basic foods by the Department of Ethnic Policies of the Regional Administration. Officials of Evenkia report a similar picture.

Other problems, some of which existed during the Soviet regime as well, include:

- *Poor living conditions leading to abandonment of forest settlements*. In 1989, 18 percent of those employed in forestry and logging were living in forest settlements. These settlements had an average population of 470 people, 37 percent of whom were working in the sector (Rezultaty 1990). When many of these logging enterprises ceased operation, much of the population was forced to relocate and social physical infrastructure (schools, shops, hospitals, public transportation and roads) deteriorated.

- *Low salaries*. Salaries in forestry enterprises have always been low, and surveys in 1989 showed that only 11 percent of employees in the sector were satisfied with their incomes. The average monthly salary in the USSR in 1988 was around 200 rubles, while salaries in the forest sector ranged from 116 to 170 rubles (the high end reserved for trained specialists in the forestry and logging industries). Much of the work done by these employees is hard, unskilled manual labor and much of the equipment is inappropriate or inadequate, making working conditions difficult. About 14 percent of workers and forest guards and 15 percent of specialists would like to change their occupation; only 15 percent would like their children to work in the same occupations (Rezultaty 1990).

- *The need for second occupations, mainly in agriculture, and some in hunting, fishing and gathering*. The result is reduced time, energy, and productivity in their "official" jobs. Surveys indicate that official salaries made up only 41 percent of total incomes, the remainder coming from agriculture and pensions or other payments to family members. Forest sector employees were working two to three hours a day in agricultural production in private households, a level comparable to that of agricultural workers (Rezultaty 1990).

- *Poor trade and supply of consumer goods, medical services, and recreational activities*. Thirty-one percent of employees in forestry and logging enterprises live in villages with a population of fewer than 500, 34 percent in settlements of 500 to 1000 persons, and 5 percent in isolated farmsteads. A third of these employees consider poor supply to be the most serious problem (Rezultaty 1990).

Migration is occurring from the northern to the southern districts of Siberia and the Far East or back to European parts of the former Soviet Union. Most of these emigrants are of the former migrant groups. Approximately 10,000 people (2,500 families) left northern districts of Krasnoyarsk Kray in 1994 alone, half of them from rural areas. In many cases, the entire employed population around a single enterprise emigrated. Experts estimate that up to one-third of the present population of the northern districts of the Far East will eventually leave.

While this emigration will have some positive effects, there are many negative effects, mainly on the aboriginal groups and other indigenous communities. These include the reduction or elimination of transportation links by air and water to local and regional centers and for the provision of regular supplies for local shops; declining demand for meat, fish, and furs; loss of skilled teachers, hospital, and other essential professionals; and the continued decline in employment.

Allocation of Land for Traditional Use[2]

The draft federal legislation on the legal status and rights of indigenous (small-in-number) peoples of the Russian North envisages the following:

---

2 *A detailed discussion on the recent developments can be found in Yamskov, 1996.*

- Creation of funds for the development of indigenous people at federal, provincial, (regional or republican), and district levels of administration.

- Permission for aboriginal NGOs to establish their own funds.

- Demarcation of territories exclusively for the traditional use of natural resources by aboriginal people and requiring the express agreement of the local aboriginal population to be used for any nontraditional (including logging) purpose.

- Definition of traditional occupations and a guarantee of the right to secure subsistence needs in this way for aboriginal people and nonaboriginal people that practice traditional occupations.

- Allowing nontraditional use of areas designated as areas of "traditional settlement and economic activities" only with the agreement of the local aboriginal population, with compensation for any economic losses incurred and requiring the sustainable use of any biological resources to be exploited.

Two other federal documents address aboriginal land rights. A joint resolution of the Government speaks of "priority development of traditional occupations," "exclusive rights for the use of biological resources in areas inhabited mainly by these people," and the creation of "territories for traditional use of natural resources by the aboriginal population." A recent Presidential decree requires provincial administrations to cooperate with associations of aboriginal peoples (NGOs) in demarcating territories for traditional use of natural resources.

The Krasnoyarsk region has not formally adopted similar legislation, but a draft law defines traditional occupations and declares that the territories are to be allocated for "indigenous ethnic groups" only and are not to be utilized for industrial activities without the express agreement of the local population. Provisional legislation of the Turukhansk and Yeniseysk districts provides for sixteen clan communities and has allotted them roughly 6 million hectares of territory (about 20 percent of the total area of the districts) as communal lands for an unspecified time. The communities have the right to approve or disapprove logging, mining, construction, or geological surveys on these lands, but they have no right to collect compensation for any of these activities.

Evenkia's draft "Land Law" defines "territories for the traditional use of natural resources by small-in-number peoples." Laws governing game management and hunting, territories for traditional use of natural resources, and clan communities are under review. Many clan communities have been organized in Evenkia, most consisting of five to fifteen working members. Russian Old Settlers and Yakut communities have the right to organize cooperatives or private farms, but land allocation preference will be given to Evenks and Kets.

The Republic of Yakutia passed legislation in late 1992 that allows aboriginal and other indigenous ethnic groups engaged in traditional occupations to form clan communities. The laws also provides that the land, renewable natural resources, and agricultural, hunting, and fishing grounds, along with forests and internal waters, will be leased to these communities for "indefinite use" at no cost and that no industrial or other use will be allowed without the community approval. The law also provides for demarcation of lands reserved for the establishment of new aboriginal communities in every district with a population engaged in traditional occupations. No such information is available for Taymyr or Khakasia.[3]

The Case of Khabarovsk Region

The regulations adopted by the Executive Committee of the Regional Parliament in 1991 define traditional occupations and territories for traditional use to include reindeer pastures, hunting and fishing grounds, areas for collecting berries and cedar nuts, forests, spawning lakes, rivers and sea inlets, and places for traditional religious ceremonies. These territories are allocated to aboriginal ethnic groups, represented by district or village associations, for indefinite use. Industrial development is not allowed on these lands, and the forests are reclassified as "Group I" forests, precluding any further final cutting. Other articles allow commercial hunting and fishing by nonaboriginal people with the agreement of the aboriginal population, the gathering of nontimber forest products and fishing for personal consumption without payment to the aboriginal people, and the cutting of timber for consumption by the aboriginal population or their enterprises, as regulated by the forestry service.

There are currently two types of land reserve for aboriginal people: territories for traditional use and communal lands. Territories for traditional use are reserved for traditional activities such as hunting, fishing, and reindeer breeding. The aboriginal population is given priority in choosing certain parts of these lands as communal lands, to be allocated exclusively for their use. Communal lands are leased by the state to particular aboriginal clans, families, or communities and are intended mainly for economic activities. These clans operate essentially as a cooperative enterprise, and only "working members" (those working at traditional occupations employing these lands) are allocated rights to the communal lands. The area of the communal land is determined by the number of workers in the clan, and each member has exclusive rights to some portion of these lands, as well as the right to bequeath that land to a son or daughter. The aboriginal spouse of a working member is eligible for a portion of this land so long as he or she pursues traditional occupations on this land but not if he or she is working, say, in town.

In applications for these communal lands, aboriginal groups have priority rights in choosing the land parcels, exemption from land rents or taxes on the use of natural resources, and free licensing for certain types of hunting and fishing for members of the clan who work in the state or collective enterprises in the traditional sector. Members of the clan may not grant or lease any part of the allocated lands to any other organization or individual, may not use any mineral or timber resources of the communal lands except for construction and personal fuelwood needs, may not sell licenses for the use of the land by others, may not leave these lands without use for more than a specified period of time (two-three years), and may not violate the seasons for hunting and fishing or regulations against the capture of designated species.

---

3 *Recent reports indicate that as of December 1995, 195 clan communities had been formed in the Republic of Sakha (Yakutia) — more than twice the number at the end of 1993. However, funding has not been forthcoming to support these communities, and many of them have begun to consolidate in order to function. Given that they are at an experimental or formative stage, their numbers may contract (or expand) depending upon government support, private investment, and other factors (communication from Gail Osherenko, Institute of Arctic Studies, Darmouth College, 23 May 1996).*

The benefits of belonging to a clan, family or community include extended lease of the lands to the community, the self-management of all aspects related to that lease, and the psychological benefit of working and living together with people who share common attitudes toward work, nature, and society.

In Khabarovsk region today, 34 million hectares are classified as "territories for traditional use;" of these, 13.5 million hectares have been designated as communal lands. By comparison, the total area of natural reserves (zapovednik) is only 1.3 million hectares of a total 77 million hectares of forest land throughout the region. In certain districts, the declaration of lands as "territories for traditional use" has resulted in a substantial decline in the volume of cutting, one reason why the former federal Ministry of Environmental Protection and Natural Resources considers these areas to be one of twelve types of protected areas.

Despite these formally legislated conditions, the actual situation is quite different. Final cutting still takes place on forests designated as Group I (where final cuttings are banned). Forestry specialists and timber industry specialists ignore these provisions because of the absence of any federal law. Few aboriginal groups protest this misuse of resources, because the logging enterprises provide them with badly needed jobs, transport links to district centers, and supplies of goods for local shops. Indeed, some communities such as the Ulch clan community in the Vanino district are doing the final cutting themselves (actually contracting migrant logger labor), despite its being expressly forbidden. The local forest service refuses to enforce the law, in order to make the point that these lands should be exploited for logging. As a result, only the forests immediately surrounding aboriginal villages are being spared final cutting.

Policy Recommendations

Ameliorate social conditions in areas of emigration. In addition to the aboriginal population and the other indigenous groups that are likely to stay in affected areas, some employees of forestry, game and fish management, and hydro-meteorological services are likely to remain as well. To make this possible, there is a need to protect social services, including transportation links, perhaps through travel subsidies for emergencies or for professional training and education. Alternatively, the relocation of the population, including accommodations and professional training in their new areas, should be provided through the district authorities.

Improve the functions of forestry and other natural resource management services. In general, the salaries of forestry personnel need to be upgraded, and targeted subsidies for transportation for employees working in remote areas should be provided. Training facilities should be established for members of aboriginal and other indigenous groups who might work as foresters and forest guards.

Develop the traditional sector of the economy. Foremost is the need to revitalize the transportation links that enable the local population to sell their products. Enterprises such as tourism, the breeding of fur animals, or the processing of non-timber products will require some start-up capital.

Ensure the land rights of aboriginal groups. Any financial assistance should be tied to further clarification and adoption of the federal laws on the status and rights of aboriginal people. Such assistance might also advocate the right of these communities to receive fair compensation for use of their lands by outsiders, especially in cases of depletion of nonrenewable resources. Also, the strict definition and implementation of protected territories will serve both social and ecological functions.

Assist aboriginal nongovernmental organizations. A fund should be established, linked to the goals and objectives of the NGOs, to assist in training members of aboriginal communities in forestry and game and fish management; to finance the college and university education of members of the aboriginal groups; to assist in the creation of processing industries in the traditional products sector; to provide special courses and training, including training in the traditional occupations; and to subsidize transportation links to district centers.

Expand targeted research activities in boreal forestry. Funding is needed for targeted research on the ecologically sustainable use of timber resources in areas inhabited by aboriginal groups, the social and economic situation in the traditional sector, and the development of a strategy for the combined use of these territories by the timber industry and the aboriginal population employed in the traditional sector. Financial assistance should be provided to the laboratories doing related research.

Organize and implement sociological surveys for all future projects. A regular and comprehensive survey by sociological, demographics, and economics staff in district administrations should be carried out to obtain up to date and detailed information on the current situation. Prior to formulating projects, field studies should be carried out in villages that will be affected (an excellent source of information is the household books available from the settlement administrative offices), and interviews should be conducted with the head of the village administration, as well as other village officials and local residents. These studies should be participatory in nature and should seek development strategies and options based on consultation with all segments of the society, including nomadic and isolated populations and village and town residents.

References

Bruk, S.I. 1981. Naselenie mira. Etno-demograficheskiy spravolchnik [Population of the World. Ethno-Demographic Handbook]. Moscow: Nauka Press.

_______. 1994. "Racial Composition of Russia's Population," In Narody Rossii (Peoples of Russia). Moscow: Rossiyskaya Entsiklopedia Press. pp. 37-41.

Butanaev, V. 1993. "Ethno-Political and Ethno-Cultural Processes in the Republic of Khakasia," in Issledovania po prikladnoy i neotlozhnoy etnologii [Studies in Applied and Urgent Ethnology]. Moscow: Institute of Ethnology and Anthropology. Paper Number 38.

_________. 1994. "Khakas" In Narody Rossii (Peoples of Russia). Moscow: Rossiyskaya Entsiklopedia Press. pp. 374-380.

Gorokhov, S.N. 1994a. "Evenks." In Narody Rossi (Peoples of Russia). Moscow: Rossiyskaya Entsiklopedia Press. pp. 416-419.

___________. 1994b. "Yukagirs." In Narody Rossi (Peoples of Russia). Moscow: Rossiyskaya Entsiklopedia Press. pp. 428-429.

Gulevsky, A. and Y. Simchenko. 1994. Economy of Peoples of Russian North: History and Contemporaneity. Moscow: Institute of Ethnology and Anthropology.

Ivanov, A. 1994. Ethno-Political Situation in the Republic of Sakha (Yakutia). In Issledovania po prikladnoy i neotlozhnoy etnologii. Moscow: Institute of Ethnology and Anthropology. Paer Number 61.

Ivanov, V. 1994. "Yakuts." In Narody Rossi. Moscow: Rossiyskaya Entsiklopedia Press. pp. 430-432.

Kaapcke, G. 1994. "Indigenous Identity Transition in Russia: An International Legal Perspective." In *Cultural Survival Quarterly*. Vol. 18, No. 2-3. pp. 62-68.

Khabarovsk Regional Department of Statistics. 1994. Sostoyanie okruzhayushchey sredy v Khabarovskom kraye v 1993 godu [State of Environment in the Khabarovsk Region in 1993]. Khabarovsk: Khabarovsk Regional Department of Statistics.

Klokov, V.F. and A.V. Koryukhina, A.V. 1994. Major Problems in Social and Demographic Development and Employment of the Peoples of the North." In *Etnograficheskoe obozrenie [Ethnographic Review]*. Number 5. pp. 64-76.

Krasnoyarsk Regional Department of Health. 1994. Narodnoe Khoziaystvo Krasnoyarskogo kraya v 1993 godu [Economy of the Krasnoyarsk Region in 1993]. Krasnoyarsk.

________________________________. 1991. Osnovnie demograficheskie pokazateli naselenia Krasnoyarskogo kraya [Major Demographic Characteristics of Population of the Krasnoyarsk Region. Krasnoyarsk.

Kuznetsov, A.I. and L.I. Missonova. 1993. "Ethno-Social Position of Evens in the Eveno-Bytantayskiy district of Yakutia." In Issledovania po prikladnoy i neotlozhnoy etnologii. Moscow: Institute of Ethnology and Antrhopology. Paper Number 35.

Kryazhkov, V.A., compiler. 1994. Status malochislennykh narodov Rossii (pravovye akty i dokumenty) [Status of Small-in-Number Peoples of Russia (Legal Acts and Documents)]. Moscow: Yuridicheskaya Literatura Press.

Messhtyb, N.A. 1994. "Nanays." In Narody Severa i Sibiri v usloviyakh ekonomicheskih reform i demokraticheskih preobrazovaniy [Peoples of the North and Siberia under Conditions of Economic Reforms and Democratic Transformations]. Moscow: Institute of Ethnology and Antrhopology. pp. 374-389.

Natsionalniy sostav. 1990. Natsionalniy sostav naselenia RSFSR po dannym Vsesoyuznoy perepisi naselenia 1989 goda [Ethnic Composition of Population of RSFSR, According to the All-Union Population Census of 1989]. Moscow: Republican Informational and Printing Center.

______________. 1990. Natsionalniy sostav naselenia Khabarovskogo kraya [Ethnic Composition of Population of the Khabarovsk Region]. Khabarovsk: Khabarovsk Regional Department of Statistics.

_______________. 1991. Natsionalniy sostav naselenia SSSR po dannym Vsesoyuznoy perepisi naselenia 1989 goda [Ethnic Composition of the USSR Population, According to the All-Union Census of 1989]. Moscow: Finansy i Statistika Press.

Pika, A.I. and B.B. Prokhorov, editors. 1994. Netraditsionalizm na rossiyskom Severe [Neotraditionalism in the Russian North]. Moscow: Institute of Economic Prognosis.

Plant, R. And M. Tomei. 1994. Prava na zemlyu korennykh i vedushchikh plemennoy obraz zhizni narodov v otdelnykh razvitykh i razvivayushchikhsia stranakh: Obzor voprosov prava i politiki, a takzhe tekushchey deyatelnosti [Rights to Land of Indigenous and Tribal Peoples in Some Developed and Developing Countries: Review of Legal Problems and Policies and of Current Activities]. Geneva: International Labour Office.

Professionalniy sostav. 1992. Prefessionalniy sostav naselenia korennykh i naibolee mnogochislennykh natsionalnostey Rossiyskoy Federatsii po dannym perepisi naselenia 1989 goda [Occupational Structure of Population, Belonging to Indigenous and Most Numerous Nationalities of Russian Federation, according to 1989 Census]. Moscow: Republican Informational and Printing Center.

Puchkov, P.I. 1994. Religious Composition of Russia's Population." In Narody Rossii (Peoples of Russia). Moscow: Rossiyskaya Entsiklopedia Press. pp. 41-43.

Shnirelman, V.A. 1993. "The Bikin Udegeys: Politics and Ecology." In Issledovania po prikladnoy i neotlozhnoy etnologii. Moscow: Institute of Ethnology and Anthropology. Paper Number 43.

Shnirelman, V. 1994. "Hunters and Gatherers at the End of the 20th Century." In *Etnograficheskoe obozrenie [Ethnographic Review]*. No. 4. pp. 140-144.

Sirina, A.A. 1994. "Scientific Report on the Expedition to Verkhnekolymsk Yukagirs in 1993." In Narody Severa i Sibiri v usloviyakh ekonomicheskih reform i demokraticheskih prebrazovaniy. Moscow: Institute of Ethnology and Anthropology. pp. 260-333.

Smolyak, A.V. 1994a. "Negidals." In Narody Rossii (Peoples of Russia). Moscow: Rossiyskaya Entsiklopedia Press. pp. 244-246.

__________. 1994b. "Oroches." In Narody Rossii (Peoples of Russia). Moscow: Rossiyskaya Entsiklopedia Press. pp. 260-262..

___________. 1994c. "Ulches." In Narody Rossii (Peoples of Russia). Moscow: Rossiyskaya Entsiklopedia Press. pp. 366-369.

Sokolova, Z.P. 1990. "Problems of Ethno-Cultural Development of Peoples of the North." In Rasy i narody (Races and Peoples). Moscow: Rossiyskaya Entsiklopedia Press.

__________. 1994. "Peoples of Russia's North under Conditions of Economics Reforms and Deomocratic Transformations." In Narody Severa i Sibiri v usloviyakh ekonomicheskih reform i demodraticheskih preobrazovaniy. Moscow: Institute of Ethnology and Antrhopology. pp. 16-49.

Taksami Ch. 1981. "Nivkhs." In Rasy i narody (Races and Peoples). vol. 11. pp. 212-220.

USSR State Committee on Forests. 1990. Rezultaty sotsiologicheskogo issledovania predpriyatiy lesnogo khoziaystva [Results of Sociological Study of Forest Sector Enterprises]. Moscow.

Vainshtein, S.I. 1994. "Kets." In Narody Severa i Sibiri v usloviyakh ekonomicheskih reform i demokraticheskih preobrazovaniy. Moscow: Institute of Ethnology and Anthropology. pp. 355-373.

Vasiliev, V.I. 1994a. "Dolgans." In Narody Rossii. Moscow: Rossiyskaya Entsiklopedia Press. pp. 149-150.

__________. 1994b. "Nenets." In Narody Severa i Sibiri v usloviyakh ekonomicheskih reform i demokraticheskih preobrazovaniy. Moscow: Institute of Ethnology and Anthropology. pp. 412-440.

__________. 1994c. "Selkups." In Narody Rossii. Moscow: Rossiyskaya Entsiklopedia Press. pp. 312-314.

Vasiliev, V.I. and S.M. Malinovskaya. 1993. "The Concept of Ethno-Political, Economic and Cultural Development of Small-in-Number Peoples in the North of Tomsk Province." In Issledovania po prikladnoy i neotlozhnoy etnologii. Moscow: Institute of Ethnology and Antrhopology. Paper Number 54.

Yamskov, Anatoly N. 1996. "Conflicts over Defining and Allocating Territories for the Traditional Use of Natural Resources by Aboriginal Peoples in Russia", Joint IUAES/IGU Congress, Linkoping, Sweden, August 22, 1996.

Zykov, F. 1994. "Ethno-Political Situation in the Republic of Sakha Before and After the Elections of December 12, 1993." In Issledovania po prikladnoy i neotlozhnoy etnologii. Moscow: Institute of Ethnology and Antrhopology. Paper Number 71.

ANNEX H

STATUS OF THE PROTECTED AREA SYSTEM FOR THE FOREST SECTOR

The vast landscapes of the Russian Federation represent one of the last opportunities on earth to conserve relatively intact ecosystems large enough to allow ecological processes and wildlife populations to fluctuate naturally. The unique assemblages of species in the Greater Caucasus and the Russian Far East surpass in diversity and level of endemism that found in temperate forests anywhere in the world.

Scope of the Protected Areas System

A proportion of this biodiversity is protected by Russia's nature reserve system, which covers nearly 6 percent of the country. It is the largest, one of the most important, and until recently one of the best organized systems in the world. It consists of strict nature reserves (zapovedniks) used for research and biosphere conservation, occupying 1.42 percent of Russia; national parks which are protected, but allow limited tourism, agriculture, and grazing, occupying 0.38 percent of Russia; special purpose reserves (Zakazniks), established to safeguard certain flora or fauna populations, usually for a specified period, occupying 4 percent of Russia; and natural monuments (pamyatniki Prirody).

In 1995, Russia had 89 nature reserves, covering an area of 29 million hectares, and 28 national parks, covering nearly 6.5 million hectares. A 1991 inventory showed more than 1,000 special-purpose reserves with a total area of 44 million hectares; 69 of them are at the federal level, occupying 11.4 million hectares.

Although nature reserves have been established in all thirteen of the physical-geographic zones (Arctic, Fenno-Scandinavia, Russian plain, Caucasus, Urals, Western Siberia, Caspian-Turgaiskaya, Central Siberia, Southern Siberian mountains, Yano-Kolyma, Baikal-Djugdjur mountain region, Amur-Sakhalin, Northern Pacific region), they are unevenly distributed. For example, twenty four nature reserves have been established in the Russian plain region, while the Arctic zone has only two.

The eighty-two nature reserves administered by the State Committee for Environmental Protection (formerly by the Ministry of Environmental Protection and Natural Resources) make up more than 40 percent of the world's strict scientific reserves (IUCN Category I). Russia has a distinguished history of research in these reserves, sixteen of which are part of the UNESCO Biosphere Reserve Program, and has amassed an enormous amount of scientific data about them over the decades.

Russian nature reserves protected a significant number of species, many of them listed in Russian and International Red Data Books of Rare and Endangered Species. Box H.1 provides additional information on species representation in the protected areas system.

Box H.1: Species Protected in Russia's Nature Reserves

The most recent reliable data on the number of species protected in strict nature reserves were recorded in 1987, when there were fifty-nine nature reserves. Many more nature reserves have been created since then, so these figures are only indicative of the importance of protected areas in habitat protection. In 1987 nature reserves protected:

- One hundred sixty eight species of terrestrial mammals (69 percent of terrestrial mammals found in Russia). Of the sixty-five mammal species listed in the Red Data Book of Russia, twenty-five (three marine species) were identified in nature reserves.

- Five hundred fifteen species of birds (83 percent of the birds found in Russia). Of the 109 birds listed in the Red Data Book of Russia, 60 were identified in nature reserves.

- Forty species of reptiles (61 percent of reptiles found in Russia). Of the eleven reptiles listed in the Red Data Book of Russia, five were identified in nature reserves.

- Twenty-six species of amphibians (96 percent of amphibians found in Russia). Of the four amphibians listed in the Red Data Book of Russia, three were identified in nature reserves.

Little information is available on species diversity and ecosystem types in national parks. However, rough estimates indicate that up to 800 vascular plants and up to 200 vertebrates (190 birds and 50 mammals) have been recorded in national parks.

Reliable data on species diversity in special purpose reserves and natural monuments are not available.

Problems of the Protected Areas System

This historic reserve system represents a systematic and comprehensive attempt to maintain and protect a significant sample of the world's biodiversity. But the system now faces serious threats. At least half the nature reserves and one-third of the national parks are in or are approaching a critical state, and the system itself is in jeopardy. Exploitation of natural resources is increasing, often supported by local administrations. Increasing use and access to public lands under privatization and deregulation have intensified the threats to protected ecosystems, while adjacent lands are often subject to clear-cutting, mining, agriculture, and pollution from industrial activities. There are no clear and consistent laws to guarantee the long-term survival and financing of the protected areas system (see Box H.2). Compounding these threats is the precipitous drop in the levels of funding to support the protected area networks. In real (constant price) terms, financial support for the nature reserves network has declined to less than 20 percent of the 1985 level.

Box H.2: The Law on Protected Areas

The Law on Protected Areas of March 1995 creates a framework for strengthening and coordinating protected areas system. This is the first national law dedicated solely to protected areas. It describes legal aspects for planning and management of all types of reserves. The law divides responsibilities for different types of protected areas between federal and regional authorities. Among the strengths of the new law are:

- Empowerment of the ranger (enforcement) service in nature reserves and national parks to an authority comparable to that of the police.

- Prohibition against privatizing property on the territory of protected areas.

Definition of the educational role of nature reserves, in addition to conservation and research. The law is weak, however, on defining the financial rights and responsibilities of protected area managers. For example, it does not provide clear guidance on how the protected areas administration can use fines and other payments collected from violators of protective regimes, including both individuals and organizations.

Institutions and Management

The ability of the protected area system to respond to Russia's new and changing realities is being hampered by serious institutional failures, in addition to severe reductions in funding. Shortcomings are apparent at all levels of protected area management: interagency cooperation, departmental functions, and the operation of individual protected areas. Management structures within the responsible federal agencies are weak and fragmented.

Protected Area Operations

Planning for conservation programs in individual reserves is inadequate, and neither nature reserves nor national parks are required to develop management plans. There is little incentive for much-needed innovation in planning or for projects encouraging sustainable use of natural resources. Work conducted by scientists in nature reserves is poorly integrated into management and policy formulation. Even the limited funds available for individual protected areas are not being used effectively. Virtually all reserve budgets are spent on wages and salaries, which do not even reach subsistence levels. Maintenance of infrastructure is ignored. Offices, laboratories; vehicles, and other equipment are deteriorating. As a result, many protected areas have become almost defenseless against the growing pressures around their borders.

Training for Protected Area Staff and Management

Most directors of nature reserves and national parks lack specific experience or training in protected area management, although they often have a diverse and valuable range of skills. There is a severe lack of training programs for protected area staff and management to build on their skills and to provide a common understanding of the purpose of nature reserves. Changing circumstances and the prospect of continued financial cutbacks call for urgent attention to training in new approaches to protected area management and planning. Staffing policies need to be developed based on smaller numbers of more flexible and better-trained staff.

Public Support

The Russian population knows little about the protected area network, and few communities have benefited from protected areas. Building public support has never been part of the philosophy and policy of Russia's protected areas. As a result, society as a whole hears, sees, and knows little about the great natural treasures of Russia. The lack of public support can be partly attributed to the general exclusion of people from protected areas. The viability of protected areas depends on public support from the Russian people as a nation, from local communities surrounding protected areas, and from regional and local governments. Such support is minimal at present.

Need to Expand the Protected Area Network

If Russia's protected area network is to provide adequate protection for biodiversity, the system will require significant additions. During the next several years, while land ownership relationships are still shifting, the government has a unique opportunity to set aside large tracks of land for free or virtually for free. However, land prices are currently being established, and they are especially high in areas rich in natural resources. These prices are expected to continue to rise as resource use and privatization accelerate. Effective action must be taken in the next few years to conserve large, unprotected wilderness areas that are not yet sufficiently represented in the protected area network. It may soon become financially impossible for the federal Government to create new protected areas, and the importance of government vision and commitment in matters of environmental protection and conservation cannot be overstated.

ANNEX I

WILDLIFE MANAGEMENT AND SUSTAINABLE FOREST DEVELOPMENT

Wildlife Management at the Federal Level

The Game Department

Before 1992, the Department for Hunting was an autonomous agency with representatives in each region and with direct access to the USSR's Council of Ministers. In an attempt to reduce the bureaucracy, the Government of the Russian Federation created the Ministry of Ecology in 1991, combining Russia's major resource agencies under the same administrative umbrella. In 1992, two decrees separated the industrial, profit-making committees from resource-protection committees. The Game Department, which fell into the first category, was subsequently removed from the Ministry of Ecology (later, and now the former, Ministry of Environmental Protection and Natural Resources or MEPNR; now split into the State Committee for Environmental Protection and Ministry of Natural Resources) and incorporated into the Ministry of Agriculture and Food, where it remains. Its official name is the Department of Protection and Rational Use of Hunting Resources. The head of the department is a Deputy Minister of Agriculture.

Functions and responsibilities of the Game Department are defined by the Law on the Protection and Use of Wildlife (1982), which provide the department's legal framework. Minor changes and amendments to these laws have been made over time, mostly related to the classification of game animals. In essence, the department is responsible for the management of approximately seventy legally defined game species on all lands except for designated protected areas such as zapovedniks. The principal responsibilities of the Game Department are summarized in Table I.1.

The resolution “On Specially Authorized State Organs of the Russian Federation in the Domain of Environmental (Nature) Protection” (September 1993) defines the former MEPNR’s rights and responsibilities for game animals. Apart from law enforcement and control, the former MEPNR approved quotas on major commercially exploited game animals in cooperation with the Game Department. Fish resources fall under the jurisdiction of the State Committee of Fisheries, an autonomous body reporting directly to the Government.

The “Order on the Protection and Regulation of the Utilization of Wildlife” gives MEPNR the authority to p*rovide for/ secure/ guarantee the protection and regulate the utilization of wildlife objects, excluding those found on the attached list of game species, or appointed/stated to have commercial demand* (translated). The term “wildlife,” however, is not clearly defined. The order does not state explicitly whether all nongame species, including the 250 animal and 500 plant species listed in Russia's Red Book (1984 status), are under the jurisdiction of the MEPNR. To date, nongame species do not enjoy any legal protection. The Red Book lists are currently being updated by the MEPNR.

Table I.1: Principal Responsibilities of the Game Department

Federal level	*Regional level*
• Manage and protect wildlife resources (game species only) • Approve hunting quotas • Respond to interagency referrals as related to wildlife matters at the federal level • Assist in resolutions of land and resource use conflicts • Produce and provide regions with hunting licenses and other related paperwork	• Conduct, commission, and take part in wildlife inventories • Propose and distribute hunting quotas among user groups • Distribute and sell hunting licenses • Assemble and provide hunting statistics • Enforce hunting regulations and wildlife laws, prosecute violators, collect fines • Represent Game Department on regional interagency committees • Arrange and administer commercial and other hunting leases

Although the former Ministry of Environmental Protection and Natural Resources (MEPNR) has changed its name since its creation in 1988 (and has now been split into two organizations, the State Committee for Environmental Protection and the Ministry of Natural Resources), its mission is still the protection of the environment. Without legal mandate, the former MEPNR made several attempts to gain legal authority over the protection of flora and fauna. Earlier draft legislation covering all of Russia's flora and fauna, prepared by the MEPNR, has not been approved by the Council of Ministers. Parliament has prepared its own version, but it too has not been approved. According to MEPNR, the old legislation on the management of wildlife contradicts the new Constitution.

Russian Association of Hunters and Fishermen

The Russian Association of Hunters and Fishermen (Rosokhotrybolovsoyuz), founded in 1945, is the oldest and largest nongovernmental organization (NGO) in Russia. With a membership of 3 million, the association is represented through seventy-eight regional chapters within each of Russia's seventy-eight "subjects" of the federation (shorthand for republics, territories, krays, and autonomous regions). Some regional societies date back more than 100 years. The association supervises an area of 250 million hectares of land and 4 million hectares of water bodies (leased for hunting purposes).

The main functions of the association are to lobby the interests of its members on national and regional levels, to support local chapters, and to market hunting and fishing-related equipment through regional chapters. The association has been instrumental in formulating Russia's hunting legislation. It has successfully lobbied for laws on gun ownership, contributed draft legal and regulatory documents for consideration by the Federal Game Department, and organized and implemented international conferences on hunting and fishing (for example, Atlantic Salmon Conference in collaboration with Canada and the United States), It is affiliated with several international hunting and fishing organizations.

The only other hunting-related NGO is connected to the military, which still has its own hunting areas throughout the federation. No data are available on these areas. According to the Federal Game Department, there are over 4,000 hunting and fishing-related sport clubs in Russia and 500 independent game hunting enterprises.

Wildlife Management at the Regional Level

The Krasnoyarsk and Khabarovsk regions were selected as representative areas on wildlife management for Siberia and the Far East. Some statistical information is presented in Table I.2.

Table I.2: Game-Related Data for the Krasnoyarsk and Khabarovsk Krays, 1994

Category	*Krasnoyarsk Kray*	*Khabarovsk Kray*
Total size of kray (hectares)	237 million	82 million
Number of districts	52	17
Distances (kilometers)		
North to South	3,000	2,000
East to West	1,300	400
Economy (by priority)	Gold mining Weapons industry Forestry Hunting and trapping	Gold mining Forestry Hunting and trapping
Employment		
Forest sector (number)	3,600	2,700
Forest land in ha	80 million	48 million
Commercial forest (hectares)	52 million	n. a.
Annual allowable cut in cubic meters	54 million	29 million
Actual cut	8 million	6 million
Number of forest fires	1000	700
Zapovedniks (hectares)	31.8 million	1.3 million
Total number of hunting blocks	105	n. a.
Number of game inspectors	86	76
Wildlife related violations	4,500	837
Population	3.03 million	1.5 million
Cities	2.19 million	1.2 million
Country	0.84 million	0.3 million

Sources: Krasnoyarsk Kray and Khabarovsk Kray Forest Committees, 1995.

Game Departments

Krasnoyarsk Kray is composed of forty-four districts. The headquarters of the kray's Game Department is in Krasnoyarsk. Six regional offices supervise the forty-four district offices, which are staffed by eighty-six game inspectors. An additional operational unit provides logistical support to the six regional offices. The major functions and responsibilities of the game inspectors are to enforce the hunting and wildlife management regulations applied to the kray and to control inventories implemented by leases and commercial hunting operations. The game inspectors are entitled to 50 percent of the fines resulting from wildlife-related violations, an incentive to apprehend violators as well as an open invitation to corruption. Corruption may become a serious problem if the wages paid to enforcement personnel do not keep up with inflation. In 1995, the average salary of a game inspector in Krasnoyarsk Kray was 84,000 rubles a month compared with 300,000 rubles a month for a forest inspector. The field personnel of the Game Department are poorly equipped, without money for vehicle maintenance, gas, uniforms, or other essential tools of the trade. Staff morale is low, and there is little motivation or enthusiasm for the tasks at hand.

The wildlife section of the former MEPNR's Regional Committee works parallel to the Game Department in its control function for wildlife use, although hunting quotas are established jointly. Relatively close ties are established with wildlife user groups and with the Regional Center for Registration and Prognosis of Hunting Resources, an advisory body to the Game Department. In general, the Krasnoyarsk Game Department is understaffed, poorly equipped, and underbudgeted. As a result, communications between districts and headquarters have broken down.

Of the Game Department's staff of eighty-eight, twelve work at headquarters and seventy-six in the seventeen district offices. Depending on size and the importance of a its wildlife, each district is served by one to three inspectors. The districts cover some 87 million hectares. According to the Chief of the Game Department, the average size of a control area per inspector should be no larger than 20,000 hectares, due to constraints in transportation and field equipment. This would require 4,350 inspectors for the kray, which is an unrealistic figure under current budget constraints.

Khabarovsk Kray has twenty zakazniks, with a total of 20 million hectares, under its jurisdiction, fifteen are of territorial and five of federal significance. The zakazniks are closed to hunting but not to logging. Logging is permitted if it does not adversely affect game populations, but in fact harvesting rules and silvicultural prescriptions are widely ignored due to lack of enforcement. The twenty zakazniks are managed by a staff of thirty-one and financed through the territorial fund. This fund is composed of revenues from the sale of hunting licenses, fines for wildlife violations, and donations. Of the 400 million rubles in the fund in 1994, 120 million went to the districts for wildlife protection and 180 million for operational costs of headquarters and Zakazniks. The constraints of the Khabarovsk's Game Department are the same as in Krasnoyarsk. The former MEPNR's Regional Committee works parallel to the Game Department, with even less interaction than in Krasnoyarsk. The relationship with the local Wildlife Research Institute, which provides the baselines for game harvest quotas, seems equally poor.

In general, management personnel and game inspectors are well-educated. Management positions are usually filled by professionals with university degrees in biology or related areas or degrees from one of Russia's two training institutions for game management. The institutions, in Kirov and Irkutsk, turn out approximately fifty graduates a year each. Game inspectors and other field personnel are trained mostly at Russia's two technical schools, in Irkutsk and Balshiha, each graduating approximately thirty students annually. Some game inspectors were formerly professional hunters.

Inventories, Quotas, Harvests, and Poaching

Inventories of game species in both krays are the responsibility of the "juridical bodies", with legal rights to the utilization and marketing of game species in designated hunting areas. Species-specific inventories are to be implemented according to inventory techniques and guidelines developed by the wildlife research institutes.

Russia's traditional system of wildlife inventories is unique, involving all stakeholders in a three-tiered process. Under the old system, inventories were controlled by game inspectors and scientific staff from the regional offices of the Game Department. Each region had its own independent institute for game science and game statistics, which conducted annual inventories and the research needed to determine species-specific harvest quotas. Based on the pooled results of the three-tiered inventories and research, quotas were determined on a district level. The only thing missing in the system was biophysical wildlife habitat maps for estimating habitat-specific biodiversity capabilities.

With privatization and other changes, the entire support structure of the wildlife management sector has deteriorated. Formerly well-organized commercial hunting operations, state-owned cooperatives, fur farming associations, state-financed wildlife research institutes, and game management authorities have been dissolved or left without leadership. Many highly skilled and experienced professionals have lost their jobs. The new system enables private persons, clubs, or groups to lease hunting blocks for commercial wildlife exploitation. In the absence of strict controls and proper guidelines, this provides an ideal medium for nepotism and corruption.

Hunting Regulations and Statistics

The Krasnoyarsk and Khabarovsk Game Departments issue an annual hunting guide with general information on legal aspects of hunting, the use of dogs, falconry, species-specific seasons, bag limits, nuisance species, and penalties and fines. Noteworthy are regulations regarding the commercial capture of songbirds (which is still legal), the right to hunt any wildlife for subsistence when working in the forest, the right of native people to exercise their traditional rights (subsistence hunting), and the right to market wildlife products. Specified animal products that may be marketed include meat, fur, velvet antlers, hard antlers, scent glands, gall bladders, and songbirds. All species that are not on a quota system can be harvested at will unless bag limits are specified by hunting regulations.

Harvest rates range from 10 to 20 percent of a population, depending on the species. In Krasnoyarsk and Khabarovsk Krays, harvest rates for hoofed animals are 10 percent. The Krasnoyarsk Game Department permits a harvest rate of 20 percent. Quotas are calculated for each district by inventoried species. The quotas identified by the research institutes are submitted to the regional Game Departments. The quotas are then discussed with the former MEPNR Regional Committee, adjusted, and submitted to the headquarters of the Game Department in Moscow. The quotas are then passed down to the district level through the regional game departments and then allocated to the leaseholders. This is a highly bureaucratic process.

The decision on quota allocation is left to the district administrators. According to the Khabarovsk Hunter and Fishermen Association, the bulk of the quotas goes to local hunters, and some are sold to international trophy hunters. There are no official guidelines on quota allocations, leaving the process open to corruption and abuse.

The harvesting of game species that are assigned a quota in Krasnoyarsk Kray is documented in Table I.3. The estimated harvest includes illegal hunting. Poaching is mostly for subsistence (Krasnoyarsk Game Department), except for the highly marketable sable, muskdeer, brown bear, and beaver. Protection for these species is urgently needed. Harvest statistics of game species for Khabarovsk Kray in 1994 indicate that the level of poaching, in particular of muskdeer and bear, could soon endanger the local populations of these two species (Table I.4).

Table I.3: Harvest of Game Species in Krasnoyarsk Kray

Species	*1991*	*1992*	*1993*	*1994*		
				Legal quota	*Reported harvest*	*Estimated harvest (including poaching)*
Moose	2,143	2,360	1,255	3,500	1,091	4,000
Reddeer	404	332	375	800	362	1,000
Roedeer	511	753	1,200	2,000	1,132	10,000
Reindeer	41,503	63,102	251	1,000	183	500
Muskdeer	85	70	91	protected	0	2,000
Wild boar	36	63	60	400	72	240
Br. bear	61	152	130	500	75	300
Sable	48,282	34,865	22,504	63,960	16,072	50,000
Beaver	189	121	53	258	54	2,000

Sources: Krasnoyarsk Kray Game Department and the Krasnoyarsk Wildlife Research Institute.

Statistics on local market value of game animals show that ungulate species are hunted mostly for meat (with the exceptions of some ungulates for their velvet antlers and muskdeer for muskglands) and furbearers mostly for fur (with the exceptions of brown bears for their gall bladders and beaver for their musk). The total black market value of the estimated game harvest in Krasnoyarsk Kray in 1994 was approximately 28 billion rubles; the real market value might be considerably higher.

It is very difficult to provide a proper economic perspective on the value of game animals in Siberia and the Far East. Approximately 90 percent of all furs produced in the former Soviet Union originated from these two areas. After the collapse of the former Soviet Union, the major commercial wildlife users disappeared. Illegal hunting undoubtedly accounts for a large part of wildlife harvests, often exceeding the legal quota many times over. There is little doubt that the wildlife at this point in Russia's market economy provides a livelihood to many people. In rural areas, game meat and fish are staple foods and critical to survival. Proper integration of wildlife management into forest resource management is therefore essential.

Table I.4: Harvest of Game Species in Khabarovsk Kray for 1994

Species Category	*Population size*		*Legal quota*	*Game Department reported harvest*	*Wildlife Research Institute*		*Price of permit per animal (Rubles)*	*Total revenue (mill. rubles)*
	Game Department	*Research Institute*			*Estimated harvest*	*Poaching (% of estimated harvest)*		
Moose	25,200	17,444	1,700	900	1,007	100	41,000	82,574
Reddeer	95,000	9,500	700	350	373	120	30,750	25,233
Reindeer	14,800	14,867	1,500	140	134	20	20,500	3,296
Roedeer	7,600	7,589	400	350	protected		20,500	
Muskdeer	18,000	18,051	1,000	160	115	500	14,350	9,901
Wild boar	4,300	4,372	500	320	109	20	28,700	3,753
Sable	110,000	107,500	35,000	23,000	21,856	50	2,050	67,207
Otter	3,800	3,847	250	70	65	100	1,230	1,599
Brown bear	4,500	4,530	550	156	156	150	41,000	82,574
Lynx	--	unknown	--	--	5	1000	--	--
Wo!verlne	--	unknown	--	--	27	unknown	--	--
Slb.marten	--	23,108	--	--	6,454	40	--	--
Mlnk	--	15,658	--	--	1,416	90	--	--
Coondog	--	2,989	--	--	664	50	--	--
Fox	--	2,079	--	--	56	100	--	--
Wolf	--	1,283	--	--	30	unknown	--	--
Fisher	--	11,664	--	--	483	unknown	--	--
Squirrel	--	200,000	--	--	51,800	30	--	--
Muskrat	--	11,885	--	--	7,745	40	--	--
Hare	--	32,324	--	--	2,764	unknown	--	--
Hazelgrouses	--	207,000	--	--	unknown	unknown	--	--
White sheep	2,000	--	--	--	24	unknown	--	--

Sources: Khabarovsk Kray Game Department and Khabarovsk Wildlife Research Institute.

Regional Wildlife Research Institutes

Before 1994, game management-related research in Russia was mainly the responsibility of the independent Scientific Research Institute of Hunting, headquartered in Kirov and with branches in each economic zone. For example, the Krasnoyarsk Institute is responsible for Krasnoyarsk Kray and the Khabarovsk Institute for the Far East covers the krays of Khabarovsk and Primorsky and the oblasts of Sachalinsk and Amurskaia. After 1994, the Scientific Research Institute of Hunting was transferred to the Russian Academy of Agricultural Sciences (RAAS). Each institute had the option of integrating into the new structure or staying independent. The Krasnoyarsk Institute chose independence and is now called the Regional Center of Registration and Prognosis of Hunting Resources. The Khabarovsk Institute opted to stay under the umbrella of the Russian Academy of Agricultural Sciences, hoping for greater budget security (only 10 percent of the institute's budget is provided by the academy). It is now called the Scientific Research Institute for Wildlife Management and Fur Farming (the Wildlife Research Institute of the Far East, for short).

A major responsibility of the research institutes has been to compile baseline data on populations of game animals, rare and endangered species, migratory birds, and wildlife habitats. Data collection was species-specific rather than habitat-oriented. Species other than "game" animals were studied on an as-needed basis. The institutes were well-funded under the old system and conducted extensive annual aerial censuses of large mammals, waterfowl, and habitats. In addition, fieldwork focused on research related to the determination of species-specific population structures (age class distribution, sex ratios, fertility rates, reproductive behavior, mortality rates, and other pertinent information). The information was used to determine harvest quotas, bag limits, and hunting seasons. Most of the data were collected by staff members, complemented through biological specimens and data supplied by professional hunters and other commercial wildlife users.

Since 1994, the institutes have become virtually immobilized as a result of dramatic cuts in government funding (up to 90 percent for Krasnoyarsk and Khabarovsk institutes) and loss of staff. The institutes have to find their own financing and depend heavily on grants from the regional committees of the former MEPNR and the ecological committees of the Khabarovsk and Krasnoyarsk Kray administrations; they also receive some contract funding from the regional game departments for the determination of annual harvest quotas. In effect, the institutes have lost their independence and are at the mercy of other agencies with their own agendas.

The situation is aptly summarized by Dr. Savchenko, the head of the Krasnoyarsk Research Institute:

> *Fifteen years of good quality ecological and biological baseline data, which have been collected systematically by twenty highly skilled and experienced professionals on all major game animals and rare and endangered animal species from throughout Krasnoyarsk Kray, are jeopardized through the lack of funds and the disintegration of the support structure. There will be no continuity of data flow. Surveys currently concentrate on lands to be leased, neglecting most other areas due to lack of funds. The core of the Institute's research team is now working full time at the University of Krasnoyarsk at the same time doing the most essential wildlife inventory/research work on an ad hoc, contract basis for the local Game Department.*

The Krasnoyarsk Wildlife Research Institute increasingly relies for its data on questionnaires filled out by leaseholders of lands that contain major hunting blocks. There are no funds for checking the validity of the responses. Inventories of nongame species, always a relatively low priority, have virtually ceased to take place in Krasnoyarsk Kray, except for some work on migratory birds.

The Khabarovsk Wildlife Research Institute seems somewhat better off. It employs six full-time research scientists, three lab technicians, and six research assistants (it employed twenty-five before 1992). Its 1994 budget was 64 million rubles, of which 29 million was spent an wages. Only 6 million rubles were provided by the Russian Academy of Agricultural Sciences. Budget shortages have forced the Institute to shut down most of its field stations and drastically scale down its fieldwork. Their current functions include monitoring game populations, conducting economic evaluations of game resources, developing special research projects in nature reserves and national parks, developing hunting guidelines, monitoring and assessing the economics of nontimber forest products, and implementing environmental impact assessments. The Institute also develops technical guidelines and criteria for the inventories of game species implemented through questionnaires for leaseholders of hunting blocks.

The Institute's staff members have established close ties with international NGOs such as the World-Wide Fund for Nature (tiger project, protected area work) and the Homocker Foundation. Current international support is provided to work on rare and endangered species and the identification of ecosystems with special protection needs. This work, based on data provided by interdisciplinary work groups under the auspices of the Institute, mainly involves compiling the ecological baseline data for the institute's ecological data bank. The institute has also developed high-quality geographic information system (GIS) capability that is being applied to the expansion of the network of protected areas, to habitat delineation for prominent endangered animal species such as the Amur tiger, and to the monitoring of sustainable resource use in the Kray.

Union for Fur Farming and Hunting Cooperatives

In the old system, the commercial operations of fur farming, trapping, and hunting were under the Far East special branch of Union for the Fur Farming and Hunting, called "Tsentrosoyuz," an affiliate of the State Game Department. A special section was responsible for inventories of game animals, which were conducted every ten years by expeditions typically composed of a wildlife ecologist, a professional hunter, and an assistant. The inventory system was based on sample plots of 1,000 to 2,000 hectares. Surveys were conducted in mid-winter along permanent transect lines. The wildlife inventory transects frequently coincided with the transects used for forest inventories (forest inventories are also implemented in a ten-year cycle).

The inventories served as the basis for general wildlife management plans, similar to the general forest management plans. The wildlife management plans provide guidelines on areas that are to be permanently or temporarily excluded from hunting and on species-specific management. The district-level inventory data are compiled at the district offices of the Game Branch, passed on to their headquarters in Krasnoyarsk and Khabarovsk, and from there to the regional wildlife research institutes for processing and archiving.

Since 1994, the inventory expeditions have been out of work. Some groups selected their own hunting areas, which have to be leased from the Game Department; others have offered their expertise on the free market as consultants. In Khabarovsk Kray, one three-person expedition team is loosely affiliated with the Russian Far Eastern Timberlands Survey and Inventory Enterprise, a subsidiary of the Russian Federal Forest Service.

Wildlife Users

Before the collapse of the former Soviet Union, wildlife users belonged to state-owned commercial hunting enterprises, hunting cooperatives, or hunting clubs. With the adoption of the Privatization Program, many state-owned operations have collapsed, and some have been replaced by leaseholds. There has been considerable confusion during the transition, and it will take time to get things under control.

Mandatory Inventories. Inventories of game species have long been a responsibility of wildlife users in Russia. Today, wildlife users have to lease hunting areas, and the leaseholders are required to conduct annual inventories of specified game species. The inventories required by the Game Department cover only species for which a harvest quota is calculated. The Wildlife Research Institutes in Khabarovsk and Krasnoyarsk implement their own annual inventories on additional species.

The inventories no longer cover all of the area of the krays, but only the areas that are being leased. Inventories are carried out in late winter and early spring using methods similar to those of the expeditions. Inventory data are due in the district offices of the Game Department by April 15. Inventory data on bear are due either in June (after bears have come out of hibernation) or in the fall. The late winter-early spring inventories are "carryover" counts, used to estimate population size after winter mortality. Beavers are subject to inventories in Krasnoyarsk Kray. The very low population estimate of 2,000 for the entire kray is indicative of large-scale habitat destruction (dredging rivers and creeks for gold, large-scale clearcut logging) and overharvest.

Juridical Hunting Bodies. Gospromkhoz are state-owned commercial hunting and trapping operations with rights to legally defined areas. In the past, gospromkhozes were found mostly in northern Siberia and the Far East, with responsibility for huge tracts of land. Currently, three outfits are still in operation in Khabarovsk Kray, covering an area of 4 million hectares with 200 staff -- 120 professional hunters and 80 administrative and marketing personnel.

Coopzveropromkhozes are cooperatives with commercial hunting and trapping privileges in designated hunting areas. They were the most common juridical hunting bodies in the former Soviet Union, controlling game harvests in over 80 percent of Khabarovsk Kray alone. Although most cooperatives have collapsed, ten still function in Khabarovsk Kray, with an area of approximately 20 million hectares and providing employment to about 500 persons in economically disadvantaged areas.

Hunting and Fishing Associations. Russia's traditional hunting and fishing associations are of local importance. Although every resident of Russia with a valid hunting license has the right to hunt anywhere in the federation, land access permits are required for the area in which the hunter wishes to hunt. Access permits are provided by the legal user of that parcel of land or through a hunting club that has rights to specially designated areas. Hunting and fishing associations cater to sport hunters only, who purchase licenses on a seasonal basis.

The Khabarovsk Hunting and Fishing Association has 39,000 members and a total land lease of 8 million hectares. Although most members hunt for pleasure and personal use of game (fur and meat), they are legally permitted to sell the products of the animals they kill. Annual membership dues are approximately US$2. Wildlife support programs of the associations include supplementary winter feeding of ungulates in harsh winters, the establishment and maintenance of saltlicks, and the taking of wildlife inventories.

Other Users. Other users include aboriginal people, individual leaseholders, and partnership leases. Eventually, all gospromkhozes and coopzveropromkhozes will be replaced by the new leasing system. The legal requirements and rights as specified in the hunting regulations and bylaws for

Krasnoyarsk and Khabarovsk Krays are the same for all user groups except aboriginal people (who hunt for subsistence free of charge). Special agreements are expected to be made with native communities.

All user groups are obliged to implement annual inventories, protect wildlife resources against poachers, implement habitat enhancement programs (establishment of crop fields, planting of shrubs and fruit trees), provide saltblocks in strategic locations, implement supplementary feeding programs on demand, use wildlife resources rationally and sustainably, prohibit hunting in designated areas within each hunting block on a rotation basis, and control predators and other dangers to wildlife.

Leases of Hunting Blocks

Leases of hunting blocks are negotiated by district authorities. In the absence of official guidelines, decisions on who qualifies for a lease, the optimum size of a hunting block, the reproductive potential of wildlife for the leasehold under negotiation, and the price of the lease are left to the discretion of the local administration. Aptly summarized by a high-ranking representative of the Khabarovsk Hunting and Fishing Association, "leases are provided through the old boys' network."

The Khabarovsk Game Department has developed a document on the "Decision on the Use of Territorial Hunting Areas in Khabarovsk Kray" which is binding for all lease agreements. It stipulates that leases can be provided to individuals, partnerships, and hunting clubs that meet its requirements. The leaseholder has to have proven qualifications as a professional hunter and on ability to meet the requirements for annual wildlife inventories. In Krasnoyarsk Kray, the requirements include the successful completion of a hunter training course.

The Decision also provides guidelines on the size of leaseholds, which range from 50,000 to 80,000 hectares in the northern section of the kray and 10,000 to 25,000 hectares in the southern section. Leaseholds are larger in the north because of lower wildlife productivity. A large section of the Decision deals with the proposed pricing structure, allocation of quotas, transfer of leases and rights, lease cancellation, legal definitions of technical terms, and violations and penalties.

Khabarovsk Kray has allocated 120 leaseholds so far (54 to individuals), and many more are being negotiated. The millions of hectares formerly covered by state commercial enterprises are rapidly being parceled out (the Khabarovsk District Ayano-Maiski, with 17 million hectares owned and operated by one leaseholder in the past, has been divided into seventeen individual leases). No data are available on the number of leases for Krasnoyarsk Kray. Leases are ten years in Krasnoyarsk Kray and twenty-five years in Khabarovsk Kray.

Price Structure of Leases and Licenses

Leasing prices for hunting blocks in Krasnoyarsk Kray are set and negotiated by the district administrators, and prices may range from 5 to 1,000 rubles per hectare (1995 prices), depending on accessibility, demand, and game species diversity and abundance. In Krasnoyarsk Kray, guidelines on prices are provided by the Decision on the Use of the Territorial Hunting Areas. This document stipulates that 11 percent of the current federally established minimum wage be charged per 1,000 hectares in the northern part of the Kray and 35 percent per 1,000 hectares in the south. Charges per 1,000 hectares may go as high as 80 percent of the minimum wage.

The current pricing structure for hunting licenses and royalties is chaotic and in urgent need of revision. Regional authorities would prefer to have transparent and straightforward federally approved guidelines on prices. The price structure for species tags (animals on quotas) and royalties in both krays is based on percentages of minimum wages. This system is confusing and complicated. In Krasnoyarsk Kray, licenses issued to commercial hunters generally cost twice as much as those issued to hunting clubs. For example, species tags for reindeer equal 0.7 percent of the minimum wage for commercial operators and 100 percent of the minimum wage for sports hunters. Wild boar costs 1.4 percent of the minimum wage for commercial operators and 100 percent for sports hunters. The cost to hunt a brown bears is twice the minimum wage for both user groups and the cost to hunt a moose, maral, and roedeer is three times the minimum wage. In Krasnoyarsk Kray, sable and beaver may be harvested by commercial operators only. Half the royalties and fines go to the regional ecological fund, the other half to the game inspectors.

In Khabarovsk, a moose tag is 200 percent of the minimum wage, and fees for red deer, roedeer, reindeer, muskdeer, snowsheep, wild boar, brown bear, sable, and otter are 150 percent of the minimum wages. All other game animals are free of charge, including valuable furbearers such as lynx and marten. However, the fee structure and royalties are not very transparent. Fees seem to change frequently in response to inflation, the general economic situation, and ad hoc decisions by administrators.

ANNEX J

INTERNATIONAL BEST PRACTICES IN SUSTAINABLE FOREST DEVELOPMENT

There are no legally binding international standards on sustainable forest management and sustainable forest development. However, in many countries, there has been a growing challenge to the traditional sustained yield industrial forest management paradigm. There is now an increasing emphasis on the sustainable management of forest ecosystems as a basis for sustainable development of the sector.

Standards for Sustainable Forest Development

Clarification of what sustainable forest ecosystem management might mean for forest sector development has occurred through various international initiatives that have tried to define criteria and indicators of sustainability. Internationally, these issues first arose in the context of tropical forest management. The International Tropical Timber Organization adopted a series of guidelines for natural forests (ITTO 1991, 1992, 1993a) and planted forests (ITTO 1993b) at the intergovernmental level. While not binding on member countries, the guidelines were adopted as an international reference standard from which individual countries could develop their own more specific guidelines, standards, and best practice.

The forest principles of the United Nations Conference on Environmental Development (UNCED) emphasized the need to address forest management issues in a holistic manner, with logically consistent principles of sustainable forest management and development for all forests and all countries. Much of the international focus in the 1980s had been on tropical forests, but by the 1990s it had became apparent that temperate and boreal forest also had global significance and that the sustainability of many management practices in these forests was also subject to considerable uncertainty (Botkin and Talbot 1992; Dudley 1992).

The Working Group on Criteria and Indicators for the Conservation and Sustainable Management of Temperate and Boreal Forests was formed in Geneva in 1994 to advance the development of internationally agreed criteria and indicators for the conservation of temperate and boreal forests. This exercise formed part of what was known as the "Montreal Process." Participants included Australia, Canada, Chile, China, Japan, the Republic of Korea, Mexico, New Zealand, the Russian Federation, and the United States. Several international organizations, nongovernmental organizations, and other countries also participated in meetings of the Working Group.

In February 1995, in the "Santiago Declaration," the Working Group endorsed a comprehensive set of criteria and indicators for forest conservation and sustainable management. While the criteria and indicators were not adopted under any international legal instrument, they do have significance for forest management because the Working Group countries account for 90 percent of the world's temperate and boreal forest. These criteria and indicators set the international reference standard for best practice and provide a logical framework for discussion.

Criteria and Indicators for Sustainable Management of Temperate and Boreal Forests

Seven criteria and associated indicators were agreed to characterize the conservation and sustainable management of temperate and boreal forests. They relate specifically to forest conditions, attributes or functions, and the benefits associated with the environmental and socioeconomic goods and services that forests provide. No priority is implied in the following list of criteria and their indicators.

Criterion 1: Conservation of biological diversity

Ecosystem diversity

(a) Extent of area by forest type relative to total forest area.

(b) Extent of area by forest type and by age class or successional stage.

(c) Extent of area by forest type in protected area categories as defined by the World Conservation Union (IUCN) or other classification systems.

(d) Extent of areas by forest type in protected areas defined by age class or successional stage.

(e) Fragmentation of forest types.

Species diversity

(a) The number of forest-dependent species.

(b) The status (threatened, rare, vulnerable, endangered, or extinct) of forest-dependent species at risk of not maintaining viable breeding populations, as determined by legislation or scientific assessment.

Genetic diversity

(a) Number of forest-dependent species that occupy a small portion of their former range.

(b) Population levels of representative species from diverse habitats monitored across their range.

Criterion 2: Maintenance of productive capacity of forest ecosystems

(a) Area of forest land and net area of forest land available for timber production.

(b) Total growing stock of both merchantable and nonmerchantable tree species on forest land available for timber production.

(c) The area and growing stock of plantations of native and exotic species.

(d) Annual removal of wood products compared to the volume determined to be sustainable.

(e) Annual removal of nontimber forest products (furbearers, berries, mushrooms, game), compared to the level determined to be sustainable.

Criterion 3: Maintenance of forest ecosystem health and vitality

(a) Area and percentage of forest affected by processes or agents beyond the range of historic variation (insects, disease, competition from exotic species, fire, storm, land clearance, permanent flooding, salinization, and domestic animals).

(b) Area and percentage of forest land subjected to levels of specific air pollutants (sulfates, nitrate, ozone) or ultraviolet B that may cause negative impacts on the forest ecosystem.

(c) Area and percentage of forest land with diminished biological components indicative of changes in fundamental ecological processes (soil nutrient cycling, seed dispersion, pollination) or ecological continuity (monitoring of functionally important species such as fungi, arboreal epiphyses, nematodes, beetles, wasps).

Criterion 4: Conservation and maintenance of soil and water resources

(a) Area and percentage of forest land with significant soil erosion.

(b) Area and percentage of forest land managed primarily for protective functions (watersheds, flood protection, avalanche protection, riparian zones).

(c) Percentage of stream kilometers in forested catchments in which stream flow and timing have deviated significantly from the historic range of variation.

(d) Area and percentage of forest land with significantly diminished soil organic matter or changes in other soil chemical properties.

(e) Area and percentage of forest land with significant compaction or change in soil physical properties resulting from human activities.

(f) Percentage of water bodies in forest areas (stream kilometers, lake hectares) with significant variance of biological diversity from the historic range of variability.

(g) Percentage of water bodies in forest areas (stream kilometers, lake hectares) with significant variation from the historic range of variability in pH, dissolved oxygen, levels of chemicals (electrical conductivity), sedimentation, or temperature.

(h) Area and percentage of forest land experiencing an accumulation of persistent toxic substances.

Criterion 5: Maintenance of forest contribution to global carbon cycles

(a) Total forest ecosystem biomass and carbon pool, by forest type, age class, and successional stages, if appropriate.

(b) Contribution of forest ecosystems to the total global carbon budget, including absorption and release of carbon (standing biomass, coarse woody debris, peat and soil carbon).

(c) Contribution of forest products to the global carbon budget.

Criterion 6: Maintenance and enhancement of long-term multiple socioeconomic benefits

(a) Value and volume of wood and wood products production, including value-added through downstream processing.

(b) Value and quantities of production of nonwood forest products.

(c) Supply and consumption of wood and wood products, including consumption per capita.

(d) Value of wood and nonwood products production as a percentage of GDP.

(e) Degree of recycling of forest products.

(f) Supply and consumption of nonwood products.

Recreation and tourism

(a) Area and percentage of forest land managed for general recreation and tourism, in relation to the total area of forest land.

(b) Number and type of facilities available for general recreation and tourism, in relation to population and forest area.

(c) Number of visitor days attributed to recreation and tourism, in relation to population and forest area.

Investment in the forest sector

(a) Value of investment, including investment in forest growing, forest health and management, planted forests, wood processing, and recreation and tourism.

(b) Level of expenditure on research and development and on education.

(c) Extension and use of new and improved technologies.

(d) Rates of return on investment.

Cultural, social, and spiritual needs and values

(a) Area and percentage of forest land managed to protect the range of cultural, social, and spiritual needs and values, in relation to the total area of forest land.

(b) Nonconsumptive use forest values.

Employment and community needs

(a) Direct and indirect employment in the forest sector, and forest sector employment as a proportion of total employment.

(b) Average wage rates and injury rates in major employment categories within the forest sector.

(c) Viability and adaptability to changing economic conditions of forest-dependent communities, including indigenous communities.

(d) Area and percentage of forest land used for subsistence purposes.

Criterion 7: Legal, institutional, and economic framework for sustainable forest management

Legal framework

(a) Property rights, appropriate land tenure arrangements, customary and traditional rights of indigenous people, and means of resolving property disputes by due process.

(b) Periodic forest-related planning, assessment, and policy review that recognizes the range of forest values, including coordination with relevant sectors.

(c) Opportunities for public participation in public policy and decision-making related to forests and public access to information.

(e) Best practice codes for forest management.

(f) Management of forests to conserve special environmental, cultural, social, and scientific values.

Institutional framework

(a) Public involvement and public education, awareness, and extension programs and provision of forest-related information.

(b) Periodic forest-related planning, assessment, and policy review, including cross-sectoral planning and coordination.

(c) Development of human resource skills across relevant disciplines.

(d) Efficient physical infrastructure to facilitate the supply of forest products and services to support forest management.

(e) Enforcement of laws, regulations, and guidelines.

Economic framework

(a) Investment and taxation policies and a regulatory environment that recognize the long-term nature of investments and permit the flow of capital in and out of the forest sector in response to market signals, nonmarket economic valuations, and public policy decisions in order to meet long-term demands for forest products and services.

(b) Nondiscriminatory trade policies for forest products.

Measurement and monitoring of change

(a) Availability and extent of up-to-date data, statistics, and other information important to measuring or describing indicators associated with all seven criteria.

(b) Scope, frequency, and statistical reliability of forest inventories, assessments, monitoring, and other relevant information.

(c) Compatibility with other countries in measuring, monitoring, and reporting on indicators.

Research and development

(a) Development of scientific understanding of forest ecosystem characteristics and functions.

(b) Development of methods for measuring and integrating environmental and social costs and benefits into markets and public policies and for reflecting forest-related resource depletion or replenishment in national accounting systems.

(c) Development of new technologies and the capacity to assess the socioeconomic consequences associated with the introduction of new technologies.

(d) Enhancement of ability to predict impacts of human intervention on forests.

(e) Enhancement of ability to predict impacts on forests of possible climate change.

Explanatory Notes on Selected Criteria and Indicators

The following notes explain what is meant by selected criteria and indicators and why they are considered important for assessing forest conservation and sustainable management. No single criterion or indicator alone is an indication of sustainability. Rather, individual criteria and indicators should be considered in the context of other criteria and indicators.

Criterion 1: Conservation of biological diversity

The objective of the conservation of biological diversity is the survival of species and of genetic variability within species. Viable breeding populations of species and their natural genetic variation are part of interdependent physical and biological systems or processes. The condition and distribution of forest communities are important to fundamental ecological processes and systems and the future of biological diversity associated with forests.

Ecosystem diversity

(a) The ecological processes and viable populations of species that are characteristic of forest ecosystems are usually dependent on a contiguous ecosystem or ecosystems of a certain minimum size. Genetic diversity within a species population depends on the maintenance of subpopulations and the existence of forest ecosystems covering a large part of their natural range. Forests may constitute all or a part of the habitat necessary to species survival.

(b) Ecological processes and the species associated with those processes within any forest ecosystem or forest type are associated with vegetative structures (age of the vegetation, its diameter and height) and successional stages (variable species of vegetation).

(c) The amount of a forest ecosystem reserved in some form of protected area is a measure of the priority society places on maintaining representative areas of that forest ecosystem.

(d) The fragmentation of a forest type may disrupt some ecological processes and availability of habitat. Such fragments of forest may be too small to maintain viable breeding populations of species. Distances between forest fragments can interfere with pollination, seed dispersal, and wildlife movement between patches of forest and breeding.

Ultimately, excessive fragmentation can contribute to the loss of plant and animal species that are unable to adapt to these conditions. In areas converted to agricultural purposes, remnant fragments of the original forest cover may provide refuges for many, although not all, components of the original diversity.

Species diversity

(a) Surveys of species numbers are necessary in order to estimate biological diversity.

(b) Ecological processes and the species associated with those processes may vary according to the extent, condition, or fragmentation of the specific forest type.

Genetic diversity

(a) Forest-dependent species with low population levels or significantly reduced range run the risk of losing important genetic traits (alleles) from their gene pools. In the case of species with a dispersed natural range, this can happen at the level of locally adapted sub-populations (provenances), resulting in a reduced ability by species to adapt to environmental changes.

(b) Monitoring the population levels of species representative of identified habitats or ecosystems across their range provides an indicator of the ability of those habitats to support species and subpopulations of those species that depend on similar habitat.

Criterion 2: Maintenance of productive capacity of forest ecosystems

(a) In many countries, the traditional calculation of the potential production of timber products is based on the forest area available for the production of commercial forest products. Forest lands are not available for timber harvesting if they do not meet minimal acceptable regeneration standards, economic growing rates, or accessibility. Spiritual, recreational, scientific, or educational values may also be deemed a higher priority than commodity production. Comparison of net forest land available for timber production with total forest land will provide a measure of the suitability or availability of forests for commercial forest production to meet society's demands for wood products.

(b) Measurements of merchantable and nonmerchantable growing stock provide an indication of timber supply opportunities.

(c) Planted forests can be an important source of forest products and can replace or augment the use of natural forests for the production of wood and nonwood forest products. Some countries use natural forest management as an alternative to planted forests. The area of forest plantations provides one measure of forest management efficiency and reduced future dependence on natural forests for commercial forest products. In addition, some believe that planted forests are also an indication of forest areas whose ecological and genetic character may be different. Many planted forests have been established to reclaim degraded lands, where the ecological and genetic character of the original forest had been lost.

(d) Monitoring the volume of wood and nonwood forest products annually removed relative to the amount that could sustainably be removed provides an indication of a forest's ability to provide a continuing supply of forest products and economic and forest management opportunities.

Criterion 3: Maintenance of forest ecosystem health and vitality

(a) Human impacts on forest ecosystems include land conversion, harvesting, species introductions, suppression of natural fire cycles and floods, and the introduction of nonnative species, especially pathogens. These influence ecological processes and ultimately forest-dependent plant and animal species.

(b) Air pollutants are suspected of having a significant cumulative impact on forest ecosystems by affecting regeneration, productivity, and species composition. Correlating forest inventory and health statistics with air pollution data will provide more information on the effects of these pollutants. Increased ultraviolet radiation, caused by changes in the earth's atmosphere, also has been shown to damage plants.

(c) The monitoring of forest structure or macro species such as vertebrates (criterion 1) will tend to detect changes in ecological processes decades after they have begun. Monitoring very short-lived species associated with specific ecological processes such as decomposition and nutrient cycling provides a more immediate indication of changes in ecological processes with potential importance to forests.

Criterion 4: Conservation and maintenance of soil and water resources

(a) The soil resource is a basic component of all terrestrial ecosystems. The loss of soil will influence the vitality and species composition of forest ecosystems. Extensive areas of soil erosion can have a major effect on recreational opportunities, potable water supplies and the lifespan of river infrastructure, and aquatic ecosystems associated with forests.

(b) Measurement of forest land managed primarily for protective functions provides data on the protection of valuable environmental amenities associated with clean air, water, soil, and flood and avalanche protection (public health and safety functions).

(c) Forests are an important part of the earth's hydrological cycles. They are particularly important in the regulation of surface and ground water flow. Changes in historic stream flow and the timing of flow, resulting in flooding or dewatered streams, can affect the health of aquatic ecosystems and the management and conservation of associated forest areas and downstream agriculture areas.

(d) Soil organic matter is important for water retention, carbon storage, and soil organisms and is an indication of soil nutrient status. Changes in soil organic matter can affect the vitality of forest ecosystems through diminished regeneration capacity of trees, lower growth rates, and changes in species composition.

(e) Nutrient and water availability to forest vegetation is dependent on the physical ability of roots to grow and access nutrients, water, and oxygen from the soil. This in turn is dependent on soil texture and structure. Subsurface hydrology can also be affected by soil compaction resulting from extensive human activities.

(f) This is frequently a measure of benthos populations (organisms that live at the bottom of water bodies). Benthos fauna are sensitive to a variety of possible changes in aquatic ecosystems such as silt, oxygen levels, and temperature. These changes may be the result of changes in upland forest areas.

(g) Monitoring water quality over large areas serves as an initial indication that activities inside or outside a forest area may be affecting ecosystem health.

Criterion 5: Maintenance of forest contribution to global carbon cycles

(a/b) The accumulation of biomass as living vegetation, debris, peat, and soil carbon (carbon pool) is an important forest function in regulating atmospheric carbon. The production rate of biomass is also a measure of forest health and vitality.

(c) The ecological and sustainable management of production forests and the long-lasting use of forest products can be a factor in controlling the amount of carbon entering the world's atmosphere.

Case Studies on Sustainable Forest Management

The International Model Forest Program

With the shared goal of preserving the world's forests for future generations, Canada and Russia have established a cooperative program to define and implement working examples of sustainable forest management. Supported by the Federal Forest Service of Russia and the Canadian Government's Green Plan International Initiatives, special forest areas have been designated in both countries to form part of a network of working models for sustainable forest management. The program is intended to foster change in the long-term management of forests to ensure future productivity, healthy regeneration, and ecological diversity based on social, economic, and environmental values.

Within the model forest network, the traditional concept of forest management is expanded to include wildlife and fish habitats, genetic diversity, and cultural history, which are recognized as important elements in determining how a forest will be managed. In addition, the management approach gives local communities an active role so that forests will benefit those who live in and near them. This broad management perspective helps ensure that use of the forest today does not compromise for its use and enjoyment by future generations.

Gassinski Model Forest (Khabarovsk Kray). The Gassinski Model Forest in Khabarovsk Kray is part of an international network of working that includes ten in Canada, two in Mexico, and potential sites that are being identified in Malaysia, the United States, and other countries. Together the network covers the boreal forests of Russia and the major ecological regions in North America and Southeast Asia. This model forest network will demonstrate how diverse ecosystems and complex socioeconomic issues can be managed to achieve sustainable forest development.

The Gassinski Model Forest is sponsored in Russia by the Forestry Administration, Khabarovsk Kray; the Federal Forest Service of Russia; and the Khabarovsk Kray Administration, Department of Natural Resources. Knowledge gained from the Gassinski Model Forest will be shared with members of the model forest network, with those managing other forests in Russia, with local individuals and organizations, and with the international community. This will be done through technology transfer and public awareness programs.

The Gassinski Model Forest covers 384,000 hectares of Russia's boreal forests within the boundaries of Nanaiski District and is bordered by the Sikhote-Alin Mountains and the Amur River. The landscape combines hilly and mountainous sections, interspersed with lowlands and flatlands. The forest is in the most populated region of the Central Amur lowland. The six villages within and beside the Gassinski Model Forest have a total population of approximately 4,700 Indigenous people (approximately 40 percent of the population). The major occupations of the inhabitants are linked to the utilization of forest resources.

The predominant species of the model forest include Yeddo spruce, Manchurian birch, and Korean pine. Other important species include larch, linden, ash, elm, oak, and poplar. Nut production is an important economic forest activity, and over 55,000 hectares are protected for this purpose. Other forest areas are protected to safeguard valuable salmon spawning grounds. Forests managed for timber production cover 208,000 hectares and support six forest harvesting and wood processing enterprises in the Nanaiski District.

Other important economic activities in the model forest include agriculture, hunting and wildlife management, fishing, and harvesting of nonwood forest products, including honey, medicinal plants, fruits and berries, and natural resins and oils. With its highly diversified wildlife, including such species as the Siberian tiger, wild boar, and moose, tourism and recreational opportunities can also be developed. The model forest will work to support these economic activities while preserving the natural environment.

Research activities will include forest ecology, adequate ecosystems, wildlife and fish habitat, fire prevention, and forest management. Environmental, social, cultural, and economic factors will be integrated to define new approaches to sustainable development in the area.

The success of any model forest project depends on support from a variety of interested groups. For this project, a partnership has been formed among representatives from all levels of government, the Nanai indigenous people, and industry, research, and international organizations. It is hoped that this collaboration will result in a balanced program of conservation and development of benefit to all local communities.

Through the international network, groups involved in the Gassinski Model Forest will exchange technical expertise and assistance with members of the McGregor Model Forest in Prince George, British Columbia, Canada. The McGregor Model Forest partners will provide assistance and training on all aspects of forest management. The links between model forests will foster a sharing of knowledge, skills, and techniques among interested groups to benefit forest management around the world.

Role of Model Forests in Sustainable Forest Management Strategy[1]

Russia has a large number of organizations that in one way or another deal with forests. Coordination of their activities lags behind the pace of the current reforms, and financing is limited. Interbranch relationships have been disrupted. Decisions approved at the federal level are often not followed up at the subnational level. Real authority is at the local level in the districts (rayons) -- and so is the real forestry. Practical measures for the good of the forests depend on the administration of the rayons, the directors of state forestry enterprises (leskhozes), and foresters. It is necessary to look for compromises among a range of interests -- forestry, the forest industry, agriculture, fisheries and water management, extractive industries, ecological agencies, nongovernment organizations, commercial structures, and private enterprises based on open democratic discussion to find solutions to the interrelated problems on the status and utilization of Russia's forest resources, the ecological consequences of forest exploitation, and the maintenance of biodiversity. The model forests of Russia are an example of such a compromise.

The preservation of Russia's forest requires effort on the part of the Government and others to inform the public that the forests are a vitally important part of land utilization. It is necessary to find new approaches to the preservation of forests, the maintenance of biodiversity, and the regulation of climate.

---

1 *This section is based on documents prepared by the Russian Federal Forest Service.*

With the approved 1993 Principles of the Forest Legislation of the Russian Federation and the forest conservation and management issues of the "Agenda of the 21st Century" taken into consideration, achieving these goals is possible through:

- Creation and realization of the National Plans of Action for Forests, in accordance with national traditions and forest management experience and international experience in the preservation of forests and their sustainable management.

- Improvement of the national forest policy based on criteria and indicators of the preservation and sustainable management of forests, developed within the framework of the Helsinki, Montreal, and other international protocols to promote the preservation and sustainable management of forests.

- Assistance in the development and liberalization of international trade in forest products.

- Creation of information systems for monitoring the preservation and sustainable management of forests at local, regional, national, and global levels.

- Creation of national and international systems of certification of forest products, based on the approved criteria of sustainable management of forests (ecolabelling).

The preservation and sustainable management of forests at the national and local levels implies the more extensive inclusion of forest-related problems of national ecological and economic importance in the process of forest conservation and management, with the global importance of the forests of each country taken into consideration.

Several other goals for the management of Russia's forest resources derive from Russia's participation in international proceedings:

- To formulate the principles of Russia's foreign policy relating to international proceedings on forests and to articulate Russia's interests in international discussions of forests and the forest sector.

- To coordinate at the international level the criteria and indicators for the preservation and sustainable management of Russia's forests.

- To create a national system of certification of forest products and to ensure Russia's participation in the international system of forest product certification based on the criteria of sustainable forest management.

- To ensure the technical and technological independence of the forest sector of Russia's economy.

Russia's forest management has long been based on the principle of the inexhaustibility of forest resources. Developed over almost three centuries, the formulation of this principle was included in the "Principles" (1993) and in documents that regulate the activity of the state forest management authority, the Federal Forest Service of Russia, such as the "Provision of Inexhaustible and Continuous Utilization, Reproduction, Preservation, and Protection of Russian Forests."

It is natural to ask whether "sustainable forest management" is synonymous with "the principle of inexhaustible and continuous utilization, reproduction, preservation, and protection of Russian forests." There is no single answer to this question, because the structure and quality of areas officially classed as forest are so different in the various regions of Russia. It is clear, however, that the idea of management is broader than the idea of utilization.

Nobody objects to the idea that forest management can and should ensure and maintain the ecological functions of the forests and their economic bounties. However, the differences in the distribution of forest resources, their utilization capacities, and the demand for forest products in any country, including Russia, make continuous commitment and compromises between all partners of the project a necessity. This is the way to sustainable development, which can be secured by sustainable management under market conditions. A model forest can become a testing ground for studying methods of conflict resolution and working out agreement between different organizations and with the local populations that use the forest resources of a particular territory.

Sustainable Forest Management and the Model Forest

Analysis of Canada's model forest system by a group of the Federal Forest Service specialists from the Khabarovsk Kray and Moscow in December 1993 and the establishment of the Gassinsky Model Forest in the Khabarovsk Kray provided an example of the model forest concept. The following formulation was achieved following discussion and debate:

> *A working model of sustainable forest development intended to function as a forestry enterprise based on multiresource forest management, including on-site processing of timber and nontimber resources, the development of the corresponding economic structures with the interests of all partners taken into consideration, primarily the local population and native peoples, without detriment to the ecological functions and properties of the forests or the biodiversity of the territory.*

The model forests of Russia should be regarded as a testing ground for scientific research and the introduction of new technologies in the key problem areas of the forest sector, including the development of technologies for forest utilization and timber processing and more complete utilization of nontimber forest resources and the study of the market demand for forest products.

The forest sector is in need of new technologies and machinery, both to fulfill Russia's international commitments to the sustainable development of all types of forests and to bring the forest sector out of its regeneration crisis. The model forest is a realistic attempt to find a new approach to the management of Russia's total forest area and the utilization of the forest resources.

The Canadian experiment with model forests shows how an organized partnership of diverse groups (government, industry, and private enterprise) makes it possible to achieve compromises among partners for sustaining the capacity of forests to fulfill their economic, social, spiritual, cultural, ecological, and environmental functions.

In deciding whether to establish a national network of model forests, several issues must be analyzed and discussed (ownership, forest research projects, preservation and protection of biodiversity) and strategic goals identified:

- Using information on the state of the forested lands where the model forests are to be located to determine the conditions and prospects for investments in the forest, agricultural, and related sectors of the economy for the purpose of balancing their development in a specific territory.

- Formulating regional models of forestry, agricultural, and agroforestry development in the territory of the model forests and developing entrepreneurship based on all forms of ownership.

- Creating new enterprises in infrastructural development, forest cultivation, forest utilization, wood conversion, paper production, wood chemistry, agriculture, and other types of activities based on various forms of ownership in the territory of the model forests.

- Contributing to the maintenance of biodiversity associated with forests and cooperating in the prevention of a global climate catastrophe through the cultivation of new forests to act as carbon sinks.

Sustainable Management and Problems of Ownership

Sustainable forest management depends on the balanced use of forest resources and the preservation of forest functions and properties that are beneficial to current and future generations. Sustainable development requires balancing the interests of various groups of the population, industry, and forest management authorities responsible for the utilization of forest resources, including timber and nontimber resources, and the development of appropriate economic structures and employment, without detriment to the ecological qualities and biodiversity of the forests.

Achieving this will require modification of the organizational structure of forest management. The modified structure must ensure the continuity of data on forests, including information on the supply and demand for forest products. For Russia, which is undergoing conversion to a market system and reform of state administrative bodies, improving the structure of forest management is closely related to preserving state ownership of the total forest area.

The state ownership of forests that has evolved in Russia constitutes a realistic base for combining the interests of the regions and the state in the form of a balanced forest policy based on the clearcut distribution of rights and responsibilities between the federal and regional levels of forest management, as stipulated in Russia's forest legislation. Considering the size and characteristics of the Russian forest (low productivity, no modern infrastructure), only the state has the necessary financial and material resources to ensure a forest management structure with qualified specialists, modern machinery and technology, and investments in forestry infrastructure.

Sustainable Forest Management and Science

In December 1994, the "International Political Dialogue on Problems of Science, Forestry and Sustainable Development" (Indonesia) established that forest science is still incapable of providing the reliable and conclusive information needed for timely decisionmaking. Decisions based on incorrect or inadequate information can have a detrimental effect on efforts to ensure sustainable development. Therefore, scientific research is needed to provide adequate information to guide decisionmaking at all the levels. It should be accessible, well-timed, and cost-efficient.

Acknowledging the pressing nature of this problem, experts from various countries have concluded that forest researchers should broaden their horizons and adopt the following priorities:

- Management, preservation, continuous development, and improvement of all types of forests in an effort to meet the needs of the population.
- Establishment of criteria and indicators for sustainable management of forests.
- Identification of problems of trade and management.
- Selection of approaches to the mobilization of financial resources and ecologically friendly technologies.
- Establishment of organizational (institutional) ties.
- Participation in forest management making this partnership accessible to nongovernment organizations and private individuals.
- Interagency relationships and integration.

The reason for identifying measures for the preservation and management of forest resources and their ecological functions is to bring together scientific research establishments and specialized educational establishments in developing training programs and systems for the management of forests and forest inventory control and encouraging active national dialogue on the fate of forests.

Various groups of the population should be involved in the discussion of problems facing forest conservation, the maintenance of biodiversity, and the climate-regulating role of forests. Drawing them into work on forest inventories and improvement of forest utilization and regeneration technologies that contribute to the maintenance of biodiversity and the climate-regulating role of forests should help to establish a relationship between the population and the forests.

The many years of forest exploitation have altered the quality of the forest resources in a number of regions of Russia. Russia's forestry crisis has resulted in lower employment of the population in the zone of logging enterprises. The preservation and maintenance of the traditional way of life of the local population should be guaranteed by the new forest policy aimed at securing sustainable management of Russian forests.

Sustainable Forest Management and the Maintenance of Biodiversity

The maintenance of biodiversity through the preservation of landscapes (soil, topography, and vegetation), habitats, and ecological niches that together determine the organization of living organisms at the genetic, species, and ecosystemic levels requires more information than is currently available. Inventories are required of the types of forest ecosystems and habitats in various forest zones.

In exploited parts of forests, the mosaic of habitats formed in the course of evolution and history that determines the biodiversity of a forest ecosystem is complicated by the presence of various stages of successional dynamics. It is necessary to promote the preservation of the existing dynamic assemblages, with their species and genetic diversity, which are developing toward a climax level. Sustainable management in forests of this type should be based on computer model predictions of the results of logging of various intensity and in different areas and times.

Under the conditions of intense anthropogenic pressure on forests, the preservation of climax forests and the remnants of virgin forests with their wild flora and fauna becomes particularly difficult. The creation of protected forest territories in different natural conditions is the most suitable method of preserving the genetic and species diversity of climax or near-climax forests. It is advisable to include such territories in model forests. An important part of maintaining biodiversity is the detection of forest ecosystems and landscapes at risk of irreversible changes. Such landscapes can also be included in model forests.

Protected areas should include forests that are important to the preservation and maintenance of biodiversity, as well as forests that are culturally and historically important. The highly protected areas of forests should include forest reserves and virgin forests and forests inhabited by aboriginal peoples who depend on them to maintain their traditional way of life, (hunting, fishing, harvesting). Protected areas should also include forests with unique species composition, productivity, and genetic properties and forests that are part of the ranges and habitats of species threatened by extinction. It is advisable to include these highly protected areas of forest in the territories of model forests.

Global Significance of Forests

The global significance of forests becomes increasingly clear as the forest cover disappears. The 1992 United Nations Conference on the Environment and Development in Rio de Janeiro made clear that the age-old question of utilization of the renewable resources such as timber can no longer be considered separately from the nontimber and nonmarket resources of forests. Russia possesses one-fifth of the world's forest resources (based on timber reserves). That means that the sustainable management, utilization, protection, and reproduction of Russia's forest resources are not only a national problem, but also a global one. A national network of model forests can make a large contribution to the realization of Russia's new forest policy.

References

Botkin, D.B., and Talbot, L.M. 1992. "Biological Diversity in Forests." In N.P. Sharma, ed., *Managing the World's Forests: Looking for the Balance Between Conservation and Development*. Dubuque, Iowa: Kendal-Hunt Publishing Company.

Dudley, N. 1992. *Forests in Trouble: A Review of the Status of Temperate Forests Worldwide*. Gland, Switzerland: World Wildlife Federation.

ITTO (International Tropical Timber Organization). 1991. *Guidelines for the Sustainable Management of Natural Tropical Forest*. Policy Development Series No. 1. Yokohama, Japan: International Tropical Timber Organization.

________. 1992. *Criteria for the Measurement of Sustainable Tropical Forest Management*. Policy Development Series No. 3. Yokohama, Japan: International Tropical Timber Organization.

________. 1993a. *Guidelines for the Establishment and Sustainable Management of Planted Tropical Forests*. Policy Development Series No. 4. Yokohama, Japan: International Tropical Timber Organization.

________. 1993b. *Guidelines on the Conservation of Biological Diversity in Tropical Production Forests*. Policy Development Series No. 5. Yokohama, Japan: International Tropical Timber Organization.

ANNEX K

DONOR PROGRAMS IN RUSSIA'S FOREST SECTOR

Russia has a relatively well-developed forest infrastructure, highly-trained scientists, a structure of forest enterprises, and some protective and regulatory measures that can serve as a framework for rapid and productive development of the sector. Still needed are essential investments directed at modernization, technical support, and basic materials (especially technological) to enhance the ability of the staff to promote sustainable development of the forest sector. Most international assistance in the sector is directed toward increasing forest productivity and sustainability and improving forest resource management.

Carbon Offset Forestry and Ecological Protection

The Carbon Offset Forestry and Ecological Protection project (1993-96), a joint effort of Oregon State University, the Saratov Forest Management District, and the International Forestry Institute, aims to conserve and sequester carbon and provide for the ecological protection of the Saratov region. This would enable Russia to receive credit toward its greenhouse gas reduction obligations under the Framework Convention on Climate Change.

Oregon State University is assisting its Russian partners in establishing forest plantations and improving forest management and is promoting the sharing of information quantifying the biological, economic, and industrial benefits of these improvements. The project will also identify barriers to private investment and ways to overcome them. The first phase of the project is the establishment of a joint implementation pilot project in Saratov, the development of contacts, and the resolution of institutional issues between collaborating partners. Especially in this arena of institutional arrangements and guidelines, the Environmental Defense Fund has been working with the former Ministry of Environmental Protection and Natural Resources and the Russian Institute for a Market Economy. The second phase of the project is a forestry model for the Far East.

Rational Use of Forest Resources of Siberia

The Russian Academy of Sciences and the Federal Forest Service are collaborating with the International Institute for Applied Systems Analysis (IIASA in Laxenburg, Austria) on a project to quantify the economic and social functions of Siberia's forest ecosystems and to develop a detailed strategy for the sector to the year 2000. The three-year project (1993-96) is jointly financed by IIASA, some external international funds, and various Russian sources (including federal and local governments) for an anticipated total of US$3-5 million.

Project activities include analysis of the condition of Siberian forests using project-generated databases; assessment of the biospheric role of Siberian forests, their influence on global change, the gas composition of the atmosphere, and carbon circulation; development of an analytical method for the dynamic modeling of the development of Siberian forests; and the formulation of strategies for the development of industry, infrastructure, and society in the forest sector. The database has now been created, including information on soils, climate, forest industry, and socioeconomic features. The goal is to integrate the database into a geographic information system (GIS) and to analyze forest resources and utilization, forest industries and markets, and the greenhouse gas balance and climate change.

Gassinski Model Forest Project

Following a workshop in early 1993 in Khabarovsk, the International Model Forest Network accepted a proposal for the Gassinski Model Forest in Khabarovsk Kray (see Annex J). The Canadian Government is contributing US$3 million to this project. The terrain is characterized by flood plain and rolling hills, with four major rivers. Spruce, birch, pine, and larch species predominate. Forestry activities are the primary contributor to the local economy, along with agriculture and inland fisheries. The local population includes a high percentage of indigenous peoples. The 1994-95 work plan includes the development of a GIS, a broad inventory of forest resources, improved silvicultural techniques, and forest fire protection and pest management. The development of a nontraditional forest products industry and tourism is also envisaged.

Sustainable Natural Resources Management Project in the Far East

Funded by the U.S. Agency for International Development (USAID), this project will be run by project coordinating committees with representatives of Khabarovsk and Primorye Krays, environmental and forestry-related government and nongovernmental institutions, and other interested parties. The proposed budget is US$16.7 million, excluding Russian counterpart contributions, other donor contributions, and training and equipment provided through various U.S. in-kind programs. The goals are to promote sustainable, multiple-use natural resources management of forests and endangered species and critical habitat in the Sikhote-Alin Mountain region and to build a strong institutional framework to support integrated management planning and demonstration.

The project hopes to develop a framework to reduce the policy, legal, and institutional barriers to sustainable private sector forest management and biodiversity conservation through the establishment of twenty or more small forest-related enterprises and fifty or more small businesses in related services or processing. The project also intends to strengthen the voice of local communities and NGOs in policy and program decisions, through partnership with the local and regional government bodies.

Monitoring the Asian Gypsy Moth, Pink Gypsy Moth, and Nun Moth

This cooperative project is intended to eradicate the threat of exotic pests introduced as a result of increased foreign trade from forest areas surrounding the ports of Vladivostok, Nakhodka, and Vostochny. Already, gypsy moths of various species have taken hold in Canada and the United States, and the U.S. Forest Service estimates that losses from the Asian Gypsy Moth could exceed US$3.5 billion. The $200,000 project is a cooperative effort of the U.S. Forest Service, the U.S. Animal and Plant Health Inspection Service, the Russian Federal Forest Service, the Moscow Forest Protection Agency, the Primorye Kray Forest Management Department, and the Far East Research Institute for Forestry. Some in-kind services will also be provided by the Russian Federal Forest Service.

The objectives of the project are to gather information on when control measures are needed to reduce the likelihood of infestation of ships and containers in port and on when the ships are at greatest risk of infestation, to develop and improve survey techniques for these destructive species of moth, and to improve communications and information transfer related to pest risk assessment and control.

Experimental Reforestation in the Far East

In 1989, the Khabarovsk Kray administration, the Far East Research Institute for Forestry, Koppinsky Lesokombinat, and the U.S. firm Weyerhaeuser agreed to conduct a reforestation experiment near Port Vanino, on the western side of Tatar Strait. The experiment is intended to establish the potential for growing high-quality seedlings of desirable tree species under nursery conditions and to create an information base for the development of artificial reforestation technologies and the use of the seedlings to plant clear-cut and burn areas. The objective is to supplant the natural regeneration of less-desirable species such as birch and aspen.

Thus far, seedlings have been grown in the greenhouses of Weyerhaeuser's Reforestation Center and delivered to Koppinsky Leskhoz and other enterprises for experimental plantation. Between 1991 and 1994, over 135,000 seedlings were delivered, and Weyerhaeuser has provided assistance in purchasing equipment for a seed storehouse (US$240,000). Sixteen greenhouses near Khabarovsk City provide 13 million seedlings a year now, enough to meet the needs of all of Khabarovsk Kray.

Establishment of Experimental Pine and Spruce Forest Seed Plantations

In cooperation with the Ministry of Agriculture and Forestry of Finland, the then-Soviet State Committee for Forestry (now divided between the Russian Federation and Ukraine) agreed to establish sites for experimental forest seed plantations of high-value pine and spruce clones in the Yaroslav, Kostroma, and Smolensk regions. Projected to continue for twenty years, the project aims to develop high-quality seeds for reforestation under the environmental conditions of Finland and Northern Europe by improving the hereditary properties (intensified and accelerated fruiting, seasonable physiological seed maturation, and the like) of the seedlings. The estimated total project budget within the Russian Federation is approximately 4 million Finnmarks.

The forest enterprises implementing the project have already prepared the soil and taken over the fencing, protection, and silvicultural responsibilities for the seedlings. They are now completing construction of forest cordon buildings, improved roads, and pine and spruce sanitary cuttings within the buffer zone of the seedling plantations.

Scientific and Technical Project TAIGA

The TAIGA project (Taiga Aerospace Investigations Using GIS Analysis), initiated through an agreement between the National Aeronautics and Space Administration (NASA) of the United States and the Russian Academy of Sciences, will establish a high-resolution picture transmission satellite receiving station in Krasnoyarsk and a Russian-supplied ground truth dataset on Russian boreal forests, in GIS form. The information will be used to study forest productivity, forest health, fire risk, and fire history in the context of the global carbon cycle.

Sikhote-Alin Project

This project is a component of the USAID funded sustainable Natural Resources Management Project. It covers an area of about 500,000 hectares in the Sikhote-Alin Mountains along the Tatar Strait, seeks to protect the endangered tiger population and promotes the socioeconomic development of the indigenous Udege population. At an estimated cost of US$1 million, this project is designed to provide an ecological description and inventory of the tiger population and habitat and will introduce measures for the conservation of the tiger population. It also seeks to define the socioeconomic problems of the Udege people, in anticipation of international financial assistance becoming available for their development.

Recreational Resources and Development of Ecotourism in Khabarovsk Kray

A joint project of the Canadian Forest Service, the Khabarovsk Kray Forest Management Department, the Far East Research Institute for Forestry, and various environmental organizations, this project assists in the development of ecotourism through the creation of a GIS for recreational resources, the organization of a tourism center, and the development of a conceptual and functional model for the management of ecotourism and other recreational uses of the natural resource base. The Canadian contribution to the project budget will be a maximum of 3 million Canadian dollars.

Development of Methods of Space Images and GIS for Forest Inventory and Monitoring

A joint project between the French Research Institute of Agriculture and Forestry (CEMAGREF) and the Russian International Forest Institute, this project is a product of an agreement between the two nations' space agencies. The French will give the Russians data received from its "SPOT" satellite at no charge. The purpose of the project is the collection of satellite information to aid in developing a forest inventory for mapping and accounting for changes in the forest fund as a result of anthropogenic activity (forest cutting) and forest fires.

World Bank/GEF Biodiversity Conservation Project

The Government of the Russian Federation, through its State Committee for Environmental Protection, and with participation of the Federal Forest Service, is implementing a Biodiversity Conservation Project funded in part by the World Bank through the Global Environment Facility (GEF) Grant of the equivalent of US$20.1 million. An additional US$1.1 million is provided by a grant from the Swiss Government through the WWF.

The Project includes a program of activities to support biodiversity conservation within the country and is also associated with the Environment Management Project funded by the World Bank. The main objective of the GEF project is to assist the Russian Federation maintain optimum levels of biodiversity in accordance with the principles of economic and environmentally sound sustainable development. The project will assist in ensuring the enhanced protection of biodiversity, within and outside protected areas, in conformance with the Government's obligations under the Convention on Biological Diversity. More specific objectives include: (i) supporting the development of federal and regional biodiversity strategies; (ii) developing and implementing mechanisms and approaches which will mainstream biodiversity conservation and environmental protection into the policy making process; (iii) assessing the Protected Area institutional framework and subsequently strengthening its effectiveness; (iv) enabling the participation of all interested stakeholders, including aboriginal peoples and local communities into biodiversity conservation; and (v) developing an inter-regional demonstration of inter-sectoral biodiversity conservation and environmentally sustainable natural resource management in the Lake Baikal Region (Republic of Buryatia, Irkutsk and Chita Oblasts).

Natural Resource Management in the Baikal Water Basin

The Natural Resource Management in the Baikal Water Basin Project (in short, Baikal Project) funded by the TACIS program of the European Commission (ECU 2.8 million) will assist the Government of the Republic of Buryatia and the Irkutsk Oblast Administration in securing the region's sensitive natural resources through improved forest and range land management for sustainable development. Demonstration actions on natural resource planning, improvement of harvesting techniques, and ecologically sound range land models are included in the project. The project will improve sustainable forest management, improve silvicultural techniques, improve the efficiency and profitability of the forest industry in the region, and demonstrate balanced ecological management of range lands.

Sustainable Development of the Lake Baikal Region

This USAID-funded project aims to develop the Lake Baikal basin, an area that includes over 4.5 million hectares of forest land. The project includes components for the sustainable development of wildlife areas, reserves, and national parks; the development of ecotourism; the sustainable management of forestry and agriculture; the production of forest-related products; technical assistance in land utilization practices; and the development of a system of protected territories. The project aims to create partnerships between Russian private enterprises and U.S. companies that can provide investments, technologies, and marketing expertise for domestic and export production.

Commercial Forestry Industry Assistance

In addition, the Russian forest sector has also benefited from assistance provided by commercial interests around the world, in particular from U.S., Finnish, and other European firms.

Distributors of World Bank Publications

Prices and credit terms vary from country to country. Consult your local distributor before placing an order.

ARGENTINA
Oficina del Libro Internacional
Av. Cordoba 1877
1120 Buenos Aires
Tel: (54 1) 815-8354
Fax: (54 1) 815-8156

AUSTRALIA, FIJI, PAPUA NEW GUINEA, SOLOMON ISLANDS, VANUATU, AND WESTERN SAMOA
D.A. Information Services
648 Whitehorse Road
Mitcham 3132
Victoria
Tel: (61) 3 9210 7777
Fax: (61) 3 9210 7788
E-mail: service@dadirect.com.au
URL: http://www .dadirect.com.au

AUSTRIA
Gerold and Co.
Weihburggasse 26
A-1011 Wien
Tel: (43 1) 512-47-31-0
Fax: (43 1) 512-47-31-29
URL: http://www .gerold.co/at.online

BANGLADESH
Micro Industries Development
Assistance Society (MIDAS)
House 5, Road 16
Dhanmondi R/Area
Dhaka 1209
Tel: (880 2) 326427
Fax: (880 2) 811188

BELGIUM
Jean De Lannoy
Av. du Roi 202
1060 Brussels
Tel: (32 2) 538-5169
Fax: (32 2) 538-0841

BRAZIL
Publicacões Tecnicas Internacionais Ltda.
Rua Peixoto Gomide, 209
01409 Sao Paulo, SP.
Tel: (55 11) 259-6644
Fax: (55 11) 258-6990
E-mail: postmaster@pti.uol.br
URL: http://www .uol.br

CANADA
Renouf Publishing Co. Ltd.
5369 Canotek Road
Ottawa, Ontario K1J 9J3
Tel: (613) 745-2665
Fax: (613) 745-7660
E-mail: renouf@fox.nstn.ca
URL: http:// www .fox.nstn.ca/~renouf

CHINA
China Financial & Economic Publishing House
8, Da Fo Si Dong Jie
Beijing
Tel: (86 10) 6333-8257
Fax: (86 10) 6401-7365

COLOMBIA
Infoenlace Ltda.
Carrera 6 No. 51-21
Apartado Aereo 34270
Santafé de Bogotá, D.C.
Tel: (57 1) 285-2798
Fax: (57 1) 285-2798

CYPRUS
Center for Applied Research
Cyprus College
6, Diogenes Street, Engomi
P.O. Box 2006
Nicosia
Tel: (357 2) 44-1730
Fax: (357 2) 46-2051

CZECH REPUBLIC
National Information Center
prodejna, Konviktska 5
CS – 113 57 Prague 1
Tel: (42 2) 2422-9433
Fax: (42 2) 2422-1484
URL: http://www .nis.cz/

DENMARK
SamfundsLitteratur
Rosenoerns Allé 11
DK-1970 Frederiksberg C
Tel: (45 31) 351942
Fax: (45 31) 357822

EGYPT, ARAB REPUBLIC OF
Al Ahram Distribution Agency
Al Galaa Street
Cairo
Tel: (20 2) 578-6083
Fax: (20 2) 578-6833

The Middle East Observer
41, Sherif Street
Cairo
Tel: (20 2) 393-9732
Fax: (20 2) 393-9732

FINLAND
Akateeminen Kirjakauppa
P.O. Box 128
FIN-00101 Helsinki
Tel: (358 0) 12141
Fax: (358 0) 121-4441
URL: http://www .akateemninen.com/

FRANCE
World Bank Publications
66, avenue d'léna
75116 Paris
Tel: (33 1) 40-69-30-56/57
Fax: (33 1) 40-69-30-68

GERMANY
UNO-Verlag
Poppelsdorfer Allee 55
53115 Bonn
Tel: (49 228) 212940
Fax: (49 228) 217492

GREECE
Papasotiriou S.A.
35, Stournara Str.
106 82 Athens
Tel: (30 1) 364-1826
Fax: (30 1) 364-8254

HAITI
Culture Diffusion
5, Rue Capois
C.P. 257
Port-au-Prince
Tel: (509 1) 3 9260

HONG KONG, MACAO
Asia 2000 Ltd.
Sales & Circulation Department
Seabird House, unit 1101-02
22-28 Wyndham Street, Central
Hong Kong
Tel: (852) 2530-1409
Fax: (852) 2526-1107
E-mail: sales@asia2000.com.hk
URL: http://www .asia2000.com.hk

INDIA
Allied Publishers Ltd.
751 Mount Road
Madras - 600 002
Tel: (91 44) 852-3938
Fax: (91 44) 852-0649

INDONESIA
Pt. Indira Limited
Jalan Borobudur 20
P.O. Box 181
Jakarta 10320
Tel: (62 21) 390-4290
Fax: (62 21) 421-4289

IRAN
Ketab Sara Co. Publishers
Khaled Eslamboli Ave.,
6th Street
Kusheh Delafrooz No. 8
P.O. Box 15745-733
Tehran
Tel: (98 21) 8717819; 8716104
Fax: (98 21) 8712479
E-mail: ketab-sara@neda.net.ir

Kowkab Publishers
P.O. Box 19575-511
Tehran
Tel: (98 21) 258-3723
Fax: (98 21) 258-3723

IRELAND
Government Supplies Agency
Oifig an tSoláthair
4-5 Harcourt Road
Dublin 2
Tel: (353 1) 661-3111
Fax: (353 1) 475-2670

ISRAEL
Yozmot Literature Ltd.
P.O. Box 56055
3 Yohanan Hasandlar Street
Tel Aviv 61560
Tel: (972 3) 5285-397
Fax: (972 3) 5285-397

R.O.Y. International
PO Box 13056
Tel Aviv 61130
Tel: (972 3) 5461423
Fax: (972 3) 5461442
E-mail: royil@netvision.net.il

Palestinian Authority/Middle East
Index Information Services
P.O.B. 19502 Jerusalem
Tel: (972 2) 6271219
Fax: (972 2) 6271634

ITALY
Licosa Commissionaria Sansoni SPA
Via Duca Di Calabria, 1/1
Casella Postale 552
50125 Firenze
Tel: (55) 645-415
Fax: (55) 641-257
E-mail: lic[illegible]@ftbcc.it
Url: http://www .ftbcc.it/licosa

JAMAICA
Ian Randle Publishers Ltd.
206 Old Hope Road
Kingston 6
Tel: 809-927-2085
Fax: 809-977-0243
E-mail: irpl@colis.com

JAPAN
Eastern Book Service
3-13 Hongo 3-chome, Bunkyo-ku
Tokyo 113
Tel: (81 3) 3818-0861
Fax: (81 3) 3818-0864
E-mail: svt-ebs@ppp.bekkoame.or .jp
URL: http://www .bekkoame.or.jp/~svt-ebs

KENYA
Africa Book Service (E.A.) Ltd.
Quaran House, Mfangano Street
P.O. Box 45245
Nairobi
Tel: (254 2) 223 641
Fax: (254 2) 330 272

KOREA, REPUBLIC OF
Daejon Trading Co. Ltd.
P.O. Box 34, Youida
706 Seoun Bldg
44-6 Youido-Dong, Yeongchengpo-Ku
Seoul
Tel: (82 2) 785-1631/4
Fax: (82 2) 784-0315

MALAYSIA
University of Malaya Cooperative
Bookshop, Limited
P.O. Box 1127
Jalan Pantai Baru
59700 Kuala Lumpur
Tel: (60 3) 756-5000
Fax: (60 3) 755-4424

MEXICO
INFOTEC
Av. San Fernando No. 37
Col. Toriello Guerra
14050 Mexico, D.F.
Tel: (52 5) 624-2800
Fax: (52 5) 624-2822
E-mail: infotec@rtn.net.mx
URL: http://rtn.net.mx

NEPAL
Everest Media International Services (P.)Ltd.
GPO Box 5443
Kathmandu
Tel: (977 1) 472 152
Fax: (977 1) 224 431

NETHERLANDS
De Lindeboom/InOr-Publikaties
P.O. Box 202
7480 AE Haaksbergen
Tel: (31 53) 574-0004
Fax: (31 53) 572-9296
E-mail: lindeboo@worldonline.nl
URL: http://www .worldonline.nl~lindeboo

NEW ZEALAND
EBSCO NZ Ltd.
Private Mail Bag 99914
New Market
Auckland
Tel: (64 9) 524-8119
Fax: (64 9) 524-8067

NIGERIA
University Press Limited
Three Crowns Building Jericho
Private Mail Bag 5095
Ibadan
Tel: (234 22) 41-1356
Fax: (234 22) 41-2056

NORWAY
NIC Info A/S
Book Department
P.O. Box 6125 Etterstad
N-0602 Oslo 6
Tel: (47 22) 57-3300
Fax: (47 22) 68-1901

PAKISTAN
Mirza Book Agency
65, Shahrah-e-Quaid-e-Azam
Lahore 54000
Tel: (92 42) 735 3601
Fax: (92 42) 758 5283

Oxford University Press
5 Bangalore Town
Sharae Faisal
PO Box 13033
Karachi-75350
Tel: (92 21) 446307
Fax: (92 21) 4547640
E-mail: oup@oup.khi.erum.com.pk

Pak Book Corporation
Aziz Chambers 21
Queen's Road
Lahore
Tel: (92 42) 636 3222; 636 0885
Fax: (92 42) 636 2328
E-mail: pbc@brain.net.pk

PERU
Editorial Desarrollo SA
Apartado 3824
Lima 1
Tel: (51 14) 285380
Fax: (51 14) 286628

PHILIPPINES
International Booksource Center Inc.
1127-A Antipolo St.
Barangay, Venezuela
Makati City
Tel: (63 2) 896 6501; 6505; 6507
Fax: (63 2) 896 1741

POLAND
International Publishing Service
Ul. Piekna 31/37
00-677 Warzawa
Tel: (48 2) 628-6089
Fax: (48 2) 621-7255
E-mail: books%ips@ikp.atm.com.pl
URL: http://www .ipscg.waw.pl/ips/export/

PORTUGAL
Livraria Portugal
Apartado 2681
Rua Do Carmo 70-74
1200 Lisbon
Tel: (1) 347-4982
Fax: (1) 347-0264

ROMANIA
Compani De Librarii Bucuresti S.A.
Str. Lipscani no. 26, sector 3
Bucharest
Tel: (40 1) 613 9645
Fax: (40 1) 312 4000

RUSSIAN FEDERATION
Isdatelstvo <Ves Mir>
9a, Lolpachniy Pereulok
Moscow 101831
Tel: (7 095) 917 87 49
Fax: (7 095) 917 92 59

SINGAPORE, TAIWAN, MYANMAR, BRUNEI
Asahgate Publishing Asia Pacific Pte. Ltd.
41 Kallang Pudding Road #04-03
Golden Wheel Building
Singapore 349316
Tel: (65) 741-5166
Fax: (65) 742-9356
E-mail: ashgate@asianconnect.com

SLOVENIA
Gospodarski Vestnik Publishing Group
Dunajska cesta 5
1000 Ljubljana
Tel: (386 61) 133 83 47; 132 12 30
Fax: (386 61) 133 80 30
E-mail: belicd@gvestnik.si

SOUTH AFRICA, BOTSWANA
For single titles:
Oxford University Press
Southern Africa
P.O. Box 1141
Cape Town 8000
Tel: (27 21) 45-7266
Fax: (27 21) 45-7265

For subscription orders:
International Subscription Service
P.O. Box 41095
Craighall
Johannesburg 2024
Tel: (27 11) 880-1448
Fax: (27 11) 880-6248
E-mail: iss@is.co.za

SPAIN
Mundi-Prensa Libros, S.A.
Castello 37
28001 Madrid
Tel: (34 1) 431-3399
Fax: (34 1) 575-3998
E-mail: libreria@mundiprensa.es
URL: http://www .mundiprensa.es/

Mundi-Prensa Barcelona
Consell de Cent, 391
08009 Barcelona
Tel: (34 3) 488-3492
Fax: (34 3) 487-7659

SRI LANKA, THE MALDIVES
Lake House Bookshop
100, Sir Chittampalam Gardiner Mawatha
Colombo 2
Tel: (94 1) 32105
Fax: (94 1) 432104

SWEDEN
Wennergren-Williams AB
P. O. Box 1305
S-171 25 Solna
Tel: (46 8) 705-97-50
Fax: (46 8) 27-00-71
E-mail: mail@wwi.se

SWITZERLAND
Librairie Payot
Service Institutionnel
Côtes-de-Montbenon 30
1002 Lausanne
Tel: (41 21) 341-3229
Fax: (41 21) 341-3235

ADECO Van Diermen Editions
Techniques
Ch. de Lacuez 41
CH1807 Blonay
Tel: (41 21) 943 2673
Fax: (41 21) 943 3605

TANZANIA
Oxford University Press
Maktaba Street
PO Box 5299
Dar es Salaam
Tel: (255 51) 29209
Fax: (255 51) 46822

THAILAND
Central Books Distribution
306 Silom Road
Bangkok 10500
Tel: (66 2) 235-5400
Fax: (66 2) 237-8321

TRINIDAD & TOBAGO, AND THE CARRIBBEAN
Systematics Studies Unit
9 Watts Street
Curepe
Trinidad, West Indies
Tel: (809) 662-5654
Fax: (809) 662-5654
E-mail: tobe@trinidad.net

UGANDA
Gustro Ltd.
PO Box 9997
Madhvani Building
Plot 16/4 Jinja Rd.
Kampala
Tel: (256 41) 254 763
Fax: (256 41) 251 468

UNITED KINGDOM
Microinfo Ltd.
P.O. Box 3
Alton, Hampshire GU34 2PG
England
Tel: (44 1420) 86848
Fax: (44 1420) 89889
E-mail: wbank@ukminfo.demon.co.uk
URL: http://www .microinfo.co.uk

VENEZUELA
Tecni-Ciencia Libros, S.A.
Centro Cuidad Comercial Tamanco
Nivel C2
Caracas
Tel: (58 2) 959 5547; 5035; 0016
Fax: (58 2) 959 5636

ZAMBIA
University Bookshop
University of Zambia
Great East Road Campus
P.O. Box 32379
Lusaka
Tel: (260 1) 252 576
Fax: (260 1) 253 952

ZIMBABWE
Longman Zimbabwe (Pte.)Ltd.
Tourle Road, Ardbennie
P.O. Box ST125
Southerton
Harare
Tel: (263 4) 6216617
Fax: (263 4) 621670

02/21/97

IBRD 28354
FEDERATION
LICY REVIEW
ND RESEARCH INSTITUTIONS
SELECTED CITIES
NATIONAL CAPITAL
RIVERS
ECONOMIC REGION BOUNDARIES
OBLAST, KRAI OR REPUBLIC BOUNDARIES
AUTONOMOUS OBLAST, OKRUG OR REPUBLIC BOUNDARIES
INTERNATIONAL BOUNDARIES
UNITED STATES OF AMERICA
Bering Strait
Chukchi Sea
Bering Sea
Anadyr
Pevek
East Siberian Sea
Laptev Sea
Kolyma R.
Indigirka R.
Ossora
Tiksi
Magadan
Petropavlovsk Kamchatskiy
Sea
Khatanga
Lena R.
Sea of Okhotsk
Norilsk
Yakutsk
Arctic Circle
Nikolayevsk na Amure
Amur R.
Vanino
Yuzhno Sakhalinsk
Tynda
JAPAN
Khabarovsk
Enisei R.
Angara R.
Blagoveshchensk
Tomsk
Bratsk
Lake Baikal
Krasnoyarsk
Chita
Amur R.
Sea of Japan
Nakhodha
Vladivostok
Irkutsk
Ulan-Ude
Abakan
CHINA
Kyzyl
-Altaysk
MONGOLIA
D.P.R. OF KOREA
OCTOBER 1996

RUSSIAN
FOREST PC
FOREST MANAGEMENT A
This map was produced by the Map Design Unit of The World Bank. The boundaries, colors, denominations and any other information shown on this map do not imply, on the part of The World Bank Group, any judgment on the legal status of any territory, or any endorsement or acceptance of such boundaries.
FOREST INVENTORY ENTERPRISES
FEDERAL FOREST SERVICE RESEARCH INSTITUTIONS
FOREST RESEARCH INSTITUTES OF RUSSIAN ACADEMY OF SCIENCES
FOREST RESEARCH INSTITUTES OF THE MINISTRY OF AGRICULTURE AND FOOD
FORESTRY GRADUATE SCHOOLS (UNIVERSITIES, ACADEMIES AND INSTITUTES)
Norwegian Sea
North Sea
Barents Sea
Kara
Baltic Sea
Gulf of Bothnia
Black Sea
Caspian Sea
Aral Sea
UNITED KINGDOM
NORWAY
SWEDEN
FINLAND
NETHERLANDS
DENMARK
GERMANY
RUSSIAN FED.
ESTONIA
LATVIA
LITHUANIA
POLAND
CZECH REP.
SLOVAK REP.
HUNGARY
BELARUS
ROMANIA
MOLDOVA
UKRAINE
TURKEY
GEORGIA
ARMENIA
AZERBAIJAN
ISLAMIC REP. OF IRAN
SYRIAN ARAB REP.
IRAQ
KAZAKSTAN
UZBEKISTAN
Kaliningrad
St. Petersburg
Novogorod
Petrozanodsk
Arkhangelsk
Murmansk
Kandalaksha
Vorkuta
Vologda
Kostroma
Syktyvkar
MOSCOW
(3) (6)
(1) (2)
Bryansk
Nizhniy Novgorod
Voronezh
Kazan
Perm
Khanty-Mansiysk
Ob R.
Yekaterinburg
Tyumen
Tobol R.
Saratov
Volga R.
Samara
Ufa
Chelyabinsk
Rostov na Donu
Volgograd
Novorossiysk
Sochi
Astrakhan
Makhachkala
Omsk
Novosibi
Gor
0 100 200 300 400 500 MILES
0 200 400 600 800 KILOMETERS

IBRD 28353

RUSSIAN FEDERATION

FOREST POLICY REVIEW

FOREST FIRE PROTECTION

OCTOBER 1996

This map was produced by the Map Design Unit of The World Bank. The boundaries, colors, denominations and any other information shown on this map do not imply, on the part of The World Bank Group, any judgment on the legal status of any territory, or any endorsement or acceptance of such boundaries.
FOREST F
HIGH P
LOW P
UNITED KINGDOM
Norwegian Sea
North Sea
NORWAY
SWEDEN
Barents Sea
NETHERLANDS
DENMARK
Gulf of Bothnia
Murmansk
Kandalaksha
GERMANY
FINLAND
Kara
Baltic Sea
RUSSIAN FED.
Kaliningrad
ESTONIA
LATVIA
CZECH REP.
POLAND
LITHUANIA
St. Petersburg
Petrozanodsk
Arkhangelsk
Novogorod
SLOVAK REP.
BELARUS
Vorkuta
HUNGARY
Vologda
Kostroma
Syktyvkar
Ob R.
ROMANIA
MOLDOVA
UKRAINE
MOSCOW
Bryansk
Nizhniy Novgorod
Kazan
Voronezh
Perm
Khanty-Mansiysk
Yekaterinburg
Tyumen
Black Sea
Saratov
Volga R.
Samara
Ufa
Rostov na Donu
Volgograd
Chelyabinsk
Tobol
Novorossiysk
Sochi
Omsk
Novosibi
Astrakhan
TURKEY
GEORGIA
KAZAKSTAN
Makhachkala
ARMENIA
Caspian Sea
Aral Sea
Gorno
SYRIAN ARAB REP.
ISLAMIC REP. OF IRAN
AZERBAIJAN
IRAQ
UZBEKISTAN
0 100 200 300 400 500 MILES
0 200 400 600 800 KILOMETERS

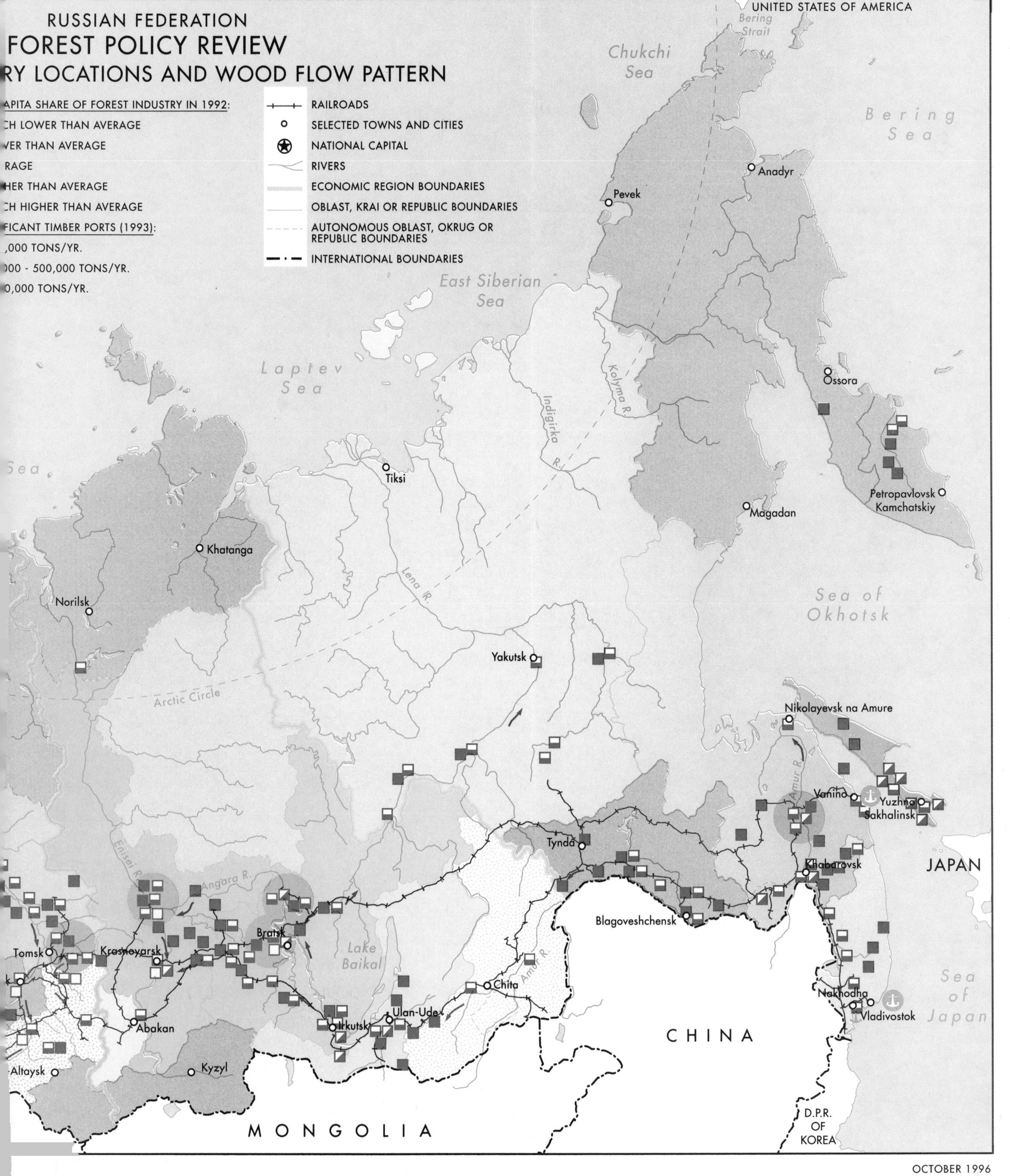
IBRD 27087R
RUSSIAN FEDERATION
FOREST POLICY REVIEW
RY LOCATIONS AND WOOD FLOW PATTERN
APITA SHARE OF FOREST INDUSTRY IN 1992:
CH LOWER THAN AVERAGE
VER THAN AVERAGE
RAGE
HER THAN AVERAGE
CH HIGHER THAN AVERAGE
FICANT TIMBER PORTS (1993):
,000 TONS/YR.
000 - 500,000 TONS/YR.
0,000 TONS/YR.
RAILROADS
SELECTED TOWNS AND CITIES
NATIONAL CAPITAL
RIVERS
ECONOMIC REGION BOUNDARIES
OBLAST, KRAI OR REPUBLIC BOUNDARIES
AUTONOMOUS OBLAST, OKRUG OR REPUBLIC BOUNDARIES
INTERNATIONAL BOUNDARIES
UNITED STATES OF AMERICA
Bering Strait
Chukchi Sea
Bering Sea
Anadyr
Pevek
East Siberian Sea
Laptev Sea
Kolyma R.
Indigirka R.
Ossora
Tiksi
Petropavlovsk Kamchatskiy
Magadan
Khatanga
Lena R.
Sea of Okhotsk
Norilsk
Yakutsk
Arctic Circle
Nikolayevsk na Amure
Amur R.
Vanino
Yuzhno Sakhalinsk
Enisei R.
Angara R.
Tynda
Khabarovsk
JAPAN
Bratsk
Blagoveshchensk
Tomsk
Krasnoyarsk
Lake Baikal
Amur R.
Chita
Ulan-Ude
Irkutsk
Abakan
Nakhodka
Vladivostok
Sea of Japan
CHINA
Altaysk
Kyzyl
MONGOLIA
D.P.R. OF KOREA
OCTOBER 1996

This map was produced by the Map Design Unit of The World Bank. The boundaries, colors, denominations and any other information shown on this map do not imply, on the part of The World Bank Group, any judgment on the legal status of any territory, or any endorsement or acceptance of such boundaries.
WOOD INDUST
WOOD INDUSTRY LOCATIONS:
LOGGING
WOOD PROCESSING
PULP AND PAPER
WOOD CHEMICALS FACILITIES
WOOD PROCESSING CENTERS
PRODUCT FLOWS
UNITED KINGDOM
Norwegian Sea
North Sea
NORWAY
SWEDEN
Barents Sea
NETHERLANDS
DENMARK
Gulf of Bothnia
GERMANY
FINLAND
Kara
Baltic Sea
RUSSIAN FED.
Kaliningrad
CZECH REP.
POLAND
ESTONIA
LATVIA
LITHUANIA
St. Petersburg
Petrozanodsk
Arkhangelsk
Murmansk
Kandalaksha
Novogorod
Vorkuta
SLOVAK REP.
BELARUS
HUNGARY
Vologda
Kostroma
Syktyvkar
MOSCOW
Bryansk
Vladimir
Nizhniy Novgorod
ROMANIA
MOLDOVA
UKRAINE
Voronezh
Kazan
Perm
Khanty-Mansiysk
Ob R.
Black Sea
Saratov
Samara
Yekaterinburg
Tyumen
Ufa
Rostov-na-Donu
Novorossiysk
Volgograd
Volga R.
Chelyabinsk
Omsk
Sochi
Novosibi
Astrakhan
TURKEY
GEORGIA
KAZAKSTAN
ARMENIA
Makhachkala
Caspian Sea
Aral Sea
SYRIAN ARAB REP.
ISLAMIC REP. OF IRAN
AZERBAIJAN
IRAQ
UZBEKISTAN
0 100 200 300 400 500 MILES
0 200 400 600 800 KILOMETERS

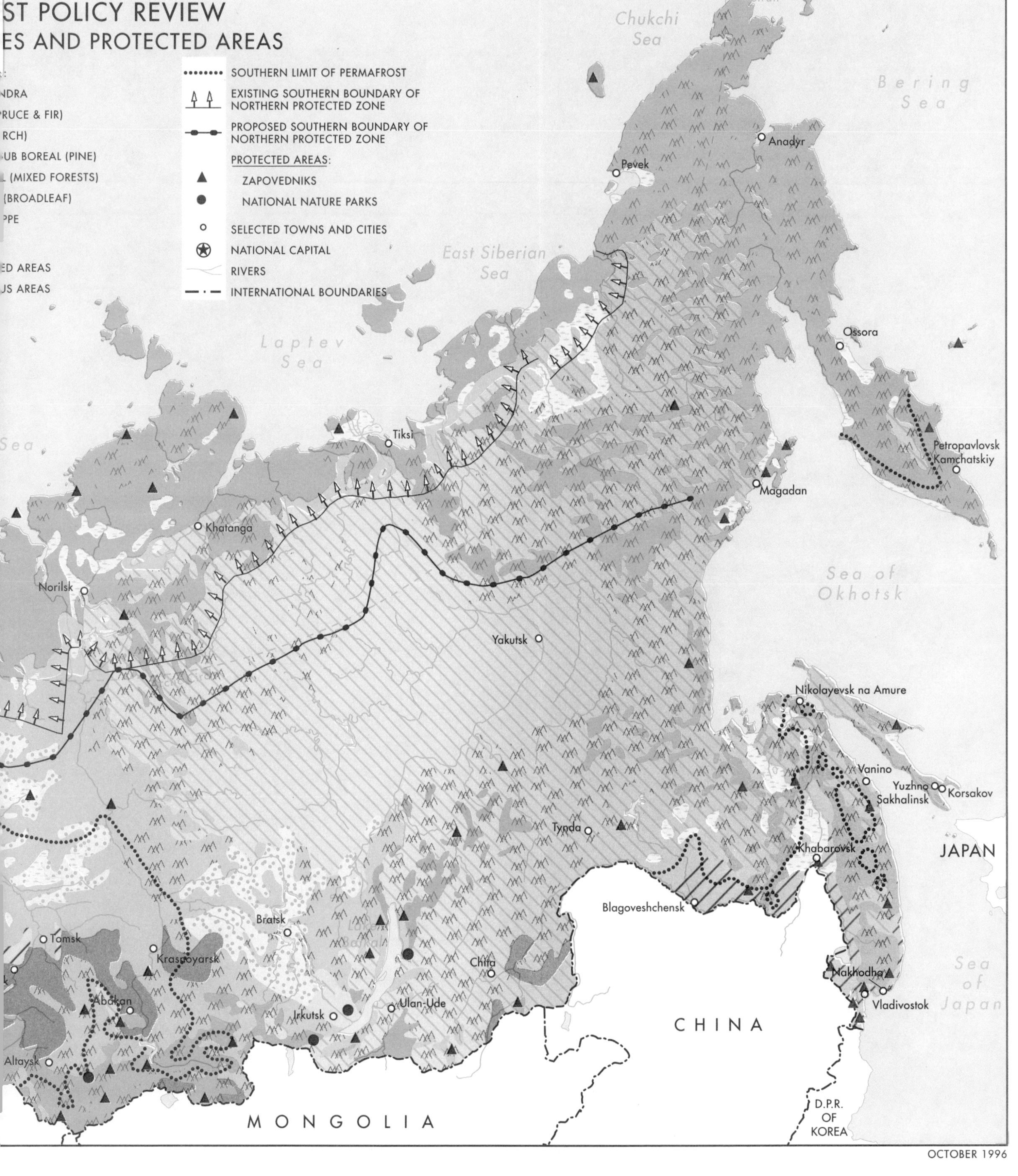
IBRD 27086R
SSIAN FEDERATION
ST POLICY REVIEW
ES AND PROTECTED AREAS
NDRA
RUCE & FIR)
RCH)
UB BOREAL (PINE)
(MIXED FORESTS)
(BROADLEAF)
PPE
ED AREAS
JS AREAS
SOUTHERN LIMIT OF PERMAFROST
EXISTING SOUTHERN BOUNDARY OF NORTHERN PROTECTED ZONE
PROPOSED SOUTHERN BOUNDARY OF NORTHERN PROTECTED ZONE
PROTECTED AREAS:
ZAPOVEDNIKS
NATIONAL NATURE PARKS
SELECTED TOWNS AND CITIES
NATIONAL CAPITAL
RIVERS
INTERNATIONAL BOUNDARIES
UNITED STATES OF AMERICA
Bering Strait
Chukchi Sea
Bering Sea
Anadyr
Pevek
East Siberian Sea
Laptev Sea
Sea
Ossora
Tiksi
Petropavlovsk Kamchatskiy
Magadan
Khatanga
Norilsk
Sea of Okhotsk
Yakutsk
Nikolayevsk na Amure
Vanino
Yuzhno Sakhalinsk
Korsakov
Tynda
Khabarovsk
JAPAN
Blagoveshchensk
Bratsk
Tomsk
Krasnoyarsk
Chita
Nakhodka
Sea of Japan
Abakan
Irkutsk
Ulan-Ude
Vladivostok
CHINA
Altaysk
MONGOLIA
D.P.R. OF KOREA
OCTOBER 1996

FOREST TYP
FOREST TU
BOREAL (S
BOREAL (L
BOREAL &
SUB BOREA
TEMPERATE
FOREST-STE
MARSH
NON FOREST
MOUNTAINO
This map was produced by the Map Design Unit of The World Bank. The boundaries, colors, denominations and any other information shown on this map do not imply, on the part of The World Bank Group, any judgment on the legal status of any territory, or any endorsement or acceptance of such boundaries.
Norwegian Sea
North Sea
Barents Sea
Kara
Gulf of Bothnia
Baltic Sea
Black Sea
Caspian Sea
Aral Sea
UNITED KINGDOM
NORWAY
SWEDEN
FINLAND
NETHERLANDS
DENMARK
GERMANY
RUSSIAN FED.
Kaliningrad
CZECH REP.
POLAND
LATVIA
ESTONIA
LITHUANIA
SLOVAK REP.
BELARUS
HUNGARY
ROMANIA
MOLDOVA
UKRAINE
TURKEY
GEORGIA
ARMENIA
ISLAMIC REP. OF IRAN
SYRIAN ARAB REP.
IRAQ
AZERBAIJAN
UZBEKISTAN
KAZAKSTAN
Murmansk
Kandalaksha
St. Petersburg
Onega
Arkhangelsk
Petrozanodsk
Novogorod
Vorkuta
Vologda
Kostroma
Syktyvkar
MOSCOW
Bryansk
Vladimir
Nizhniy Novgorod
Kazan
Perm
Khanty-Mansiysk
Voronezh
Yekaterinburg
Saratov
Samara
Ufa
Tyumen
Rostov na Donu
Volgograd
Chelyabinsk
Novorossiysk
Omsk
Sochi
Novosibir
Astrakhan
Makhachkala
Gorno
0 100 200 300 400 500 MILES
0 200 400 600 800 KILOMETERS